W9-CCP-913

# USING BENCHMARKING, NEEDS ASSESSMENT, QUALITY IMPROVEMENT, OUTCOME MEASUREMENT, AND LIBRARY STANDARDS

## A How-To-Do-It Manual® with CD-ROM

Rosalind Farnam Dudden

*A Medical Library Association Guide*

### HOW-TO-DO-IT MANUALS FOR LIBRARIANS

### NUMBER 159

NEAL-SCHUMAN PUBLISHERS, INC.
New York                    London

Published by Neal-Schuman Publishers, Inc.
100 William St., Suite 2004
New York, NY 10038

Published in cooperation with The Medical Library Association.

"A How-To-Do-It Manual®" and "A How-To-Do-It Manual for Librarians®" are registered trademarks of Neal-Schuman Publishers, Inc.

Printed and bound in the United States of America.

The paper used in this publication meets the minimum requirements of American National Standard for Information Sciences—Permanence of Paper for Printed Library Materials, ANSI Z39.48–1992.

**Library of Congress Cataloging-in-Publication Data**

Dudden, Rosalind Farnam
    Using benchmarking, needs assessment, quality improvement, outcome measurement, and library standards : a how-to-do-it manual® with CD-ROM/ Rosalind Farnam Dudden.
        p. cm. – (How-to-do-it manuals)
    "A Medical Library Association Guide."
    Includes bibliographical references and index.
    ISBN 978-1-55570-604-3 (alk. paper)
    1. Libraries—Evaluation. 2. Medical libraries—Evaluation. I. Title.
Z678.85.D83 2007
027—dc22
                                                        2007007899

*I dedicate this book to all hospital librarians.*

*Hospital librarians work every day*

*to organize and locate information to*

*increase the knowledge of biomedical professionals*

*so that they make a difference in the health of people.*

*Hospital librarians serve the people who serve the sick.*

# CONTENTS

# LIST OF FIGURES

# FOREWORD

The Medical Library Association (MLA) has long been recognized in the library community for its exceptional professional development program, which encompasses both continuing education and credentialing. In 1999, the MLA launched a new program to define, develop, and evaluate a coordinated and comprehensive Web-based medical library benchmarking tool. This initiative was designed to provide opportunities for hospital, academic, and specialty health libraries to learn more about the benchmarking process, compare data, establish best practices, and identify and work with a benchmarking partner. Now known as the Benchmarking Network, the program began with hospital libraries and now includes libraries in research institutions, libraries serving health sciences programs, consumer health information services, veterinary libraries, and other related corporate and association libraries.

Almost 400 libraries participated in the second benchmarking survey, launched in 2004. In the increasingly competitive healthcare environment, benchmarking studies are excellent advocacy tools. Librarians have successfully used study results to increase library materials, budgets, staffing, and even space.

In 2004, Rosalind Dudden, an MLA fellow and a distinguished member of the Academy of Health Information Professionals, received the National Library of Medicine Grant for Scholarly Works in Biomedicine and Health to enable her to write a comprehensive book about evaluating library services for librarians in small-library settings. *Using Benchmarking, Needs Assessment, Quality Improvement, Outcome Measurement, and Library Standards* is an outgrowth of her work on the MLA Benchmarking Network project. She chaired the outcomes team for the first study and has been a tireless promoter of the Benchmarking Network both regionally and nationally.

*Using Benchmarking, Needs Assessment, Quality Improvement, Outcome Measurement, and Library Standards* provides an overview of related literature and theory. It also serves as a how-to guide for analyzing the results of measurement and evaluation techniques and for cogent communication of these results to your parent institution's administration. As such, it is an important contribution to the literature of evaluation and assessment. We encourage you to use this guide to measure, sustain, and improve the quality—and the relevance—of your library's services.

Carla J. Funk, CAE, Executive Director, Medical Library Association Betsy L. Humphreys, AHIP, Deputy Director, National Library of Medicine

# PREFACE

In library school, we learned that effective evaluation can help a library run smoothly, offer improved services and programs, and prove its worth and value to administrators. But in real life, in busy, often-understaffed work environments, assessment can become a low priority. Even doing the necessary background reading is daunting. Though there are many valuable works on the subject, they are often highly theoretical and lack practical application. As a result, librarians often come up short when searching for a book that will quickly teach them what they need to know.

I wrote *Using Benchmarking, Needs Assessment, Quality Improvement, Outcome Measurement, and Library Standards: A How-To-Do-It Manual®* as a "real-life" guide to results-oriented library evaluation. My primary aims for this book are to explain the most important and popular assessment techniques in straightforward language and to use uncomplicated step-by-step instructions to teach the reader how to perform evaluation studies with skill and competence.

This book combines my 35 years of experience, including more than 10 years of work with the MLA Benchmarking Network Initiative, with two years of intensive research, supported by a grant from the National Library of Medicine (NLM). This grant gave me the time to read widely from the extensive literature available on the subject of library evaluation. From the beginning, my intent was to create a bridge between the theory of evaluation and the practicalities of execution by writing a book that would speak to the concerns of working professionals. As I wrote, I asked myself: Could I do this project in a reasonable amount of time? Would I have the necessary skills? Could I follow the examples? I have tried to provide a set of tools that any reader, no matter how busy, can use to assess his or her services.

Librarians in any setting can learn from the explanations and use the workbooks and checklists. Because evaluation can seem even more challenging in a small library, I have made sure that the advice can be used even with the smallest staff. Librarians in single-staff settings often have the most to gain from evaluation. Changes in economic climate and technological advances have put small libraries in danger. Technical skills alone will not necessarily save a library from closure or downsizing. Effective evaluation adds another layer of defense in a librarian's battle against downsizing and closure. If a library is threatened, showing proof of its positive impacts may be the needed ammunition to save it. My goals for *Using Benchmarking, Needs Assessment, Quality*

*Improvement, Outcome Measurement, and Library Standards* will have been achieved if readers can answer two vital questions about the basics of assessment and the five core methods: How do I do it? and How do I apply the results within the time constraints of a full-time job?

*Using Benchmarking, Needs Assessment, Quality Improvement, Outcome Measurement, and Library Standards* is divided into three parts. Part I, "Evaluating Library Quality and Performance," prepares the reader by examining related management theory. Chapter 1, "Why Evaluate?" covers the purposes of assessment in today's environment of social, economic, and technological change. Chapter 2, "The Effective Library," defines the attributes of an ideal library and examines how to develop a culture of assessment. Chapter 3, "Library Measures," contrasts new and old paradigms of information collection. It explains what one should measure and what various measurements mean.

Part II, "Working with Evaluation Methods," details five core methods (needs assessment, quality improvement, benchmarking, library performance standards, and outcomes measurement) and their real-world applications, followed by a quick overview of other quality improvement and evaluation systems. Each chapter contains background information and a step-by-step explanation, illustrated through real-life examples. The workbook found at the end of each chapter is also reproduced on the accompanying CD-ROM.

Chapter 4, "Method 1: Needs Assessment," discusses the assessment of customer needs, which drives evaluation projects and helps focus future goals. Chapter 5, "Method 2: Quality Improvement," explains how to improve the processes that serve customer needs, highlighting the differences between efficiency and effectiveness. Chapter 6, "Method 3: Benchmarking," addresses a common emphasis in industry and health care. This method can help librarians look beyond their own projects and take part in corporate initiatives. Chapter 7, "Method 4: Library Performance Standards," is particularly important for academic and health sciences libraries. This chapter compares standards for college libraries and hospital libraries to develop a universal set of performance-based evaluation questions. Chapter 8, "Method 5: Outcome Measurement," demonstrates three strategies for discovering and reporting outcomes: logic models, surveys, and categorization. Since outcomes vary extremely by setting, this chapter discusses the uses of this method for public, academic, special, and medical libraries. Chapter 9, "Other Systems for Quality Improvement and Evaluation," presents an overview of 11 other industry and library methods of quality improvement measurement.

Part III, "Tools for Doing Evaluation," will help librarians carry out any type of study and effectively communicate the results. Chapter 10, "Data Collection and Analysis Methods," describes techniques such as surveys, focus groups, observation, interviews, sampling, and questionnaire design. Chapter 11, "Skills for Communicating in Evaluation Projects," covers listening, interviewing, presenting, writing, PowerPoint presentations, and teamwork. Chapter 12, "Tools for Improvement and Evaluation," focuses on ways to analyze and present data.

The accompanying CD-ROM contains a variety of resources, arranged in folders by chapter. The workbooks for the five core chapters, along with supporting materials not printed in this manual, are included for easy editing and use. The glossary and an extensive list of recommended readings with hot links can also be found on the CD-ROM.

The greater message of *Using Benchmarking, Needs Assessment, Quality Improvement, Outcome Measurement, and Library Standards* is the importance of a culture of assessment, a concept detailed in Chapter 2. Even the smallest libraries can strive to create a culture where evaluation is a valued part of everyday library operations.

# ACKNOWLEDGMENTS

I would like to acknowledge the help and support of the institutions and people who assisted me in my effort to write this book. The idea for this book came in the fall of 2003. I thought that if practicing hospital librarians and other librarians in small-library settings could have a guide to use to evaluate their library service, they would have a major tool in their management arsenal to defend against downsizing and closure. But there did not seem to be such a book on the market, at least not one that could be quickly put to use by a practicing librarian. Since 1999, I have been very involved in the creation of the Medical Library Association Benchmarking Network Survey. This survey was intended as a tool for use in defending the hospital library. My idea was to write a "cookbook" to tell me in a few steps how to do the kind of evaluation that would assess the needs of my users or would communicate the value or worth of the library to my administration. I had never heard of such a book, and if I needed one, other practicing librarians might also.

So, being an industrious person, I wrote a research grant application and was awarded a two-year grant that funded 50 percent of my time. I want to acknowledge that receiving this grant (#5-G13LM008520) from the National Library of Medicine made this book possible by giving me the protected time needed to write. These grants are called the NLM Grants for Scholarly Works in Biomedicine and Health. The purpose of the research grant was to prepare a book-length manuscript (or other scholarly work) of value for U.S. health professionals. The reviewers, who felt my idea was worthy and gave me the good score, offered me hope that other people thought the book would be of use to librarians in small-library settings.

I wish to acknowledge the support of my employer, National Jewish Medical and Research Center, located in Denver, Colorado. Not only was I encouraged to seek the grant, but National Jewish also has a system in place that supported me totally in administering the grant and allowing me to hire staff to replace my time spent on writing the book. My thanks go to the dedicated support staff at National Jewish who helped me.

My professional life has been shaped by the associations I have belonged to since 1971, the Medical Library Association (MLA) and the Colorado Council of Medical Librarians (CCML). The members, staff, programs, sections, chapters, and committees of these associations have supported and mentored me in my career all these years, and this book could not have been created without them. I particularly wish to acknowledge the 40 or so hospi-

**Reference: NLM Grants for Scholarly Works in Biomedicine and Health**
www.nlm.nih.gov/ep/GrantPubs.html

The National Library of Medicine (NLM) awards small grants for the preparation of book-length manuscripts and other scholarly works of value to U.S. health and biomedical professionals. Scholars in biomedical fields face competing demands for their time, including requirements for clinical care services, grant-related research, and administrative duties. Scholarly work draws upon original sources that may reside in archives, databases, libraries, or human experts around the world, in many different languages and formats. The work of scholarship—discovery, thoughtful analysis, synthesis, and lucid presentation of findings from such materials—requires protected time and support for incidental costs, including materials, staff assistance, and travel. The NLM Grant for Scholarly Works in Biomedicine and Health is intended to help defray such expenses.

tal and other librarians who worked on the MLA's benchmarking committees and continue to do so to bring this important program to the members. The program would not have been so successful had it not been for the over 500 MLA members who entered their data in the two surveys. My hat is off to all of you! Using the benchmarking results to demonstrate evaluation methods has been a major benefit to writing this book.

I must acknowledge those who helped me through this four-year process. First is the staff at the Tucker Medical Library at National Jewish, who kept the place running while I wrote. Shandra Prozko and Barb Griss kept the reference services going, while Carol Miller, Sean Crow, and LaVonne Griffie worked on the daily activities of the library. Without their dedicated and competent support, I could not have gotten this done.

I am also grateful to those who helped me with the technicalities of the book. Adelaide Fletcher, Reference Librarian at the Denver Medical Library, rescued me at the end of the process with the superb editing skills of an English major and the fresh eyes of a new graduate. Jeff Magouirk, staff member at the Biostatistics Department at National Jewish, helped at the beginning of the project with a discussion of statistical concepts and support for what I wrote about them. Thanks also to Sean Crow, staff member at the Tucker Medical Library, who helped with the glossary and benchmarking results. Other editing help in a pinch came from my friend Margi Holcomb; my daughter, Laura Dudden; and my partner, Jim Mills.

A special thanks goes to Margaret Bandy, Medical Librarian at Exempla Saint Joseph Hospital in Denver, whose unwavering support of the idea kept me going through times of doubt.

Any author needs a good meal and the support of his or her family, and I am no exception. Through all my doubts and time constraints, my partner, Jim Mills, and daughter, Laura Dudden, have supported me without question. Thanks for the meals and encouraging remarks!

Last but not least, I would like to acknowledge my late parents, George Bronson and Nancy Farnam, for their belief in quality education and service to the community, which shaped my life and made it possible for me to write this book.

# Part I

# Evaluating Library Quality and Performance

# WHY EVALUATE?

This book shows how to accomplish an evaluation or assessment project. The projects in this book are realistic and can change how the library operates. They do not have to be big. They just need to be done as part of a plan, and they have to be done with a purpose. There is no point in doing evaluation "just because you should." The first step in any evaluation project is to fully understand why you are doing the evaluation.

Consider the tables in your library. Why are the tables positioned where they are? Do you like them there? Is it time for a change? Is it "your" library? Maybe it belongs to the users of the information in the library. What would *they* say about those tables? If you asked them, would they say they are too large or too small, sticky or clean, or even in the right place?

How important are the library tables? If they are not cleaned properly, that is important—your users may not want to come to the library. If they are by the window or in a dark corner, you may know instinctively that they should be moved, and a decision is made. What information was the decision based on? Should you just move them? Should the person in charge of cleaning be contacted? Some "problems" can be solved with simple steps such as moving tables or having them cleaned more often. Other issues, such as the whole atmosphere or ambience of the library, might be turned into a needs assessment where you ask your users what they want.

Perhaps the library budget is under attack this year. What data do you have to defend it? Have you been gathering statistics or measures for several years? If so, have you been able to understand how the measures relate to the environment in which your library operates? What about the environment in which your organization is operating? What have you been able to tell the administration about the mission and value of your library?

Evaluation is all about making decisions and then defending the decisions within changing, even turbulent, environments that are influenced by both tradition and the politics of the day. The purpose of evaluation is to provide the "evidence" for:

- development of services and programs
- improvement of services and programs
- informed decision making
- accountability to show others that the services and programs are effective
- demonstration of value or worth of an information service to the user's life or work

**Definition: Culture of Assessment**

A Culture of Assessment can be achieved by creating systems and structures that are based on continuous assessment and evaluation in an organizational culture that is customer-focused and uses assessment systematically (Lakos and Phipps, 2004).

Evaluation allows you to learn to do things better and to do better things. In some cases, an evaluation project seeks to improve the quality of the system being evaluated. In other cases, it can provide a statement of value or worth. Decisions are best when they are informed by timely, accurate information gleaned from a relevant evaluation. Having a culture of assessment improves the likelihood that learning and decision making will be enhanced because everything will be driven by the desire to improve. But the desire to improve does not guarantee actual improvement. It takes staff involvement, customer focus, and a systematic plan. Traditions and politics are powerful forces in virtually every environment and need to be met head-on in a systematic way.

# TYPES OF EVALUATION

## FOR PLANNING

Evaluation projects measure what the library is doing in relation to its mission and vision. If your library has not written down its mission, it is best to do so before starting an evaluation project of any kind. The Logic Model, covered in Chapter 8, is a planning model that includes evaluation and can be used for strategic planning, as suggested in a recent Rand Corporation technical report (Greenfield, Williams, and Eiseman, 2006). The ideas of strategic planning are briefly covered in Chapter 9. A needs assessment, as outlined in Chapter 4, is the kind of evaluation that will impact and help begin your planning process

Discovering what the library user or customer needs and then planning to meet those needs will inform your mission and plan. It will either confirm that you are on the right track or it will indicate the need for a course adjustment.

**Definition: Needs Assessment**

A systematic process for determining discrepancies between optimal and actual performance of a service by reviewing the service needs of customers and stakeholders and then selecting interventions that allow the service to meet those needs in the fastest, most cost-effective manner.

**Definition: Quality Improvement**

An approach to the study and improvement of the processes that provide services to meet needs of customers. A quality improvement program is a group of activities undertaken to identify opportunities for improvement and take action to improve the quality of the services and their outcomes.

## FOR IMPROVEMENT

Providing quality programs and services is the obvious goal of any library or organization. Evaluating your programs and services will help you assess how well you are doing and help you do better. By learning more about it and by asking what is and what is not working, you can improve the system and demonstrate the quality of your processes. Quality improvement studies of your library systems and processes, as outlined in Chapter 5, as well as benchmarking studies as outlined in Chapter 6, either will find ways to improve them or they will be judged to be of quality.

**Definition: Benchmarking**

The ongoing comparison and review of one's own process, product, or service against the best-known similar activity, so that realistic goals can be set and effective strategies can be identified and implemented to work toward their attainment (CHLA/ABSC Benchmarking Task Force, 1998).

**Definition: Library Performance Standards**

Something that is established by authority or by the custom of general consent to be as a model or example to be followed. An explicit statement of expected quality. Standards represent performance specifications that, if attained, will lead to the highest possible quality in the system.

**Definition: Outcomes Measurement**

A type of performance measure that demonstrates the benefits to people: specifically, achievements or changes in skill, knowledge, attitude, behavior, condition, or life status for program participants. They assess the impact of a program on people and society (Institute of Museum and Library Services, 2006).

## FOR DECISION MAKING

All methods of evaluation lead to enhanced decision making. Every management decision could be supported by evidence to back it up, either from the literature or from an evaluation project. Directors, through their own interests in assessment and an organizational culture that demonstrates a concern for service quality and staff expertise, incorporate assessment data into their decision-making activities. Data are needed for decisions about developing policies, allocating staff, building collections, and planning service delivery. Decisions are made using formal assessments, survey results, anecdotal information, focus groups, staff surveys, and interviews (Beck, 2003).

## FOR ACCOUNTABILITY

Those who fund the library and those who use the library hold it accountable for providing quality services and programs. Evaluation can provide funding bodies with evidence of success and users with evidence of quality. These accountability pressures from parent institutions are a significant factor for institutions and "the use of assessment data provides the library with an opportunity to highlight its accomplishments with credibility and integrity" (Beck, 2003: 30). Benchmarking studies, as described in Chapter 6, and library performance standards, as described in Chapter 7, can help the library staff demonstrate how they compare with other libraries and with national standards of best library practices.

## FOR VALUE AND WORTH

Measuring the impact of library services is now a requirement in some agencies and institutions. Administrators want to know what value there is to your services and how they impact a person's life or, in the case of corporations, an employee's work. As described in Chapter 8 on outcomes measurement, even a small library operation can draw on the theories and studies of others to show their value and worth.

While there are evaluation methods that can be adapted to smaller settings, this type of evaluation is evolving, and in the future, there will be better ways of doing studies at the local level to show local impacts.

# EVALUATION STAKEHOLDERS

**Definition: Stakeholders**

Stakeholders are individuals, groups, or organizations that have a significant interest in or expect certain levels of performance from the program being evaluated. They are interested in the results of the evaluation or what will be done with results of the evaluation. They can be administrators, sponsors, staff, or customers. They may be internal or external to the organization.

An evaluation project has many stakeholders. All of them will benefit from an evaluation project but in very different ways. They also are influential in the design and purpose of an evaluation project. The starting point of any evaluation project is to identify the stakeholders. Jennifer Cram has divided them into four groupings (Cram, 1999)

- Customer groups
  The library customers should always be a stakeholder in any evaluation project. They are the reason the library exists. As an evaluation project is planned, one of the questions to ask at the start should always be, "How does this problem affect the customer and how important is it to that customer?" Customers can be divided into subgroups based on their needs, which are often based on their role at the institution. Since the point of doing the evaluation is to improve or modify a service or program to bring it more into line with what the customer needs, the customers will benefit from improved services targeted to their needs.

- Functional groups
  These groups include the people who affect the daily routine of the library, provide services, and operate the library. This includes the staff, external suppliers, and service providers. The staff are almost always a stakeholder in that a task they do, or a task connected to what they do, may be the process being evaluated. They benefit by participating in the evaluation and seeing that their job is an important part of the whole library system.

- Normative groups
  According to Cram, these groups provide authority for the library to function and set general rules and regulations. These stakeholders would include the government in some cases, funding bodies and boards, professional and industry associations, and senior management inside and outside the library. The library administration is a stakeholder in that it is they who must support the project with time and other resources. They benefit by being supplied with evidence to use in decision making. Immediate supervisors in the area of the library being evaluated benefit by seeing more efficient systems in place. They can also see how their area is connected to the larger mission

of the library. Upper administration benefit by being supplied with evidence to support decisions they need to make in relation to the resources supporting the library. Most outside funding agencies or sponsors now require measurement of the outcomes of a funded program. This evaluation is now usually a required part of any grant proposal. These bodies benefit from a well-organized evaluation by being able to report to their stakeholders that the funds they supplied created the change they wanted to see, or the desired outcome. For more on outcomes measures, see Chapter 8.

- Diffused groups
  This includes community members and special-interest groups as well as the media. In a public library setting, these groups benefit from an evaluation because it gives them a chance to see whether their interests are being met. In the corporate world, this set of stakeholders could be other departments or even the company's customers, who indirectly benefit from the company's having a library. As an example, patients in a hospital library benefit since their health-care providers have better knowledge because they used a library. In either case, communicating that your evaluation project has confirmed the quality and value of your service can be beneficial to this larger community.

## WHY EVALUATION MATTERS

> "The heart of Library 2.0 is user-centered change. It is a model for library service that encourages constant and purposeful change, inviting user participation in the creation of both the physical and the virtual services they want, supported by consistently evaluating services" (Casey and Savastinuk, 2006; 1).

Each part of the library is a system. Each system is in place to produce a product or service for the user. The systems all connect to one another within the bigger system called the library. The library is part of an organization, be it a corporation, a hospital, a school, or a city government. All of those organizations are interconnected within larger and larger systems, from the local community to the world at large. What happens in these larger systems has an effect on what happens in the library.

The rapid pace of change in the world today is affecting all libraries. Some authors, using computer software lingo, are calling today's library "Library 2.0," a whole new version of the old one. As these changes are introduced, librarians will need skills in evaluation to make decisions that proactively navigate through these changes, rather than passively reacting to them. Changes in the medical library field are discussed below, but many of these impact all libraries. How will your library react to these changes? Evaluation skills will help you adapt and adopt.

How did the administration of your hospital or corporation decide to have a library? Even if they have a record of such a decision, the individual members probably have no recollection of it or may not have even been present when it was made. As part of your evaluation plans, you can figure out how to remind them. If your budget is only .17% of the corporate budget, it does not have much influence. But if you can show quality, efficiency, or effectiveness in the products of the library service, they may agree it is a good decision to keep your service well funded.

If you never report to your administration what a good job the library is doing, how will they know what the library contributes when budget time comes around? If you do not tell your granting agency how successful the project it paid for was, how are you going to get your next project funded?

If you do a small evaluation of a process, the staff involved can feel good that they are doing a quality job, either because the quality was shown or because improvements were made to make it a quality process. In the end it is the library user who benefits most because the library systems will be operating at a higher level of quality, all owing to evaluation and assessment.

Evaluation has everything to do with context. Libraries divide themselves into various categories. The largest divisions are academic, public, school, and special. Each category then subdivides on various parameters of size, purpose, subject, and funding source. Evaluation projects in each environment will necessarily be different. Each environment has its own challenges and resource mix, so it is difficult to adopt an evaluation plan verbatim from another library. Other projects reported in the literature can serve as models or examples. Each evaluation project is carefully planned around available resources in the context of that library. In the past, evaluation was the prerogative of management. It was not necessary for survival. Most libraries would do an evaluation, yet no one would notice except those working in the part of the library being evaluated. Processes were improved, customer needs were met, and while not rich, libraries in general were supported. Libraries were considered "essentially good," and it was thought: Why evaluate something that is going to exist anyway because of its basic value to society or the corporation? Today, the climate has changed.

The library has been described as a social construct. Today, *society* dictates what a public, a university, or even a special library *is*. In Western culture, tradition has it that the free public library at the turn of the century was intended to provide materials for an educated public so that they could participate in a democracy. The university library was to provide the students with learning resources. In each case, the social, economic, and political environments of the time influenced these libraries (Calvert, 1994).

Since the early 1990s, the library's place in this environment has been questioned and jostled. While there is still a need to preserve the scholarly record, and in this digital age preserve access to it, various types of libraries are being asked how they contribute to the missions of the agencies, institutions, or corporations that fund them. Derived from a social services model, libraries are being asked how the services they provide with the funds they are given have an impact on the lives of the people who ultimately provided those funds. What is the "outcome" of the library's existence in relation to the community, school, or corporation?

Public librarians are asked if they changed the life of the user. In universities and other school settings, librarians are being asked not just whether they provided learning resources but also if their service contributed to the success of the student. In special libraries, the result of the use of a library by a worker might not be a change in his or her personal life but might make the person contribute more to the bottom line. In health care, the product translates to better patient care. Assessing how the library contributes to better patient care has been studied and the positive contributions reported (Weightman, 2005).

Meanwhile, as all this change is going on, we are still being asked to report what it is we do. Annual reports from major public libraries or networks contain information about not only what they did but also what their customers say about the value of the service. Communicating our activities, value, and worth is necessary to get the point across to those who supply the funding. While these stakeholders may be requiring evidence of outcomes, often they have not made a full transition to the new paradigm. They still want to see the old activity reporting as well as the new outcomes reporting. Learning and using evaluation strategies in all areas are more important than ever.

## CONSTANT CHANGE

The pace of change is relentless and will not be slowing down. In the ten years between 1996 and 2006, the Internet and World Wide Web have revolutionized information transmission, among other things. While researching this book, I found many excellent articles in the library literature in print but quite a few noteworthy additions available only on the Internet. Many of the print articles were found, delivered, and even read without ever putting them on paper. Filing PDF (Portable Document Format) copies became as difficult as filing paper copies. I even wondered, why file? Because of the Internet, I could just get it again from the source if needed.

Futurists today say that employees will one day be retrained in their job every three to five years. I look at my career and see this in the past. These futurists were not working in libraries for the last 35 years or they would know that this is part of our past as well as our future. Certainly, every 5 years something new came up and transformed my job.

The readers of this book may not have been around for the past 35 years and may not realize that the rapid pace of change is nothing new but, rather, something librarians have lived with for a long time. Here are some examples from my own career. I have worked in a hospital library since 1971.

First I worked in a hospital-based school of nursing, a type of education no longer offered. Then as the school closed, I worked in the hospital library of a general community hospital for 14 years. I now manage the library at the National Jewish Medical and Research Center, which is a combination clinical service and research institution specializing in two subjects, immunology and respiratory medicine.

> **Did You Know: New in the Past 35 Years**
>
> Catalog card production
> OCLC ILL
> Copy Machines
> Computerized union lists of serials
> Online searching
> DOCLINE
> Microcomputers
> Word processing
> Spreadsheets
> Online Public Access Catalogs (OPACs)
> Integrated library systems (ILS)
> The Internet
> The World Wide Web
> End-user searching
> Library Web sites
> Electronic journals
> Electronic books
> Multimedia articles in journals

- In 1971, I took over a small hospital library from a librarian who was retiring at age 75. I was charged to improve and enlarge it in keeping with the growth of community hospitals, the trend at the time. Many hospital libraries were started in the early 1970s. I continued to use accession numbers for my books for two years until I asked myself why I was doing it and discontinued the practice. No one noticed.
- In 1975 we banded together in a consortium and shared services and cooperated. We started cataloging on OCLC as a group. With the local library school, we developed a computerized union list of serials, replacing the card file that was started in the 1950s.
- In 1980 we learned to search our first online database, MEDLINE on the old ELHILL search language, maybe a little later than some communities, but our 300-baud-rate (300-bytes-per-second) machines hummed with excitement at this new technology. We even used them to exchange

interlibrary loan requests on a local bulletin board. My first terminal was in the purchasing department, and I went to the storeroom to use it.

- In 1985 we studied integrated library systems (ILS) and started a shared online catalog with the university in 1987. We started using OCLC for interlibrary loan.

- In 1990 we were finishing our use of OCTANET, a precursor to DOCLINE, and moved to DOCLINE at about that time. By 1990 we had migrated from dumb terminals to microcomputers using word processing and a modem to connect to the world. We started using e-mail on the Internet.

- In 1995 we were expanding our use of the shared ILS, having migrated our records twice between systems, and we expanded from five libraries to nine. The Internet developed with the World Wide Web, and many of us were involved in developing Web sites for our institutions and libraries. Modems started to disappear as WANs (wide area networks) and LANs (local area networks) took over. Our users were starting to do their own MEDLINE searches on BRS Colleague and Grateful Med.

- In 2000 having a library Web site was a requirement and most of our users were doing their own searches on PubMed or Ovid or Silver Platter. Reference librarians became library educators and Web site developers. The first electronic journals were becoming widely available.

- In 2005 few libraries were buying print-only journals. We purchased a serials listing service to supplement the ILS and track our electronic journal titles. Over one-half of the journal collection was received as online only, and we "owned" over 125 electronic books. Through the e-journal open-access initiatives and the purchase of aggregations, our serials list exploded to over 5,000 titles. End users are now being educated in evidence-based medicine, a special way of constructing queries to find articles that provide structured evidence of proper treatment or diagnosis, a new idea since about the late 1990s.

- Today, we are expected to be involved in informatics initiatives to connect the electronic patient health record with the knowledge-based information traditionally purchased by libraries. Users are asking for seamless interfaces at their desktop from the patient record to any article, just a few clicks away.

**Definition: Informatics**

Informatics, a newer word for information science and technology, especially when computers are involved, is concerned with the collection and organization of information (gathering, manipulating, storing, retrieving, and classifying recorded information) using computers and statistical methods. Bioinformatics is the information science of biology; medical informatics, the information science of the practice of medicine.

With each new technological addition to the infrastructure of libraries, librarians have adapted. Decisions were made as each new idea was evaluated, before installation and after. Nina Matheson, in her Janet Doe lecture in 1994, talked about the "fundamental idea of the library" and how it must change to survive. She proposed that instead of a keeper of books and journals, a repository for second hand knowledge, the library would be a "knowledge server, an encyclopedic source of knowledge," a manager of first hand knowledge. In the changes that have taken place and the changes that are going to come, Matheson proposes that "many libraries will wither and disappear because they are too small to be cost-effective or to find a role as a useful player in the larger restructuring taking place in the scholarly communication system" (Matheson, 1995: 6).

In the same article, Matheson does not see research into library systems and library management efficiencies as useful in redefining the role librarians will play. New roles are being developed for librarians by pressures from the outside environment. While some libraries still will be needed to act as archives of past knowledge, new forms and technologies of knowledge production will develop and librarians need to be poised to be part of them. They need to be "a useful player in the larger restructuring" (Matheson, 1995: 5).

To follow Matheson's advice on how to find a new idea for a library and be a useful player, you need to be proactive in your decisions. Being proactive is acting in advance to deal with an expected or observed difficulty. It requires followers to be engaged and concerned with what is happening, to be intelligent about the big picture. The proactive organization's genius is found in the ways in which leaders engage followers in an enterprise that builds on their own and their effective followers' values and motivations (Lubans, 2006).

## THE FUTURE OF EVALUATION AND ASSESSMENT

How can a library become a "useful player"? How knowledge is structured is one of many variables coming into play since 1994. Carla Stoffle has written a series of articles about the future of academic libraries and the intricate challenges faced by them. Some of the outside pressures and challenges she notes that will change the face and function of the library are:

---

**Did You Know: Strategies to Be Proactive (Lubans, 2006: 30–33)**

- For new hires, stress credentials less, spirit and independent thinking more.
- Increase integrated decision making, decrease top-down decisions. Solutions emerge when intelligent people engage in open and honest discussion.
- Flatten the administration; spread out administrative responsibility.
- Make clear your organizational values: how they treat each other, what the library aspires to be. Say them, mean them, do them, every day.
- Experiment more: Find out by doing. Make more mistakes in pursuit of best solutions.
- Use self-managing teams or other constructs that require critical thinking and decision making by followers.
- Increase staff development budgets to train everyone in soft and hard skills. Replace formal performance evaluation meetings with career development conversations.

**Further Reading: The Future**

Association of Research Libraries, Office of Leadership & Management Services. "The Keystone Principles." www.arl.org/newsltr/207/keystone.html (last updated: December 1999; accessed September 28, 2006).

Stoffle, C. J., B. Allen, and D. Morden. "Continuing to Build the Future: Academic Libraries and Their Challenges." *Portal*, 3, no. 3 (2003): 363–380.

Stoffle, C.J., B. Allen, and J. S. Fore. "Predicting the Future: What Does Academic Librarianship Hold in Store? *C&RL News*, 61, no. 10 (2000): 894–901.

Stoffle, C.J., R. Renaud, and J. R. Veldof. "Choosing Our Futures." *College & Research Libraries*, 57, no. 5 (1996): 213–233.

1. Uncertainty about how information and knowledge will be structured and used in the future by a generation that has always used computers.
2. Technology changes on all levels and the need to upgrade equipment, a cost that will impact the budget in other areas.
3. The World Wide Web and the new technologies of the Internet causing relentless pressure to adapt services to a new technological environment. Whether a college library using text messaging for reference or a special library informing users with a blog, libraries are pushed to provide new service methods while still having to maintain the old system.
4. Conflicting pressures to create a library focused on customers' needs while at the same time maintaining the traditional library focused on materials.
5. Demands for accountability from the agencies, institutions, or corporations that fund libraries. How do you show the library's impact on the user or your effect on the bottom line?
6. The need to look for the "value added" services that support institutional priorities and a system to report these.
7. Economic pressures on the agencies and institutions that fund libraries. City and state government have less money to go around and more competition for it. Corporations are always looking at the bottom line.
8. Economic pressures on libraries, shrinking budgets and the need to do more with less.
9. High cost of information in a chaotic, unpredictable, and often unreasonable market.
10. Problems recruiting and retaining the best in the profession when salaries are not keeping up and the environment is challenging.
11. New technical positions being filled with nonlibrarians. This might have an impact on our professional values.
12. Response to competition inside and outside the institution from those who are in the information business. Outside commercial services are selling products directly to our customers that mimic traditional library services. Inside information systems departments are providing services we could provide and, in many cases, with little coordination with us.

To respond to all these pressures and more, there is a need to continually examine what a library is today and tomorrow. Many groups are trying to reinvent or reconceptualize the library. Martha Kyrillidou from the Association of Research Libraries (ARL) discusses how libraries have gone from concentrating on the workings of the library to examining users and seeing how they can use the library and what they need. This is not unlike many of the business quality initiatives discussed in Chapter 9. One new model she quotes is that the "library serves as a physical presence, a memory institution, a learning center, a community resource and an invisible intermediary" (Kyrillidou, 2002: 42). It is through constant evaluation that we will be able to set the course to the new library.

There are many initiatives on many levels that are addressing these changes. Each initiative has implications for all libraries and needs to be supported across boundaries of association and library type. The examples listed below are just a few of the many that exist, but each covers a different challenge.

- How to measure the new information environment: The Association of Research Libraries has its New Measures Initiatives which includes (ARL, 2006):
  - LibQUAL+(TM) (Measuring Library Service Quality)
  - DigiQUAL (Measuring Digital Library Service Quality)
  - E-Metrics (Measures for Electronic Resources)
  - COUNTER (Counting Online Usage of Networked Electronic Resources)
- How to explain the new environment to others: The Association of Academic Health Sciences Libraries (AAHSL) Charting the Future Task Force has written a vision of the library's involvement in knowledge management entitled: *"Building on Success: Charting the Future of Knowledge Management within the Academic Health Center"* (AAHSL, 2003).
- How to measure the new political environment: The Institute of Museum and Library Services has a granting program for outcome-based evaluation that has already produced some significant results, as discussed in Chapter 8: (Institute of Museum and Library Services, 2006).
- How to influence the new technical environment: The Medical Library Association, as well as most other library and information science associations, has been involved in the issue of scholarly publishing by advocating for libraries and the users to create an equitable system. Their Internet resource page links to many of the initiatives that are involved (MLA, 2006).

It would be nice to say that evaluation and assessment will ensure the library you work in will transform and survive, but this is not a given. In our library communities, we hear about libraries, big and small, that are coping with staff reductions and closures. Some of these changes are at the whim of the administration. Some are due to mergers and acquisitions. These changes carry a personal toll on the librarians and staff involved. Michael Schott has written a book about these problems, *Medical Library Downsizing: Administrative, Professional, and Personal Strategies for Coping with Change*, which can help prepare for this and cope with the aftermath (Schott, 2005). If you feel that downsizing is a possibility, it might be good to look at this book. At the same time, you can be proactive and start an assessment and evaluation plan for your library. You can choose to base your management decisions and management style on evidence found in evaluation.

Blaise Cronin, then the dean at the Indiana University School of Library and Information Science, in his contribution to the book, *Applying Research to Practice: How to Use Data Collection and Research to Improve Library Management Decision Making*, talks about the characteristics of a good researcher. Skills such as clear writing, numerical skill, respect for deadlines and funding sources, and objectivity are important and necessary, but mostly, managers and researchers both need a "well-developed awareness that most people, especially researchers, have got it wrong most of the time" (Cronin, 1992: 132). The approach to evaluation taken in this book, that evaluation will tune a library so it is effective and survive, may be off the mark. Certainly evaluation will not save the day every time it is used. But a library management system based on service quality and a staff that is dedicated to finding the evidence certainly will go a long way toward communicating with administration.

Librarians who choose to work in small settings can learn to use assessment and evaluation. Practicing librarians in small settings need to be generalists. They hire, fire, and evaluate personnel, but they are not human resources experts. They develop budgets and financial plans, but they are not accountants. They develop mission statements and strategic plans, but they are not planning experts. They can learn to do evaluation and assessment without being experts in those fields. They are experts in information storage and retrieval and meeting the needs of information users, with all the details that involves. The experts in the field of library and information science evaluation and assessment will help all of us respond to these future issues and we will be able to carry out assessment and evaluation, develop needed services, improve the services we have, make decisions based on the evidence, and demonstrate that our effective library service has value and worth in the life and work of our users.

# REFERENCES

Association of Academic Health Sciences Libraries (AAHSL) Charting the Future Task Force. 2003. "Building on Success: Charting the Future of Knowledge Management within the Academic Health Center." Association of Academic Health Sciences Libraries. Available: www.aahsl.org/document/CTFprint.pdf (accessed December 18, 2006).

Association of Research Libraries. "ARL New Measures Initiatives." Association of Research Libraries. Available: www.arl.org/stats/newmeas/index.html (accessed July 10, 2006).

Beck, S. J. 2003. "Data-Informed Decision Making." *ARL* (230/231): 30.

Calvert, P. J. 1994. "Library Effectiveness: The Search for a Social Context." *Journal of Library and Information Sciences*, 26: 15–21.

Casey, M. E., and L. C. Savastinuk. 2006. "Library 2.0." *Library Journal*, 131, no. 13: 40–42.

CHLA/ABSC Benchmarking Task Force, Canadian Health Libraries Association/Association des bibliothèques de la santé du Canada. 1998. *CHLA/ABSC Benchmarking Tool Kit*. Toronto: Canadian Health Libraries Association/Association des bibliothèques de la santé du Canada.

Cram, J. "'Six Impossible Things before Breakfast': A Multidimensional Approach to Measuring the Value of Libraries" (last updated August 27–31, 1999). Available: www.alia.org.au/~jcram/six_things.html (accessed June 20, 2006).

Cronin, B. 1992. "When Is a Problem a Research Problem?" In *Applying Research to Practice: How to Use Data Collection and Research to Improve Library Management Decision Making*, edited by L. S. Estabrook. Urbana-Champaign, IL: University of Illinois Graduate School of Library and Information Science.

Greenfield, V.A., V. L. Williams, and E. Eiseman. 2006. "Using Logic Models for Strategic Planning and Evaluation: Application to the National Center for Injury Prevention and Control." Rand Corporation. Available: www.rand.org/pubs/technical_reports/TR370/ (accessed January 5, 2007).

Institute of Museum and Library Services. "Outcome-Based Evaluation Overview: New Directives, New Directions: Documenting Outcomes in IMLS Grants to Libraries and Museums." Institute of Museum and Library Services. Available: www.imls.gov/applicants/basics.shtm (accessed July 7, 2006).

Kyrillidou, M. 2002. "From Input and Output Measures to Quality and Outcome Measures, or, from the User in the Life of the Library to the Library in the Life of the User." *Journal of Academic Librarianship*, 28, no. 1/2: 42–46.

Lakos, A., and S. Phipps. 2004. "Creating a Culture of Assessment: A Catalyst for Organizational Change." *Portal*, 4, no. 3: 345–361.

Lubans, J. 2006. "Balaam's Ass: Toward Proactive Leadership in Libraries." *Library Administration & Management*, 20, no. 1: 30–33.

Matheson, N. W. 1995. "The Idea of the Library in the Twenty-First Century." *Bulletin of the Medical Library Association*, 83, no. 1: 1–7.

Medical Library Association. "MLA Scholarly Publishing Resources." Medical Library Association (last updated March 13, 2006). Available: www.mlanet .org/resources/publish/pub_resources.html (accessed September 22, 2006).

Schott, M. J. 2005. *Medical Library Downsizing: Administrative, Professional, and Personal Strategies for Coping with Change*. New York: Haworth Information Press.

Weightman, A. L. 2005. "The Value and Impact of Information Provided through Library Services for Patient Care: A Systematic Review." *Health Information and Libraries Journal*, 22, no. 1: 4–25.

# 2 THE EFFECTIVE LIBRARY

If the library you manage is doing all the right things and doing things right, and it is well used and well supported, what adjective would you use to describe the library? *Good? Ideal? Flawless? Exceeds standards?* Or is the library *efficient, competent,* or *effective? Skilled, qualified, capable, impressive? Quality, high caliber, superior? High ranking, preeminent, leading, greatest?* By using a thesaurus, especially the mesmerizing Visual Thesaurus (www.visualthesaurus.com/), you can come up with many words. What about being a "right-on-target" library, a library that provides just the right mix of services and resources for the customer? This library would not be so large that it risked getting downsized, nor so small that it could not provide the needed services. The appropriate sports analogy from basketball might be "nothing but net." You throw the ball and it doesn't hit the rim but goes straight down, touching only the net. Perfect! To be so perfect, the library would need to have a specific direction and be constantly evaluating its course to reset it to that direction. This library would communicate its perfection to its stakeholders. This library could adapt and adopt in the constantly changing technological and economic environment of the 21st century.

The word used in the literature to describe this quality library is effective. While you know you are doing a good, great, or perfect job, those may not be the words to use. How does a library get to be effective, and how does it show that it is? These questions are covered in the library evaluation literature written by experts in the field. The depth of the thought that has gone into attempting to define and measure an effective library can soon overwhelm the practicing librarian in a small-library setting. Can a small library demonstrate its effectiveness, or is this reserved for large libraries with a specialized and expert staff? Some authors advocate establishing a "culture of assessment." Can a small library or even a one-person library have such a culture?

This book is an attempt to help the practicing librarian manage an effective library, establish a culture of assessment, and communicate its effectiveness to the administration. So, where to start? Calvert points out that researchers in this field operate in a "semantic jungle" (Calvert, 1994: 17) This is partly because the words used to describe evaluation and assessment are common and have various meanings.

Lee-Thomas makes an excellent distinction between assessment and evaluation (Lee-Thomas and Robson, 2004: 7):

- Assessment is the gathering of meaningful or purposeful data that will provide information that informs, improves, or confirms.
- Evaluation is assigning merit, value, or worth to the findings.

Calvert brings forward definitions for some words that he finds are sometimes used as synonyms: (Calvert, 1994: 17)

- Measurement: The process of ascertaining the extent or dimensions or quantity of something
- Performance: The doing of something, an activity
- Evaluation: The process of determining whether something is what you want it to be
- Effective: Something that does well what it is supposed to do

He then puts these words together in a sentence that shows how they can differ:

> "The results of *measurement* can be used to *evaluate* the *performance* of a library and thereby determine whether or not it is *effective*" (Calvert, 1994: 17).

# THE CULTURE OF ASSESSMENT

**Definition: Culture of Assessment**

An organizational attitude that can be achieved by creating systems and structures that are based on continuous assessment and evaluation. A culture that is customer focused and uses assessment systematically.

The idea of a "culture of assessment" was created as a response for the need for organizational change to meet the challenges facing libraries today. As outlined by Lakos and Phipps in articles and workshops, the idea is that libraries must support the values of quality and quality management in a new culture. Responding to the pressures of the external environment, they state:

> Libraries are challenged to be nimble, innovative, responsive, proactive and, most of all, able to demonstrate their value. Libraries must be able to measure their outcomes and systematically make technology, budget allocation, service and policy decisions based on a range of data—needs assessment, customer evaluation data, stakeholder expectation data and internal process and organizational effectiveness data. Pressure to offer value-added service

is mounting in intensity, and the rate of change is relentless." (Lakos and Phipps, 2004: 346–347)

In response to this pressure, they recommend developing a culture of assessment. Lakos has a tool kit on the Web that gives the definition and a basic list of the organizational components that need to exist and the support systems that must be in place. He doesn't mince any words:

> Libraries, librarians and information professionals have to implement services and systems which are highly effective and focused on customer outcomes and impacts. Librarians have to care that their systems are designed, planned, implemented, maintained and renewed with the goal of exceeding customer expectations as the primary value. Librarians have to create customer-responsive environments that are designed to enhance service quality and maintain superior standards of service. This can only be achieved by creating systems and structures that are based on continuous assessment and evaluation. Libraries and librarians have to create organizational cultures that are customer focused and use assessment systematically. (Lakos, accessed: 2006)

Phipps discusses the initiative at the University of Arizona Library called the Performance Effectiveness Measurement System (PEMS). The new culture that the system promotes changes the organizational environment so that the library becomes a "learning and listening organization." What the library measures and how the measurement is conducted also changes. The new measures of library effectiveness are not compatible with the structure and culture of traditional internally focused organizations. The library must "become an acting organization—experimenting, seeking new perspectives and new methodologies, and designing new organizational systems that involve, engage, develop, and increase the commitment of staff and partner with customers to design the future they need that includes library values and visions" (Phipps, 2001: 657).

Lakos and Phipps define a culture of assessment:

> A Culture of Assessment is an organizational environment in which decisions are based on facts, research and analysis, and where services are planned and delivered in ways that maximize positive outcomes and impacts for customers and stakeholders. A Culture of Assessment

exists in organizations where staff care to know what results they produce and how those results relate to customers' expectations. Organizational mission, values, structures, and systems support behavior that is performance and learning focused. (Lakos and Phipps, accessed: 2006)

While Lakos and Phipps are working in an academic library environment, their principles of organizational change and development can be applied to the smaller library setting. Based on the principles of total quality management (TQM) and the learning organization, this "organizational change or shift" is seen as essential to creating an effective library service through continuous assessment. Below is an adaptation of the Lakos and Phipps list of what it takes to create this culture, giving illustrations for implementation in a small-library setting.

## MANAGEMENT SYSTEMS FOR THE CULTURE OF ASSESSMENT

1. The organization's mission, planning, and policies are focused externally—on supporting the customer's need for access to information.

   In most of the evaluation projects discussed in the rest of this book, it is always emphasized that the project must be tied to the mission of the library and the strategic planning process. It is difficult for a librarian in a small setting to take the time to write a strategic plan. If there is no time, at least write a mission and values statement. Your institution or organization has one. Find it and support it with a library mission statement. Develop it and discuss it with your staff. Mention the library's relationship to the customer! The ideas of strategic planning are briefly covered in Chapter 9.

2. How performance measures will be assessed is included in organizational planning documents such as strategic plans and unit goals.

   You have a written mission. Start writing goals and objectives for your plan, one service or program at a time. Using the SMART format described in Chapter 12, indicate any performance measure you can reasonably collect. At first, do not look at the details of the total library, since it will be overwhelming. Your mission looks at the whole. Start with one service and writing one small goal at a time. Relate it to the mission.

---

**Organizational changes for creating a culture of assessment are recommended in the following works:**

Kovel-Jarboe, P. 1996 "Quality improvement: A Strategy for Planned Organizational Change." *Library Trends* 44, no. 3 (Winter): 605–630. Marshall, J. G. 2000 "Determining Our Worth, Communicating Our Value." *Library Journal* 125, no. 19 (November 15): 28–30.

---

**Definition: Strategic Planning**

A practical action-oriented planning process with set goals and resource allocation plans that will affect strategic issues of vital importance to the organization that have been identified by the study of internal and external factors.

See Chapter 9 for more details about strategic planning. See Chapter 8 for a workbook on how to use a logic model for planning and evaluation, including strategic planning.

---

**On the CD-ROM: Mission Statements**

In the Chapter 2 folder: NNLM Mission Statements.doc A sample of mission statements gathered by the Outreach Evaluation Resource Center (OERC) of the National Network of Libraries of Medicine.

After a while, you will have a total plan. While strategic planning is not covered in this book, the planning model called the Logic Model is covered in Chapter 8. The Logic Model is a planning model that includes evaluation, and it can be used for strategic planning. The ideas of strategic planning are briefly covered in Chapter 9.

3. Leadership commits to, and financially supports, assessment activities.

   Commit to this idea. You are the administrator of the library. Educate your supervisor about the culture of assessment and get him or her to support the idea. Show your staff that you are committed and you appreciate their help with the plan.

4. Staff recognize the value of assessment and engage in it as part of their regular assignments. Individual and organizational responsibility for assessment is addressed explicitly—in job descriptions or is otherwise communicated formally.

   As you are leading the effort to write your plan that includes assessment in each function, include the staff members involved in the function and make it clear to them that it is their responsibility to carry out the assessments that have been jointly decided on. Give them the tools, skills, and time to accomplish the new tasks that are included in the assessment. If you are the only one, give these to yourself. Tell your supervisor you need them.

5. Relevant data and user feedback are routinely collected, analyzed, and used to set priorities, allocate resources, and make decisions.

   As part of your planning, you schedule different kinds of assessments. You may do a needs assessment every year if it is required, but other assessments may be every two or three years. Continuous communication does not mean every day or even every month. But every time you finish a scheduled evaluation, you should have a plan as to how to communicate the results to interested parties. Just as you are going to work on your strategic plan one service at a time, so too you would schedule evaluations over a period of time. This organizational change will take you several years. Meanwhile your services and programs will be evolving faster than your plan. This will be one of your biggest challenges.

## SUPPORT SYSTEM FOR THE CULTURE OF ASSESSMENT

6. Assessment activities are supported by a Management Information System (MIS) or Decision Support System (DSS).

   A Management Information System or Decision Support System is a computer system that can generate statistics for various library units and activities in a systematic way that supports planning and decision making. This is a good idea, but these systems have yet to be developed commercially for libraries. They are complex, and those in development are already reported to be benefiting the libraries developing them, such as the PEMS system at the University of Arizona Library, mentioned above. Because of the complexity of a total system, your goal here would be not to develop one yourself but at least to be systematic in your data collection. Use a spreadsheet or a database program and keep all your statistics in the same place. Some parts of the library will report monthly, others quarterly or yearly. Develop your system to accommodate this. If you have an integrated library system, there will be statistical reports you can run, but they cover just part of the library operation. If you do a special evaluation project, integrate your findings into your system. Your goal of any system would be analysis and reporting of the data. Can your system produce an annual report? Can it analyze trends? If working on this mega-file of data is more than you can do, at least keep all your statistical reports in the same directory or folder on your computer. Whenever you are asked to respond to a survey, keep those data there also. And watch the literature for any library MIS or DSS systems that might develop in the future.

7. All services, programs, and products are evaluated for quality, impact, and efficiency.

   This is your overriding goal, but it is not accomplishable without planning activities and organizational structures, such as those outlined above. When you have had the time to touch every service, product, or program with your strategic plan, then you will have a system that can support this statement. This is the part where you carry out evaluation projects using your planning documents and assessment measures. Using the Logic Model as explained in Chapter 8 as a planning document will help with this effort. As covered in Chapter 1, the evaluation projects will provide the "evidence" for

- development of services and programs
- improvement of services and programs
- informed decision making
- accountability to show others that the services and programs are effective
- demonstration of the value or worth to the user's life or work

8. Staff are given support to continually improve their capability to serve customers and are rewarded for this.

All staff members should know that it is their responsibility to continuously monitor their processes to ensure they are done in a quality way. They should receive training in quality improvement techniques, such as those discussed in Chapter 5, as well as any training specific to their duties. A system of rewards could be set up with the help of human resources so that people are acknowledged for the work they do for quality service.

9. Staff are rewarded for work and the application of new learning that demonstrates improved service quality and better outcomes for customers.

Staff development activities and support for and appreciation of staff to learn more about assessment and about their job activities are essential to creating this culture. Part of this organizational change is becoming a learning organization, as promoted by Peter Senge in his book *The Fifth Discipline: The Art and Practice of the Learning Organization* (Senge, 2006) which was published in 1990 and revised in 2006. Senge talks about an organization where personal mastery, a shared vision, team learning, and systems thinking are part of every team and where people are constantly learning to do a better job of serving the customer. See Chapter 9 for more details on Senge's ideas. Lakos and Phipps's work is based on these management principles. By working with human resources, you may be able to set up a recognition system.

10. Ongoing staff development in measurement, evaluation, and assessment is provided and supported.

Even if the library has only two or three staff members, each person needs to be educated on what it takes

**Did You Know: University of Maryland Libraries Comprehensive Learning Curriculum**

- Introduction: Development of the Organization
- Defining Customer Service
- Measurement, Evaluation, and Continuous Improvement for Planning and Decision Making
- Development of Self, Teams, and Workgroups
- Exploring Leadership and Followership
- Individual Improvement
- Computer Skills
- Library Basic Skills
- Leadership Development
- Train-the-Trainer

to carry out assessments and evaluations. This includes education on the organizational changes needed to have a culture of assessment. By discussing this with your supervisor, you can start planning what courses you and your staff can take, either in-house or though other organizations. The human resources department can assist you in finding courses as well as professional library organizations. The book *The Tell It! Manual: The Complete Program for Evaluating Library Performance*, goes over basic evaluation techniques and outlines a course of study (Zweizig, et al., 1996). The University of Maryland Libraries has posted its comprehensive learning curriculum on the Web, and it serves as an example of the types of skills you might plan to learn. Focusing on individual and organizational advancement, it is a plan "for all library staff to develop the skills needed to become members of teams and to improve the way we operate as an organization" (University of Maryland Libraries Learning Curriculum, accessed: 2006). This list can give you an idea of the types of areas the staff need to concentrate on.

11. Units within the library have defined critical processes and established measures of success.

    This is easier to imagine in a large library with a staff that often deal with only one process per person. In smaller libraries, the staff have many processes listed in their job descriptions. In the case of one-person libraries, one person does them all. If you take the above approach of tackling one process at a time, you can work your way through the system over an appropriate period of time, usually several years. Developing your management information system at the same time helps keep track of your plans and measures.

12. Individual staff members develop customer focused SMART goals in annual planning processes and monitor progress regularly.

    The SMART acronym helps you remember the parts of a well-constructed goal. SMART stands for specific, measurable, attainable, results-oriented, and timely. The concepts involved in SMART goal setting are covered in Chapter 12. In this new culture of assessment, the emphasis of all goals is that they be customer focused more than process oriented.

# MODELS OF ORGANIZATIONAL EFFECTIVENESS

Lakos and Phipps place emphasis in their writing on the culture behind an organizational structure that facilitates evaluation. Their approach is modeled on TQM and the learning organization. They use a wide variety of evaluation methods, a system of evaluation. The traditional division of library functions may not work in today's environment. The traditional top-down model of managing an organization may not be conducive to this new approach. What is the model of an organization that will be effective in a library with a culture of assessment? How you organize your library will affect what you evaluate, how you report your evaluation, and which stakeholders might be influenced by the evaluation.

How would you organize the parts of a library? Using their studies of New Zealand, Calvert and Cullen isolated 13 parts and called them dimensions of library effectiveness, as listed in Figure 2.1 (Calvert, 1994). Later, Cullen goes on to assign evaluation methodologies to each dimension, also shown in Figure 2.1 (Cullen, accessed: 2006). So now, using these theories, you can determine which evaluation methodology goes with which dimension.

| **Figure 2.1:** Models of Organizational Effectiveness and Dimensions of Library Effectiveness | | |
|---|---|---|
| **Model** (Cameron) | **Dimensions of Library Effectiveness** (Franklin, Cullen) | **Systems of Evaluation** (Cullen) |
| The Goal Attainment Model | Range and Depth of Services<br>Access Services<br>Reference and Information Services<br>Customer Services<br>Programs and Events | Goals and Objectives<br>Benchmarks<br>Standards<br>Output Measures<br>Citizen's Charter |
| The External Systems Model | Financial Inputs<br>Physical Environment<br>Staffing | Input Measures<br>Library Statistics<br>Benchmarks<br>Standards |
| The Internal Process Model | Management Culture and Direction<br>Collection Management<br>Technical Processes | Management Information Systems<br>Decision Support Systems<br>TQM—Total Quality Management<br>ISO9000/9001, and so forth |
| The Strategic Constituencies Model | Community Use and Satisfaction<br>Relations with Councilors and Council Management | Service Quality<br>Customer Satisfaction<br>Total Quality Management<br>ISO9000/9001, and so forth<br>Gap Reduction<br>Marketing |
| Adapted and combined from Franklin (accessed: 2006), Cameron (1986), Cullen (accessed: 2006), and Cullen and Calvert (1996). | | |

When you do an evaluation, what area of your environment are you influencing? Several resources discuss the work of Kim Cameron (1986), who proposed a multidimensional construct with four models of organizational effectiveness (Cullen, accessed: 2006; Franklin, accessed: 2006). Cullen matches the dimensions of library service to these four models. Cameron's four models can be described this way:

1. *The Goal Attainment Model:* Here the organization assesses its effectiveness in terms of achieving its goals and objectives. Resource allocation is often based on which goals are achieved. There is a focus on increasing outputs and through them, goal achievement.
2. *The External Systems Model:* Here the organization measures its effectiveness in terms of gaining resources from its environment. Successful libraries are those that secure more extensive resources from their environment and translate them into those inputs that are considered desirable.
3. *The Internal Process Model:* Here the organization measures the efficiency with which it converts inputs into outputs. Using ratios of transactions per staff member or number of items added to stock per staff member, and so forth, the library sees continuous improvement as showing effectiveness.
4. *The Strategic Constituencies Model:* Here the organization looks outward to its different constituencies or stakeholder groups. It is effective if the needs of the different identified constituencies are met. This is a marketing model where each constituency is shown how its needs have been met.

As an example of these models, Franklin, in his 2002 Web document *Organizational Assessment: An Academic Library Case Study*, discusses the multidimensional approaches to organizational assessment taken by the University of Connecticut Libraries (Franklin, accessed: 2006). Figure 2.1 compares the four models developed by Cameron, the 13 dimensions developed by Franklin and Cullen, and the evaluation methodologies reported by Cullen. It allows you to see that if you were to do an evaluation study using performance benchmarking comparing your budget and purchases with others, you would be using the External Systems Model, and you would be able to show how you translated your financial resources into knowledge resources.

These four models are described here to give you some ideas for rethinking your library organization in a smaller library setting. While you will not be making seven functional areas, each with multiple internal team structures, as they did when they reorganized at the University of Connecticut Libraries, you may want to rethink how you structure your services. Will you be evaluating your goals or processes or user satisfaction? Each one will require a different kind of evaluation project. How they relate to one another and the whole will influence your decision on how to evaluate them.

In a related concept, Wallace and Van Fleet talk about a culture of evaluation in the first chapter of their book *Library Evaluation: A Casebook and Can-Do Guide.* (Wallace and Van Fleet, 2001). While the terms *assessment* and *evaluation* are often used interchangeably, remember the distinction between assessment and evaluation noted in the introduction above: (Lee-Thomas and Robson, 2004: 7).

- Assessment is the gathering of meaningful or purposeful data that will provide information that informs, improves, or confirms.
- Evaluation is assigning merit, value, or worth to the findings.

Lakos and Phipps advocate a culture of assessment where an organization is in place that promotes the continuous gathering of data to improve the quality of all dimensions of the library. Wallace takes a more technical systems approach to the interactions within a library. "In an ideal situation, evaluation becomes a basic social and societal system of the library and a culture of evaluation permeates the library and all its functions and activities" (Wallace and Van Fleet, 2001: 10). Building this culture must be deliberate and also requires an understanding and appreciation of the fundamental characteristics of evaluation. Wallace lists them as

1. Evaluation results from design, not accident.
2. Evaluation has a purpose.
3. Evaluation is about quality.
4. Evaluation is more than measurement.
5. Evaluation does not have to be big.
6. There is no one right way to evaluate.

These theories help you achieve an "ideal" library, a library that is "nothing but net," an effective library, by having you commit to a bigger picture. Evaluation is not just about how many of this or that activity was done. It is about the whole interactive system. You can not choose one of the organizational models listed in Figure 2.1 and look at your library from only that point of view. You should not focus only on your goals and ignore what is happening in the external environment, in the boardroom, or in the technological climate that will affect the operation of the library. If you spend too much time measuring internal processes, have you forgotten to ask the customers what they want? If you are constantly trying to find out what the customer wants, have you neglected to focus on the inputs to the library and let your support slip? If you focus on getting inputs and resources, how are you going to know what to spend the money on when you get it? It is a balancing act.

Cullen proposes a new matrix for examining focus, value, and purpose (Cullen and Calvert, 1996). When the library is viewed as a social construct, performance measurement becomes a social construct also. Within the context of your library's environment, discuss the present focus of your management and follow that with a discussion of value and purpose. From this discussion with your staff and supervisor, you can start looking at the kinds of assessments that can be done to be meaningful in your environment.

Looking at organizational models is a complex and multidimensional process. The idea is to balance your activities with an overall plan that looks at all dimensions, to create a culture where all aspects of the library are assessed and evaluated. How you see the "dimensions" of the library service will have an effect on how you plan to assess and evaluate them. How well you learn the skills in accomplishing an evaluation will be important also. It is hoped that the five evaluation methods described in this book, with their step-by-step instructions, will assist you. But this is just a "cookbook." As you prepare to do your evaluation project, always think of the bigger picture and where the library service being evaluated fits in.

# THE EFFECTIVE LIBRARIAN

Using the definitions above, an effective librarian would be someone who does well what he or she is supposed to do. To be effective, the librarian needs certain competencies and skills. Why address this in a book about evaluation? The following reasons demonstrate why:

- Evaluation and assessment are an important part of your competency and skill set.
- If you are going to have a culture of assessment, you and your staff need a variety of skills and competencies.
- Which skills and competencies should you pursue?

This section gives you an overview of the resources available to make your decision.

There is a lot of literature on competencies, and many librarians are being asked to write them for their staff as part of the job description performance evaluation system at their institution. Writing from scratch is a difficult proposition, but utilizing the literature and the available lists will help you get started. Holloway and her team at the University of Arizona Library give an excellent review of their experience writing competencies (Holloway, 2003: 94). The author advises that writing core competencies should be a team effort, but the results can be used to:

- Define work expectations across groups of librarians with similar responsibilities
- Build job descriptions
- Provide measures for performance evaluations
- Inform interview questions for candidates, and
- Provide directions for new areas of learning and growth at the mastery level

`Studying competencies in relation to evaluation and assessment is part of providing directions for new areas of learning and growth for you and your staff. Since you are reading this book, you are to be congratulated for taking a step forward to gain a new skill or competency! You have probably seen surveys from library associations asking what continuing education course you would want to take. Some have over 35 "skills" listed. How do you decide which ones are most important? First understand the terms involved in a review of core competencies. Holloway has graded the different levels competencies and skills in this way (2003: 95):

- *Professional competency*—knowledge in the areas of collection development and needs assessment, information resources development, education, and reference, and the ability to use these areas of knowledge to provide library and information services
- *Personal competency*—roles, attitudes, and values that enable librarians to work effectively and efficiently in a team-based environment, focus on continuous learning, and demonstrate the value-added nature of their contributions
- *Expectation*—minimum levels of activity or behavior that demonstrate competencies
- *Skill*—a developed aptitude or ability, such as computer skills, language ability

Next, review lists of competencies and read about the issues involved. Do an inventory of your own personal and professional competencies and your skills. Decide where you excel and make sure your supervisor is aware of your knowledge and abilities. Decide where you could improve and seek out education and experiences that will enable you to do so. Stretch your abilities by taking on unfamiliar projects.

This section could have a long list of competencies and skills that make an effective librarian. But many of these are readily available in articles and Web pages. For small special libraries, the most referenced is the *Competencies for Information Professionals of the 21st Century*, first developed in 1996, extensively revised in 2003, and available on the Web. The list has two parts including personal competencies and professional competencies. Professional competencies are divided into four major sections as well as applied scenarios to illustrate many of the roles and responsibilities performed by information professionals:

- Managing information organizations
- Managing resources
- Managing services
- Applying information tools and technologies

"Professional Competencies relate to the practitioner's knowledge of information resources, access, technology and management, and the ability to use this knowledge as a basis for providing the highest quality information services" (Abels, 2003).

In parts of sections A and C, the skills for evaluation and assessment are defined:

A. *Managing Information Organizations*
   A.2. Assesses and communicates the value of the information organization, including information services, products and policies to senior management, key stakeholders and client groups.
C. *Managing Information Services*
   C.4. Develops and applies appropriate metrics to continually measure the quality and value of information offerings, and to take appropriate action to ensure each offering's relevancy within the portfolio.
   C.5. Employs evidence-based management to demonstrate the value of and continually improve information sources and services.

**Reference: Competencies for Information Professionals of the 21st Century.**

Abels E, R. Jones, J. Latham, D. Magnoni, and J. G. Marshall. 2003. *Competencies for Information Professionals of the 21st Century.* Special Committee on Competencies for Special Librarians. Special Library Association. Available: www.sla.org/content/learn/comp2003/index.cfm. (accessed September 21, 2006).

*Applied Scenario*

> Uses evidence-based management to present reasoned evidence of a service's value and an organization's abilities. Develops and applies measures of service/product usage, client satisfaction and the organizational or client impact of services and products. Regularly assesses clients' information wants and gaps using market research tools including questionnaires, surveys, interviews, focus groups and observation.

In a review of the recent literature on core competencies, the following examples were found, many of which provide a list or reference lists that you could use for your inventory:

- Moran discusses how core competencies relate to the future in this interesting overview. He discusses the ALA *Draft Statement of Core Competencies 2005*, and he connects the values of librarians to the rapidly emerging technologies (Moran, 2005; American Library Association, accessed: 2006).
- Lougee's work for the Council on Library and Information Resources (CLIR) titled *Diffuse Libraries: Emergent Roles for the Research Library in the Digital Age*; here she states that she believes technology has opened possibilities for broader and deeper involvement for libraries and librarians in education and learning (Lougee, 2002).
- Holloway, who was already quoted above, describes the difference between core and mastery-level professional competencies and how they were developed and used at her institution. They used the SLA competencies and those from the Association of Southeastern Research Libraries (Holloway, 2003; Abels, 2003; Association of Southeastern Research Libraries, accessed: 2006). A list of those developed at the University of Arizona is included in an appendix.
- Van Wert reports on a survey of special and academic librarians in Colorado (Van Wert, 2004). Using competency lists can help librarians inventory their skills and look for training in areas where they are lacking. She points out that linking competencies to staff development helps with evaluating staff-training needs and with justifying the expense of meeting those needs. She points out that finding the budget money can be difficult. (As reported in the MLA Benchmarking Network survey 2004, of the 281 libraries

reporting their annual expenditures for professional development and travel, the mean was $1,784 and median was $1,409. These figures could be used to ask for funds.) Van Wert mentions three useful Web lists:
- Competencies of Law Librarianship (American Association of Law Libraries, accessed: 2006)
- Library Staff Competencies: Administrators, Librarians, Paraprofessional Support Staff (Library Staff Competencies, accessed: 2006)
- Managerial Competencies for Small and One Person Libraries (accessed: 2006)

- Beck gives an overview of specialized competencies for public services staff. She lists competencies in the technology area, which may be helpful to someone who has to develop a competencies list for a technical position. There is also a list of where to find lists of competencies on the Web and in print (Beck, 2002).
- Press and Diggs-Hobson provide us with a list of the characteristics of a culturally competent librarian, hereby giving all of us some food for thought about how we interact with our users, especially those from a different culture (Press and Diggs-Hobson, 2005).
- Stanley put together some "Hospital-Specific Examples" for each of the 1996 SLA competencies. These were discussed at a 1999 symposium for hospital librarians and published here (Stanley, 2002).
- Helmick and Swigger report on a project to list the competencies of the "library practitioner," a person defined in this project as someone working as a director of a small public library, usually an independent library in a small community, who "do not have accredited master's degrees in librarianship and usually have had little or no formal training in librarianship, as well as little or no work experience in public libraries prior to assuming the role of director" (Helmick and Swigger, 2006: 54). Because of economic, geographic, and educational issues, over two-thirds of western states public libraries are managed by such library practitioners (Western Council of State Libraries, accessed: 2006). The core competencies are grouped in seven major categories and give detailed lists of expected knowledge. While developed for the public library setting, this list could be used by the special librarian in a small setting as a competency and skills inventory.

## GOALS OF EVALUATION

This is a lot of information to absorb, and there is no fast and easy way to develop a culture of assessment. The first step is to decide if this idea will work for you and your environment or social context. Study some of the work cited here. Discuss it with your supervisor. Does he or she understand the challenges facing libraries today?

Survival of libraries is not necessarily self-centered. Yes, we want to keep our jobs, and, yes, as a profession, we believe that libraries have a place in the world. But we also want to:

- Have services and programs that are developed to meet the information need of the users
- Do the best job possible with the most cost-efficient systems.
- Make decisions for the library services that are based on evidence.
- Show that the services and programs provided by the library have been effective in achieving the mission of the organization.
- Demonstrate that library service has value in the user's life and work.

If these sound familiar, they are the purposes of evaluation. No one can ever ensure their survival, but by developing a culture of assessment and a learning environment, you will know you have given it your best shot. Maybe your shot will be nothing but net!

## REFERENCES

Abels, E., R. Jones, J. Latham, D. Magnoni, and J. G. Marshall. 2003. *Competencies for Information Professionals of the 21st Century*. Special Committee on Competencies for Special Librarians. Special Library Association. Available: www.sla.org/content/learn/comp2003/index.cfm (accessed September 21, 2006).

American Association of Law Libraries. "Competencies of Law Librarianship." American Association of Law Libraries (last updated March 2001). Available: www.aallnet.org/prodev/competencies.asp (accessed June 12, 2006).

American Library Association. "Draft Statement of Core Competencies 2005." American Library Association (last updated July 2005). Available: www.ala.org/ala/accreditationb/Draft_Core_Competencies_07_05.pdf (accessed September 21, 2006).

Association of Southeastern Research Libraries. "Shaping the Future: ASERL's Competencies for Research Librarians." Association of Southeastern Research Libraries (last updated November 10, 2000). Available: www.aserl.org/statements/competencies/competencies.htm (accessed September 21, 2006).

Beck, M. A. 2002. "Technology Competencies in the Continuous Quality Improvement Environment: A Framework for Appraising the Performance of Library Public Services Staff." *Library Administration and Management*, 16, no. 2: 69–72.

Calvert, P. J. 1994. "Library Effectiveness: The Search for a Social Context." *Journal of Librarianship and Information Science*, 26: 15–21.

Cameron, K. 1986. "A Study of Organizational Effectiveness and Its Predictors." *Management Science*, 32: 87–112.

Cullen, R. "Measure for Measure: A Post-Modern Critique of Performance Measurement in Libraries and Information Services" (last updated June 1–5, 1998). Available: http://iatul.org/conference/proceedings/vol08/papers/cullen.html (accessed September 22, 2006).

Cullen, R., and P. J. Calvert. 1996. "New Zealand University Libraries Effectiveness Project: Dimensions and Concepts of Organizational Effectiveness. *Library and Information Science Research*, 18, no. 2: 99–119.

Franklin, B. "Organizational Assessment: An Academic Library Case Study." Available: www.lib.uconn.edu/~bfranklin/orgassess.doc (accessed September 12, 2006).

Helmick, C., and K. Swigger. 2006. "Core Competencies of Library Practitioners." *Public Libraries*, 45, no. 2: 54–69.

Holloway, K. L. 2003. "Developing Core and Mastery-Level Competencies for Librarians." *Library Administration and Management*, 17, no. 2: 94–98.

Lakos, A. "Culture of Assessment – Toolkit." Available: http://personal.anderson.ucla.edu/amos.lakos/CUtoolkit.html (accessed September 21, 2006).

Lakos, A., and S. Phipps. 2004. "Creating a Culture of Assessment: A Catalyst for Organizational Change." *Portal*, 4, no. 3: 345–361.

Lakos, Amos, and Shelley Phipps. "Defining a 'Culture of Assessment'" (last updated 2002). Available: http://personal.anderson.ucla.edu/amos.lakos/assessment/CulAssessToolkit/Assessdef3-new.doc (accessed September 21, 2006).

Lee-Thomas, G., and J. Robson. 2004. "The Questions of Academic Library Assessment." *Indiana Libraries*, 23, no. 1: 6–10.

"Library Staff Competencies: Administrators, Librarians, Paraprofessional Support Staff." Available: http://librarysupportstaff.com/4competency.html (accessed June 12, 2006).

Lougee, W. P., and the Council on Library and Information Resources. 2002. "Diffuse Libraries: Emergent Roles for the Research Library in the Digital Age." Council on Library and Information Resources. Available: www.clir.org/pubs/reports/pub108/pub108.pdf (accessed September 21, 2006).

"Managerial Competencies for Small and One-Person Libraries." Arrowhead Library System, MN. Available: www.arrowhead.lib.mn.us/renewal/managerial.htm (accessed June 12, 2006).

Moran, R. F., Jr. 2005. "Core competencies." *Library Administration and Management*, 19, no. 3: 146–148.

Phipps, S. E. 2001. "Beyond Measuring Service Quality: Learning from the Voices of the Customers, the Staff, the Processes, and the Organization." *Library Trends*, 49, no. 4: 635–661.

Press, N. O., and M. Diggs-Hobson. 2005. "Providing Health Information to Community Members Where They Are: Characteristics of the Culturally Competent Librarian." *Library Trends*, 53, no. 3: 397–410.

Senge, P. M. 2006. *The Fifth Discipline: The Art and Practice of the Learning Organization*. New York: Doubleday/Currency.

Stanley, E. 2002. "Competencies for Hospital Librarians." *National Network*, 24, no. 2: 12–13, 20.

University of Maryland Libraries. "University of Maryland Libraries Learning Curriculum." Available: www.lib.umd.edu/pub/learning/curriculum.html (accessed September 21, 2006).

Van Wert, L. 2004. "How Do We Know What We Don't Know? Competencies and Staff Development in Special Libraries. *Colorado Libraries*, 30, no. 2: 10–14.

Wallace, D. P., and C. J. Van Fleet. 2001. "The Culture of Evaluation." In *Library Evaluation: A Casebook and Can-Do Guide*, edited by D. P. Wallace and C. J. Van Fleet. Englewood, CO: Libraries Unlimited.

Western Council of State Libraries. "Library Practitioner Core Competencies." Continuum of Library Education, Western Council of State Libraries (last updated October 20, 2004). Available: www.westernco.org/continuum/final.html (accessed September 21, 2006).

Zweizig, D. L., D. W. Johnson, J. Robbins, and the American Library Association. 1996. *The TELL IT! Manual: The Complete Program for Evaluating Library Performance*. Chicago, IL: American Library Association.

# LIBRARY MEASURES

When did you last measure your library? What measure did you choose? You have just read about why it is important to evaluate, how to create a culture of assessment, and what skills are needed to do so. Now you need to look at your library and start by picking something to measure. You might begin with a simple measure of activity, perhaps count interlibrary loans or circulation. These are traditional activities to count. You should first think about trying to explain a relationship between the two activities to your supervisor or even what they individually mean. And what relationship do they have to your budget and to your users? If you were given more money to buy books, would your circulation go up and would increased circulation prove this to be a worthwhile expenditure? Maybe, maybe not. In this chapter we will be discussing the controversies involved in how measures are decided on and how they relate to one another.

## LIMITATIONS OF MEASUREMENT

In 1988, Deborah Goodall reviewed the substantial research done on performance measurement in the 1970s and 1980s. She points out that while plenty had been written, the studies were mostly modifications and not improvements on the system of evaluating libraries. She lists these difficulties with making improvements in evaluation methods (Goodall, 1988: 140–141):

- Difficulty in finding suitable measures for individual services and even if found, there is a problem synthesizing them into a whole picture of your library.
- Simple numerical measures, such as circulation or interlibrary loan, may give a misleading picture, but complex approaches like outcomes measurement may be too difficult to do.
- Systematic collection of data over time may be too costly and small samples less accurate or useful.
- While data is needed for better management and for budget justification, the same data may not satisfy these two needs.
- While there are qualitative library standards in some specialized settings, as covered in Chapter 7, since there are no established quantitative standards for libraries that

specify the exact measure and quantity of that measure, collecting comparative data may be the way to go. This can allow you to view trends over time and to compare different libraries across the board. Interpretation of findings would be up to the individual library.

- Librarians are not motivated to do performance measurement because many measurement tactics are complex and impractical.
- Librarians fear that when compared with others, they might be at the bottom or at the top. Those at the top fear they will be cut back, and those at the bottom fear being viewed as failures. Both need to realize their opportunity. Those at the top can set an example and can be viewed and promoted as a "best practice" library. Those toward the bottom can take the opportunity to learn from others and to demonstrate the need for more support to reach "standard" levels of service.

Jennifer Cram also finds the literature of evaluation full of problems and performance measurement still needing improvement in practice. Some of her grievances are similar (Cram, 1996: 231):

- It is hard to see where all the bits fit together; that is, evaluation strategies are usually not holistic.
- Evaluation projects often rely too much on statistical measurement; that is, too much that really is important is ignored or discounted in the interest of neatness.
- The collection of data is focused on process and transactions and not on outcomes of service.
- There is significant underperformance on the part of librarians in extracting information from the data collected, partly due to a lack of an overall picture.
- Customer satisfaction data is approached as a report card in its most negative sense rather than as a source of information about areas where improvement or further investigation is needed.

Gorman responds with the advice that librarians need to be aware that (Gorman, 2000: 119):

- Meaningful data are contextual.
- Meaning depends on interpretation.
- Meaning is derived from variables that are complex and difficult to measure.
- Understanding is an inductive process.

---

**Definition: Inductive Reasoning vs. Deductive Reasoning**

Inductive reasoning: drawing a general conclusion based on a limited set of observations; a system of reasoning based on observation and measurement.

Deductive reasoning: The process of reasoning from general principles to particular examples; a system of reasoning based on definitions and premises.

This differs from, but is not necessarily in conflict with, the traditional quantitative approach that the statistician takes. That position consists of identifying and measuring variables, which can be done in a relatively straightforward manner, as well as the fact that norms and consensus can be derived from the data by a deductive process. Since the "norms and consensus" of managing a library are not totally agreed upon, establishing a set of measures for your particular library can be more of an art than a science.

These problems with evaluation practices will remain with us. As you embark on your road to a culture of assessment, you should be aware of them. Luckily we have many national and international initiatives aimed at assessment and evaluation issues, and many good ideas and tools are being developed to deal with these problems.

# TYPES OF MEASURES

Chapter 1 discussed the change in the social or cultural context in which the library exists. This affects the kind of measures that a library chooses to use. In the stereotypical library, there were only three types of measures, as illustrated in Figure 3.1.

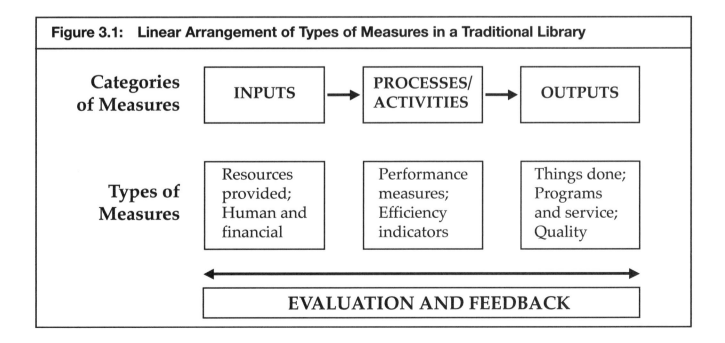

**Figure 3.1: Linear Arrangement of Types of Measures in a Traditional Library**

| Categories of Measures | INPUTS | → | PROCESSES/ ACTIVITIES | → | OUTPUTS |

| Types of Measures | Resources provided; Human and financial | | Performance measures; Efficiency indicators | | Things done; Programs and service; Quality |

**EVALUATION AND FEEDBACK**

Historically, libraries would compare how big they were in terms of inputs like budget, staff, and collection. Bigger was considered better. Then when business management practices were starting to be applied to libraries, the actual processes of the library were measured for efficiency. Next, external stakeholders starting asking what libraries were doing with all the resources given to them. So libraries started to report all their activity, their circulation, interlibrary loans, and reference questions, their outputs. Although it is quite hard to prove in a library setting, the linear relationship among these three entities—inputs, processes, and outputs—is taken from manufacturing. The more raw material you have, the more efficient your process is, the greater your output and thereby your outcomes and your profit. A feedback loop is also seen to exist where, through evaluation of outputs, you could adjust your inputs or processes, as shown in Figure 3.1.

In the last ten years, to add to the problems of measurement, libraries have been asked to demonstrate that the activities produced by the resources they are allotted have made a difference in the life or work of the recipient of those activities, called, variously, the patron, user, client, or customer. The next step is to show how this changed person impacted the community or organization.

The Institute of Museum and Library Services (IMLS), a leader in measuring such impacts, defines outcomes as "benefits to people: specifically, achievements or changes in skill, knowledge, attitude, behavior, condition, or life status for program participants" (IMLS, accesses: 2006). In a university setting, libraries are being asked how their programming contributes to the learning outcome of the student or the research effort of the institution. Chapter 8, "Outcomes Measurment," gives more background on the social pressures that have led to the use of outcomes measures and more on the initiatives to respond to them. In most descriptions of outcomes measurement, outcomes is a category of measures tacked on near the end of a linear continuum, as shown in Figure 3.2.

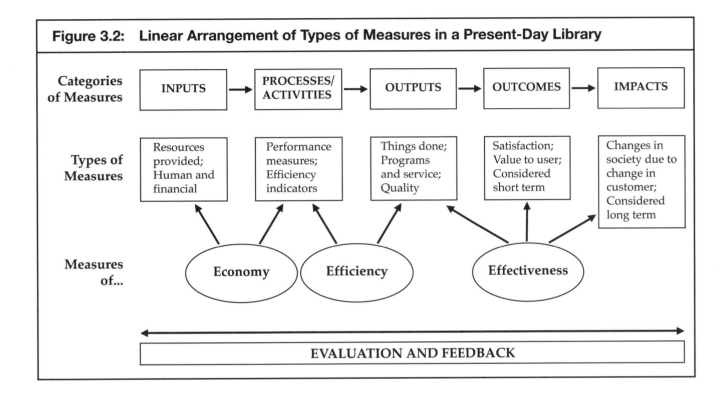

Figure 3.2: Linear Arrangement of Types of Measures in a Present-Day Library

Martha Kyrillidou, as shown in her essay on the issues involved in this continuum, believes that the relationship is not necessarily linear. *All* of these categories could have an effect on one another, perhaps in a circular pattern with connections even haphazardly across the middle. She uses as an example the complex information-seeking behavior of a graduate student where the physical library and even the virtual library are just two points on a complex interaction of information sources accessed. If you add motion to the model, she sees a "more dynamic and flexible model, moving users and information resources into a spiral swirl up and down into the depths of knowledge, exploration, and experience" (Kyrillidou, 2002: 45).

Whichever type of measure you select to use in your evaluation project, whether counts of inputs or outputs or surveys of outcomes or customer satisfaction, the idea is to think broadly about the activities being measured. Be sure the purpose of your project is clear and its relationship to your strategic mission is written down.

# MEASUREMENT PLANNING

As mentioned in Chapter 2, as part of an overall plan for improvement, you are going to develop a culture of assessment. You are going to start by developing or reviewing the mission of the library to see if it is in line with the organization's mission. You will be involving your staff and your supervisor. Next you start by selecting one small area in which to do your first evaluation project and understanding how that area fits into the larger whole. Using strategic planning methods or SMART goals, as described in Chapters 9 and 12, or a logic model, as described in Chapter 8, and other resources in this book, you start your evaluation plan in one area. Then you move on to other areas using the same methods, and after a while you will have an evaluation plan for the whole library. Review various lists of traditional measures such as the ones listed below to help decide which measures to start to collect. You may already be collecting some of these, so you should congratulate yourself.

As part of the planning process, you would explain *why* you are collecting the measure, describe *what* each measure is, and detail *how* it is collected and stored.

- Why: Relate the measure to an objective or goal that is named in the overall mission.
- What: Write some definitions about the measure or parameters to describe the measure, for example, what constitutes a reference question.
- How: Write a procedure describing where the measure comes from and how it will be collected.

You could go from the mission to the measure or from the measure up to the mission. Start small with an overall plan in mind and execute it part by part. At first, a part-by-part process might be a little disjointed. If you start with the mission, after examining it you could choose a mission-critical part of the operation to evaluate and write all the supporting goals and objectives and evaluation plans for it. Or you could start with a specific problem and after relating it to the mission, write the plan for its evaluation. After doing this over time for enough parts of the library operation, you will have a strategic plan with mission, goals, objectives, and measures. An example of this from another industry could be the interstate highway system's new method of design and build. Instead of spending years writing a total strategic plan (or highway design), you design and build each part of the plan separately (each highway interchange) and in the end, you have a whole plan (or highway). Whichever way you go, using the Logic Model as described in Chapter 8, will help you with your planning efforts. The ideas of strategic planning are briefly covered in Chapter 9.

This planning system mostly applies to your traditional activities, such as interlibrary loan and circulation. When you start working on your "new" measures of outcomes and impacts, deciding what to collect and when becomes more complex. With the traditional measures, you can usually get the data from existing sources, such as budgets and activity counts. For outcomes, you will probably need to do a survey, focus group, or other data-gathering method, described in greater detail in Chapter 10. This type of evaluation should be written into your overall plan and carried out on a regular basis (that is, annually or biannually).

Remember, the goal is to develop a culture of assessment that allows you to make decisions based on evidence. From that evidence, you can write reports so others will understand your library's contribution to the institutional mission. The evaluation project is never the end in itself. Communicating your evaluation findings to various stakeholders is discussed in greater detail in Chapters 11 and 12.

Another important issue in the "what to measure" category is the issue of using quantitative or qualitative measures. For more techniques for collecting data for these two types of measures, see Chapter 10. Based on the problems listed above, it may be considered easier to use quantitative measures because of the difficulty in gathering qualitative measures. Often stakeholders think in terms of hard numbers, but these may not work for library systems. G. E. Gorman, who has authored books on both methods (Gorman, et al., 2005; Clayton and Gorman, 2003), wants librarians to strike a balance between the two methods and use both. He gives this advice (Gorman, 2000: 118):

- Look seriously at the genuine shortcomings of quantitative data collection and analysis methods and seek to incorporate qualitative methods that permit deeper understanding of library users, collections and services.
- Focus less on users as a genus, more on specific categories of users and profiles of their wants and needs.
- Focus less on numerical aspects of collections and more on acceptable indicators of collection quality.
- Focus less on simple user enquiries and more on the nature and level of these enquiries.
- Employ qualitative data collection methods in full awareness of the problems associated with achieving value-free

> "The distinction between efficiency and effectiveness is critical. Efficiency is a measure of cost. Effectiveness is a measure of outcome. Efficiency describes the relationship between a program's outcome and the resources expended to achieve the outcome. Efficiency is clearly important—the more efficient an organization, the more outcome it can generate from the same expenditure of resources—but it is always subsidiary to effectiveness. What effectiveness describes is the relationship between a program's outcome and the expectation with which that program was undertaken in the first place. Effectiveness is a measure of DID IT REALLY WORK?" (Weil, 2000: 10–11).

use of these methods, i.e., cultural or value bias in the answers you get.

- Foster awareness among stakeholders that efficiency and effectiveness are not equivalent concepts, and that effectiveness in the information sector is a greater good than efficiency.
- Work with software developers in creating qualitative data software programs that are more acceptable in terms of user friendliness and analytical capabilities.

Depending on what type of library you manage, you will find different lists of possible measures, both qualitative and quantitative. By reviewing any of them, you can get ideas of measures that might be useful or meaningful in your context. Some of the programs mentioned below have instructions and/or term definitions that will help you define the measure you are looking into collecting.

- *The Association of Research Libraries (ARL) Statistics & Measurement Program* (www.arl.org/stats/)

  This program has been an example to other library groups. By reviewing ARL's survey form, an older version of which is available on its Web site to nonmembers, you can see the instructions and the kinds of data they are asking for. Martha Kyrillidou has five criteria for "measures that matter." She advises, "Measure what is important, not just what is measurable, because what you measure is what you will pay attention to and work toward" (Kyrillidou and Askew, accessed: 2006).
- *The Association of Academic Health Sciences Libraries (AAHSL)* (www.aahsl.org/)

  The AAHSL survey is not on the Web but has been reported in the literature. An article by Gary Byrd and James Shedlock gives a list of all the different data items reported over time for this survey (Byrd and Shedlock, 2003). Although there are no definitions, it is a comprehensive list of inputs, outputs, and university library customers.
- *The Medical Library Association Benchmarking Network Surveys 2002 and 2004 (MLA)* (www.mlanet.org/)

  The work sheets and definitions used for this survey include 12 parameters for measuring the size of a hospital library and 73 measures of library inputs and outputs. In the 2004 version there were attempts to collect parameters for other types of libraries. These are available in

---

**Did You Know: Measures That Matter Should:**

- Be consistent with the organizational mission, goals, and objectives
- Integrate with program review processes as established in the culture of assessment
- Balance customer, stakeholder, and employee interests and needs
- Establish accountability
- Be collected and used only when the data are reliable and valid (Kyrillidou and Askew, accessed; 2006)

---

**On the CD-ROM: Sample of a List of Measures**
In the Chapter 6 folder: MLA BN Survey Worksheets Folder
The questionnaire and definitions for the MLA Benchmarking Network Surveys 2004

the members-only section of the MLA Web site and also on the CD-ROM in the folder for Chapter 6 included with this book. The 2002 work sheet is also available as an electronic appendix to the article on the subject by Dudden, which can be downloaded from PubMed Central (Dudden, et al., 2006b).

- *Indicators of Outcomes in Colleges*

  Bonnie Gather Lindauer has published lists of student learning outcomes and indicators for colleges and community colleges in her publications. In her 1998 article she also reports outcomes and indicators in various categories (Lindauer, 1998), as well as the performance indicators for the university library study in New Zealand by Cullen and Calvert (Cullen and Calvert, 1995). In her 2004 manual, *Measuring What Matters: A Library/LRC Outcomes Assessment Manual*, written for California community colleges, she has lists of possible outcomes indicators for this type of library (Lindauer, 2004).

- *Indicators of Outcomes in Public Libraries*

  Institute of Museum and Library Services (IMLS) has funded two projects to look at outcomes in public libraries. These are described more fully in Chapter 8. One is the Counting on Results (CoR) program, which developed a method to survey outcomes and count them. This project developed six questionnaires that addressed 13 "service responses." These are available on its Web site (Colorado State Library Library Research Service, accessed: 2006).

  The other project is a research program of the Information School of the University of Washington and the University of Michigan. Now named IBEC: Information Behavior in Everyday Context, its slogan is "helping maximize the impact of information in communities" (IBEC, accessed: 2006). On the Web-based *Outcomes Toolkit* is included sample surveys that show the questions other projects asked (Durrance and Fisher, accessed: 2006).

  Another major list that has both traditional measures and outcomes measures can be found in Appendix A of Joseph R. Matthews's book *Measuring for Results: The Dimensions of Public Library Effectiveness* (Matthews, 2004).

- *Indicators gathered from surveys by state agencies and accrediting bodies*

  Much of the literature, especially regarding measures for college and university libraries, discusses the expectations of accrediting bodies. Public libraries look at state surveys from library or education agencies. Library leaders recommend that librarians be part of the team that develops these questions so that the measures requested are in tune with what libraries are doing today. These expectation need to reflect not just the libraries' outputs but also their outcomes and impact. Lindauer, in her article "Comparing the Regional Accreditation standards: Outcomes Assessment and Other Trends" discusses these issues and trends (Lindauer, 2002).

# WHAT TO MEASURE

As you think of your library and its management, how do you categorize it? Since you are a librarian, you are probably already doing this. Traditionally the three standard categories of library work have been public services, technical services, and administration. Today these have been renamed client satisfaction, collections and usage, and strategic alignment (Henczel, 2006). The semantic difference is amazing.

- *Public service* emphasized the fact that the library is performing a service and to evaluate it you would simply look at the service. *Client satisfaction* refers to the user or customer. To evaluate that concept, you have to look at what they need or want and if they considered that what they got was of quality. The focus changed from the service to the customer.
- *Technical service* refers to the process of storing and retrieving material that is in the collection. To evaluate this you might do a quality improvement project analyzing the efficiency of a process, as discussed in Chapter 5. *Collections and usage* refers to the content of a library, whether on a shelf or over the network, not just the process that got it there. It also implies that usage is important, not just the process of storage. The focus again has moved to the customer.
- *Administration* is a word that is thought of as managing budgets, personnel, and facilities. It is an internal word, implying that the library is an isolated place. Analysis is therefore done internally and looks at internal trends and quality. *Strategic alignment* is an external concept. Where does the library fit into its environment, its context? The

stakeholders that control this external environment of the library are more important than ever. By evaluating the concept of strategic alignment, a library can find ways to communicate with these stakeholders. By doing so they might be able to increase their resources (budget, personnel, and resources) to manage information and knowledge or at least maintain them.

The Association of Research Libraries (ARL) is leading the way in developing systems for gathering and analyzing measures that will describe the effective library of the future with all the changes it is going through. One of ARL's eight strategic objectives is "performance measures," with the goal "to describe and measure the performance of research libraries and their contribution to teaching, research, learning and community service." In 1999, they introduced the ARL New Measures Initiative in response to the following needs (ARL New Measures Iniative, accessed: 2006):

- Increasing demand for libraries to demonstrate outcomes/ impacts in areas important to the institution
- Increasing pressure to maximize use of library resources by benchmarking best practices to save or reallocate resources

All of the ARL initiatives can be found at the New Measures Initiative Web site, which identifies eight areas where new measures will be needed by the library of the future. These new measures can align with the three new categories of library work mentioned above:

- *Client Satisfaction*
  1. User Satisfaction
  2. Library Impact on Teaching and Learning
- *Collections and Usage*
  3. Ease and Breadth of Access
  4. Library Impact on Research
  5. Library Facilities and Space
- *Strategic Alignment*
  6. Market Penetration
  7. Cost Effectiveness of Library Operations and Services
  8. Organizational Capacity

Librarians who work in small library settings may well say, "But the libraries that belong to ARL are the biggest libraries in world! What has this got to do with my small library?" But it

**Reference: ARL New Measures Initiatives**

The initiatives that address these areas are reviewed by Julia Blixrud:

Blixrud, J.C. "Mainstreaming New Measures." *ARL*. 230/231 (2003): 1–8. Available: www.arl.org/ newsltr/230/

Also in white papers from the 1999 retreat found on the Web at: www.arl.org/stats/ newmeas/nmbackground.html really is just about scale. You may have only a few square feet and a few public computers, but you still need to evaluate their strategic importance to the mission of the library and how they serve its customers. By reading about what the ARL libraries are thinking concerning facilities and space, with their huge buildings and hundreds of computers, you may get some ideas about how to describe the strategic importance of a new computer for your library. And by looking at these areas that have been identified, you may start thinking of your library in a new way.

The ARL is one example of forward thinking about the structure of libraries. OCLC is also going to look at the future of libraries. It was announced in November 2006 that OCLC was awarded a $1.2 million grant from the Bill and Melinda Gates Foundation to develop a national marketing campaign to increase awareness of the value of libraries and the need to support them. With the funds, OCLC will conduct research, develop strategies, create materials, and test elements of a national marketing campaign to demonstrate the value of libraries, and the need to increase support for libraries to meet the changing needs and expectations of library users at local, state, and national levels.

Studies indicate that most people are unaware of all the types of information and services libraries make available to their patrons. *Perceptions of Libraries and Information Resources*, a report issued in December 2005 (OCLC Online Computer Library Center, accessed: 2006), noted that U.S. residents do not have a current view of library services or technology offerings. Most residents hold a nostalgic view of libraries, associating libraries overwhelmingly with "books." While 99% of libraries now provide free Internet access and most provide electronic collections and online services, many residents are unfamiliar with these services and do not see libraries as providing services that fit with their current lifestyles.

Again this is on a grand scale compared with your small operation. But the same pressures come into play. How many of your users "perceive" the resources they access at their desks as being supplied by the library? While this OCLC plan is talking about marketing, tuning your evaluation program to these new paradigms should be an important part of your plans.

# COMPARATIVE DATA INITIATIVES

Both ARL and AAHSL collect library statistics or measures on a national level. These data collection initiatives started when comparing inputs and outputs across like institutions was a standard method of evaluation. The goal was to use the raw data or ratios to facilitate comparative benchmarking techniques to see how they compared to others.

Being the leaders in these efforts, library directors first had to find a way to make the data gathered in different institutions truly comparable. Definitions of what each measure meant were developed over time. Libraries that participated needed to agree on the definitions and then start collecting the data in the recommended manner. Over time, they added new measures and deleted ones that were no longer useful.

Today both the ARL and the AAHSL have initiatives to describe the new world of electronic resources. As an example, the ARL E-Metrics and COUNTER projects are efforts to explore the feasibility of defining and collecting data on the use and value of electronic resources. Another example is the Institute of Museum and Library Services (IMLS) funded *E-Metrics Instructional System* (EMIS) at the Information Use Management Policy Institute and the School of Information Studies at Florida State University. The EMIS provides public librarians with multifaceted Web-based instruction regarding the usage of and uses for networked information resources (E-Metrics Instructional System, accessed 2006). The EMIS program has an excellent downloadable report (*Electronic Resources and Services Annual Report*) that can be copied and adapted for your situation. Both of these initiatives will allow practicing librarians eventually to be able to measure the new electronic resources available in their library and understand how to communicate the measures to their administrator.

In a 1981 study Nina Matheson and Suzanne Grefsheim criticized the use of these comparable quantitative statistics to measure local library quality. They saw these data-collection efforts as merely measuring resource allocations. They also questioned their use in surveys by accrediting bodies. Even as early as 1981, they called for "a means to evaluate the effectiveness of that allocation by determining its worth and its impact on users" (Matheson and Grefsheim, 1981: 300). Even with such early criticism, the data-collection programs of these associations have continued.

---

Resource on the Web:
*Electronic Resources and Services Annual Report.*
www.ii.fsu.edu/EMIS/annualReport.cfm.

This Web site includes downloadable examples of the use of e-metric data in annual report format. The examples represent public libraries of different sizes.

Annual report templates are available to use with your own data. There are four files that work together to allow you to create your annual report:

- An MS Word file containing instructions and tips for developing an annual e-metrics report using your own data
- An Excel spreadsheet where you will enter your library's data
- An MS Word file containing the draft annual report on the Library's Electronic Resources and Services
- An MS Word file containing the annual report appendices related to method.

The EMIS would like to see your completed annual report. It can be sent as an attachment to *emis@lis.fsu.edu*

In 2003, James Shedlock, then chair of the *Annual Statistics* editorial board of the AAHSL, states "The *Annual Statistics* continue to serve the members as a highly regarded and essential management tool. . . . Consistent data are highly valued, because trend analysis is an important component in the management of local resources" (Shedlock, 2003: 184). The rise of benchmarking as a management tool also has encouraged the use of tools such as the AAHSL *Annual Statistics*. Chapter 6 describes the use of the national data collection initiatives for performance benchmarking and identification of benchmarking partners. The comparative statistics can be used for service comparisons, to establish best practices, for management decisions, or for research projects.

Hospital and other special library members of the Medical Library Association (MLA) in the past had neither the organization nor the impetus to gather comparable statistics about their activities. Local and regional surveys have been done in the past and sporadically reported in the literature (Van Toll and Calhoun, 1985). Activity in the late 1980s in the Hospital Libraries Section (HLS) of the MLA inspired the American Hospital Association (AHA) librarians to push for a survey of hospital libraries. AHA survey results reported the type of services in hospital libraries but not any measures of those services (Wakeley and Foster, 1993).

In the late 1990s, health-care economic forces were causing many hospital libraries to be closed. Market forces, especially managed care and its emphasis on cost control, transformed the health care industry, especially the hospital sector. Many hospitals embraced plans for mergers as a strategy to decrease costs. It was reported that in 1996 a record number of 768 hospitals merged (Japsen, 1996). As more hospitals merged, many departments were consolidated across hospitals. This departmental consolidation trend affected some hospital libraries drastically. The hospital library literature of the 1990s contains a number of examples of libraries that were consolidated, downsized, or eliminated following a merger (Schott, 1996; Williamson, 1997).

In response MLA leaders began investigating the feasibility of providing comparative data to hospital libraries. The MLA Benchmarking Network Surveys of 2002 and 2004 were modeled on the survey example of the AAHSL *Annual Statistics* and the Canadian Health Libraries Association/Association des Bibliothèques de la Santé du Canada (CHLA/ABSC) benchmarking tool kit, which was developed to assist their members in collecting and analyzing data (CHLA/ABSC Benchmarking Task force, 1998). The development and results of the MLA

Benchmarking Network Survey 2002 are reported by Dudden et al. (2006a; 2006b).

There are other examples of national data collection efforts, many of which use the Web to collect the data. This has cut down on the sometimes prohibitive costs of mailing and data entry of such surveys. The problem still remains of defining the data so it is truly comparable. One library's count of items used in the library or categories of primary users may be completely different from another's, even though they appear to collect similar numbers. Also, the issue of outcomes and impacts has not been integrated into these efforts, but it is hoped that in the future there will be development in this area.

It is difficult to say that one should exactly measure this or that, since there are so many variables in the context of any given library. In today's environment, you will need to measure a variety of inputs, processes, outputs, and outcomes, all with different methodologies, and each measurement will be reported to different stakeholders. In the future, new technologies will require new sets of measures. This book attempts to give you the tools to use evaluation to accomplish an effective library service using meaningful measures.

In these first three chapters, you have read about where evaluation might fit in the life of your library and some of the controversies and problems involved in deciding to do evaluation. In the next chapters you will learn about methods for needs assessment, quality improvement, benchmarking, library performance standards and outcomes measurement. Each type of evaluation has its place, and you do not need to do all of them. You may already know which is best for your situation, and you should read only what you need. The chapters in Part III will provide you with tools to get the job done, the mechanics of data collection and reporting. Above all, no matter which measure you decide to use as an indicator of a quality process, service, or outcome, it is recommended to look at the *why, what, and how*. Think strategically. Why are you doing this evaluation? Be specific to your goals. What method are you going to use to evaluate which goal? Improve your skills technologically. How are you going to carry out the evaluation?

# REFERENCES

"ARL New Measures Initiative." Association of Research Libraries (last updated October 24, 2005). Available: www.arl.org/stats/newmeas/ (accessed September 22, 2006).

Byrd, G. D., and J. Shedlock. 2003. "The Association of Academic Health Sciences Libraries Annual Statistics: An Exploratory Twenty-Five-Year Trend Analysis." *Journal of the Medical Library Association*, 91, no. 2: 186–202.

CHLA/ABSC Benchmarking Task Force, Canadian Health Libraries Association/Association des bibliothèques de la santé du Canada. 1998. *CHLA/ABSC Benchmarking Tool Kit*. Toronto: Canadian Health Libraries Association/Association des bibliothèques de la santé du Canada.

Clayton, P., and G. E. Gorman. 2003. *The Information Professional's Guide to Quantitative Research: A Practical Handbook*. London: Facet.

Colorado State Library Library Research Service, University of Denver College of Education Library and Information Science Program. "Counting on Results." Available: www.lrs.org/CoR.asp (accessed July 12, 2006).

Cram, J. 1996. "Performance Management, Measurement and Reporting in a Time of Information-Centred Change." *Australian Library Journal*, 45, no. 3: 225–238.

Cullen, R., and P. J. Calvert. 1995. "Stakeholder Perceptions of University Library Effectiveness." *Journal of Academic Librarianship*, 21: 438–448.

Dudden, R. F., K. Corcoran, J. Kaplan, J. Magouirk, D. C. Rand, and B. T. Smith. 2006a. "The Medical Library Association Benchmarking Network: Development and Implementation." *Journal of the Medical Library Association*, 94, no. 2: 107–117.

Dudden, R. F., K. Corcoran, J. Kaplan, J. Magouirk, D. C. Rand, and B. T. Smith. 2006b. "The Medical Library Association Benchmarking Network: Results." *Journal of the Medical Library Association*, 94, no. 2: 118–129.

Durrance, J. C., and K. E. Fisher. "Outcomes Toolkit 2.0." Ann Arbor, MI and Seattle, WA: University of Michigan and University of Washington (last updated 2002). Available: http://ibec.ischool.washington.edu/default1024.aspx?subCat=Outcome%20Toolkit&cat=Tools%20and%20Resources (accessed June 12, 2006).

"E-Metrics Instructional System (EMIS)." Information Use Management Policy Institute, School of Information Studies, Florida State University. Available: www.ii.fsu.edu/EMIS/ (accessed September 22, 2006).

Goodall, D. L. 1988. "Performance Measurement: A Historical Perspective." *Journal of Librarianship*, 20, no. 2: 128–144.

Gorman, G. E. 2000. "Collecting Data Sensibly in Information Settings. *IFLA Journal*, 26, no. 2: 115–119.

Gorman, G. E., P. Clayton, S. J. Shep, and A. Clayton. 2005. *Qualitative Research for the Information Professional: A Practical Handbook*. 2nd ed. London: Facet.

Henczel, S. 2006. "Measuring and Evaluating the Library's Contribution to Organisational Success: Developing a Strategic Measurement Model." *Performance Measurement and Metrics*, 7, no. 1: 7–16.

"IBEC: Information Behavior in Everyday Context." Ann Arbor, MI and Seattle, WA: University of Michigan and University of Washington (last updated 2006). Available: http://ibec.ischool.washington.edu/ (accessed July 12, 2006).

Institute of Museum and Library Services. "Outcome-Based Evaluation Overview: New Directives, New Directions: Documenting Outcomes in IMLS Grants to Libraries and Museums." Institute of Museum and Library Services. Available: www.imls.gov/applicants/basics.shtm (accessed July 7, 2006).

Japsen, B. 1996. "Another Record Year for dealmaking: Activity among Medium-Size Companies Fuels Continued Drive toward Consolidation." *Modern Healthcare*, 26, no. 52: 37–38, 40–41, 44–46.

Kyrillidou, M. 2002. "From Input and Output Measures to Quality and Outcome Measures, or, from the User in the Life of the Library to the Library in the Life of the User." *Journal of Academic Librarianship*, 28, no. 1/2: 42–46.

Kyrillidou, M., and C. Askew. "Old and New Measures . . . Why Bother?" Association of Research Libraries (last updated February 24, 2003). Available: www.arl.org/stats/newmeas/index.html (accessed September 22, 2006).

Lindauer, B. G. 2002. "Comparing the Regional Accreditation Standards: Outcomes Assessment and Other Trends. *Journal of Academic Librarianship*, 28, no. 1/2: 14–25.

Lindauer, B. G. 1998. "Defining and Measuring the Library's Impact on Campuswide Outcomes." *College & Research Libraries*, 59, no. 6: 546–570.

Lindauer, B. G. 2004. *Measuring What Matters: A Library/LRC Outcomes Assessment Manual*. Revised edition. CA: Learning Resources Association of California Community Colleges.

Matheson, N. W., and S. F. Grefsheim. 1981. "National Rankings as a Means of Evaluating Medical School Library Programs: A Comparative Study." *Bulletin of the Medical Library Association*, 69, no. 3: 294–300.

Matthews, J. R. 2004. *Measuring for Results: The Dimensions of Public Library Effectiveness*. Westport, CT: Libraries Unlimited.

OCLC Online Computer Library Center Inc. "Perceptions of Libraries and Information Resources." OCLC Online Computer Library Center (last updated 2005). Available: www.oclc.org/reports/2005perceptions.htm (accessed December 15, 2006).

Schott, M. 1996. "Corporate Downsizing and the Special Library (Getting Tired of Lemons)." *MLA News*, no. 284: 1, 8–9.

Shedlock, J., and G. D. Byrd. 2003. "The Association of Academic Health Sciences Libraries Annual Statistics: A Thematic History." *Journal of the Medical Library Association*, 91, no. 2: 178–185.

Van Toll, F. A., and J. G. Calhoun. 1985. "Hospital Library Surveys for Management and Planning: Past and Future Directions." *Bulletin of the Medical Library Association*, 73, no. 1: 39–42.

Wakeley, P. J., and E. C. Foster. 1993. "A Survey of Health Sciences Libraries in Hospitals: Implications for the 1990s." *Bulletin of the Medical Library Association*, 81, no. 2: 123–128.

Weil, S. E. 2000. "Transformed from a Cemetery of Bric-a-Brac." In *Perspectives on Outcome-Based Evaluation for Libraries and Museums*, edited by B. Sheppard. Washington, DC: Institute of Museum and Library Services. Available: www.imls.gov/pdf/pubobe.pdf

Williamson, D. F. 1997. "Going with the Flow: Managed Care, Mergers, and Partnerships." *MLA News*, no. 297: 19.

# Part II

# Working With Evaluation Methods

# 4 METHOD 1: NEEDS ASSESSMENT

The phrase *needs assessment* often causes anxiety among librarians in small settings. You think of large surveys and difficult interpretations with no definite conclusions. A needs assessment is a way to prove that a gap in services exists at your library, whether you know it already or not. Some needs assessments are quick and easy to conduct, while others may take considerable time. Following every step outlined here could be a yearlong project, but the extra time is worth it in the long run because a carefully done needs assessment will yield results that apply for more than a year. Reading this chapter will also let you know what you are not going to get if you want to do a quick needs assessment.

Why do a needs assessment at all?

- As a management tool, the results can be used to advocate for more funding or to write a grant.
- Budgeting and planning can benefit from knowing what users need.
- The results can be used to explain services to users or to communicate with those with budget or funding authority.
- A needs assessment is the foundation for evaluating the program of the library as a whole.
- A needs assessment may be recommended or required by an accrediting body or library association standards.

While Chapter 7 covers library standards in detail, needs assessments are usually part of a library standards document. The Association of College and Research Libraries (ACRL) 2004 standards include the statement "Comprehensive assessment requires the involvement of all categories of library users and also a sampling of non-users" (ACRL College and Research Libraries Task Force, 2004). For hospital libraries, the Joint Commission on Accreditation of Healthcare Organizations (JCAHO) standards recommend that need assessments be done regularly (JCAHO, 2006). Standard IM.1 requires planning to meet both internal and external information needs. The *MLA Standards for Hospital Libraries 2002* have designated a standard for needs assessment as well, Standard 6, as shown in Figure 4.1 (Gluck, et al., 2002; Hassig, et al., 2005).

---

| **Figure 4.1 Standard 6: From the MLA Standards for Hospital Libraries 2002** |
| --- |
| "The librarian provides evidence of an ongoing assessment of the knowledge-based information (KBI) needs of the organization and the development and implementation of a plan to provide appropriate resources, services, and technology to meet those identified needs.<br><br>Intent: The librarian uses a variety of tools and techniques, both formal and informal, to assess the KBI needs of the hospital and medical staff. The needs assessment should address the timeliness of information services and document delivery. In response, resources and services are made available to meet those identified needs. Techniques may include, but are not limited to: focus groups, surveys, analysis of usage patterns, budget and strategic planning, inventory of collections, and one-on-one conversations with health care leaders regarding clinical and organizational information needs. Tools to be used include recognized guidelines, standards, lists of recommended resources, and benchmarking resources appropriate to the size and scope of the organization. Examples include MLA's benchmarking survey, the "Brandon/Hill Selected List of Print Books and Journals for the Small Medical Library," and other recognized resource guides for health sciences specialties" (Gluck, et al., 2002: 470). |

Attention to customer needs is important in any service profession. As covered in Chapters 2 and 5, the culture of assessment and the philosophies of total quality management (TQM) promote the change in library management to a customer-focused operation. To be customer focused, carrying out a periodic customer needs assessment is an essential part of the program of assessment and planning. Having a strategic plan with a mission statement has been mentioned. As part of the planning process, use of the Logic Model, as explained in Chapter 8, will integrate evaluation with the planning process including needs assessment. The ideas of strategic planning are briefly covered in Chapter 9.

Any good administrative report would indicate how you are meeting your customers' needs. But where do you find the time to learn about the process of assessing those needs? You would perhaps start with a survey of the literature only to find few examples of needs assessment in smaller libraries available. Lynn Westbrook's *Identifying and Analyzing User Needs* gives an in-depth overview of the needs assessment process and is geared to larger libraries (Westbrook, 2001). The article by Annabeth Crabtree, which is presented as a case study from the literature at the end of the chapter, is one of the few we found (Crabtree and Crawford, 1997). An in-press article describes an assessment process at Via Christi Health System in Wichita, Kansas (Perley et al., 2007). The project was funded in part by a grant from the

National Network of Libraries of Medicine. The study was conducted on behalf of the Via Christi libraries for the purpose of developing an evidence-based, user-centered long-term plan. A consultant was hired to plan and analyze the study and prepare the final report of the study.

Recommendations were organized to address the primary questions:

> **On the CD-ROM: Needs Assessment Final Report and Appendices**
>
> In the Chapter 4 Folder: Via Christi Folder
> Thanks go to Via Christi's administration for giving permission for this final report and appendices to be placed on the CD-ROM. This is a hard-to-find document and is a useful example for all small libraries of a comprehensive needs assessment project report.

- How can the Via Christi librarians best serve their patrons, given realistic limitations on time, resources, and personnel?
- Given these limitations, how can they best assist the medical center in terms of improving patient care and outcomes?

Most books on the subject are focused on either human resources training needs, educational needs, or larger sociological needs. It would take time to translate these procedures to a library setting or to translate the recommendations or examples to fit your setting. This chapter was developed with the practicing librarian in mind. The needs assessment process is simplified into twelve steps. It can be done quickly in as little as four weeks, or it can be a fully funded year long program using outside help. The scope of the assessment and the amount of resources available will determine the time you can spend on your project.

## WHAT IS A NEEDS ASSESSMENT?

> **Definition: Needs assessment**
>
> A systematic process for determining discrepancies between optimal and actual performance of a service by reviewing the service needs of customers and stakeholders and then selecting interventions that allow the service to meet those needs in the fastest, most cost-effective manner.

In the social sciences, a needs assessment is a study that answers questions about the social conditions a program is intended to address and the need for the program. In libraries, a needs assessment studies the nature of the information need that a specific information service is intended to address and the need for that service or another service to meet the perceived need. Needs assessments have been described using three models (McKillip, 2003):

- gap in services
- marketing
- decision-making

The gap in services model measures ideal services against what is being offered, or against user evaluation of what the user perceives as being offered. The marketing model looks at the match between what users want and what the library can provide instead of the ideal situation. In the decision-making model, you take the survey results and weigh them using a scale to make decisions about the program being evaluated. In Step 10 below, scales are described where to reach a decision you compare the results, which can easily be implemented to the results, which will have the most impact. All of these models have pieces that can be used by libraries. The gap model is the most widely used.

Using the gap model, needs assessment theorists in the social sciences define a need as a gap between a real condition that can possibly be changed and an ideal condition that is acknowledged as valuable (Reviere, et al., 1996). In the library world, an ideal condition might be that every user can access the library's electronic journal collection. You perceive, through your needs assessment that the real situation might be that only one-half of potential users have access to a computer that has Adobe Acrobat Reader on it, which means that up to one-half of them are unable to download and read full-text articles. The gap here is technological. Can the situation be changed to close the gap? Or you might find out that the interface to the electronic journals is not easily accessible or understood. The gap here is both a technological one and an educational one. Can either gap be closed?

A broader observation might be that you perceive there is a gap between the real condition that few allied health staff members use library services, the ideal condition being that a good percentage of allied health staff use the library. What is the "gap" that prevents them from using library services? If you do not know what it is, you need to ask them by doing a needs assessment. In the real life evaluation example from the literature described below, the author does just that.

To find out if your professional assessment of the gap between the ideal situation and the real situation is more than an assumption, you perform a needs assessment. The final list of needs is prioritized and a plan drawn up to attempt to change systems and services to close the gap. The literature is adamant that this is not the end of the process. The final step is to redo the assessment to see if the changes in the program have modified the gap.

Be committed to the idea that if you identify a client need, you will be prepared to act. There is no point in doing an assessment and then filing it away with no plans for a change. For many reasons, this actually happens. Sometimes there is political pressure not to change. Sometimes the team loses its momentum and does not have the energy to finish. Make sure it is understood by all stakeholders involved that doing the needs assessment will most likely result in changes.

If you undertake a needs assessment, your users will assume that if an unmet need is identified, library services and systems will be changed to meet that need. Asking the library users questions about services raises their expectations of these services, and if nothing happens, the library system would be seen as nonresponsive. Is your library system or your organization open to change?

One of the guiding rules of needs assessment is that it should be "in context." The context is your library and your customers. This need for context means that there is no cookie-cutter technique that will fit all libraries. Reading the literature can give you some ideas about the issues and problems, but you will not be able to replicate exactly what was done in their project. It is still worth reading some of the few examples that discuss their specific project. Whether a large academic library survey that uses major resources and data-gathering assistance, such as the University of Iowa Libraries's undergraduate user needs assessment, or an example from a smaller library, such as reported by Crabtree and by Perley, you will be able to get few ideas from their experience (Crabtree and Crawford, 1997; Perley, et al., 2007; Clougherty, Forys, and Lyles, 1998).

There are various levels of needs assessment in every situation. There are macro-assessments of the whole library service and micro-assessments of one service or new program. Something as simple as a free trial on an expensive online resource that was broadcast on a company wide e-mail list to solicit opinion could be considered a mini-needs assessment and could be reported as such.

## THE 12 STEPS OF A NEEDS ASSESSMENT PROJECT

A needs assessment project has three critical components:

- A strategy to identify what you need to know about your users' information needs
- A set of methods to find out this information
- A way to integrate what you learned into your library planning and service provision

At the end of the chapter there is a step-by-step workbook that can save you time and effort and give you useful results. The process outlined in the workbook can be applied to whatever type of needs assessment you do as well as whatever type of library you are in. How any needs assessment progresses will depend on the question being asked and the resources expended. You can use this workbook to do a quick or a comprehensive project. There is a copy on the CD-ROM in the Chapter 4 folder in word-processing format so you can fill it out as you do your planning.

# PREPARE FOR THE PROJECT: STEPS 1–3

As you start your plan, you can use steps 1 through 3 to prepare. You could involve a few people but not a large, formal group at this time. In laying this groundwork, you can make preliminary decisions about cost, feasibility, and time frames involved.

## STEP 1. DEFINE YOUR PURPOSE OR QUESTION

In the first step, you write down your purpose:

- What do you perceive the need to be?
- Why are you doing this needs assessment?
- Who is asking you to evaluate this need?
- How does the need fit with your mission or strategic plan?
- What resources will be needed to conduct the needs assessment?
- How important is the need?

Answers to these questions will drive the use of your time and resources. As the manager deciding to do the assessment, you would want to briefly answer these questions. They will form the basis of your decision to proceed with the project. Once this is done, you can begin gathering the team of advisers and coworkers to plan and carry out a detailed plan for a needs assessment.

## What Do You Perceive the Need to Be?

Write a brief description for yourself of the problem you see in your system. You may have an idea of what is wrong, but you have a feeling it would be best to have your idea verified by your users or customer base. Can you articulate the problem? If not, how are you going to evaluate it? This does not have to be extensive, just a few ideas you can bring to a team you will be forming to do the project.

## Why Are You Doing This Needs Assessment?

This is the first question to ask as you start your plan. From time to time new ideas and technologies come up that are interesting. But does your library system "need" them? Sometimes change happens so fast that the whole system needs to be evaluated. Is this assessment going to test whether your mission is being met in the light of the new technologies? Sometimes you are mandated from above to find out if your department is meeting the needs of its clients in a general way. Or perhaps your administration takes the Joint Commission on Accreditation of Healthcare Organizations (JCAHO) standards seriously and requires evidence of a periodic needs assessment.

## Who Is Asking You To Evaluate This Need?

Asking "why" will lead to the question: Who wants the assessment done? It might be you, the head librarian, asking if your customers need an expensive resource. It might be an outside agency or the upper administration. Just as in a reference interview, the purpose of the person asking the question greatly affects the answer. His or her exact request needs to be clarified.

## How Does the Need Fit with Your Mission or Strategic Plan?

It is also important to ask if the proposed needs assessment fits with the library's strategic plan. An ideal needs assessment is really just part of the larger planning and assessment process. As described in Chapters 1 and 2, plans involved in the culture of assessment come into play. Having a mission statement and plans to develop a strategic plan are critical to the process. Using tools such as the Logic Model described in Chapter 8 and the SMART goals described in Chapter 12 is useful.

A needs assessment project is done within the context of the organization the library is part of. If you know your company cannot afford an expensive resource, there is no point in asking if people need it. The administration expects resources allotted to the library to be spent to provide specific services to meet the information needs of the organization. You have an overall plan in mind about how you are going to spend the budget allotted to the library, even if it is not written down. One could say, then, that a needs assessment is really just part of the budgeting process.

The most important part of a strategic plan is a definition of a vision and mission statement for the library. The mission drives the expenditure of funds and thereby the plan, even if the plan is not written down. If your library does not have a mission, get together with your staff and/or supervisor and write one. As you

---

**On the CD-ROM: Mission Statements**

Found in the Chapter 2 folder, NNLM Mission Statements .doc is a sample of mission statements gathered by the Outreach Evaluation Resource Center (OERC) of the National Network of Libraries of Medicine.

start this process, you will find that you have always had a mission. You just never articulated it or wrote it down. Can you describe in 30 seconds what your library does? That would be your mission. Study your company's mission and strategic plan and see where you can provide services to meet it. Model your plan on theirs. It should be brief and discussed by the whole library staff. A needs assessment project can help you reassess your mission statement and strategic plan. It can guide plans for capitol investment, discover technologically driven shifts, and identify trends, emerging environmental concerns, and unexpected opportunities, all of which will affect the direction you and your library should take.

### What Resources Will Be Needed to Conduct the Needs Assessment?

What information, and how much, will be required to assess and analyze the need? This question will affect how many resources you put into your assessment. Sending out an e-mail to get opinions on an expensive resource uses far fewer resources than a pretested print survey that goes out to 700 people. But there are problems with Web surveys, too. Each has its place. Refer to Chapter 10 on data collection for more on deciding which method best fits your needs assessment.

### How Important Is the Need?

Finally, how much importance will be attached to the results of the assessment? How important is it that we do or do not buy the resource? If you have the budget, the results of your e-mail survey are important in the decision as to whether to purchase the resource. If you do not have the money and if the results are positive for buying the resource, the results will need to be presented to ask for a budget variance to buy the resource. This gives added importance to the assessment.

### STEP 2. GATHER YOUR TEAM

It is best not to do a needs assessment alone. Professionals in many settings know a lot about their customers' needs and work hard to meet them. But they also can make assumptions that are not totally on target. It is best to involve a steering committee in the needs assessment project.

The steering committee would consist of library staff members and staff members from around the institution who have an interest or stake in the project you are undertaking. For example, if your project involved some educational component, you would

**Definition: Steering Committee**

While a team is a group of interacting individuals sharing a common goal and the responsibility for achieving it, a steering committee is a special type of team that is usually interdisciplinary and includes stakeholders from different levels. It has a broader view of the project and helps guide its development and implementation. Some members might be advisory, and some might be part of a working group.

want to include any other employees who have a role in education in your institution. If your project involved physicians, you would want to have some physicians on your steering committee. If you were planning a community outreach program, you would want to have members of the community involved. If appropriate, you could involve librarians from a nearby institution as advisers.

If you are in a one-person setting, ask interested coworkers or neighboring librarians to help out. Think of your extended network. This could include library school professors and students, consultants from your state library, or librarians from other types of libraries. You could have steering committee members who are consulted only by e-mail. As a library professional, you probably already have a pretty good idea of what you are going to look into. You could write up some preliminary plans and present them to your new steering committee as ideas, getting input from that point as to how to accomplish this project. You prepared for the first meeting in Step 1, but you need to be open to revision of your ideas once the team meets. At your first meeting you can discuss your ideas, the potential timeline, and an idea of the resources available for the project. Chapter 11 has some communication tips on working with teams such as the steering committee.

## STEP 3. IDENTIFY STAKEHOLDERS AND INTERNAL AND EXTERNAL FACTORS

**Definition: Stakeholders**

People, groups, or organizations that have a significant interest in how well a program performs or who are interested in the results of the assessment or what will be done with results. They may be staff members, supervisors, administrators, sponsors or funders, personnel who do parallel functions in the company, or the users or customers of the service. They may be internal or external to the organization and may not actually use the service being evaluated.

The library does not exist in a vacuum. Depending on what you are planning to measure, you should be able to identify parties who will be affected. If you are planning an assessment of a new program or technology, there will be people in the institution who have some involvement in it even before you start. If you were planning a systemwide needs assessment where the entire hospital is involved, your stakeholders would be interdisciplinary. Stakeholders have a vested interest in your plans and should help with the planning of the design. Stakeholder involvement in the planning phase will greatly facilitate their acceptance of changes that are made as a result.

Any needs assessment project requires the support of your management. Since being able and willing to change is a vital part of the needs assessment process, the support of management in that change is essential. After having done preliminary planning, as described in Step 1, it would be best to discuss the plans with your immediate supervisor. If it is a larger plan whereby you are planning to ask for more budget money, you could inform other management on a higher level that you are doing the assessment. They are, of course, very busy people, and your library is one of

**On the CD-ROM: SWOT Analysis**

Found in the Chapter 12 folder: SWOT Analysis Med Lib.doc and SWOT Analysis—NNLM.doc

A SWOT (strengths, weaknesses, opportunities, and threats) analysis is a type of environmental scan. It is an analysis and evaluation of key internal and external conditions to develop an understanding of the current environment that may affect how the organization functions. An explanation and two examples are on the CD-ROM.

many departments vying for their attention. It is best not to bring up the results for the first time during the budget preparation time, since this is one of the busiest times. If you have reported the results to them previously, they might have had time to review them.

It would also be good to identify with the steering committee what internal and external factors exist that could influence your plans. This is called an environmental scan, or SWOT analysis. Analyze the strengths, weaknesses, opportunities, and threats that surround the problem. Using this technique is described in Chapter 12, and there is an example on the CD-ROM in the Chapter 8 folder.

The external review can determine which departments could be affected by the project. Is your project technological, and does it require interaction with the information systems department of your institution? If your project might result in an expansion of services, it would be good to determine which departments could be affected. When we were doing a mini needs assessment to decide whether to purchase a portable computer classroom to be used for educational programming, we found that other departments had a use for such technology as well. There were also plans for audiovisual consolidation. If acted upon, these plans would have impacted our program. Internal factors might include your budget and staff. Is your budget going to cover the project, or will you need more funds? Your staff should be consulted on various plans so that they are not surprised. How will the outcome of this needs assessment impact their jobs? Discussing possible outcomes with your staff in advance might help minimize staff anxiety. Change can be a very stressful thing to library staff who may feel that their jobs could be replaced with new technologies. Also enlisting staff members to help out is a wise use of resources, since they often know the systems being assessed well and are stakeholders in the outcome of the assessment.

# PLAN THE PROJECT AND CONDUCT THE NEEDS ASSESSMENT: STEPS 4–8

Now that you have determined your purpose, identified stakeholders, scanned the environment, and gathered a steering committee, you and your steering committee can plan and carry out the project. This is no different from any project involving resources, timelines, and committees. Steps 4–7 can actually be done by the steering committee simultaneously. Then you can progress to Step 8 and begin to gather data.

## STEP 4. DEFINE THE QUESTIONS

With the preliminary planning done and the purpose of the needs assessment determined, you now want to see if what you are planning to measure *can be* measured. With your steering committee, you now develop the questions that you will ask to get at the opinions of or facts about your users. These are the research questions that will drive your assessment.

This research question definition will affect your decision on what method to use to gather data. The research question should not be as generic as: Do customers need educational programs? To be meaningful the question needs to be much more specific. A more measurable, and therefore more meaningful, question might be: What is the need for more instruction in using the online full-text journal collection? This assumes you know why you need to ask this question. Have there been complaints? Do people seem confused? Did the library staff observe patron frustration in finding materials? Which patrons seem to be having the most trouble? All these questions will influence how you structure your research question or questions.

One of the problems for needs assessment, or any kind of research, is determining what data you will need to answer your chosen question. Berkowitz has developed a master matrix for designing needs assessments (Berkowitz, 1996). She matches these four parts:

- each research question
- the data that will answer it
- the data source that will be needed
- an analysis plan for that data source

**Figure 4.2   Matrix for Designing an Instructional Program Needs Assessment**

| (1)<br>Research Question | (2)<br>Data Element(s) | (3)<br>Data Source(s) | (4)<br>Analysis Plan(s) |
|---|---|---|---|
| 1. What is the need for an instructional program for using the online full-text journal collection? | Reported service questions at the circulation desk | Observational report form administered for 4 weeks | Listing of types of observed barriers to finding the article |
| 1.1. Which types of barriers are encountered most often? | Number of times a barrier is encountered | Internet survey of barriers encountered (developed from observational report above) sent to e-mail group of selected customers | Tabulation and analysis of numbers of barriers encountered |
| 1.2. What types of patrons have the most problems? | Number of people responding from each patron type | Internet survey of barriers encountered (developed from observational list) sent to e-mail group | Cross tabulation of barriers and patron type |
| 1.3 Will an instructional program be useful? | Opinions of library customers | Telephone survey of selected customers who were selected as non-users of e-journals | Narrative opinions of those interviewed |

(Matrix adapted from Berkowitz, 1996: 22–27)

Figure 4.2 illustrates how such a matrix would look. Using the structure of a table will help you arrive at a research question that can actually be answered. It will also help you determine how the analysis can be done. The data analysis section of Chapter 10 can help you with this process. You will then be able to see how your data will appear in the end. While this exercise may seem to be a backward approach, it will help you avoid wasting time on a poorly formed question.

In this example, based on recent reports in the literature and in talking to your colleagues, you are interested in starting an education program. You feel your users are not making the most of your e-journal collection, and you would like to shift some of your staff time to teach people how to access it more efficiently. But first you want to verify your opinion with a needs assessment. Figure 4.2 is a matrix for some possible research questions to measure this need and gap.

## STEP 5. DETERMINE RESOURCES AVAILABLE

Resources are most often figured monetarily. How much employee time will be expected? Employee time costs money. Can you afford to hire an outside consultant? If you are planning to do a survey, how much money will it take to print and distribute a survey or to do an online survey with a commercial vendor? Each data-gathering method has some expenses. Focus groups require time to organize, meet, and report. Computerized surveys may require a subscription fee. If you have some idea about the resources available before you start, you will not waste committee time planning something you cannot afford. The steering committee can develop a formal budget or an informal spending plan for smaller projects. This would include internal staff time, consultants, printing, mailing, computer and/or software expenses, and possible incentives, such as drawings or gifts for participation. This budget plan would be drawn up and shared with all stakeholders. A section in Chapter 12 on budget planning has a list of activities to use for itemizing the budget. While most costs of evaluation are for staff time, there are other expenses. This extensive list can be edited. It is included on the CD-ROM in the Chapter 12 folder as a spreadsheet for easy development into a budget.

## STEP 6. DEVELOP A TIMELINE

Timelines can be very short or very long. As the manager doing the preliminary planning for this project, you probably have some idea how long the project will take, or perhaps how long you want it to take. It is best to inform your steering committee members as you ask them to join the committee about how long you expect the project to take. This will aid in their personal planning and help you find members who are committed to seeing the project through to the end. If it is a long project, they need to know this so they can plan to dedicate more time to it. You can write up a preliminary timeline and present it to the steering committee for revision and comments. Since other employees are involved, this timeline should be very specific as to how many meetings are needed. This will help you avoid the tendency to hold too many unnecessary meetings or meetings that go longer than they should. The planned work that takes place between meetings by different members of the group could also be listed.

---

**Definition: Gantt Chart**

A Gantt chart is a type of bar chart used in a process or for project planning and control to display planned work targets for completion of work in relation to time. Typically, a Gantt chart shows the week, month, or quarter that each activity will be completed and sometimes the person or persons responsible for carrying out each activity.

For more involved projects, develop a Gantt chart to plan your timeline. See an example of a Gantt chart in Step 6 in the Workbooks below and more in detail in Chapter 12.

## STEP 7. DEFINE YOUR CUSTOMERS

Library customers are more than just the people who walk in the door. In today's networked world, some of our customers may never even see the library. In a corporate setting, you could view every employee as a customer. In a hospital setting, this could be expanded to include patients and persons in the surrounding community who are seeking health information. Exhaustive lists of various groups of employees or the public usually do not help determine what services to offer and how to design services, however. Most services are defined by primary, or targeted, customers. These main customers would be mentioned in your library mission statement. *Target population* is a term used in market research and sociological research to describe a population you want to observe. This group is the total population from which information is needed, the population intended to be identified and served by the program. For example, in a medical library, one target population might be all active medical staff and another target might be all nurses. If you asked the same questions of these two groups, the answers would be different and not necessarily comparable.

One can define the library's primary customers and then rank others as secondary customers. As more resources become available to the library, existing services can be extended to the secondary customers. Or, if the needs of the secondary customers are assessed or surveyed, resources can be requested specifically to meet their needs, thereby elevating them to primary customers. Figure 4.3 gives an example of defining your target population.

---

**Figure 4.3　Choosing Your Target Population Example**

In a needs assessment reported by Crabtree, the library had a defined set of services for its primary customers, physicians. It was observed by the library staff that another set of customers, allied health personnel, were not using the library services much. The needs assessment was done to see what barriers existed for this population that caused them not to use the library. After the results were analyzed, the library was able to modify its services. As an example of one result, 20% of the respondents felt the collection was deficient in their subject area. The library responded by modifying its collection development policy and purchasing more materials in this area (Crabtree and Crawford, 1997).

While a target population would be the population you *want* to observe, a survey population is the population you *can* observe. In most cases you cannot talk to every member of a target population, so you rely on a survey of a sample of the target population to assess needs. How to select a sample population is discussed in Chapter 10. Remember that if you choose to conduct a voluntary survey, it will be inherently biased because those who fill out the survey have selected themselves into it. You will be hearing from those who want to be heard and will miss those who refuse to be heard. This is called a self-selection bias.

The purpose and goals of the needs assessment project will indicate the population to be assessed. The steering committee should spend some time discussing who these people are, why you want to know what they need, and how you define them.

## STEP 8. GATHER DATA FROM IDENTIFIED SOURCES

Now that you have defined your question, gathered a steering committee, and made a plan, you are finally ready to gather data to assess the situation you are interested in. To most people, the term, *needs assessment,* means conducting a survey, but you can do a needs assessment without performing a survey. Data for needs assessment are generally divided into two types: primary and secondary.

### Primary Data

- Primary data for the project are data gathered at the time of the project for the first time using: surveys, focus groups, interviews, and, observations.
- Secondary sources of data come from records or sources you already have, such as locally gathered statistics, national surveys, literature searches, previous needs assessments, or comments from a suggestion box.

Many of the books available on needs assessment have chapters on methodologies for gathering the different kinds of primary data such as surveys, focus groups, observation, interviews as well as questionnaire design. Chapter 10 of this book was developed to give the reader more detailed information on these topics. If you collect primary data by asking people questions, this is considered research with human subjects. You should check with your Institutional Review Board (IRB) for the protection of human subjects to see if you need approval.

> **Warning: Primary Research on Human Subjects**
>
> If you work in a hospital or research setting, your institution may have an Institutional Review Board, or IRB. An IRB is a group that has been formally designated to review and monitor biomedical research involving human subjects, in accordance with Food and Drug Administration (FDA) regulations. An IRB has the authority to approve, require modifications in (to secure approval), or disapprove research. This group review ensures protection of the rights and welfare of human research subjects. If you are planning a primary data-gathering project of hospital employees, they might be considered "human subjects" and their privacy and other issues may need to be protected. It is best to check to see if a review is necessary so as not to be stopped by regulations in the middle of the project. Of course, you also want to know that you are correctly protecting your subjects, and the IRB office can advise you on this. Once your data–gathering plans (or research protocols, as they might call them) are decided upon, the plans can be presented to the IRB.

## Secondary Sources

Secondary sources of data are everywhere once you start looking for them. Some places to look are

- Previously gathered local statistics
- Previous needs assessments
- Participation in corporate quality committees and initiatives
- Library or technical standards
- Comments from a suggestion box or user comments
- Literature search for journal articles and a Web search
- National or local surveys such as the MLA Benchmarking Network surveys
- Participating in corporate committees, reading corporate communications, or consulting with persons in key positions and/or with specific knowledge

You should try to acquire secondary data first. Primary data are expensive and time consuming to collect. Sometimes your secondary data can identify a gap without your having to gather any primary data. On the other hand, primary data from a survey or other data-gathering plan may need to be supplemented by secondary data. Either way, it will take you less effort to collect secondary data, and then move on to primary data if necessary.

### Previously Gathered Local Statistics

Are you gathering any statistics in your library already? If not, what statistics should you begin to gather? Association surveys such as the MLA Benchmarking Network survey, the AAHSL survey, or the ARL survey can be used as background for establishing the need to do a needs assessment by identifying gaps in your services by comparing your numbers or services with others.

The MLA Benchmarking Network survey, the work of a committee of hospital librarians in 2002 and 2004, has a work sheet for the measures that are traditionally asked about libraries in relation to inputs and outputs. It includes more than 45 questions about the service practices of nonacademic health sciences libraries so they could be compared using various evaluation techniques. Figure 4.4 gives examples of a few of the measures of library activities from the MLA Benchmarking Network survey.

---

**Reference: See Chapters 3 and 6 for Information about These Surveys:**

- The Medical Library Association Benchmarking Network Surveys 2002 and 2004 (MLA) (*www.mlanet.org/*) On the CD-ROM in the Chapter 6 folder.
- The Association of Academic Health Sciences Libraries (AAHSL) (*www.aahsl.org/*)
- The Association of Research Libraries (ARL) Statistics & Measurement Program (*www.arl.org/stats/*)

---

| **Figure 4.4 Sample Measures Gathered for the MLA Benchmarking Network Survey** |
|---|
| Reference Questions<br>Mediated Searches<br>Patient Care Mediated Searches<br>Reference Questions for Consumers<br>Educational Program Sessions<br>Educational Program Session Participants<br>Monographs Circulated<br>Items Received from Outside Sources (Borrows)<br>Items Sent to Outside Sources (Lends)<br>Print Monographs<br>Print Monographs Purchased<br>Monographic Titles with Electronic Full-Text Access<br>Externally Produced Bibliographic Databases for End Users |
| Note: The complete 2002 and 2004 questionnaires, which cover many more statistics, can be found on the CD-ROM in the Chapter 6 folder, and the 2002 set is an electronic appendix to the article on the project (Dudden, et al., 2006). |

This survey was conducted in 2004, however, and in today's electronic world, it is difficult to pin down which statistics to collect about your electronic resources, because they shift constantly. As discussed in Chapter 3, the IMLS-funded E-Metrics Instructional System (EMIS) provides a Web-based course regarding the usage of and uses for networked information resources (EMIS, accessed: 2006). The EMIS program also has a downloadable *Electronic Resources and Services Annual Report,* which can be copied and adapted for your situation.

The issues involved in measurement of library activity are covered in Chapter 3. While they are controversial and in transition, if you have not been gathering any statistics, it might be a good time to start. Without any measures of activity, how are you going to answer questions from the administration? Part of the culture of assessment described in Chapter 2 is having a management information system. It can be a simple spreadsheet or database. The idea is to collect your data systematically. How measures are reported can differ greatly. For example, they may be reported monthly, quarterly, or annually. You can use a spreadsheet or database to collect different statistics and compare them more easily by normalizing different units. Columns or rows can be arranged by month so data can be pulled out for annual reports by the calendar year or budget year. This should be kept up-to-date so they can be pulled out any time someone should ask you to provide them. Assuming you have already gathered measures, what do they show for the purposes of needs assessment? If compared over time they might show an increase or a decrease in activity. How does this change in activity relate to the information needs of the customer? These types of statistics might be a justification to do a needs assessment.

### Previous Needs Assessments

When was your last needs assessment? Did you institute new services to fill the gap identified at that time? Did they fill the gap? Can you ask if the user still needs some of those items you could not accomplish before? As an example, in our case study from the literature, one of the needs identified at St. John's Regional Health Center in Springfield, Missouri, was for a better library facility. That was in 1995. In 2005 perhaps the electronic revolution has negated that need. Instead of more space, maybe they need to redesign their space to accommodate more computers. Maybe they need to put funds into the Web site to provide better navigation. Maybe they need to investigate a proxy server for off-campus access. These questions came up by analyzing a previous needs assessment result and determining what had changed.

### Participation in Corporate Quality Committees and Initiatives

Participation in corporate quality programs can generate data that might be useful and also give you experience in research. Chapter 5 covers the concepts of quality improvement (QI) and its use as an evaluation technique. Your library could do evaluations while participating in the hospitalwide quality improvement program. These might reveal a gap. Your quality improvement project can sometimes be restructured and reported as a needs assessment. Serving as a resource to the quality committee members can help raise the visibility of the library services.

### Library or Technical Standards

Comparing your library operations and collections with published standards can be a form of needs assessment. Using standards for evaluation is covered in Chapter 7, with enumeration and details about the Medical Library Association's *Standards for Hospital Libraries 2002, revised 2004* (Gluck, et al., 2002; Hassig, et al.,

**On the CD-ROM: Standards for Hospital Libraries 2002, Revised in 2004**

In the Chapter 7 folder: 2004 MLA Hospital Standards Folder
While these standards are available on the Web, MLA has given permission to include them on the CD-ROM.

**Definition: Knowledge-Based Information (KBI) Services**

KBI consists of systems, resources, and services to help health professionals acquire the knowledge and skills needed to maintain and improve competence; support clinical, managerial, and business decision making; support performance improvement and activities to reduce risk to patients; provide needed information and education to patients and families; and satisfy research-related needs (Gluck, et al., 2002).

2005). In relation to a needs assessment, you could review appropriate standards and use the results to identify a gap in services or processes. Standards can be classified as technical or performance. Technical standards have to do with cataloging codes or interlibrary loan codes. Associations or government agencies often write performance standards to recommend best practices for a particular type of library.

The Medical Library Association has had a long history of writing both technical and performance standards. Its hospital library standards were first written in 1970, then rewritten in 1984, 1994, and 2002. The *Standards for Hospital Libraries 2002, revised in 2004* detail ten areas where a librarian could compare the library's operations or situation with what is considered a standard. Doing ongoing needs assessments is recommended in Standard 6. So if you are not doing needs assessments, the standard is pointing out a gap in your library service. Of course doing a needs assessment to see if you should be doing one is a little odd! However, if you found *another* gap and needed to convince someone that a needs assessment should be done, this standard would back you up.

Standard 7 states that "the library actively promotes KBI services and resources to all user groups and provides evidence thereof" (Gluck, et al., 2002: 468). There is a list of user groups and promotion activities. If there is a group you are not actively serving or a promotional activity you are not doing, this would identify a potential gap to be assessed. One promotional activity mentioned in the standard is "participation in new employee orientations." Figure 4.5 demonstrates a mini needs assessment to see if there is a need for participation in new employee orientation, as mentioned in the standard.

---

**Figure 4.5   Mini Needs Assessment on New Employee Orientations**

---

*A. Prepare for the Project.*
Step 1. Define your purpose or question:
   Is it important for the library to be mentioned in the new employee orientation?
Step 2. Identify stakeholders and internal and external factors:
   Human Resources Department which holds the new employee orientation; the new employees.
Step 3. Gather your team—Who is going to do what:
   Ask to meet with HR and involve some of your staff.
*B. Plan the project and conduct the needs assessment.*
Step 4. Define the goals and objectives:
   Goal is to let new employees know what the library does.
Step 5. Define resources available:
   The employee orientation program has very little time to give to each department. There is a booklet that library materials could be included in. There is a tour that could point out the library.
Step 6. Time line:
   The tour could be modified immediately. The booklet is reassembled in December and republished in January.
Step 7. Define your customers:
   The new employee; the HR staff that conducts the orientation.
Step 8. Gather data from identified sources:
   Ask via e-mail what several libraries are doing in your state or region.
*C. Analyze the data and recommend a plan of action*
Step 9. Analyze the data:
   Review what HR can provide; review what other libraries are doing.
Step 10. Make a decision and a plan of action:
   Plan to include a welcome letter from the library and a data form for circulation in the New Employee booklet. Have the tour stop by the library. Put it on the calendar to update the welcome letter every December if necessary.
Step 11. Evaluate the needs assessment process and report to administration:
   Report to your administrator the review and the actions taken.
Step 12. Repeat needs assessment in the future to see if the gap is smaller:
   Monitor how many circulation forms come in from the Orientation booklet.

---

### Comments from a Suggestion Box or User Comments

What if you did an extensive needs survey and found out that a high percentage of the respondents found the library computer chairs to be uncomfortable. Did you really need to do an extensive survey to find this out? A suggestion box might be just as good. Many libraries have comment forms where on the top the user makes a comment and on the bottom the library staff responds. This can easily be done on the Web. Do an Internet search on "library suggestion box" to see what creative methods other libraries are using. A periodic report compiling the suggestions by topic and the library's responses can be summarized for the administration. This could be considered a type of assessment of user needs if you described it that way.

### Literature Search/Web Search

If you were planning a needs assessment to target a specific group or service, it would be natural to survey the literature to see if there was something published on the topic. Finding relevant articles can guide your project and save you some time. Perhaps you have thought up a new service after having lunch with some nurse managers. It came out that they felt the staff nurses were not using the online resources enough. Before doing a full-blown assessment to prove that this was the case, you might find enough evidence in the literature that there is a need to educate nurses in online resources. If you did a PubMed search on "Education, Nursing AND Online Systems AND library," you would find an article by Jody Wozar that discusses a program to teach nurses about the available resources (Wozar and Worona, 2003). The author has done a needs assessment and a postinstructional assessment. Using this article, you could meet with a nursing staff development coordinator to discuss ways to teach the nurses in your own institution. Again, you could verify the need and respond to it without performing a formal assessment. You could report to your supervisor your activity in this area in the form of a needs assessment.

### National or Local Surveys

Reviewing a survey of library activity in general can give you ideas about what other services or programs you might consider offering. If your planned needs assessment has a comparable question on the survey, you can use that data as well as any original data you collect. For example, you might be performing a needs assessment on starting a program of library education, showing users how to use e-journals and how to search MEDLINE. You would want to do a survey to see what the need is in your institution. You can also look at the MLA Benchmarking survey to see what the common practice is nationwide. You can construct a chart from the MLA Benchmarking Network survey by copying the data from the Web or from the documents on the CD-ROM in the Chapter 6 folder. Figure 4.6 shows that if you are a hospital with 1,500 FTEs (full-time employees), you could expect to hold 11 sessions a year attended by 84 people or more, up to 12 people a session. This is based on a group of 37 to 40 hospital libraries of like size. The median number is used and not the mean, because the data is widely dispersed and the median is a more robust measure than the mean when the data has a wide range. If your planning for the program indicated that your hospital needs a computer lab with 12 computers, these figures could support that phase of the plan.

| Figure 4.6 Educational Programs in Hospitals with 1,500 Hospital FTEs | | | | | | |
|---|---|---|---|---|---|---|
| **Range descriptions for hospital FTEs** | **Qualified answers** | **Mean** | **Median** | **Third quartile** | **Maximum** | **Minimum** |
| Number of Educational Program Sessions by Number of Hospital FTEs | | | | | | |
| Range 4: 1,350 to 1,824 | 40 | 26 | 11 | 21 | 445 | 1 |
| Number of Educational Program Session Participants by Number of Hospital FTEs | | | | | | |
| Range 4: 1,350 to 1,824 | 37 | 133 | 84 | 200 | 439 | 10 |
| Number of Educational Program Session Participants per Session by Number of Hospital FTEs | | | | | | |
| Range 4: 1,350 to 1,824 | 37 | 15 | 12 | 17 | 55 | 1 |

If you were to hold 11 or 12 sessions a year, what would the staffing needs be for such a program? You can construct another table using the MLA Benchmarking Network survey, as shown in Figure 4.7, based on the library FTE and see what the median numbers are. Note that the MLA charts can all be read the same way. This kind of data would supplement and enrich any other data that you might gather. It can also give you a jumping-off point and save you the effort of gathering basic information. You do not need to determine how many educational programs are appropriate for a library with 1.5 to 2.4 FTEs, for example, because the MLA Benchmarking survey gives you that number. Instead, you can go a step beyond and try to discover what resources you need to *accomplish* that level.

**Figure 4.7   Educational Programs in Hospitals with 2.3 Library FTEs**

| Range descriptions for library FTEs | Qualified answers | Mean | Median | Third quartile | Maximum | Minimum |
|---|---|---|---|---|---|---|
| Number of Educational Program Sessions by Total Library FTE | | | | | | |
| Range 4: 1.5 to 2.4 | 51 | 24 | 12 | 22 | 243 | 1 |
| Number of Educational Program Session Participants by Total Library FTE | | | | | | |
| Range 4: 1.5 to 2.4 | 45 | 145 | 100 | 200 | 718 | 10 |
| Number of Educational Program Session Participants per Session by Total Library FTE | | | | | | |
| Range 4: 1.5 to 2.4 | 43 | 15 | 10 | 19 | 55 | 1 |

### *Other People as Sources*

At managers meetings and other corporate committee meetings, keep your ears open for questions that show an information need. If you hear an announcement of a community health education series, for example, speak up and ask if there is a need for a course on finding health information on the Web. You have found from reading the professional literature that finding quality information on the Web is frustrating to the general public. Instead of trying to start your own community program, you could be part of an institutionwide effort. When suggesting your participation in the community program to your administrator, state your case in the language of needs assessment and how your participation fills a community need, as shown in the literature. Keeping informed about what is going on in the company is overall a useful activity, but it can also be used to identify gaps in library service or resources.

### Primary Data

The effort involved in collecting primary data is one reason many small libraries do not do extensive needs assessments. The skills necessary for the various parts can be daunting, but it can be done. Be sure to check to see what help is available. Some large institutions have statistics departments. Ask around and see if any of the other managers have the skills needed to advise you. Many people are willing to mentor or advise their colleagues as long as they do not have to actually tabulate any figures. Your supervisor or human resources personnel may know who could help. All of the methodologies listed below require skills in identifying your target population, determining your sample, developing questions, and analyzing the results. Chapters 10 and 12 cover these methods in greater detail. These are skills the average manager or librarian will have to learn anyway. Planning, budgeting, and communicating are skills most managers already have, and they can easily be applied to this task. A suggested planning method is the Logic Model, explained in Chapter 8. There is a section on budget planning in Chapter 12. Chapter 11 is all about different communication channels, including writing evaluation reports. So do not dismiss out of hand your ability to collect primary data. The rest of this chapter summarizes four primary data collection methods and how to analyze and act on the data they yield. Be sure to read Chapter 10 for more specific information on each data collection method.

### Surveys

Formal or informal surveys can provide quantitative data for a numerically oriented question. For example: How many of the medical staff physicians use PubMed daily, weekly, or monthly? This kind of question can be quantified using a statistically valid sample and a well-designed questionnaire. An informal survey that costs less money can give you results that improve your understanding of the situation. The kind and quality of the survey you do will depend on the importance of the assessment to the stakeholders who are financially supporting the assessment. The techniques and resources outlined in Chapter 10 will assist you in developing a survey for your project. On the CD-ROM in the Chapter 4 folder, there are four examples of needs assessment questionnaires that librarians were kind enough to share.

### Focus Groups

Focus groups are a qualitative method of finding out about your users' perceptions. They are useful in situations where opinions are important, for example, to help you plan building renovations or to discover general needs you have not thought of. In a focus group, selected groups of people, usually from a subcategory of users, are brought together to answer a developed set of questions, and their opinions are recorded. This is useful if you are already planning on introducing a new product or service and want to fine-tune it. They can also be used as a preliminary investigation for a more extensive survey when you are not exactly sure what questions will give you the most useful information. Chapter 10 covers focus groups in greater detail.

---

**On the CD-ROM: Needs Assessment Questionnaires**

In the Chapter 4 folder: Four Folders with sample questionnaires from:

- Camillia Gentry, Via Christi Libraries, Wichita, KS 67218
- Nancy Goodwin, Tremaine Library, Middlesex Hospital, Middletown, CT 06457
- Mary Peters, Medical Library, Texas Scottish Rite Hospital for Children, Dallas, TX 75219–3993
- Penny Worley, BioMedia Services, Scott & White Memorial Hospital, Temple, TX 76508

### Observation

The qualitative techniques of observation can be used in specific situations where what is *actually taking place* is important. Observation can be used in a situation where what people report is not a reliable indicator. How well is a class going? How are people using the library computer center on a given day? Setting up a planned observational study with a checklist of selected questions for the observer to consider with space on the form for a narrative comment can produce some interesting results. Refer to Chapter 10 for more information.

### Interviews

Interviews are an effective way to determine the opinions of your customers. Interviews can be used to ask one question of one person at a time at the circulation desk, or a set of questions can be developed to ask a sample of a population. Use of a set of predetermined questions, but allowing for personal interaction with the interviewer, can yield results that give a new understanding to the situation at the same time as collecting some quantitative data. By using the principles of good survey and questionnaire design as outlined in Chapter 10, this technique can yield rich and useful results. Issues of communication involved in interviewing are covered in Chapter 11.

### Questionnaire Design

All primary data collection methods require sound questionnaire design. Chapter 10 goes over these principles and refers you to many resources in print and on the Internet.

# ANALYZE THE DATA AND RECOMMEND A PLAN OF ACTION: STEPS 9–12

## STEP 9. ANALYZE THE DATA

Once data has been gathered from secondary and/or primary sources, each source of data needs to be analyzed separately according to the structure of the data-gathering technique. Various charts such as run charts, bar charts or histograms, and scatter plots can be developed from data to illustrate trends and gaps. Descriptions of these charts can be found in Chapter 12. Using these analytical methods, within each source of data, you can identify the needs or gaps that you were looking for. The needs or gaps identified would then be listed along with any figures or dimensions that show the extent of need. This list could be based on the percentage responding that they have the need. If more than one data-gathering method was used, the different results should be compared. The matrix in Figure 4.3 will guide your analysis of the various data sources. For example, you could do side-by-side comparisons between data gathered in a focus group that had been categorized and data gathered in a survey.

Usually, you will discover the needs of various population groups are different. As an example, medical staff members may need more access to mediated searches, while assistants or medical students may need more education on the e-journal access system. Sometimes the most pressing needs cannot be funded or are impractical. They should not be discarded, however, but kept for future analysis. You should bring them to the attention of your administration even though they may not be able to be acted on in an timely manner. By documenting that a need has existed for some time, your case will be stronger when there *are* resources available for the service you wish to implement.

You could expand the needs assessment committee at this point to include some other management personnel with an interest in the topic. These might be people who have some influence on the implementation of new programs. They do not need to be part of the data-gathering portion of the needs assessment, but they could supply valuable information when it comes to setting priorities to remedy the needs.

Westbrook outlines a four-step process for analyzing results (Westbrook, 2001):

- Developing an overview of the data
- Running the statistical analysis
- Running the narrative analysis
- Drawing conclusions

The whole steering committee would be involved in Steps 1and 4, but individuals or smaller groups could run the two analyses. Review Chapter 10 for an overview of data analysis issues and techniques and Chapter 12 for an overview of some tools of data display. The conclusions most likely would consist of a list of identified information needs of the group being studied. In the case study from the literature, the gaps identified were ranked by percent of respondents, as shown in Figure 4.9 (p. 88).

## STEP 10. MAKE A DECISION AND A PLAN OF ACTION

Now is the time to make a decision and rank the results by assigning them a priority for implementation. It is interesting to note that most needs assessment literature centers on data collection and analysis and then seems to skirt over the decision-making process. Altschuld and Witkin discuss this in their book called *From Needs Assessment to Action: Transforming Needs into Solution Strategies.* In their experience as consultants, they saw many surveys shelved with no decision made or action taken (Altschuld and Witkin, 2000). The analysis you do in Step 9 will provide you with a list of perceived needs. Now all that remains is to determine which one or ones are the best to implement, assuming you cannot have them all. One method to make this determination is to use the Ease and Impact Chart, as described by Adam Englesgjerd and Cathy Larson—shown in Figure 4.8 (Englesgjerd and Larson, accessed: 2006).

List and number the possible actions that correspond to the needs identified by your survey. Get any additional information about each action that could help you make your decision, for example, cost information or staff time. For example, some actions would affect many customers (high impact) but would seem relatively difficult to carry out (low ease). Discuss with the steering committee each item to determine impact or ease. Generally, the actions to take first are those with high-impact activities that are relatively easy. Refer to the Englesgjerd Web course for a graphic example of using the chart (Englesgjerd and Larson, accessed: 2006).

**Figure 4.8   Ease and Impact Grid**

This resource shows a step-by-step method of using an ease and impact grid. On a blank flip chart, draw two lines crossing each other to form quadrants. The vertical axis represents the impact a particular action may have. The horizontal axis represents the ease with which an action may be accomplished. With discussion, you can place your identified needs in each quadrant and rank them.

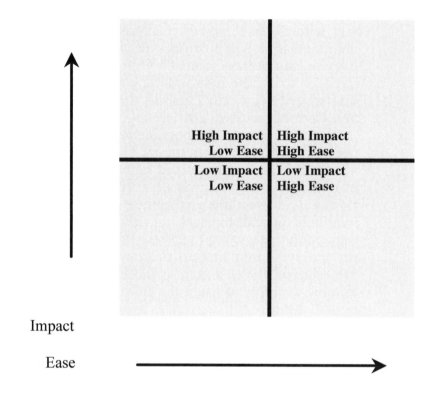

Impact

Ease

- The bottom left quadrant represents low impact and low ease
- The bottom right quadrant represents low impact and high ease
- The upper left quadrant represents high impact and low ease
- The upper right quadrant represents high impact and high ease

[Grid adapted from Englesgjerd and Larson (accessed: 2006)]

In the Crabtree real life evaluation from the literature, the following needs were identified during the analysis and ranked by percentage responding:

1. More library hours (20% wanted)
2. More materials for allied health and nursing (10%)
3. Improved library facilities (10%)
4. More library visibility, especially information about resources (4%)
5. Improved location needed (3%)

The needs were then rated in terms of ease of implementation and impact on the library users. Figure 4.9 demonstrates how these needs can be reordered using the Ease and Impact grid. The listed needs are described in column B, column A shows their rank according to the grid of ease and impact, and column C shows the rank on the Ease and Impact grid. The resulting list ranks differently from the list above, which is ranked only on percentage of response. This type of analysis allows the steering committee to make specific recommendations for action. It can result in small incremental changes or large sweeping ones, depending on the analysis.

**Figure 4.9  Ranking of Needs by Ease and Impact**

| A | B | C |
|---|---|---|
| | **Ranking re-ordered based on Ease and Impact analysis** | |
| | **Need being evaluated** | **Scale** |
| **1** | **2. More materials for allied health and nursing (10%)** | |
| | **EASE:** Would need to re-adjust the collection development policy and a lot more money to these resources. These resources are generally less expensive than medical resources. | HIGH |
| | **IMPACT:** A need identified by a large percentage. Would serve more allied health personnel. | HIGH |
| **2** | **4. More library visibility, especially information about resources (4%)** | |
| | **EASE:** More staff effort and some photocopying or printing of posters and flyers. | HIGH |
| | IMPACT: Would encourage more users to use the services. | HIGH |
| **3** | **5. Improved location needed (3%)** | |
| | **EASE:** Same as number 3 **below** but perhaps could respond with more electronic resources that could be accessed from the desktop. | MEDIUM |
| | **IMPACT:** If more electronic resources accessed from the desktop, more people would be able to use library resources. | HIGH |
| **4** | **1. More library hours (20%)** | |
| | **EASE:** Need more staff to fill hours. Would be costly and hard to get. | LOW |
| | **IMPACT:** Highest ranked need for personnel who work the swing or night shift or for those who want to stop by after work. Hard to know if the users would come to the library during any new hours established. | MEDIUM |
| **5** | **3. Need improved library facilities (10%)** | |
| | **EASE:** Costly and long term to implement. Would need major administrative buy-in and perhaps donated funds. | LOW |
| | **IMPACT:** A high ranked need. Would encourage users to come to the library as a place to study and research. | HIGH |

## STEP 11. REPORT TO ADMINISTRATION AND EVALUATE THE NEEDS ASSESSMENT PROCESS

Actions have been decided on based on the needs assessment and the prioritized list. Can you carry them out with your existing budget? Do you need a budget increase? Whichever is true, you now need to prepare a report that documents the whole process. In Chapter 11 and on the CD-ROM in the Chapter 11 folder, the Evaluation Report Template lists all the parts of a formal report. Charts and graphs useful in demonstrating the results are discussed in Chapter 12. The report from the Via Christi study mentioned above is available on the CD-ROM in the Chapter 4 folder and is an excellent example of a needs assessment report.

With needs assessment and other evaluation projects, there usually is one large or archival report that will contain all the data and all the documentation it took to accomplish the project. It could include documents and data on a CD-ROM. This report could be kept in the library to document the assessment for any survey activity, such as a visit from the JCAHO, or for any stakeholders to review if they choose to. If you feel that more than a few people will want to see the report, you should prepare two or three copies to circulate.

As mentioned early in the chapter, action must be taken because by doing the needs assessment in the first place, you implied your commitment to changing your practices based on the needs found. From the core report, you would prepare different reports for various audiences and stakeholders involved. The administration should get an executive summary and an offer to view the full report. The library staff would get a more detailed report and again the opportunity to view the full report. Library users might get a report that concentrates more on the vision and results than the methodology. Each report should be written using language appropriate for the audience. Chapter 11 goes over some of the issues in choosing your communication channel. The reports should tell the whole story but as briefly as possible.

## STEP 12. REPEAT NEEDS ASSESSMENT IN THE FUTURE TO SEE IF THE GAP IS SMALLER

Needs assessments can and should be an ongoing part of any library operation. If a major assessment was done, a few years later perhaps a smaller assessment could be done to see if any of the previous identified gaps were filled. This could result in a report to administration of how responsive the library is to users' needs. The main concept here is that needs are always there and a needs assessment is a continuing process. In these times of rapid change in libraries and technology, it is important to keep up with the changes in your customer's needs. Developing a culture of assessment and evaluation among your staff would allow small and large assessment projects to be carried out more easily because your library will always be open to the idea of improvement.

Periodic needs assessments can connect the library operation to its users more strongly. When this is done, ownership of the library and its services is shared with the library *customers* (Silver, 2004). How many librarians say, "My library does this or that," forgetting whose library it really is? Needs assessments help establish the customer as the center of the service and bring the librarian and the library staff back to what is at the core of a library service: What do the library customers need?

# REAL-LIFE EVALUATION: NEEDS ASSESSMENT

This example is presented in terms of the needs assessment steps delineated in this chapter. Each step is listed, and then it is indicated that these authors did that step.

Crabtree, A. B., and J. H. Crawford. 1997. "Assessing and Addressing the Library Needs of Health Care Personnel in a Large Regional Hospital." *Bulletin of the Medical Library Association,* 85, no. 2: 167–175.

Abstract: The Medical Library staff of St. John's Health System, Inc., in Springfield, Missouri, conducted a needs assessment survey to document the library needs of nonphysician health-care personnel. The intended use of the survey was threefold: first, to collect baseline data from nonphysician health-care employees; second, to gather recommendations from both library users and nonusers to be included in library planning and improvements; and third, to promote the library during the survey process. Study results, along with an implementation report detailing actions taken to enhance strengths and address weaknesses identified in the needs assessment survey, are presented. Opportunities for further investigation of library needs also are reported.

## PREPARE FOR THE PROJECT

### Step 1. Define Your Purpose or Question

The purpose was to determine user satisfaction and evaluate the needs of nonphysician health-care personnel in order to provide a baseline for future comparisons, to consider revision of the library's strategic plan, and to promote the library and encourage its use among this population. This question was decided upon to meet the requirements of the JCAHO standards. Also, while physicians had been surveyed in the past, nonphysician personnel had not.

### Step 2. Identify Stakeholders and Internal and External Factors

The hospital environment is well described. St. John's is a comprehensive health-care delivery system composed of St. John's Regional Health Center, an 886-bed acute care hospital, and Springfield Clinic, a multispecialty clinic with approximately 340 physicians located at multiple sites throughout southwest Missouri and northwest Arkansas. There are more than 3,500 hospital employees and more than 1,200 clinic employees among the St. John's Health System workforce.

### Step 3. Gather Your Team—Who Is Going to Do What

Library staff, with the help of some managers to distribute the questionnaire.

## PLAN THE PROJECT AND CONDUCT THE NEEDS ASSESSMENT

### Step 4. Define the Goals and Objectives

1.  Determine user satisfaction and evaluate the needs of nonphysician health-care personnel in order to provide a baseline for future comparisons
    a.  Use non-probability sampling (see Chapter 10)
    b.  Identify library users and nonusers
    c.  Distribute questionnaires in a personal manner
    d.  4–6 surveys distributed in each area based on number of employees
2.  Consider revising the library's strategic plan
    a.  Library personnel reviewed all comments; whenever possible, the ideas presented were taken into consideration during library planning processes.
3.  Promote the library and encourage its use among this population

    a. Provide some basic information in a cover letter and on the final page of the survey

## Step 5. Determine Resources Available

The library staff and resources of the library department.

## Step 6. Develop a Timeline

A timeline was established with the survey distribution taking place in November-December 1995.

## Step 7. Define your customers

Nonphysician health-care personnel employed at St. John's Health System.

## Step 8. Gather Data from Identified Sources

Previous needs assessments are described.

The requirement of JCAHO to do a needs assessment is mentioned.

A literature search was conducted, and articles on surveying nonphysicians were found as well as others on needs assessments.

Discussions of the Medical Library Advisory Committee show participation in carrying out the suggested results of the survey.

An extensive non-probability survey of 422 employees was carried out with a 69% return.

## ANALYZE THE DATA AND RECOMMEND A PLAN OF ACTION

### Step 9. Analyze the data

The data were analyzed in the article. Tables and percentages were displayed.

### Step 10. Make a Decision and a Plan of Action

The library's mission statement and strategic plan were revised to be more inclusive of all personnel, and a Medical Library Advisory Committee was formed to review and prioritize the results for possible action. Action plans were carried out in various areas: changing the collection development policy, promoting the services more, increasing network and computer access to the libraries online resources, and submitting requests to administration for more staff and space.

### Step 11. Report to Administration and Evaluate the Needs Assessment Process

The survey was reported to the administration and the Medical Library Advisory Committee.

### Step 12. Repeat Needs Assessment in the Future to See If the Gap Is Smaller

Further studies of more employees are planned.

# WORKBOOK FOR NEEDS ASSESSMENT

(Adapted from "Make Your Own Plan" by Adam Englesgjerd and Cathy Larson [accessed: 2006] and "Needs Assessment Guide" by Fernando Soriano [1995].)

Using this workbook, you can do a one-year comprehensive project or a three-month quick project. As you work through the plan for a quick project, there will be notes to guide you to speed up the process. There is an example of a Gantt chart for either project.

## PREPARE FOR THE PROJECT

### Step 1. Define Your Purpose or Question

Think about the purpose for conducting needs assessment. Capture that purpose here:

General Purpose: _____

_____

_____

_____

### Step 2. Gather Your Team—Who Is Going to Do What

For a quicker project, you need to find some helpers and advisors. These may be other managers or support staff. Are you going to do all the work? Can you count on them to act quickly with their help and advice? Write down some thoughts about this issue.

_____

_____

Who is responsible for which activities? Have they been released from their usual duties so they will have time to do this? Are they interested? Do they have the skills? Do they work well as a group? Who is responsible for the overall project.

| Member name | Title | Extension | Reason to be on team/ Skills |
|---|---|---|---|
|  |  |  |  |
|  |  |  |  |
|  |  |  |  |

### Step 3. Identify Stakeholders and Internal and External Factors

Your stakeholders are those people who have an interest in the project. Think of all the people and programs your assessment might impact.

| Name | Title | Extension | What is their stake in this project? |
|---|---|---|---|
|  |  |  |  |
|  |  |  |  |
|  |  |  |  |

Scan your external and internal environment quickly and jot down some thoughts about it and any implications you can think of using a SWOT analysis. Use a separate sheet. See Chapter 12.

| STRENGTHS (Internal): | WEAKNESSES (Internal): |
|---|---|
| OPPORTUNITIES (External): | THREATS (External): |

### PLAN THE PROJECT AND CONDUCT THE NEEDS ASSESSMENT

### Step 4. Define the Goals and Objectives

Based on the overall purpose of the needs assessment, with the steering committee, what are the Key Questions that will define this purpose? For a quick needs assessment you will have fewer questions.

1. _____

_____

2. _____

_____

3. _____

_____

4. _____

_____

### Step 5. Determine Resources Available

List the resources you will need to carry out the project—both personnel and materials. For a quick assessment you will not have time to ask for extra resources. Can you and your staff and budget handle the project?

Who is responsible for various parts of the process? With the team, create a Responsibility Chart listing all the tasks that need to be done and who will be doing them. Which staff members have the time and expertise? See Chapter 12 for more on Responsibility Charts.

| Responsible party → | Team member | Team member | Team member | Team member |
|---|---|---|---|---|
| Process | A | B | C | D |
| General planning and coordination | | | | |
| Designing the study | | | | |
| Collecting the data | | | | |
| Coding or preparing the data for analysis | | | | |
| Analyzing the data | | | | |
| Interpreting the results | | | | |
| Reporting the results | | | | |

R - Responsible for carrying out the task. Every task must have an R.
C - Consults with the R person for the task
A - Assists the R person with the task
I - Is informed about the status of the work

_____

_____

Refer to the section in Chapter 12 on budget planning for a list of the people, materials, and activities that make up an evaluation project budget. Having some idea of how much time it will take, as outlined in Step 6, calculate a budget to see what the expenses will be. These items have been transferred to a spreadsheet and placed on the CD-ROM in the Chapter 12 folder as an example to use for developing your own budget. Write down a few preliminary ideas here.

_____

_____

_____

## Step 6. Develop a Timeline.

Make a Gantt chart (See Chapter 12 for more on Gantt charts).
Timeline for Conducting a Quick Assessment in One Month

| Months | 1 | | | |
|---|---|---|---|---|
| Weeks | 1 | 2 | 3 | 4 |
| A. Prepare for the project | | | | |
| Step 1. Define your purpose or question | x | | | |
| Step 2. Gather your team—Who is going to do what | x | | | |
| Step 3. Identify stakeholders and internal and external factors | x | | | |
| B. Plan the project and conduct the needs assessment | | | | |
| Meeting 1 | x | | | |
| Step 4. Define the goals and objectives | x | | | |
| Step 5. Define resources available | x | | | |
| Step 6. Timeline | x | | | |
| Step 7. Define your customers | x | | | |
| Step 8. Plan to gather data from identified sources | x | | | |
| Plan for review by the Institutional Review Board (IRB) | x | | | |
| Meeting 2 | | x | | |
| Step 9. Gather data from identified sources | | x | | |
| Design instruments | | x | | |
| Test and refine instruments | | x | | |
| Administer instruments | | | x | |
| Send reminder | | | x | |
| C. Analyze the data and recommend a plan of action | | | | |
| Step 10. Analyze the data | | | | x |
| Step 11. Make a decision and a plan of action | | | | x |
| Step 12. Evaluate the needs assessment process and report action plans to administration | | | | x |
| Step 13. Repeat needs assessment in the future to see if the gap is smaller | | | | |

**Timeline for Conducting a Six-Month Assessment**

| Months | 1 | | | | 2 | | | | 3 | | | | 4 | | | | 5 | | | | 6 | | | |
|---|---|---|---|---|---|---|---|---|---|---|---|---|---|---|---|---|---|---|---|---|---|---|---|---|
| Weeks | 1 | 2 | 3 | 4 | 5 | 6 | 7 | 8 | 9 | 10 | 11 | 12 | 13 | 14 | 15 | 16 | 17 | 18 | 19 | 20 | 21 | 22 | 23 | 24 |
| A. Prepare for the project | | | | | | | | | | | | | | | | | | | | | | | | |
| Step 1. Define your purpose or question | | x | | | | | | | | | | | | | | | | | | | | | | |
| Step 2. Gather your team—Who is going to do what | x | x | | | | | | | | | | | | | | | | | | | | | | |
| Step 3. Identify stakeholders and internal and external factors | | x | x | | | | | | | | | | | | | | | | | | | | | |
| First meeting | | | x | | | | | | | | | | | | | | | | | | | | | |
| B. Plan the project and conduct the needs assessment | | | x | | | | | | | | | | | | | | | | | | | | | |
| Step 4. Define the goals and objectives | | | x | x | | | | | | | | | | | | | | | | | | | | |
| Meeting 2 | | | x | x | | | | | | | | | | | | | | | | | | | | |
| Step 5. Define resources available | | | | x | | | | | | | | | | | | | | | | | | | | |
| Step 6. Timeline | | | x | x | | | | | | | | | | | | | | | | | | | | |
| Step 7. Define your customers | | | x | x | x | | | | | | | | | | | | | | | | | | | |
| Plan for review by the Institutional Review Board (IRB) | | | | x | | | | | | | | | | | | | | | | | | | | |
| Meeting 3 | | | | | x | | | | | | | | | | | | | | | | | | | |

# Timeline for Conducting a Six-Month Assessment (Continued)

| Months | 1 | | | | 2 | | | | 3 | | | | 4 | | | | 5 | | | | 6 | | | |
|---|---|---|---|---|---|---|---|---|---|---|---|---|---|---|---|---|---|---|---|---|---|---|---|---|
| Weeks | 1 | 2 | 3 | 4 | 5 | 6 | 7 | 8 | 9 | 10 | 11 | 12 | 13 | 14 | 15 | 16 | 17 | 18 | 19 | 20 | 21 | 22 | 23 | 24 |
| Step 8. Gather data from identified sources | | | | | | | | | | | | | | | | | | | | | | | | |
| Meeting 4 | | | | | x | | | | | | | | | | | | | | | | | | | |
| Design instruments | | | | | x | x | | | | | | | | | | | | | | | | | | |
| Test and refine instruments | | | | | | | x | x | | | | | | | | | | | | | | | | |
| Administer instruments | | | | | | | | | x | x | | | | | | | | | | | | | | |
| Send reminder | | | | | | | | | | | x | x | | | | | | | | | | | | |
| C. Analyze the data and recommend a plan of action | | | | | | | | | | | | | | | | | | | | | | | | |
| Step 9. Analyze the data | | | | | | | | | | | | | x | x | x | | | | | | | | | |
| Step 10. Make a decision and a plan of action | | | | | | | | | | | | | | | | x | x | x | x | | | | | |
| Step 11. Evaluate the needs assessment process and report action plans to administration | | | | | | | | | | | | | | | | | | | | x | | | | |
| Step 12. Repeat needs assessment in the future to see if the gap is smaller | | | | | | | | | | | | | | | | | | | | | | | | |

## Step 7. Define Your Customers

Given the program or service being assessed, who are your key customers or users?

_____

_____

_____

_____

Do you have a good list of these people (a sampling frame) from which you can use to survey or draw a sample if needed? Describe the list?

_____

_____

_____

_____

Can you identify any subsets of this group? How many total people are there in each group?

_____

_____

_____

_____

Are there prospective customers (that is, those who currently are not using your services)? Who are they, and how would you find them?

_____

_____

_____

_____

## Step 8. Gather Data from Identified Sources

What would be the best methodology to reach the people you are surveying and why? Make notes by each method to decide the possible ramifications of its use.

**Secondary data identification and use**

Previously gathered local statistics _____

_____

Previous needs assessments _____

_____

Participation in corporate quality initiatives _____

_____

Library or technical standards _____
_____

Comments from a suggestion box or user comments _____
_____

Literature search/Web search for similar experiences _____
_____

National or local surveys, such as the MLA Benchmarking Network surveys _____
_____

Participating in corporate committees, reading corporate communications, or consulting with persons in key positions and/or with specific knowledge _____
_____

**Primary data**

Surveys _____
_____
_____

Focus groups _____
_____
_____

Observation _____
_____
_____

Interviews _____
_____
_____
_____

Using the design matrix from Figure 4.3, match your questions, data elements, data sources, and analysis plan.

**Matrix for Designing an Instructional Program Needs Assessment**

| (1) Research question | (2) Data element(s) | (3) Data source(s) | (4) Analysis plan(s) |
|---|---|---|---|
|  |  |  |  |
|  |  |  |  |
|  |  |  |  |
|  |  |  |  |

## ANALYZE THE DATA AND RECOMMEND A PLAN OF ACTION

### Step 9. Analyze the Data

Who on the steering committee can analyze your data? Who can you use as a resource?

| Member name | Title | Extension | Skills |
|---|---|---|---|
| | | | |
| | | | |
| | | | |
| | | | |

Plan to develop a list of the results from the analysis that will be used for decision making and prioritization. What types of ranking will be best for the listing?

_____

_____

_____

_____

### Step 10. Make a Decision and a Plan of Action

Which stakeholders will you ask to be on the steering committee to help you make decisions on your data?

| Member name | Title | Extension | What is their stake in this project? |
|---|---|---|---|
| | | | |
| | | | |
| | | | |
| | | | |

What is the list you will use to rate each need using the Impact and Ease system? Use the grid below to write down some ideas.

1. _____

2. _____

3. _____

4. _____

5. _____

Ease and Impact Grid

|  |  |
|---|---|
| **High Impact**<br>**Low Ease** | **High Impact**<br>**High Ease** |
| **Low Impact**<br>**Low Ease** | **Low Impact**<br>**High Ease** |

Impact

Ease

## Step 11. Report to Administration and Evaluate the Needs Assessment Process

Refer to Chapter 11 and the CD-ROM in the Chapter 11 folder for the Evaluation Report Template.

How will you announce your decisions to your users? _____

_____

Who will compile the project report? _____

_____

Who will write the executive summaries? _____

_____

How will you distribute the final information? _____

_____

## Step 12. Repeat Needs Assessment in the Future to See If the Gap Is Smaller

When would you plan to look at this question again to assess the impact of the assessment?

_____

_____

_____

_____

# REFERENCES

ACRL College and Research Libraries Task Force. 2004. "Standards for Libraries in Higher Education: The Final, Approved Standard." *College & Research Librarianship News*, 65, no 9: 534–543.

Altschuld, J. W., and B. R. Witkin. 2000. *From Needs Assessment to Action: Transforming Needs into Solution Strategies*. Thousand Oaks, CA: Sage Publications.

Berkowitz, S. 1996. "Creating the Research Design for a Needs Assessment." In *Needs Assessment: A Creative and Practical Guide for Social Scientists*, edited by R. Reviere, S. Berkowitz, C. C. Carter, and C. G. Ferguson. Washington, D.C.: Taylor & Francis.

Clougherty, L., J. W. Forys, and T. A. Lyles. 1998. "The University of Iowa Libraries' Undergraduate User Needs Assessment." *College & Research Libraries*, 59, no 6: 572–584.

Crabtree, A. B., and J. H. Crawford. 1997. "Assessing and Addressing the Library Needs of Health Care Personnel in a Large Regional Hospital." *Bulletin of the Medical Library Association*, 85, no. 2: 167–175.

Dudden, R. F., K. Corcoran, J. Kaplan, J. Magouirk, D. C. Rand, and B. T. Smith. 2006. "The Medical Library Association Benchmarking Network: Results." *Journal of the Medical Library Association*, 94, no. 2: 118–129.

E-Metrics Instructional System (EMIS). "Information Use Management Policy Institute, School of Information Studies, Florida State University." Available: www.ii.fsu.edu/EMIS/ (accessed September 22, 2006).

Englesgjerd, A., and C. Larson. "Needs Assessment Tutorial." Needs Assessment and Data Management Project Team, University of Arizona Library (last updated April, 2000). Available: http://digital.library.arizona.edu/nadm/tutorial/index.htm (accessed December 15, 2006).

Gluck, J. C., R. A. Hassig, L. Balogh, M. Bandy, J. D. Doyle, M. R. Kronenfeld, K. L. Lindner, K. Murray, J. Petersen, and D. C. Rand. 2002. "Standards for Hospital Libraries 2002." *Journal of the Medical Library Association*, 90, no. 4: 465–472.

Hassig, R. A., Balogh, L., Bandy, M., Doyle, J. D., Gluck, J. C., Lindner, K. L, B. Reich, and D. Varner. 2005. "Standards for Hospital Libraries 2002 with 2004 Revisions." *Journal of the Medical Library Association*, 93, no. 2: 282–283.

Joint Commission on Accreditation of Healthcare Organizations. 2006. *Comprehensive Accreditation Manual for Hospitals: The Official Handbook*. Oakbrook Terrace, IL: Joint Commission on Accreditation of Healthcare Organizations.

McKillip, J. 2003. *Need Analysis: Tools for the Human Services and Education*. 2nd edition. London: SAGE.

Perley, C. M., C. A. Gentry, A. S. Fleming, and K. M. Sen. 2007. "Conducting a User-Centered Information Needs Assessment: the Via Christi Libraries' Experience." *Journal of the Medical Library Association*, 95, no. 1: (In Press).

Reviere, R., S. Berkowitz, C. C. Carter, and C. G. Ferguson. 1996. *Needs Assessment: A Creative and Practical Guide for Social Scientists*. Washington, D.C.: Taylor & Francis.

Silver, J. 2004. "Library Needs Assessment." *Journal of Hospital Librarianship*, 4, no. 1: 99–104.

Soriano, F. I., and University of Michigan School of Social Work. 1995. *Conducting Needs Assessments: A Multidisciplinary Approach*. Thousand Oaks, CA: Sage Publications.

Westbrook, L. 2001. *Identifying and Analyzing User Needs: A Complete Handbook and Ready-to-Use Assessment Workbook with CD-ROM*. New York: Neal-Schuman Publishers.

Wozar, J. A., and P. C. Worona. 2003. "The Use of Online Information Resources by Nurses." *Journal of the Medical Library Association*, 91, no. 2: 216–221.

# 5 METHOD 2: QUALITY IMPROVEMENT

## WHAT IS QUALITY IMPROVEMENT?

Libraries have a long history with the concept of quality:

- Quality materials are selected and purchased.
- Quality standards have been written for bibliographic control and representation.
- Quality service for library patrons has been a hallmark of library management.

Today, quality has become a management imperative, with many different names and systems. Starting with the principles of total quality management, or TQM, the quality philosophy moved across the globe and from industry to health care to the public sector. As described in Figure 5.1, the six basic elements of TQM are:

1. Organizational commitment and integrated planning
2. Process focus versus employee performance
3. Employee involvement and teamwork
4. Customer mindedness or focus
5. Learning organization and continuous improvement
6. Data driven and data enhanced

In the early 1990s, libraries adopted TQM principles, and many examples of its implementation were reported in the literature. Since its inception, it has gone by many names:

- quality assurance (QA)
- continuous quality improvement (CQI)
- continuous improvement (CI)
- quality improvement (QI)
- performance measurement
- Most recently: performance improvement (PI)

The culture of assessment, discussed in Chapter 2, is another incarnation of the management principles needed to accomplish

**Reference: TQM and QI**

Two reprint collections by Jurow and Barnard and by O'Neil bring together the significant TQM literature before 1994:

- O'Neil, R.M. *Total Quality Management in Libraries: A Sourcebook.* Englewood, CO: Libraries Unlimited, 1994.
- Jurow, S.R., and S.B. Barnard, eds. *Integrating Total Quality Management in a Library Setting.* New York: Haworth Press, 1993.

a quality improvement program. The theory combines continuous quality assessment with TQM and the "learning organization," as described in Chapter 9. As outlined in Chapter 8, emphasis in the library evaluation literature has shifted from process quality measurement efforts to outcomes research to measure the impact of services on customers. However, measurement and review of the quality of the process that provides a service or product is still needed to manage effectively. Whichever method of evaluation of quality is selected, its implementation is based on the principles of TQM and QI. FOCUS-PDCA is one of the many methods of quality improvement that has descended from TQM, and it stands for find-organize-clarify-understand-select and plan-do-check-act. Benchmarking is another tool and is covered in Chapter 6.

The FOCUS-PDCA methodology for quality improvement is explained in detail followed by a workbook for implementation. We focus on FOCUS-PDCA (no pun intended) in this chapter because it can be done independently and is not part of a named management philosophy. Other management philosophies using quality improvement methodologies are reviewed in Chapter 9.

# PRINCIPLES OF QUALITY MANAGEMENT

Most of us take the importance of quality for granted. Why would you not want to sell or buy a quality product or service? The industry shift to TQM in the 1980s and 1990s had a lot to do with *when* you measure for quality and *how* you achieve quality. The revolutionary idea was really quite simple: Quality is a result of a finely tuned process. Before TQM, quality was tested only at the end of a manufacturing process. If a quality control inspector found a defect, the employee who made the defective product was disciplined or fired. Management theory was "top-down," with employees who simply took orders and had little or no input into how the job got done.

**Reference: On the Web: Deming's "System of Profound Knowledge"**

Deming's "system of profound knowledge" and his 14 points are now part of the core management literature:

- Clauson J. Deming Electronic Network Web Site. http://deming.eng. clemson.edu/pub/den/
- The W. Edwards Deming Institute®. www.deming .org/

The quality movement that led to TQM can be traced to the exceptional success of Japanese industry in the 1950s. Using its own experts and ideas and those of various American consultants, Japan increased its foreign market share by 500% by 1990. The United States, meanwhile, had lost 40% of its foreign market share (Jurow and Barnard, 1993). Japan's American consultants and theorists included W. Edwards Deming, Joseph M. Juran, and Philip B. Crosby, among others. America's Fortune 500 companies, led by Ford Motor Company and others, were so impressed that they adopted Deming's quality principles, and American management transformed itself. The health care industry adopted Deming's principles soon after. Libraries discovered TQM in the early 1990s. Figure 5.1 lists the key ideas of these three leaders as outlined by Nardina Mein.

---

**Figure 5.1   Mein's Summary of Quality Management Principles**

- *Organizational commitment:* The whole organization, including top administration and every worker, must be committed to continuous improvement of work processes. When quality improvement programs are implemented, organizations develop extensive training programs in quality improvement and in team skills to support the process.
- *Process focus:* When improving work problems, the focus is on the work process and not on employee performance. The view is that ineffective processes (not problem employees) cause problems.
- *Employee involvement:* Employees are an integral part of the procedure used to change processes. It is considered important to involve employees directly in improvement efforts because they are most familiar with work processes and possess valuable knowledge about how the processes can be improved.
- *Customer mindedness:* Organizations that are focused on quality improvement go beyond "customer feedback" to involve customers in the design of work processes and services to ensure their needs are met. The definition of customer is also broadened to include internal customers, that is, other departments and individuals within the hospital, as well as external customers, or patients.
- *Learning organization:* The leadership of quality-focused organizations seeks to establish an environment where new ideas, learning, and innovation are welcomed.
- *Data driven:* Statistical tools are used throughout the quality improvement process to provide information and analysis based on facts rather than hunches, beliefs, or intuition.

Mein, N. N. 2000. "Quality Improvement." In Holst, R., and Phillips, S. A., eds. *The Medical Library Association Guide to Managing Health Care Libraries* (56–57). Chicago, IL: Medical Library Association and Neal-Schuman Publishers. Reprinted with permission.

TQM goes hand in hand with the concept of strategic planning. Both concepts emphasize "forward thinking, teamwork, the human dimension, a culture change, enhanced productivity, and strategies for improving quality" (Riggs, 1994: 88). As mentioned in Chapter 2, having a mission statement and strategic plan can be developed over time within the culture of assessment. Integrating the principles of TQM into any developing plan would be an essential part of the process. The planning tool called the Logic Model is explained in Chapter 8 and can be used to identify processes to be evaluated as well as to develop a strategic plan. The ideas of strategic planning are briefly covered in Chapter 9.

In the health-care industry, the Joint Commission on Accreditation of HealthCare Organizations (JCAHO) was founded on the concept of quality in that its first efforts were to assure that patients in hospitals came to no harm. Standards were written in an attempt to accomplish this philosophy. In the 1980s the JCAHO rewrote its standards to emphasize processes rather than structure and instituted quality assurance (QA) programs to correct performance shortcomings. By the 1990s this had become continuous quality improvement (CQI), then quality improvement (QI) and in the early 2000s, performance improvement (PI). These program changes reflect different ideas about how to address quality in large and varied organizations.

QA and QI are often used interchangeably but have different focuses. Ideally, they are complementary.

- QA focuses on a service performance level that assures consumer protection and individual accountability. It also measures performance based on national averages and suggests areas to improve.
- Quality improvement (QI) on the other hand is more proactive. A traditional reactive mind-set is: "If it is not broken, do not fix it." The QI philosophy is proactive: "It may not be broken, but we can still improve it." Following Deming's "system of profound knowledge," with directives that include "improve every process" and "break down barriers," QI looks at internal system improvement using a team approach supported by top management.

The current focus of the JCAHO is on "performance measurement," which seeks to gather comparative measures of hospital performance on a countrywide scale. It has its roots in QA and is greatly assisted by the development of electronic health or medical records.

**Chapter 9 gives an overview of these business quality programs:**

- Balanced scorecard
- Five Ss
- Gemba processes
- Kaizen
- Lean
- Learning organization
- Six Sigma

**Reference: TQM in Any Size Library**

If you want to implement TQM in your setting, Miller has written an excellent case study in the book *Library Evaluation: A Casebook and Can-Do Guide* (Miller, 2001). While her case study is of a medium-size public library, her implementation and experience can be an example for any size library. Even a small staff can study TQM and apply its principles to the operation of the department. The case study library studied Deming's 14 points and adapted them to its organization.

To quote, its "goal was to become a quality organization that

- Focuses on customers,
- Continuously improves processes,
- Uses knowledge and skills of all staff,
- Prevents mistakes,
- Uses facts to make decisions,
- Uses statistical and analytical tools to measure success,
- Uses feedback to evaluate success, and
- Adds value" (Miller, 2001: 27–28).

# THE LIBRARIAN'S ROLE IN COMPANYWIDE PROGRAMS

If your corporation adopts a quality management program, no matter what they choose to call it, the library staff will, of course, be part of the effort. Step in early to be part of the new process so the library staff can learn what is expected in the system. By participating in the system, the library staff will perceive what kind of information needs the other departmental or interdisciplinary teams might need for their own success. Resources can be purchased to support the educational efforts of the quality program administrators. Whichever program is chosen by the administration, there will be a major employee education initiative.

Using traditional library services, the library can respond to the information needs of the quality teams. Reference services, interlibrary loan, Web site resources, and collection development will all come into play. You can also be proactive and seek out quality teams to serve on. Working with the quality program is one way to get out of the library and meet directly with library users.

# QUALITY MANAGEMENT IN THE LIBRARY

Whatever method of quality improvement you use, the management of the library needs to adopt a culture of quality management. In the best of all worlds, it would be nice if the top management of your company also did. But you can still apply TQM principles in your area, even without a companywide program.

As shown in Figure 5.2, David Orenstein, in his article "Developing Quality Managers and Quality Management: The Challenge to Leadership in Library Organizations," lists 11 ways to motivate your library to adopt a quality culture, a culture that "considers service issues, people, and challenges as simultaneous and interconnected concerns" (Orenstein, 1999: 44). His insightful article gives many practical tips on how to accomplish these management ideas. The methodology you choose, or that which is chosen for you, will work well only in a supportive management environment such as Orenstein describes. Mein also discusses the characteristics needed for a successful quality program (Mein, 2000). In Figure 5.2, Orenstein's recommendations are placed side by side with Mein's corresponding Characteristics for Quality Success.

| Figure 5.2 Characteristics of Quality Success | |
|---|---|
| **Orenstein's Eleven Ways of Looking at TQM (Orenstein, 1999: 44)** | **Mein's Organizational Characteristics for Quality Success (Mein, 2000: 63–66)** |
| 1. Build a shared vision for the library. | Mission and vision for the Health Care Organization. |
| 2. Put the needs of the customers before the politics of the organization. | |
| 3. Build cooperation among all levels of employees. | Collaborative approach to problem solving. |
| 4. Communicate. | |
| 5. Emphasize teamwork. | Empowerment of all levels of staff. |
| 6. Build trust. | |
| 7. Redesign processes and attitudes. | |
| 8. Train for quality. | Employee education and training. |
| 9. Develop leadership skills. | Executive leadership of the quality improvement. |
| 10. Manage by fact. | Information systems available to provide data. |
| 11. Motivate staff by making work enjoyable. | Reward, recognition and celebration. |

# QUALITY IMPROVEMENT MODEL: FOCUS-PDCA

As mentioned above, corporations institute various quality management programs. Whichever program your management uses, your library would participate in it and adopt its principles. If there is a companywide initiative, you will be trained in its methodology. Studying the general TQM principles discussed above would also give you an excellent background.

In the absence of an institutionwide program, one methodology widely used in health care is FOCUS-PDCA. The PDCA cycle, plan-do-check-act, sometimes called the Shewhart cycle, is represented as a cycle or wheel, implying a process of continuous improvement, as shown in Figure 5.3. Adding the FOCUS part,

**Reference: On the Web: FOCUS-PDCA**

Search for "FOCUS-PDCA" or just "PDCA" to find many current resources on the topic. Rather than my recommending specific sites, it is best to do your own search.

As an example, Kay Wagner gives a detailed overview of the FOCUS-PDCA process with several Internet references, but none of them is available today:

• Wagner, K. C. 2002 "FOCUS PDCA: A Process Improvement (PI) Tool for Libraries." *Journal of Hospital Librarianship*, 2, no. 2: 93–97.

find-organize-clarify-understand-select, uses Deming's other principles of planning and teamwork. Recently, the "check" section has been renamed, so you will also find the acronym PDSA, plan-do-study-act. Developed in 1989 and trademarked by the Hospital Corporation of America (HCA), FOCUS-PDCA appears to be in common use today, and many descriptions of it can be found on the Internet but not on the HCA site. The FOCUS-PDCA methodology grew out of Deming's expansion of the Shewhart cycle: "Plan-Do-See," developed in the 1920s. When the quality of a product varies or there is variation in service outcome, the Shewhart cycle is used as a tool to investigate that variation and make small changes in the process.

**Figure 5.3    FOCUS-PDCA Cycle**

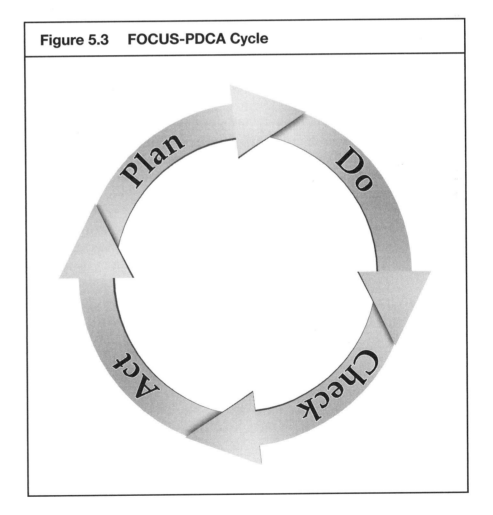

Any type of library could use this methodology, although it is best known in health care. The FOCUS-PDCA method can be used for small or large projects. Always remember that the purpose of the evaluation is to provide quality service to the customer in line with the library vision and mission. Do not get lost in the details. The PDCA system gives a structure for process improvement that avoids placing blame on the staff involved in the process. It also avoids the problem of staff discussions disintegrating into a gripe session. The individual steps in the FOCUS-PDCA process are described below. Tools for managing your team and analyzing your results can be found in Chapter 12. Following the explanation of FOCUS-PDCA, you will find a real-life evaluation example of the process. This approach is modeled on Wagner's article (Wagner, 2002).

## FIND

Find an opportunity or process for improvement. Define the problem. What is wrong? Perhaps review where you stand in the MLA Benchmarking Network survey. Find an area where your activity is significantly different from other libraries. Is this area important to customers or to the mission of the organization? Wagner suggests that after you identify an opportunity or process, you write an opportunity statement. "The opportunity statement answers the following questions:

- where does the improvement opportunity lie and
- what are the boundaries of the work,
- why is this the right time to do the work, and
- what will this effort improve?" (Wagner, 2002: 94)

## ORGANIZE

Organize and identify a team that understands the opportunity and related systems or processes.

- Who knows about this?
- Which members of the staff work with the process or have an interest in it?
- Which other departments would be involved?

Plan the team activities by developing a timeline using a Gantt chart. Assign work using a responsibility chart. Explanations of both of these can be found in Chapter 12. Chapter 11 has some tips on working with teams.

Plan a budget by referring to the "Budget Planning" tool in

Chapter 12. List the details of the types of expenses this evaluation project will incur. Some projects may be so small that they do not require a formal budget. By having a plan even for small projects, you can monitor the time spent. Sometimes projects have a way of dragging on and too much time is spent on them.

## CLARIFY

Clarify the process by collecting information about it.

- What is involved?
- Who are the customers of the process?
- Interview team members and others involved in the process.
- Do a literature search to see how others have handled the process.
- Do a flowchart.

If from your preliminary analysis, small routines can be changed, you can change them now.

## UNDERSTAND

Understand the causes of the problem. Identify root causes of the problem and address system issues. Why is it not working? Do a cause and effect, or fishbone, diagram, as shown in Figure 5.4. By naming the problem and analyzing some of the root causes, you can choose a small part of the process to improve. It is unlikely you would throw out a whole process and start over. Usually you would find a part of the process that may be causing the problem and would change it. Causes are often grouped in the large categories of equipment, people, materials, and methods. Depending on the process, there may be other large categories. In the case study we used, the large categories of policies, people, equipment, and procedures. See Chapter 12 for more information about cause-and-effect diagrams.

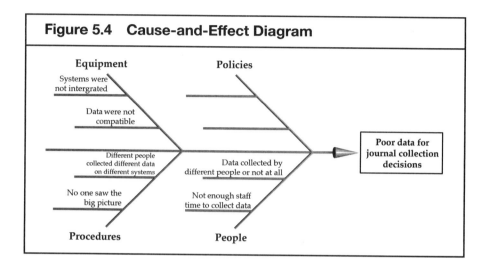

**Figure 5.4  Cause-and-Effect Diagram**

## SELECT

Select a process improvement activity:

- Where should the change occur?
- What change should be made?

Having worked through the previous steps of clarification and understanding, you may realize that improvement could happen in more than one place. You may have already made small changes. Make sure there is team consensus on which part of the process to change. Verify with management that resources are available to make the change.

## PLAN

Having identified a change in a process using FOCUS, the objectives and processes necessary to make those changes should be established. The resulting plan should include decisions about:

- Who: Team members should have roles designated, such as a team leader, someone to be in charge of training if necessary, and someone to be in charge of assessment and monitoring.
- What: Activities need to carry out the changes. Develop an activities chart, such as the one in Figure 5.5.
- When: A timeline of resources, activities, training, and target dates. Develop a Gantt chart, such as the one in Figure 5.6.
- How: Tools for monitoring the expected change should

be identified and developed, such as a data collection plan, the tools for measuring outcomes, and criteria for determining when success targets have been met. Tools are listed in Chapter 12, and techniques are covered in other chapters for these activities.

## DO

Implement the new process based on the plan set out in the previous phase. Set a date when the process will be checked or studied.

At this point the change might be temporary because you cannot assume it will be effective in solving the problem that was identified. Give the change some time to be measured.

## CHECK

Study, monitor, and evaluate the process change. This step includes both the formal and informal assessments that take place continually and the assessment at the specified end of the study. Check means to determine if the process change was a success. Examine the data collected about the process and determine if the criteria for success were met. Identify people and system issues that impacted the success of the plan and what you have learned. Report the outcome of the study to the team and to management. If the change had successful results, recommend permanent adoption of the change. The data you collected will help justify your recommendations. If the results were negative or inconclusive, go back to the clarifying, understanding, and selecting stages and decide if some other factor was perhaps more important. Assessment data from this "check" step becomes part of the input for the next step in the cycle, whether it is to "act" or return to the beginning. The data you collected will help in the redefinition of the problem.

## ACT

If you have completed all of the other steps correctly, taking action should be a simple process:

- Take action based on what you learned when you studied the results of the change.
- Review all the previous FOCUS-PDCA steps with the team. If the process modification worked, accept it. If the change did not work, go through the cycle again with a modified or different plan.
- Use what you learned to plan new improvements, beginning the cycle again, even on the same process.

- Share best practices with the staff in formal and informal settings.
- Report activities to management, whether positive or negative. Use the Evaluation Report Template as a guide, as found in Chapter 11 and on the CD-ROM in the Chapter 11 folder.
- Keep the results on file in case you wish to revisit the process in the future.

# REAL-LIFE EVALUATION: FOCUS-PDCA

This example comes from a program developed by Margaret Bandy at the Medical Library at Exempla Saint Joseph Hospital, in Denver, Colorado.

**Find**

When the journal subscriptions were reviewed each year, even without a budget crisis, the librarian felt there was not enough data to make an informed decision about adding or continuing a title. An opportunity statement reads as follows:

- An opportunity exists to bring together data we already collect to make journal collection decisions more effectively.
- The effort should improve communication with the medical and hospital staff by having available to them understandable data for the decisions.
- The process is important because collection development decisions impact the budget and service to the medical and hospital staff.

**Organize**

A team was assembled that included the technician who gathered the journal use data; the librarian at the university who was in charge of the shared integrated library system, where the data was stored; the library director, who would be presenting the data to the library committee and making the final collection decisions; and a library school intern who would be helping with the extra data gathering. This team was successful because it brought in expertise from outside the library, involved the library staff that actually did the work, and coordinated with the local library school to help get the job done.

## Clarify

The team found that decisions for journal deletions and additions were difficult to make. Data came from various sources and was not integrated. Requests for new titles had no comparison data. In case of a budget reduction, it was felt a system needed to be in place. It was felt the data was there, just not coordinated.

## Understand

The problem named in the fish bone diagram (See Figure 5.4) was that journal collection development decisions were made without enough data. Using the four main branches of the diagram the following was found:

- Policies: Could find no cause
- People:
    1. Data were collected by different people or not at all.
    2. Not enough staff time to collect all the data needed
- Equipment:
    1. Systems were not integrated.
    2. Some data were not compatible
- Procedures:
    1. Different people collected different types of data about the journals titles on different systems.
    2. No one saw the big picture of what was needed for the decisions.

## Select

The team decided to go forward with the data integration process improvement. The process selected was described: "Repackage the internal use data into a single report that contains the necessary variables, so that we can examine how journals are used in the Medical Library. This will serve as a first step in a review of the journal collection."

## Plan

For journal collection development data-gathering process improvement activity, a plan was developed. (See Figures 5.5 and 5.6)

- **Who:** Technician, student, librarian director, and shared integrated library system (ILS) manager. The major resource needed was time to organize and merge the data. A library student intern doing her 100-hour practicum at the library that quarter provided this resource. If these personnel were not available, other staff would have had to be reassigned for the project, and that would have been difficult. It was felt that once an Excel spreadsheet was developed, it could be updated annually.

- **What:** Reformat and import internal use data into an Excel spreadsheet. Collect and add new data. The sources of data were listed. Each source was analyzed for what it would contribute and how to get the data in some order. Data on the use of a journal title were gathered for each print copy of a journal by the technician by reading barcodes at the time of reshelving. It was stored in the ILS. Interlibrary loan (ILL) title data could be retrieved from two different systems. The ILL data were considered important because the library was a net lender. This count was part of the use data and needed to be subtracted. Cost data were available electronically from the subscription agent. Some data, such as the journal subject, needed to be collected and entered by the library student.
- **When:** The project needed to be completed by the end of the student's 100-hour practicum.
- **How:** The criteria for success were to be:
  - A spreadsheet available for review when needed.
  - The spreadsheet would be judged to be useful as a tool for the library committee and library director during the review.
  - The spreadsheet would be easily updated and used in following years.

**Figure 5.5 Improvement Activities Chart**

| Activity | Team member | Resources needed |
|---|---|---|
| Produce Annual Use Report by title and volume and export into Excel | Shared ILS manager | Skill at report making |
| Edit Annual Use Report for consistency | Technician | Excel skills; time |
| Enter price manually from invoice | Student | Excel skills; time; understanding the invoice |
| Enter subjects manually using the NLM Classification broad subject categories as the subjects | Student; checked by library director | Excel skills; time; some knowledge of medical subjects |
| Enter ILL loan data manually | Student | Excel skills; time |
| Do tabulations of needed data: final internal use figure; cost per internal use | Student; checked by library director | Excel skills; time |
| Sort by subject | Student | Excel skills; time |
| Do final report and charts for Library Committee | Library director | Excel skills; time |

**Figure 5.6 Gantt Chart**

| Activity / Weeks → | 1 | 2 | 3 | 4 | 5 | 6 | 7 | 8 | 9 | 10 | 11 | 12 |
|---|---|---|---|---|---|---|---|---|---|---|---|---|
| Produce Annual Use Report by title and volume and export into Excel | X | | | | | | | | | | | |
| Edit Annual Use Report for consistency | X | X | | | | | | | | | | |
| Enter price manually from invoice | | X | X | X | | | | | | | | |
| Enter subjects manually using the NLM Classification broad subject categories as the subjects | | | | X | X | X | | | | | | |
| Enter ILL loan data manually | | | | | | X | X | | | | | |
| Do tabulations of needed data: final internal use figure; cost per internal use | | | | | | | | X | X | | | |
| Sort by subject | | | | | | | | | | X | | |
| Do final report and charts for Library Committee | | | | | | | | | | | X | X |

**Do**

All the data was entered into the spreadsheet and calculations were done on the data. The final internal use figure was calculated by subtracting the ILL loans from the total use that came from the ILS. The cost per final internal use was calculated. The spreadsheet was sorted by subject category, and various other reports were made. An example of a portion of the final spreadsheet is shown in Figure 5.7.

---

**Figure 5.7  Sample from the Final Spreadsheet**

| Journal Title | Price (1999) | Total uses from ILS | ILL Loans | Number of internal uses | Cost per internal use |
|---|---|---|---|---|---|
| **QZ—Pathology and Cancer** | | | | | |
| Cancer | $437.00 | 73 | 3 | 70 | $6.24 |
| Journal of Clinical Oncology | $346.00 | 42 | 15 | 27 | $12.81 |
| Journal of the National Cancer Institute: JNCI | $210.00 | 45 | 8 | 37 | $5.68 |
| MMWR: Morbidity and Mortality Weekly Report | $79.00 | 26 | 1 | 25 | $3.16 |
| **W—Practice of Medicine** | | | | | |
| Family Practice Management | $132.00 | 2 | 0 | 2 | 66.00 |
| JAMA: Journal of the American Medical Association | $245.00 | 346 | 14 | 332 | $0.74 |
| Medical Care | $373.00 | 13 | 9 | 4 | 93.25 |
| Medical Economics | $109.00 | 19 | 3 | 16 | $6.81 |
| **WG—Cardiology** | | | | | |
| American Heart Journal | $291.00 | 48 | 2 | 46 | $6.33 |
| American Journal of Cardiology | $245.00 | 101 | 8 | 93 | $2.63 |
| Circulation | $396.00 | 248 | 11 | 237 | $1.67 |
| Clinical Cardiology | $80.00 | 52 | 25 | 27 | $2.96 |
| Journal of the American College of Cardiology | $286.00 | 128 | 10 | 118 | $2.42 |

**Check**
The new data-gathering process for journal collection development was considered effective. The criteria for success were evaluated:

- A spreadsheet available for review when needed:
  - The results were presented to the library committee on time.
- The spreadsheet would be judged to be useful as a tool for the library committee and library director during the review.
  - Using the spreadsheet, a decision was made to cancel some high-cost-per-use journals across various subjects. By grouping the journals by subject, cost per use was not the only criterion for selection or deselection. A balance across subjects could now be monitored. The process also produced other reports. The library committee was shown pie charts on the top ten subjects by use and by cost. Journals falling under the National Library of Medicine classification: WB—The Practice of Medicine—was the most heavily used, at 37% of the total. WO—Surgery—came in second, at 11%. The highest cost per use was WR—Dermatology—at $14.97 per use, followed by WH—Hematology—at $11.69.
- The spreadsheet would be easily updated and used in following years:
  - The team discussed the ease of updating the spreadsheet and decided it could be done each year.

**Act**
Action was taken on the new journal collection development data-gathering process by deciding to continue to use the spreadsheet every year and update it annually. The student wrote procedural documentation for updating the spreadsheet. The technician will prepare a journal use report annually. The team plans to streamline the use of ILL borrowing data to add this component to purchasing decisions. The library director reported the findings of the project to management. The team prepared a poster of the FOCUS-PDCA project for the hospital's annual quality fair. The library director and library committee now have a process to make collection decisions based on established data.

# WORKBOOK FOR FOCUS-PDCA

## FIND AN OPPORTUNITY OR PROCESS FOR IMPROVEMENT.

Review benchmarking or customer needs assessments, satisfaction surveys, or complaints to locate a problem area.

_____

_____

Define the problem.

_____

_____

_____

Is this area important to customers or to the mission of the organization?

_____

_____

_____

Write an opportunity statement. Where does the improvement opportunity lie? What are the boundaries of the work? Why is this the right time to do the work? What will this effort improve?

_____

_____

_____

## ORGANIZE A TEAM THAT UNDERSTANDS THE OPPORTUNITY AND RELATED SYSTEMS OR PROCESSES.

List team members and their reason for being on the team.

| Member name | Title | Extension | Reason to be on team/Skills |
|---|---|---|---|
|  |  |  |  |
|  |  |  |  |
|  |  |  |  |
|  |  |  |  |

List other departments that would have an interest in this process:

_____

_____

_____

Who is responsible for various parts of the process? With the team, create a responsibility chart listing all the tasks that need to be done and who will be doing them. Which staff members have the time and expertise? See Chapter 12 for more on responsibility charts.

| Responsible party → Process | Team member A | Team member B | Team member C | Team member D |
|---|---|---|---|---|
| General planning and coordination | | | | |
| Designing the study | | | | |
| Collecting the data | | | | |
| Coding or preparing the data for analysis | | | | |
| Analyzing the data | | | | |
| Interpreting the results | | | | |
| Reporting the results | | | | |

R—Responsible for carrying out the task. Every task must have an R.
C—Consults to the R person for the task.
A—Assists the R person with the task.
I—Is informed about the status of the work.

Plan a budget by referring to the "Budget Planning" tool in Chapter 12. List the details of the types of expenses this evaluation project will incur.

_____
_____
_____

## CLARIFY THE PROCESS BY COLLECTING INFORMATION ABOUT THE PROCESS.

Who are the customers of the process?

_____
_____
_____

Do a literature search to see how others have handled the process.

_____
_____
_____

Interview team members and others involved in the process.

_____

_____

Do a flowchart if appropriate.

_____

_____

## UNDERSTAND THE CAUSES OF THE PROBLEM.

Do a cause and effect, or fishbone, diagram.

_____

_____

_____

Discuss with the team the various parts of the process to determine what can be changed.

_____

_____

_____

## SELECT A PROCESS IMPROVEMENT ACTIVITY.

Get team consensus on which part of the process to change.

_____

_____

_____

Verify with management that resources are available to make the change.

_____

_____

_____

## PLAN. WRITE DOWN THE ACTIVITIES AND MEASURES NEEDED TO FIND IMPROVEMENTS FOR THE PROCESS IDENTIFIED USING FOCUS.

Plan activities needed to change the process and assign team members

| Activity | Team member | Resources needed |
|---|---|---|
|  |  |  |
|  |  |  |
|  |  |  |

Develop a timeline and Gantt chart for the activities. See Chapter 12 for an explanation.

| Activity                                  Weeks → | 1 | 2 | 3 | 4 | 5 | 6 | 7 | 8 | 9 | 10 | 11 | 12 |
|---|---|---|---|---|---|---|---|---|---|---|---|---|
| General planning and coordination |  |  |  |  |  |  |  |  |  |  |  |  |
| Designing the study |  |  |  |  |  |  |  |  |  |  |  |  |
| Collecting the data |  |  |  |  |  |  |  |  |  |  |  |  |
| Coding or preparing the data for analysis |  |  |  |  |  |  |  |  |  |  |  |  |
| Analyzing the data |  |  |  |  |  |  |  |  |  |  |  |  |
| Interpreting the results |  |  |  |  |  |  |  |  |  |  |  |  |
| Reporting the results |  |  |  |  |  |  |  |  |  |  |  |  |

Develop a data collection plan for monitoring tools and targets for criteria of success.

| Tool | Criteria | Team member | Resources needed |
|---|---|---|---|
|  |  |  |  |
|  |  |  |  |
|  |  |  |  |
|  |  |  |  |

## DO. IMPLEMENT THE NEW PROCESS BASED ON THE PLAN SET OUT IN THE PREVIOUS PHASE.

Set a date when the process will be checked or studied. This will determine whether to keep the process or go back to the beginning and find another process to improve that will be more effective.

_____

_____

_____

## CHECK. STUDY, MONITOR, AND EVALUATE THE PROCESS CHANGE. DETERMINE IF THE PROCESS CHANGE WAS A SUCCESS.

Examine the data collected and determine if the criteria for success were met.

| Criteria | Team member reporting | Data used |
|---|---|---|
|  |  |  |
|  |  |  |
|  |  |  |

Identify people and system issues that impacted the success of the plan and what you have learned.

| Staff members | Contribution to success | What was learned |
|---|---|---|
|  |  |  |
|  |  |  |
|  |  |  |

Report the outcome of the study to the team and management, detailing the data and making a recommendation for change.

_____
_____
_____
_____

If the results were negative or inconclusive, go back to "clarify, understand, and select" and decide if some other factor was perhaps more important. Assessment data already collected become the input for the next step in the cycle.

_____
_____
_____
_____

## ACT. TAKE ACTION BASED ON WHAT YOU LEARNED WHEN YOU STUDIED THE RESULTS OF THE CHANGE.

Review all the previous FOCUS-PDCA steps with the team.

Find: _____
_____

Organize: _____
_____

Clarify: _____
_____

Understand: _____
_____

Select: _____
_____

Plan: _____
_____

Do: _____
_____

Check: _____
_____

Make a decision as to whether the process improvement was successful.

_____
_____
_____

If the process modification worked, accept the change.

_____
_____
_____

If the change did not work, go through the cycle again with a modified or different plan. Use what you learned to plan new improvements, beginning the cycle again, even on the same process.

_____
_____
_____

Share the results with the staff in formal and informal settings.

_____
_____
_____

Report activities to management, whether positive or negative. Use the Evaluation Report Template as a guide for the reports, as found in Chapter 11 and on the CD-ROM in the Chapter 11 folder.

_____
_____
_____

Keep the results on file in case you wish to revisit the process in the future.

_____
_____
_____

# REFERENCES

Jurow, S. R., and S. B. Barnard. 1993. "Introduction: TQM Fundamentals and Overview of Contents." In *Integrating Total Quality Management in a Library Setting*, edited by S. R. Jurow and S. B. Barnard. New York: Haworth Press.

Mein, N. N. 2000. "Quality Improvement." In *The Medical Library Association Guide to Managing Health Care Libraries*, edited by R. Holst, S. A. Phillips, K. M. Bensing, and the Medical Library Association. Chicago: Medical Library Association/Neal-Shuman Publishers.

Miller, P. J. 2001. "Case Study 2.1: Implementing Total Quality Management." In *Library Evaluation: A Casebook and Can-Do Guide*, edited by D. P. Wallace and C. J. Van Fleet. Englewood, CO: Libraries Unlimited.

Orenstein, D. I. 1999. "Developing Quality Managers and Quality Management: The Challenge to Leadership in Library Organizations." *Library Administration and Management*, 13, no. 1: 44–51.

Riggs, D. E. 1994. "Strategic Quality Management in Libraries." In *Total Quality Management in Libraries: A Sourcebook*, edited by R. M. O'Neal. Englewood, CO: Libraries Unlimited.

Wagner, K. C. 2002. "FOCUS PDCA: A Process Improvement (PI) Tool for Libraries." *Journal of Hospital Librarianship*, 2, no. 2: 93–97.

# 6 METHOD 3: BENCHMARKING

**Reference: Benchmarking Resources**

Since the 1980s a multitude of books have been written about benchmarking. These are recommended:

Andersen, B., and P-G. Pettersen. 1996. *The Benchmarking Handbook: Step-by-Step Instructions*. New York: Chapman & Hall.

Muir, H. J. 1993–1994. *Library Benchmarking Notebooks: A Librarian's Guide*, 1–5: 1. *Conducting a Preliminary Benchmarking Analysis*; 2. *Developing Benchmarking Metrics*; 3. *Identifying Benchmarking Partners: Special Libraries*; 4. *Collecting and Analyzing Benchmarking Data*; 5. *Presenting Benchmarking Results*. Cincinnati, OH: Library Benchmarking International.

Spendolini, M. J. 1992. *The Benchmarking Book*. 2d ed. New York: Amacom.

Benchmarking is an evaluation tool used to measure quality, and it is one of several tools that can be used as part of the management philosophy of total quality management, or TQM. The theories of TQM have been expanded on in the business world with such programs as Six Sigma, Kaizen, and Lean, which are explained briefly in Chapter 9. Chapter 5 goes over TQM or QI principles in more detail, as well as providing background on the quality movement. Chapter 5 also covers another TQM tool called FOCUS-PDCA (find-organize-clarify-understand-select and plan-do-check-act).

There is no single best way to address quality. Quality programs are often an organizationwide initiative that comes from the board and chief executive officer (CEO). Many of these programs have a positive philosophy about learning new systems and demonstrate a willingness to change. Benefiting the customer is the primary goal of all attempts to measure quality. Benchmarking resources abound in print and on the Web. Introduced to the United States by Xerox in the late 1970s, benchmarking soon became part of the tool kit to adopt the quality principles of W. Edward Deming. For more about Deming and his quality principles, see Chapter 5.

Benchmarking has been described as a "complex" activity (Buchanan and Marshall, 1996: 2). It does require skills such as survey design, question writing, general statistics, effective analysis, and display of data, skills that are covered in Chapter 10 on data collection. Benchmarking does have a learning curve. But, by reading this chapter and supplementing what is learned with perhaps a basic book and several articles on the topic, you, the practicing librarian, can successfully do a benchmarking project that will either improve your processes and services or compare your performance to others.

If your institution has a quality department or committee, you should always check with them before embarking on benchmarking or any evaluation project for that matter. They may have tools, connections, and expertise that can be useful to you. They can also advise you about the quality culture of your organization and how your plans fit with it. If you do not find an institutional quality culture, you can still create one on your own in the library as a departmental program using the principles of TQM, as described in Chapter 5, and the ideas of a culture of assessment, as described in Chapter 2.

A recent study pointed out that evaluation of the success of quality programs and benchmarking, in particular, in libraries has not been studied (Wilson and Town, 2006). Wilson, in his attempt to study library benchmarking projects, developed a framework he called the Quality Maturity Model. It is a model that could be used to evaluate where your quality program is in relation to its development or maturity. His conclusion in his brief study is that benchmarking projects are not very successful unless your quality program is mature (Wilson and Town, 2006). You might conclude that process benchmarking should not be your first evaluation project.

## WHAT IS BENCHMARKING?

What is benchmarking, exactly? Thomas Peischl gives us the word's appealing derivation and states that it comes from "the jargon of carpenters and surveyors—a mark on a bench or a pole became the standard or measure for future repetitions of a service or task. The 'benchmark' was accepted as an indicator that some prior measure was true, acceptable, and reliable, and could be counted on to provide an indicator of a prior quality measurement" (Peischl, 1995: 99–100). As you are working on your "complex" project, try to remember that simple mark on the carpenter's bench.

Comparing your operation with others allows you to implement improvements in your own system by identifying superior performance and practices. It allows you to identify what you *could* or *should* be doing. Benchmarking allows the library staff to go beyond their own experience and find innovative activities in other libraries, the kind of activities that may help them survive. The Joint Commission for the Accreditation of Healthcare Organizations (JCAHO) leads a major benchmarking initiative in the health-care industry, and benchmarking is a chief TQM evaluation technique.

## TYPES OF BENCHMARKING

It can be said that people benchmark everyday, whether they are aware of it or not. How often have you considered which is the

**Definition: Benchmarking**

1. A tool to measure and compare your library's performance or work processes with those of other libraries.
2. The ongoing comparison and review of one's own process, product or service against the best known similar activity, so that realistic goals can be set and effective strategies can be identified and implemented to work towards their attainment (CHLA/ABSC Benchmarking Task Force, 1998: 24).
3. A continuous, systematic process for evaluating the products, services, and work processes of your organization and comparing it to other organizations that are recognized as representing best practices for the purpose of organizational improvement (Spendolini, 2000: 9).

best store, the best restaurant, the best book, and so on? If you were to write down the thought process that goes into your decision, you might see comparison benchmarking taking place. Librarians do "informal" benchmarking every time they buy something for their library. Which is the best database service, the best journal, the best computer? If you were to write down the steps you took to make one of these decisions, it could result in a small benchmarking report. Does your supervisor really know what it takes to make one of your decisions? If you wrote down these processes and showed them to your supervisor, it would not only justify your purchasing decision but also show him or her the value of your selection service to the institution.

A formal benchmarking project can be categorized with two questions (Andersen and Pettersen, 1996). Each question has three answers.

1. What do you want to compare?
   - Your overall performance (performance benchmarking)
   - A process that provides a service to customers (process benchmarking)
   - An overall look at your strategic position (strategic benchmarking)
2. Against whom are you going to compare?
   - Internal departments (internal benchmarking)
   - External organizations, libraries, or similar operations (functional benchmarking)
   - Other organizations that are your direct competition (competitive benchmarking)

When you compare the two questions in the matrix shown in Figure 6.1, there are nine types of benchmarking projects, such as internal-process, external-performance, external-strategic, and so forth. Each one has different levels of value or relevance to a library operation. Figure 6.1 gives each type a rating as to its value or relevance to libraries. Your first decision is to choose your method of benchmarking.

| Figure 6.1 | Value or Relevance of Benchmarking Type Combinations to a Library Operation | | | |
|---|---|---|---|---|
| | | Against whom are you going to compare? | | |
| | | Internal | Functional | Competitive |
| What do you want to compare? | Performance | Low | Medium | High |
| | Process | Medium | High | Low |
| | Strategy | Low | Low | Medium |
| (Adapted from Andersen and Pettersen, 1996: 7) | | | | |

"Data (performance) benchmarking measures and compares inputs and outputs of a process against a benchmark to assess performance. Process benchmarking analyzes a sequence of activities and compares them with similar functions in best practice organizations" (Henczel, 2002: 13–14).

- *Performance benchmarking* compares measures of performance to determine how good your own operation is compared with others. It involves measuring inputs and outputs of a process and comparing them with others' measurements of the same. Performance benchmarking has many other names, including comparative, data, metric, organizational, or outcomes benchmarking. *Outcomes*, however, has come to mean the effect of the service or product on the client, not the service or product itself, which is an output of the system. Outcomes measures are described in Chapter 8. Sometimes performance benchmarking is a limited collaborative exchange of information within a consortium or organization: a "best practices" collaboration, if you will. Performance benchmarking is explained in detail below using the example of finding out if you need more computer terminals for library customers.

- *Process benchmarking* compares the methods and practices, or sequence of activities, used to perform a process. It compares the processes with similar functions in partners or peer institutions that are identified as having "best-practices." Called "classic benchmarking" by Todd-Smith and Markwell, this "involves selecting benchmarking partners to compare the steps of a process to understand why other libraries may do the process faster or better" (Todd-Smith and Markwell, 2002: 86). An example of process benchmarking would be comparing record keeping for your interlibrary loan operation in the hope of having it more streamlined and using less paper.

- *Strategic benchmarking* compares your overall strategic choices with others. If usually done as part of a planning

**Reference: Strategic Benchmarking**

Strategic benchmarking compares your array of services and your position in the institution with others. Where do you stand when it comes to trends and services and resources being offered by other libraries? Nikki Poling's article on benchmarking asks, "Are you ahead or behind the curve" (Poling, 2002: 22)? That is the essence of strategic benchmarking.

process at a company level, it would involve investigating choices and plans made by other companies, usually using public information. On the departmental level, in a library, it might be a systematic review of the literature for trends to see where the profession is heading so you do not get left behind. An example of strategic benchmarking could be that you read about larger libraries purchasing and using federated search programs. Strategically would this service be a good match for the needs of your customers? It would relate to a strategic plan you have or are developing. The ideas of strategic planning are briefly covered in Chapter 9, and the Logic Model covered in Chapter 8 can be used as a strategic planning tool.

Now you should have decided what method of benchmarking you are going to do. Your second step is to decide with whom you will compare your operation. You might assume you can only benchmark against other libraries, but that is not true. You have three choices:

- *Internal benchmarking* compares your performance, process, or strategies against another department or division in your organization. This is sometimes the easiest to do and could be used to practice the benchmarking process. A support process practiced by all departments, such as purchasing or financial record keeping, could be compared to see if your systems are as efficient as they can be. You might compare how you file your financial information such as requisitions and vouchers with other departments. Maybe there are electronic means that would cut down on paperwork.
- *Functional benchmarking*, sometimes called generic benchmarking, compares the processes or functions you have chosen to analyze against organizations that have similar processes in the same or a different industry. These organizations are recognized as having state-of-the-art products, services, or processes. Can you identify a library you consider to be an example of one that uses excellent management principles? Based on your own operation, do you think the other library is more efficient? Process benchmarking is detailed below, and choosing partners is described.
- *Competitive benchmarking* compares your performance against direct competitors selling to the same customer base. This can be done with contacted partners or just

shadowing selected partners using public data. This is usually part of a company planning process. Since libraries do not compete with each other by selling a product to the same customer, this is not generally used in libraries. You could be creative and compare with booksellers or other commercial information providers. As an example, a recent OCLC report compared the daily circulation of public libraries (5.4 million) with the daily shipments from Amazon (1.5 million) (OCLC Online Computer Library Center, accessed: 2007).

# ETHICS AND ETIQUETTE

The ethics or etiquette of benchmarking is mentioned by most experts as important to be aware of. Start with finding out if your organization has a benchmarking office or perhaps a quality improvement department. If you are contacting competitors, they might want to know about your project, especially if you are contacting partners. They might already be dealing with these partners, and your project might interfere or influence theirs. They might have rules for information exchange. They may also be helpful in finding partners using their contacts with competitors. If there is no such department, at least go over the issues with your supervisor. Mainly use your common sense. As Muir says, "If it feels wrong to exchange certain types of information, it probably is" (Muir, 1994: 22). Refer to the *Benchmarking Code of Conduct*, published by APQC (accessed: 2006) and excerpted here in Figure 6.2.

---

**Figure 6.2. The Benchmarking Code of Conduct**

*Legality*: This mostly has to do with businesses due to possible acquisition of trade secrets and implications for restraint of trade, price fixing, bid rigging, or bribery. For libraries, one guideline is to not use benchmarking study findings from another library without permission of all partners.

*Exchange of information*: Be willing to give the same information as you get. Communicate well to avoid misunderstandings of what is being exchanged. Be honest and complete.

*Confidentiality*: Do not disclose any data or findings to outside parties without permission of all involved. Do not disclose the partner's participation without their permission.

*Use of information*: Do not use any data or findings for anything other than your stated purpose. Tying a partner's name to the results requires their permission. Never use the results of the study to market or sell.

*First party contact*: If necessary contact partners though a designated benchmarking contact at their institution. If you contact another librarian directly, always check to see if they need to coordinate with a benchmarking or quality office at their institution. Respect a partner's company culture, working within agreed upon procedures and prohibited communication guidelines.

*Third party contact*: If contacted by a third party, such as another library that heard about the study, do not share partners' names without permission. Also, do not use names in open forums or publications without permission.

*Be prepared*: Have a commitment to efficiency and get your work done on time. Be fully prepared for each meeting. Provide your partners with the interview or site visit guide before the arriving for an arranged site visit.

*Complete the project*: Follow through on each phase of the process in a timely manner and complete the project to the satisfaction of all partners.

*Understanding of the partner relationship*: Treat your partners as they would like to be treated and handle information in the manner agreed upon.

(Adapted from Andersen and Pettersen, 1996, and APQC, 2004)

---

# BENEFITS AND PITFALLS

There are several benefits and pitfalls to doing a benchmarking project that you should be aware of.

## BENEFITS

- The strategic goals of the library and organization are supported.

  Whether performance or process benchmarking, the evaluation will show the library's support for the mission and goals of the library and its larger organization. Part of the process would be to show the value of library activities that are often unique to a library.

- Management support will be nurtured.

    By showing your management and staff how the library compares with others and/or by involving them in process benchmarking, you will gain their support. The changes that come from a benchmarking project can be more readily accepted than can a direct order from a supervisor to change a process.

- Performance and customer service will be improved.

    Benchmarking projects grow out of a customer service focus. Whichever kind of benchmarking you are doing, you are evaluating how well you are serving your customer. Can you add a program you found when looking at the programs of other libraries? Will the customer benefit if you improve your efficiency through a process benchmarking project? By focusing on something that will make a significant difference to organizational effectiveness, a detailed examination of the process can only improve it. After experience is gained with one process, others can be brought into the system of evaluation.

- Decision making will be better.

    A benchmarking project will assist managers in identifying and prioritizing parts of their system that need improvement. Decision-making processes will improve because they will have evidence from the study to help them make their choices. The team aspects of benchmarking will help support them in their decisions.

- Professional and staff relationships will improve.

    By working together on the project, personnel will improve their relationships both internally and externally through better communication and understanding of the job being done. Benchmarking projects create opportunities for both individual and organizational development.

## PITFALLS

- Choosing a process to benchmark can be difficult.

    All evaluation projects should be tied to your overall mission and the mission of your organization. How do you determine that one process is more important than another? Is there enough room for improvement in the process to make the analysis worthwhile? Make sure the process you choose is not too large to be evaluated; it can be broken down into smaller processes, which will be easier for you to handle.

- Confusing performance and process benchmarking.

    Performance benchmarking will tell you where you rank. You may be able to show serious shortfalls that may suggest places to improve, but often these will need further study. Only by doing a process benchmarking project can you improve that process and thereby potentially improve your rank in that area.

- Choosing cost over quality.

    Your project can get fixated on cost to the detriment of quality customer service. Chapter 8 covers how to assess outcomes of services, some of which include an added value of any given service. When evaluating a process for quality, you should not just look at cost but see what quality adds to value or outcomes. Remember the intangible, as well as the tangible, benefits of the process. While it is hard to include value or outcome concepts about a process, they should not be overlooked.

- Be aware of the resources needed to do the project.

    Benchmarking takes significant resources of time and money. Make sure you spend enough time in the planning stages to select the right questions, or you will waste resources. Follow through to the end to get a result.

- Data collection decisions must be collaborative.

    Data collected by different libraries may not match. Whether collecting performance data or flowcharting a process, make sure the definitions of the data points being collected are defined. It may be difficult to agree not only on definitions but also on what to measure. Data already collected may not match across different environments and may be too limited to help you correct your performance. The data must be consistent, defined correctly, and collected accurately.

- Changing environments and innovative practices.

    Benchmarking may not take into account new technologies or new economic conditions. Also, unique environments may not be comparable. The local context must be taken into account for each project. An innovative practice in a specific environment may not lend itself to benchmarking. Do not let benchmarking stifle innovation and creativity.

- Identifying partners is difficult.

    You need to research your benchmarking partners so that you are not asking them questions you can find out in the public domain. Also, be sure the processes being measured are similar enough so that they can be compared.

Try to make sure that potential partners have excellent practices and that you are not just picking them because they are convenient.

# PERFORMANCE BENCHMARKING

## DESCRIPTION

Collecting and analyzing measures of library inputs and outputs has been discussed since the 1960s (Goodall, 1988). It is often difficult to explain the relationship between numbers gathered about your collection, your services, and your budget because there is no direct connection between inputs and outputs. These challenges are discussed in more detail in Chapter 3. The planning model called the Logic Model, discussed in Chapter 8, attempts to give some clarity to the issue. Many reports of overall library activity show each program separately, since there is little connection between the statistics gathered for each program. How do you know if your measures, inputs or outputs, are "good" or conforming to the "best practice" for the type of library you are? A performance benchmarking project can help you assess this. You would need to gather inputs and outputs from a number of similar libraries and compare them. This can be time consuming, and in some cases it is be hard to find like libraries. Several professional organizations have completed surveys for their members. They collect input measures or parameters of size, so you can find like libraries and collect measures of activities in order to assess the performance of the group of libraries.

Three associations, as described in more detail in Chapter 3, have conducted this type of survey:

- The Association of Research Libraries (ARL) Statistics & Measurement Program (www.arl.org/stats/)—Collected since the turn of the century.
- The Association of Academic Health Sciences Libraries (AAHSL) (www.aahsl.org/)—Collected since 1975 (Shedlock and Byrd, 2003; Byrd and Shedlock, 2003).
- The Medical Library Association Benchmarking Network Surveys 2002 and 2004 (MLA) (www.mlanet.org/). Aggregate results available on the CD-ROM in the Chapter 6 folder. Collected in 2002 and 2004 (Dudden, et al., 2006a, 2006b).

The surveys collect measures of institutional size, collection numbers, and service output numbers. Participants would use the data to measure their overall performance against others. All were of great service to the participants, since by using these surveys, they did not have to contact other libraries and collect the data themselves.

Performance benchmarking can be used to demonstrate whether your resources or activities are well supported. Using the MLA Benchmarking Network 2002 survey, the Northern and Southern California Kaiser Permanente libraries successfully completed such a project (Fulda and Satterthwaite, 2003; 2004). Eleven libraries in the Northern California District compared three items from their budgets (books, journals, and staff) to the median benchmarking data for other libraries of like size. They then submitted a request for additional funding, using as justification the discrepancy they found with the funding for those budget items between the Kaiser libraries and the median for libraries documented in the benchmarking data. The analysis showed that funding of book and journal expenditures and of staff for other libraries, as reported in the benchmarking data, was significantly higher than the expenditures for these items in the Kaiser library budgets. When requesting a budget increase, the librarians developed scenarios of how additional money would be spent using three different funding levels. The mid-level scenario, which increased funding by $1 million for the 11 libraries, was subsequently approved.

Examples of benchmarking that were done before the MLA Benchmarking Network survey demonstrate how difficult it is for librarians to gather their own statistics and make their own decisions on which data to gather (Goodwin, 1999; Harris, 2000). Anecdotally, there are many less-dramatic examples of libraries that have used the MLA Benchmarking Network surveys to ask for more funds and staff. Two such success stories were circulated by the MLA Benchmarking Network Editorial Board to encourage participation in the 2004 survey. They are included in full on the CD-ROM in the Chapter 6 folder.

Performance benchmarking is a simpler activity to do than process benchmarking. It is often used as a wake-up call to a funding body that something is wrong, as in the case of the Kaiser libraries, but it does not give you a definite idea or plan about what to improve to gain better quality. It should be considered a first, although major, step in a quality improvement program. It can, however, lead to what has been called the three Ds: disbelief, denial, and despair. First you do not believe the results of the comparison (how could be we *that* low?). Then you deny the re-

---

**On the CD-ROM: Benchmarking Network Survey Success Stories (in the Chapter 6 folder)**

Success #1: Value documented. The benchmarking efforts paid off because with the benchmarking data we could easily demonstrate value and return on investment (ROI). We were able to increase staff and maintain or increase budget resources by using the MLA Benchmarking data.

Success #2: We gained a permanent, half-time library assistant position. With solid statistics showing continuing large increases in patronage and services over the years, plus positive responses to a decade of annual user surveys, during the 2004 budget presentation we used data from the MLA Benchmarking Network survey to support a request for a permanent, half-time assistant. A short and simple presentation demonstrated our library was greatly understaffed when compared with hospitals like ours in three parameters: size of the medical staff, number of residency positions, and number of FTEs.

sults by claiming that the comparable libraries are not really like yours. Finally, you become paralyzed by despair because you do not know how to catch up (Andersen, and Pettersen, 1996).

If you do not fall victim to the three Ds, you will need to follow up and focus on the processes that contribute to the performance gap. Sometimes all you need to do is identify the performance difference and use it to your benefit through systematic review and open communication. The steps that follow are steps you can take to do performance benchmarking.

## STEPS FOR PERFORMANCE BENCHMARKING

### 1. Identify the measure or measures to be benchmarked and start the planning process.

Decide what you are going to benchmark and why. You will need to think about how you are going to do it, with whom, and for what purpose. It is most important to know your purpose. Some appropriate purposes would be to discover:

- Does your library operation need more money, space or resources?
- Is your staff size low or your budget low?
- How much will it cost to start purchasing electronic books or journals?
- Should you have more computer terminals?

Think about how you are going to gather measures and parameters of size:

- Are you a member of the Association of Academic Health Sciences Librarians (AAHSL), or did you participate in the MLA Benchmarking Network?
- Will you have to gather your own measurements?
- Who are your peers?
- Who would make good partners?
- How are you going to find them?

These are just preliminary thoughts to put down in order to discuss the project with your supervisor.

### 2. Establish management commitment to the benchmarking process.

Discuss with your supervisor what your needs are and how you think performance benchmarking will demonstrate them. For this you will have to be somewhat aware of the possible results of the project. Do you think you will be above or below average? This will impact how you approach the project with your supervisor. You need support, since you will be reporting the results to this person. If you get to go ahead with the project, expenses will be incurred that the supervisor will have needed to approve.

### 3. Plan the evaluation project by establishing the benchmarking team, defining a budget, and setting timelines.

In hospital libraries and other small-library settings, the team may be just you! But what other resources could you use? Does your institution have a quality improvement department that could help? They might join the team to help with data collection and analysis, as described in Chapter 10. Your team does not have to be as robust as with process benchmarking, but you should inform and involve your employees and your supervisor. Chapter 11 has some tips on team building and working with teams. Define a budget for the project, even if all the time and materials come from your own budget. Plan the expenses and how they will be covered. Refer to the "Budget Planning" tool in Chapter 12 for details of the types of expenses that evaluation projects incur. Develop a timeline using a Gantt chart and set team responsibilities using a responsibility chart, both of which are described in Chapter 12.

### 4. Identify, define, and understand the measures to be benchmarked.

This activity depends on your purpose and your strategic reason for doing the study. Which measure or measures do you want to compare? If you are using the AAHSL or MLA survey data, you can choose among many. You will need to choose the ones that relate to the project and understand the definitions applied. The MLA Benchmarking Network survey data asks how many databases there are and how much is spent on them. Would that be enough, or would you want them listed by name but with no price attached? And how would you account for the number of free databases that were tracked by a partner? If you are comparing budgets, make a decision about how much detail you would want. You can see how complicated it can get. If you plan to collect your own data, you will need to be judicious and not ask too many irrelevant questions. You will need definitions of terms. Decide what data are needed and collect it for your own institution. This will give you an idea of how hard it will be for others to do so when you ask them the questions.

## 5. Use existing surveys or plan to collect data from benchmarking partners.

If you are using the AAHSL or MLA survey, you will not need to contact partners. You will need to decide on parameters of size and activity. You will have to learn how to use and read the systems and tables presented to you by each survey. If you decide to collect data, you will have to identify partners. Be sure the data are not already available, or the partners you contact may wonder why you are bothering them. In other words, if you working with an MLA or AAHSL member and are collecting data on questions already asked in their two surveys, why are you collecting it again?

If you are asking questions not represented in these surveys, you can still use the surveys to identify benchmarking partners. By searching the available size parameters, you will get different lists of comparable institutions. You can also use listservs, associations, and library directories to recruit potential partners. Establish contact with the selected partners and gain acceptance for participation in the study. Usually for performance benchmarking, the number is between four and ten. For performance benchmarking, fewer than four would not be considered statistically significant and more than ten would be too time consuming. Explain the benefits of participating, such as access to the final report.

## 6. Collect the data from benchmarking partners if you need to.

If you are not using the AAHSL or MLA surveys, you will need to collect the data to be used for comparison. You will already have identified and defined your metrics and collected data from your own institution. Now you need to collect that data from others. Using the techniques defined in Chapter 10 on collecting data, develop a questionnaire. You might save some time by using some of the questions and definitions from the MLA Benchmarking Network survey, which are available on the CD-ROM in the Chapter 6 folder. You can administer it using paper, an online survey service, or phone interviews. A combination of those methods also might work. For example, you could send the partners a Word document via e-mail. Then they could collect the data from various sources and fill it in the paper form. Using the filled-in form, they would access the Web form, and it would be faster and easier to fill in. A follow-up phone call could be made if there are any problems with the answers. Since the aforementioned large cooperative surveys exist, it is assumed that your survey would be small and the questions complementary to the larger survey and not the same. It is also assumed that since this is performance data and not process data, a site visit would not be reasonable. Why would you need to visit if you just want to compare budgets? However, if you were benchmarking space and arrangement of space, a visit might be in order.

### 7. Analyze and present the data.

A spreadsheet is developed containing the final data. Benchmarking data can be presented as raw data or as a ratio. You could present the simple raw data points as discovered in the surveys you have access to or from the data you collected yourself. The point of analysis is to pick out the most significant data to the question at hand. If your question is simple or one dimensional, raw data may be the thing to use. Chapter 10 has a few tips on data analysis. For further study, the Web documents from the University of Wisconsin-Extension, Cooperative Extension Service are recommended. They give more extensive but still understandable explanations of quantitative and qualitative data analysis. Chapter 12 lists and describes briefly quantitative analysis tools for data display:

- Bar chart (histogram)
- Data points
- Pareto chart
- Pie chart
- Radar chart
- Run chart
- Scatter chart

Using these analysis tools, you can look at the data and find comparisons and trends. As you look at it, you decide how to present the data for decision making and reports. These are three possible approaches.

- *Using a single data point for a simple or single issue*
  In Figure 6.3, raw data from the MLA Benchmarking Network survey is used to answer a single question about how many public access terminals a library should have. Using that program, you can see data from 14 to 53 libraries. If you had gathered you own data, you would have had to call that many libraries to ask them just one question.

---

**Figure 6.3   Example of Use of Raw Data from the MLA Benchmarking Network Survey**

A patron has suggested you get more computer workstations. He states that often when he comes to the library, the terminals are all in use. You and your staff have observed peak time usage, but in general the terminals are not always full. Rather than performing a time study, you decide to benchmark what other libraries are doing, using the MLA Benchmarking Network survey.

There is a relevant question on the survey: "SP16. How many Web-accessible computer workstations do you have in your library available to end users?" You login to the site. Using the Benchmarking Network Report selection tool, you choose three parameters of size and one location parameter, your state. You copy the data into Word and convert it to a table. With some editing you can produce a table and a chart that looks like this:

| Question Number of Web-accessible end-users workstations | | | | |
|---|---|---|---|---|
| Your data | Mean (average) | Median | Third quartile (75%) | Maximum |
| **8.00**<br><br>Web-accessible end-user workstations | Compared with libraries in your state (14 libraries): | | | |
| | 5.57 | 4.50 | 8.00 | 14.00 |
| | Compared with your institutional size (55 libraries):<br>Number of hospital full-time equivalent (FTE): Employees 1850 to 2699 | | | |
| | 6.13 | 5.00 | 8.00 | 20.00 |
| | Compared with your staff (53 libraries):<br>Number of total library FTEs: 2.5 to 3.9 | | | |
| | 6.35 | 6.00 | 8.00 | 16.00 |
| | Compared to your total budget (23 libraries):<br>Total annual expenditures for the library $570,000 to $1,049,999 | | | |
| | 13.24 | 12.00 | 14.00 | 52.00 |

*(continued)*

**Figure 6.3   Example of Use of Raw Data from the MLA Benchmarking Network Survey (*Continued*)**

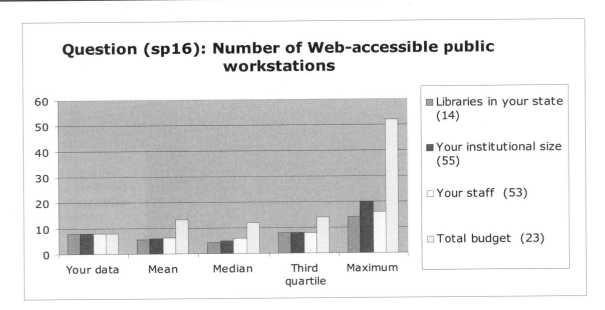

Question (sp16): Number of Web-accessible public workstations

The table shows the "performance" of the other libraries quite well. Your library matches the third quartile, or the 75%, mark on three out of four of the parameters of size you chose to look at. The third quartile is considered a "best practice" in benchmarking theory. You confer with your supervisor about the results and respond to the user complaint. Your joint response is:

"While at times the workstations are all occupied, there are many times when they are empty. We have compared our number of stations with libraries from comparable institutions and found that 75% of comparable libraries reporting had the same number of workstations that we have. At this time we do not feel justified in requesting more workstations. We will continue to monitor the situation for possible needed improvement and apologize for the inconvenience."

- *Using the results of a whole survey as a communication tool*

  The MLA Benchmarking Network survey or a survey you do yourself can also be used for broad comparisons over many activities. This example uses the MLA survey, but you could use another survey you participate in or one you did yourself among 10 or 12 partners. Figures 6.4 and 6.5 provide an example of using Web page printouts or downloads from the survey reports to discuss the general state of the library with your supervisor. These reports, presented in an organized fashion, can be used to start a dialogue about any positive and negative results found. You have to be careful of the three Ds, mentioned above—disbelief, denial, and despair—and present the analysis as either a broad overview of performance or as a preliminary study to identify areas where a process benchmarking study could be done. This kind of overall review can be a useful communication. It may be enough to point out areas for improvement.

Whichever method you use to present the data to your supervisor or others, in this example, you are using the data analyzed for you by the MLA Benchmarking Network program. In the profiles section, you get to point out how your institutional size compares with the survey. In the measures of activity sections, you would point out the positive and negative results but maybe not comment on everything. If you did decide to put the whole thing into a word processing document, you could delete sections that did not apply to your situation. In Figure 6.5, for example, if you did not have a consumer health collection, you would delete questions about this service. If you have collected your own data, you can use a spreadsheet to do most of the analysis.

### Figure 6.4 Presenting Survey Results

As an example, you have been asked by your supervisor to broadly compare your activities with libraries of like size. You have decided to present the data based on the size parameter, the number of hospital FTEs. You could also compare according to budget size or library FTEs.

Two techniques to review and present the data:

1. *Print out the Web page displays on the MLA Benchmarking Network Interactive site*
   *Print out your "single library profile."*

   - Search for each parameter of size you want.
   - Print out each for the four activity areas, (administrative, public services, technical services, and special services) for each parameter.
   - Arrange them in a tabbed notebook, one tab for each section.
   - Review the data for interesting findings. There are a lot of data here (each section is 8–10 pages long when printed).
   - Review every chart and write notes to yourself about why the data look the way they do.
   - Circle numbers of interest, good or bad.
   - Reprint the whole thing again and make neater notes to present to your supervisor.
   - You could let him or her see it before you meet to go over the figures. The printouts have graphs, which can be useful to illustrate findings.

2. *Import the data into Microsoft Word.*

   - Import MLA's Benchmarking survey data into Microsoft Word with the graphs as images by first saving the Web page using the Save As command in Internet Explorer and choosing "Webpage, Complete." Save the page using the extension .htm. This saves the text as HTML and puts the images in an attached folder. You can then open the HTML document using Word's Open command and then save it as a Word document. All the tables and graphs will be present.
   - Edit the document or not, depending on your plans.
   - The end result would be a tabbed notebook, as above, with a tab for each section but all word processed with no handwritten notes.
   - This method might be more time consuming, and deciding to do it would depend on the formality of your relationship with your supervisor.
   - The advantage is you can type any comments into your report.
   - You can also eliminate any parts of the page that are irrelevant to your question.
   - The results Web pages can be copied and pasted into a spreadsheet. This would allow you to manipulate the data with some editing and make charts, such as in the example using the raw data (Figure 6.5).

**Figure 6.5    Example of Data Presentation from the MLA Benchmarking Network Survey**

### Question ts01: Number of print monographs in library's collection

| Your data | Mean | Median | Third quartile (75%) | Maximum | Graph |
|---|---|---|---|---|---|
| 3000 | 3272 | 2386 | 4500 | 10957 | |

### Question ts02a: Monographs for use in consumer health information service (CHIS)

| Your data | Mean | Median | Third quartile (75%) | Maximum | Graph |
|---|---|---|---|---|---|
| 1350 | 340 | 50 | 500 | 3000 | |

### Question ts12: Number of monograph titles with electronic full-text access

| Your data | Mean | Median | Third quartile (75%) | Maximum | Graph |
|---|---|---|---|---|---|
| 112 | 37 | 22 | 61 | 172 | |

### Question ts02b: Print books purchased in the reporting year

| Your data | Mean | Median | Third quartile (75%) | Maximum | Graph |
|---|---|---|---|---|---|
| 280 | 220 | 150 | 260 | 1827 | |

- *Using the Canadian method for benchmarking using ratios*
  The Canadian Health Libraries Association/Association des Bibliothèques de la Santé du Canada published the *Benchmarking Tool Kit* in 1998 (CHLA/ABSC Benchmarking Task Force, 1998). The program they wrote uses ratios for comparison. Ratios are used more in process benchmarking but can also be used with performance benchmarking. If the benchmarking partners you chose vary in size, using a ratio will make the data more comparable. This can be done using the MLA Benchmarking Network survey or gathering your own data. Figure 6.6 is an example of using ratios.

**Figure 6.6    Example of Using the Ratio System from the Canadian Benchmarking Tool Kit Pilot Test Results**

**Indicator value 7:**    **Total operating expenditures per primary client. Variable 16 divided by Variable 7.**

**Scores and ranking**

| Library Code | A.1 | A.2 | S.1 | C.H.1 | T.H.3 | S.2 | T.H.1 | C.H.2 | T.H.2 |
|---|---|---|---|---|---|---|---|---|---|
| Score | $441.21 | $372.76 | $209.21 | $113.01 | $101.12 | $90.23 | $72.56 | $68.97 | $68.19 |
| Rank | 1 | 2 | 3 | 4 | 5 | 6 | 7 | 8 | 9 |

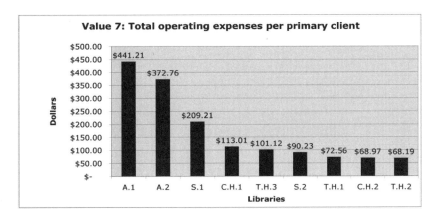

**Variable 16: Total operating expenditures (Sorted by rank)**

| Library Code | A.2 | A.1 | S.2 | T.H.3 | T.H.2 | T.H.1 | S.1 | C.H.1 | C.H.2 |
|---|---|---|---|---|---|---|---|---|---|
| Score | $1,927,902 | $1,821,775 | $499,041 | $295,762 | $256,824 | $164,700 | $106,070 | $105,722 | $83,454 |
| Rank | 1 | 2 | 3 | 4 | 5 | 6 | 7 | 8 | 9 |

**Variable 7: Total FTE primary clients (Sorted by rank)**

| Library Code | S.2 | A.2 | A.1 | T.H.2 | T.H.3 | T.H.1 | C.H.2 | C.H.1 | S.1 |
|---|---|---|---|---|---|---|---|---|---|
| Score | 5531 | 5172 | 4129 | 3766.44 | 2925 | 2270 | 1210 | 935.5 | 507 |
| Rank | 1 | 2 | 3 | 4 | 5 | 6 | 7 | 8 | 9 |

CHLA/ABSC Benchmarking Task Force. 1998. *CHLA/ASBC Benchmarking Tool Kit.* Toronto, ON: Canadian Health Libraries Association/Association des bibliotheques de la sante du Canada.

## 8. Identify areas for improvement and report your results.

A performance benchmarking project results in decisions about a service being proposed or library being evaluated. These will not be detailed changes in procedures but rather decisions to possibly pursue specific ideas for improvement. The success stories mentioned above are examples of libraries that have identified areas for improvement and reported their findings to the administration. Use the Evaluation Report Template, as found in Chapter 11 and on the CD-ROM in the Chapter 11 folder, as a guide.

Perhaps it has been suggested that you form a library advisory committee or disband the one you have. Using the MLA Benchmarking Network survey, you would find that of the libraries responding, half have one and half do not. This would indicate that to come to a conclusion, you would have to set up a small process benchmarking project and call selected libraries with a specific questionnaire about library committees.

Perhaps it has been suggested that you support the use of personal digital assistant (PDA) by the staff by exploring resources and posting them on the library Web site. Using the MLA Benchmarking Network survey, you find that of the 55 libraries in your size group, 41 do not support this activity, 12 do support it, and 2 did not answer the question. Since the PDA technology is considered by some to be the technology of the future and by others too transitional to take seriously, this report would warrant further study of your own hospital's specific programs and needs.

## 9. Continue to conduct benchmarking studies for comparative purposes over time.

The MLA Benchmarking Network survey was conducted in 2002 and 2004. It is hoped that this will continue into the future. By continuing to participate, you can mark your progress over time in specific areas of concern. If you conducted your own study, contact your partners again to refresh the data over a certain period of time, perhaps every other year or even every year if the partners find it useful.

# REAL-LIFE EVALUATION: PERFORMANCE BENCHMARKING

## THE NIST RESEARCH LIBRARY ASSESSMENT PROJECT

Overview: The National Institute of Standards and Technology (NIST) Research Library, a major government library serving scientists, guest researchers, and others with a staff of 17 and a collection of over 300,000 volumes and 1,150 journal subscriptions, initiated a benchmark study owing to a static budget and the need to cancel essential materials. Responding to an advisory committee report and with the encouragement of the director's office, the library undertook assessment projects to adopt "evidence-based practice" to support planning and decision making. In a series of three articles, the authors describe the customer survey, the benchmarking activities, and the results of these two activities as they provide direction for operational and strategic planning. For the benchmarking project a survey of 69 questions was developed to look at performance across the total program. Areas of excellence and deficiency were identified and reported. Improvements in several processes were recommended, and strategic decisions in various areas were made.

1. *Identify the measure or measures to be benchmarked and start the planning process.*

   The scope of the performance benchmarking was determined to be broad to see which programs might be excellent and which might be deficient.

2. *Establish management commitment to the benchmarking process.*

   Concerns were raised about quality of the library service due to inadequate funding, and the Director's office requested assessment activities to see if more funds were warranted. Since the Director's office initiated the request, commitment of management was present from the beginning.

3. *Identify and establish the benchmarking team.*

   The team was developed with employees of the library and employees from the management groups in the same division and met twice a month for a year.

4. *Identify, define and understand the metrics to be benchmarked.*

   The Division management provided a list of topics to address. They were very broad in scope.

5. *Use existing surveys or plan to collect data from benchmarking partners.*

Preliminary comparisons were made with Association of Research Libraries (ARL) data. The team decided to do their own data collection using the ARL measures as a model. The survey was tested by collecting data in-house to identify unclear or vague questions. The final survey had 69 questions.

6. *Collect the data from benchmarking partners if you need to.*

Benchmarking partners at similar libraries were identified using the *American Library Directory*. Fifteen were approached and seven were willing to participate. Five libraries agreed to be identified and two did not. The survey was completed in four weeks.

7. *Analyze and present the data.*

The data was compared for inconsistencies and partners were contacted for follow up questions. Each team member took an area to analyze. The July 2003 article contains figures demonstrating some of their tables. They used both raw data and ratios to make comparisons.

8. *Identify areas for improvement and report your results.*

Oral, electronic and print reports were made to various management teams. Information was put in the Division newsletter. Three areas were identified as needing improvement: overall budget, materials budget and interlibrary loan. The library excelled in areas of communication and variety of service based on a low customer per library staff ratio. The October 2003 article contains a summary of findings.

9. *Continue to conduct benchmarking studies for comparative purposes over time.*

The authors report that while their staff has always been customer-oriented, "more sophisticated methods of listening and learning are now embedded in our operations and way of thinking" (Silcox and Deutsch, 2003: 31).

# PROCESS BENCHMARKING

As part of an overall evaluation plan that you have developed within your culture of assessment, you might choose to do a process benchmarking project. Perhaps you have done a performance benchmarking project and have seen that some of your activities are lower than they should be. Perhaps you have just completed a user survey and some services received a more negative rating than they should have.

- Could this be because your actual process is inefficient?
- Are you and your staff willing to change the process?
- Is the process important to your overall library mission and goals?

If you answered yes to any of these questions, you could consider a process benchmarking project.

The actual results of a process benchmarking project are not that useful to other library operations, since each project is so specific to the immediate environment. Reports of the data would also have to be detailed to make a local comparison. Therefore, most of the literature on process benchmarking describes an assessment project in general, without much detail. One exception is described in our real-life example for process benchmarking.

Process benchmarking is "the practice of being humble enough to admit that someone else is better at something and being wise enough to try to learn how to match or even surpass them at it." This quote is attributed on the Web to Carla O'Dell, president of the American Productivity & Quality Center (APQC, accessed: 2006). It does get to the heart of the reason to do process benchmarking, and it should describe your attitude as you start your project. On the Web, Sam Walton, of WalMart fame, is quoted as saying that he spent more time in his competitors' stores than they did. He further states that many of his best ideas came from process benchmarking.

How many libraries have you visited lately? Do you visit other libraries even while on holiday? Do you visit them with a critical eye? This informal type of benchmarking is useful. What would you report to your supervisor or staff about your visits? After visiting and touring the new Seattle Public Library, you could report to your staff the many innovations and philosophies that drove their process of architectural planning and development. While not specifically applicable to a small operation, if you ever did get to redesign your space, this information would be helpful as background.

If you are about to spend a lot of time measuring and comparing a process, you will need to be willing to learn and change. The transfer of the information about the process from your partner to you is a person-to-person process. You will be building relationships and fostering the desire to learn in yourself and your employees.

The previous section on performance benchmarking laid out a nine-step plan for comparing your various activities with others'. From that, you may have identified some areas for further study, or, as part of your culture of assessment plans, you may have done a customer satisfaction survey and noted some areas where customers were not satisfied. Perhaps the process for that service could be improved. You are now interested in doing process benchmarking.

## STEPS FOR PROCESS BENCHMARKING

### 1. Identify the process to be benchmarked and start planning.

Start by doing some preliminary planning. Your major planning will go on after you form your team. As the manager, you will need to think about how you are going to do it, with whom, and for what purpose. As an example, perhaps your customer satisfaction survey identified a lack of up-to-date computers to access the Internet in the library. Is this a critical success factor for the library? Does the environment of the library require better computers? Are you planning on adding more e-resources? Brainstorm with your staff about this lack and see what preliminary ideas they have. Is this even a process? The library described in Figure 6.3 used performance benchmarking to decide that it did not need more computers, but your situation is different in that you do have fewer computers and also you feel they are not up-to-date.

You decide that having good equipment is part of the process of retrieval of online resources. It is related to the critical success factor of having consistent and error-free service. Before you can assess how much, if any, more equipment to buy, you want to do a process benchmarking project to see how other libraries of similar size and setting use their equipment.

To continue your exploration of whether to benchmark your computer equipment, you need to consider alternatives. Can you just state to the administration that you need more and better computers and get them? It does happen. You could base your request on your needs survey. A more likely situation, however, is that it will probably be part of the budget process and probably part of the capital budget. Discuss the need with your supervisor. When is the budget due? Allow time to do the project and get your supervisor's support. These are some preliminary thoughts to put down to discuss the project with your supervisor.

---

**Definition: Critical Success Factor (CSF)**

Critical success factors are those issues that are deemed important to the organization, things that must work for the organization to achieve its mission. CSFs come from specific industry characteristics, competitive strategies, environmental changes resulting from economic or technological trends, or from internal organizational needs.

### 2. Establish management commitment to the benchmarking project.

Discuss with your supervisor what your needs are and why you think a process benchmarking project will demonstrate them. Your preliminary thoughts and staff discussions will help you present an idea. Be somewhat aware of the results you may find. For example, if you are looking at computer equipment, will you be able to show that your future benchmarking partners have better computer equipment? This will impact how you approach the project.

### 3. Plan the evaluation project by establishing the benchmarking team, defining a budget, and setting timelines.

In hospital libraries and other small library settings, the team may be just you! But what other resources could you use? Does your institution have a quality improvement department that could help? They might join the team to help with data collection and analysis, as described in Chapter 10. Perhaps they subscribe to a Web survey service? In the case of the need for better computers, can you get a team member from the information technology (IT) department? If so, it is a good idea to enlist his or her cooperation. Chapter 11 has some tips on team building and working with teams.

Define a budget for the project, even if all the time and materials come from your own budget. For a process benchmarking project that includes site visits, you may need to ask for special funds. Again, maybe the quality department might help out. Or if you have enough time, ask for funds in the next budget year. Plan the expenses and how they will be covered. Refer to the "Budget Planning" tool in Chapter 12 for details of the types of expenses that evaluation projects incur. Develop a timeline using a Gantt chart and set team responsibilities using a responsibility chart, both of which are described in Chapter 12.

### 4. Define and understand the process to be benchmarked.

Before you contact partners, you have a lot of work to do in planning the project. It can be easy to get off track and tackle more than one process. In this step, you will study and examine your own process and define the data elements that characterize the process. You will identify all the inputs, outputs, and customers. If appropriate, develop flowcharts. In the example of the computers, age and operating systems would be a metric or measurement. Perhaps, your process is not just about replacing the computers because of age but the whole computer center. The computer center as a service is more than just machines. Understand and document your library computer center or area, including the equipment and the environment, such as chairs, desks, keyboard drawers, and noise. Perform a literature search about the process you are examining at and see if there are any benchmarks or standards there. What would you learn from others about their whole process of providing public access computers for their customers? First you have to be able to describe your situation in order to compare it with others.

## 5. Identify metrics and collect process data.

Which metric or metrics do you want to compare? Choose ones that relate to the project and understand the definitions applied. As in performance benchmarking, be judicious and do not ask too many questions or questions that are irrelevant or too difficult. Decide what data are needed and collect it for your own institution. This will help you see any problems with collecting the data. As you are doing this, think about planning your comparisons. What are the most effective ways to compare your practice with those of benchmarking partners? In the example of the computer center, you would want to compare technical details about the computer such as operating system, memory size, and storage size as well as the date purchased. Looking at the whole operation, perhaps you would do an observational sample of the people using the center.

## 6. Identify, rank, and implement internal process improvements.

After you have collected data on your own internal process, it is important to do a thorough analysis of your current practices. As you do this, your team may see problems in the process and be able to correct them immediately. Other problems identified may have to wait until you see what others are doing. After the studies above, you could report your findings to the IT department and ask their advice about costs of new equipment. This kind of information can be included in the final report. If you are looking at new chairs, find out how much they cost. Maybe you have the money in the budget. Then this aspect of the study need not be compared.

## 7. Identify and contact benchmarking partners.

While your team is working on defining and gathering internal metrics, they can also begin finding partners. You will need to determine how many partners you want or need. This will depend on the project time and budget. Partners can be found in local library associations and chapters and sections of national associations such as the SLA and MLA. You could also call for partners on library listservs. If you participated in the MLA Benchmarking Network surveys, you can find partners on a national level. Figure 6.7 shows a sample listing libraries based on size in the various categories available. In this way you would find libraries from like-size institutions. You can look them up in the MLA Directory to find their contact information.

---

**Figure 6.7   MLA Directory Search Results for Hospitals with 1,825 to 2,700 FTEs**

Based on your selections, there were 23 institutions that matched your criteria. (Your own, if included, is marked by an asterisk.) They are:

| | | |
|---|---|---|
| 1 | Alaska Native Medical Center | Anchorage, AK |
| 2 | Baptist Princeton | Birmingham, AL |
| 3 | Arkansas Children's Hospital | Little Rock, AR |
| 4 | Atascadero State Hospital | Atascadero, CA |
| 5 | Kaiser Permanente Medical Center | Fresno, CA |
| 6 | John Muir Medical Center | Walnut Creek, CA |
| 7 | Boulder Community Hospital | Boulder, CO |
| 8 | The Children's Hospital | Denver, CO |
| 9 | Exempla St. Joseph Hospital | Denver, CO |
| 10 | Hospital of Saint Raphael | New Haven, CT |
| 11 | Deaconess Hospital | Evansville, IN |
| 12 | St. Elizabeth's Medical Center | Boston, MA |
| 13 | Greater Baltimore Medical Center | Baltimore, MD |
| 14 | Eastern Maine Medical Center | Bangor, ME |
| 15 | Botsford General Hospital | Farmington Hills, MI |
| 16 | New York Methodist Hospital | Brooklyn, NY |
| 17 | Mercy Medical Center | Canton, OH |
| 18 | Portland VA Medical Center | Portland, OR |
| 19 | Salem Hospital | Salem, OR |
| 20 | Ft. Sanders Regional Medical Center | Knoxville, TN |
| 23 | Primary Children's Medical Center | Salt Lake City, UT |
| 23 | IHC Urban Central Reg. Health Sys. | Salt Lake City, UT |

But do these libraries represent the "best practice" in the process you are working on? Are some libraries recognized by associations and in the literature as "excellent" in the area in which you are looking? This can be considered an attribute when selecting partners. If you have put out a call on a listserv or at an association meeting, you would screen the replies by sending out a short survey about their activity and availability of data in the process you are asking about. To recruit more potential partners, one question might be: Do you know any other libraries that especially represent a best practice in this area? You could offer to share some anonymous results with those who volunteered and filled out the preliminary questionnaire but were not selected.

In studying the computer center, perhaps you got 20 responses to your call for participants on a listserv and other sources. Your preliminary questionnaire to this group revealed libraries with a wide range of resources. Since you are looking for best practices, you create a list of potential partners that includes a few more than you need and rank them by your perception of their excellence based on your questionnaire. The article used in the real-life evaluation has an example of such a questionnaire in an appendix (White, 2002). Starting at the top, you would make initial contact with each potential partner. This could be via phone, e-mail, or, in the case of larger projects, letter.

If you decided to locate partners from the MLA Benchmarking Network, a communication with a potential partner might begin like this:

> I would like to find partners to identify best practices in (your process here, in this case, providing public access computers). I have identified your library as a potential partner with which to benchmark our library process. Would you be interested in working with me in examining practices in this area? Our institutions have some similarities. (List basic similarities here.) I would like to find out more about the practice of providing this service, not just the numbers of computers a library provides.

Also, you might want to offer the partner something in return, for example, nonconfidential information from the other institutions you are contacting, if all partners agree to that. More commonly, the final report refers to other libraries in a confidential way. Mention there might be a site visit as part of the project. In process benchmarking, you might identify up to ten potential partners. You could send a more detailed survey to them. From the responses, you would select only two or three for the site visit, depending on your budget.

You could use a combination of techniques for finding partners. This is your project, and your team will be doing the majority of the work. The partners are supplying needed information and perhaps agreeing to a site visit. Negotiate who will do what and what will be in the report. The partners can participate in the survey development. In some studies, site visits might be exchanged so that your partners are able to visit you. They may also agree to share costs. Perhaps you will find a highly motivated partner in another city who will lead in gathering data in that city. Your up to ten partners could be selected in the two cities and site visits arranged in those two cities but data compared across all participants. The results would be far more powerful than with ten partners in your own city who do not match you quite as well.

Ideally you want some of your partners to be doing things better than you. Every partner will benefit from having the opportunity to view and share the report with their supervisor, but those on the bottom will find the report most useful in justifying budget increases, and so forth. Those who rank below you get the benefit of seeing how they could do things better. Those who rank highly get to have proof that they are doing a good job. All of this means that the relationships that evolve during the study will be complicated and need to be managed in a sensitive and clear way. As covered in the ethics section, above, confidentiality and communication are issues to take seriously at all times.

## B. COLLECTING AND ANALYZING INFORMATION—BENCHMARKING IN ACTION

### 8. Collect process data from benchmarking partners.

You have already collected data on your own process. Using what you learned there, you will decide the best way to collect data from your partners and what questions to ask them. Using the techniques defined in Chapter 10 on data collection and analysis, develop a questionnaire to collect statistics having to do with institution size and the metrics you have developed about the process in Step 5. You could send out a print or electronic questionnaire or do telephone interviews or a combination of all three. You could send out the questionnaire in print or as an e-mail attachment and then have your partners enter the data into an online survey. That way they can respond more efficiently by gathering the data on paper and transferring it to the Web intake form. This collection of quantitative data is not unlike any other survey but it is just the first part in the examination of the process as whole. As in any survey, some of your 4–10 partners will not be able to answer some of the questions. If the sizes of the libraries are uneven, it is best to include the size measurements on the survey, so that you can compare using ratios.

### Analyze benchmarking partners' process data and compare against internal process data.

Numbers, even after analysis, rarely tell the whole picture. Benchmarking differs from other evaluation methods in that in its structured process it may include site visits or intensive observation. To prepare for a site visit and even decide where to do the site visit, the data collected from your partners needs to be analyzed. You do not need to do a site visit with every partner. Doing that may be cost prohibitive. This is a one-way process. You have your process, and you are looking for processes in libraries that are done in a better way. It might be a waste of time to visit sites that ranked lower than yours. This is the advantage of being the one who initiates a benchmarking project.

When you compare your metrics with those of your partners, you are essentially doing performance benchmarking on a micro level, since the data usually cannot describe the process. You can analyze the actual data or you can use ratios. If the libraries vary in size, ratios are a better way to compare.

From this preliminary analysis, you can accomplish two things:

- Since you have a larger group of partners and are planning only one- or two-site visits, you will need to use these results to pick your sites.
- You can use this data to develop questions for the site visit. What details will you be looking at? What questions will you ask?

### 10. Conduct site visits or interviews and reanalyze data.

Observation is a key component of process benchmarking, and site visits are the preferred tool. Interviewing key people at the other institutions by phone can be a less expensive alternative but not as effective. Careful planning and preparation should make your site visit effective. In the management literature, warnings are given against "industrial tourism," where you are just looking and not collecting data. Do not waste time gathering data you already have from the survey. Andersen and Pettersen point out that the newcomers to benchmarking see the site visit as the exciting phase of the project and all the planning as just a necessary evil (Andersen and Pettersen, 1996). A site visit needs to be well planned to include both observation of the physical operation and structured interviews with key personnel. Your partner, not wanting to waste time any more than you do, might not be as cooperative and forthcoming if he or she perceives you are unprepared.

Using the techniques described in Chapter 10 on data collection, you can develop a questionnaire for the structured interviews. If you are working with flowcharts of a process, you might ask those at the site to be visited to prepare a flowchart of their process. Practices observed or discovered during the site visit are unique in that differences in the process may be discovered that did not come up in the written exchanges.

Andersen and Pettersen divide the information sought in benchmarking into three levels. (Andersen and Pettersen, 1996).

1.  The first level is the Performance Level. You have already gathered quantitative data to assess the performance level. How well does the partner perform when compared with you?
2.  The next level is the Practice Level, the actual process that allows the partner to reach the superior numbers. This is what you will be observing on the site visit.
3.  The third level is what they call the "Enablers" of the Practice. These are the factors that "enable" the employee to have a process that is superior. They can be discovered in the survey or site visit and include such things as better training, organization, different or better equipment used, support processes such as more help from an IT department, or more time spent on staff communication.

A debriefing session for the site visit team is essential. Also arrange for follow-up questions to clarify any details. The site visit is also a time to build relationships with partners that might result in future benchmarking and other projects.

Site visits to out-of-town libraries are obviously expensive. If this cannot be arranged as an individual trip, perhaps you could choose partners in cities where you will be attending association meetings. You can time your project around that trip and spend one extra day before or after the meeting.

If site visits are not an option, owing to cost, a structured telephone interview with comparable employees (employees doing the same tasks) at the chosen site is an alternative. If you were benchmarking interlibrary loan processes, your team should interview the technician doing the work as well as the manager. In the computer center example, you could exchange digital pictures of the computer centers and interview the partner on the phone about the pictures. These pictures could be used in your final report. You could visit local libraries and interview and exchange pictures for distant libraries.

You now have qualitative data from your survey, and quantitative data from your interview or site visit. The analysis you did before the site visit would have shown you some of the problem areas in your own process. Using what you have learned at the subsequent site visit, you could develop a best practice template, which is your ideal of how the process should operate, including the enabling factors that make it successful. Which practices, methods, and resources make it possible to achieve these performance levels?

Using this template, you can identify a list of gaps in your own system that need improvement. From this list you will make your recommendations for change.

## C. REPORTING, ADAPTING IMPROVEMENTS, AND MONITORING RESULTS—POSTBENCHMARKING
### 11. Present results, implement improvements, and monitor results.

Any change requires good communication to be successful. Your most important communication is between you and your supervisors, your employees and your benchmarking partners. During the project, the team might plan some periodic reports discussing the progress of the project. The final reports can be planned from the beginning and added to as the project moves forward. The purpose of the reports is to communicate the findings to partners as agreed upon, to show management either what resources are needed to get the process improved or to tell them what steps have been taken to improve the processes, and to make known to employees how the processes were compared and how decisions were made. Each report should be developed for its intended audience. Use the Evaluation Report Template as a guide, as found in Chapter 11 and on the CD-ROM in the Chapter 11 folder.

- *The Master Report* is a notebook containing all the plans, timelines, communications, and documents used to accomplish the project. It should be used as reference for the other reports. It should be a record of the work that other reports can refer to for further reading.
- *The Partners' Report* shows all of the comparative charts and process steps in the ideal process template. Identities may be revealed depending on what was agreed upon. The

report should acknowledge all partners' roles and cooperation in the project. It should be suitable for sharing with management and employees at their own institutions.

- *The Management Report* is often both oral and written. This is where you will show what actions you wish to take, what resources you will need, what results you would expect for the process change, and when you plan to measure the changes in the future.
- *The Employees' Report* will describe the steps in the project and the plans for the future of the process. It should include the ideal process template and the partners' to report, perhaps as an appendix. It should invite the employees to view the Master Report and encourage open communication about the planned changes.

If your institution has a quality department, you might want to submit a report to them using their established format and perhaps present the findings and process to an institutionwide quality team. The Evaluation Report Template in Chapter 11 contains some comments specific to benchmarking projects. Chapter 12 gives examples of different kinds of graphs and charts you can use in your reports.

After preparing and making all your reports, your team needs to implement the changes recommended in the report. You now get to improve your process! You know how your best practice partner became world class. The question to ask now might be: How do *we* become world class? Usually you will not copy exactly the process of your best-practice partner. The cultures of the two institutions may differ enough so that direct translation would not be possible. In your template, you "adapt" the best practice to fit your environment. As an example, you may not be able to afford some of the equipment the other library has, so the process that having that equipment enables would not be implemented; but it could be reported as a major future enhancement when the funds become available.

As part of your implementation plan, the team develops a draft implementation plan to elicit feedback from those who will be affected by proposed changes. This will allow both consultation and refinement to your plan. With that, you then set goals for adaptation and application of the information you have learned. Part of your plan will be to decide how and when to measure the impact of the proposed changes. There should be constant communication that the changes will lead your library to be a best-practices library, something every employee can be proud of.

### 12. Continue to conduct benchmarking of this process and recycle the benchmarking process for other areas or processes.

Now that you have implemented changes, you need to monitor the process periodically. How will you know you are still the best? Sometimes you will need to recalibrate the benchmarks as the environment changes. The project took a good number of resources to accomplish. Make your investment pay off by continuing to check that your system is the best.

One way to make the investment pay off is to recycle the benchmarking process and repeat it on a periodic basis in other areas of your library. The experiences and lesson learned each time you do it will lead to an efficient and effective evaluation system. You will refine this model to meet your needs as you and your team become more experienced in benchmarking. The number and names of steps are not as important as the use of an integrated, systematic approach to benchmarking. Benchmarking is a skill that can be refined so that the effort involved in doing a new project will be reduced owing to improved skill.

## REAL-LIFE EVALUATION: PROCESS BENCHMARKING

### RESHELVING TIME AND ACCURACY

White, L. S. 2002. "The University of Virginia Library's Experiment with Benchmarking." *Virginia Libraries*, 48, no. 4: 17–25. Management Information Services, University of Virginia Libraries. Available: www.lib.virginia. edu/mis/benchmarking/ (accessed 2006).

*Overview*: The University of Virginia Library set a goal to institute a process benchmarking project to learn about the evaluation tool. From an analysis of SERVQUAL and student surveys, the shelving/reshelving process was chosen as a pilot study of the benchmarking tool. The team learned how to conduct a benchmarking project. They analyzed their own process and developed metrics and a questionnaire. They looked for partners on a listserv and identified two to visit. They reported their findings and were able to improve their shelving process both in turnaround time and accuracy.

A. Planning the Study—Pre–benchmarking

1. *Identify the process to be benchmarked and start planning.*

   Upon management review of SERVQUAL, which is a purchased customer service survey with predefined service questions and based on findings from locally developed student surveys, the process of shelving/reshelving was chosen as a process that could be improved.

2. *Establish management commitment to the benchmarking process.*

   The management of the library was committed to trying out the benchmarking tool and seeing how it worked. It saw the shelving process as an important customer service that allowed customers to find needed materials quickly.

3. *Identify and establish the benchmarking team.*

   A team was chosen from several departments and service units. The team was given a charge to create a benchmarking process for the library and carry out a benchmarking project. They educated themselves on the basics of the benchmarking process.

4. *Define and understand the process to be benchmarked.*

   The team wrote a survey to define the process and, after pretesting in-house, had the 11 libraries on the campus fill it out. This helped define the process to be measured.

5. *Identify metrics and collect process data.*

   From this survey the team was able to identify some metrics such as training, number and level of employees, pay rates, pickup routines, and so forth.

6. *Identify, rank, and implement internal process improvements.*

   This preliminary survey showed that some of the UVA libraries already had excellent processes and some needed improvement. The team conducted studies of three processes for which they had no data, number of items shelved, accuracy, and turnaround time.

7. *Identify and contact benchmarking partners.*

   The team investigated whether to compare outside the "industry," such as with grocery stores or video stores, but these were found unwilling to share their operational information. Two library listservs were queried and 19 libraries were sent a short questionnaire; 13 responded. From these responses, two benchmarking partners were chosen as representing the best practice, which was a four- to five-hour turn around time and 94% or better accuracy.

B. Collecting and Analyzing Information—Benchmarking

8.  *Collect process data from benchmarking partners.*
    The two partner libraries were asked to fill out the internal process survey.
9.  *Analyze benchmarking partners' process data and compare against internal process data.*
    The analysis was done on the internal process and compared with the partners'. This helped decide what to look at during the site visit.
10. *Conduct site visits or interviews and reanalyze data.*
    Site visits were arranged. The team walked through its own process in preparation. They needed to be familiar with their own step-by-step process in order to compare it with others.

C. Reporting, adapting improvements, and monitoring results—post–benchmarking

11. *Present results, implement improvements, and monitor results.*
    The team presented reports throughout the process and in the middle brought in a consultant to present basic benchmarking information to the whole staff. The final report was submitted to the Administrative Council and made available on the World Wide Web. The new processes were implemented in five units over two years and monitored on a routine basis. The smaller units, while measured, were not in need of as much improvement.
12. *Continue to conduct benchmarking of this process and recycle the benchmarking process for other areas or processes.*
    The measures of time and accuracy continue to be monitored and have been included in the Library's Balanced Scorecard. (This library uses the management technique of the Balanced Scorecard which is described in Chapter 9.)

# WORKBOOK FOR PERFORMANCE BENCHMARKING

## 1. Identify the measure or measures to be benchmarked and start the planning process.

Using customer surveys or management directives, discuss with staff and supervisors how many aspects of the library activity to benchmark. Capture some ideas here.

_____

_____

_____

## 2. Establish management commitment to the benchmarking process.

Discuss with your supervisor the resources it will take to do the study and get a commitment to start with the project. Note here some of the issues discussed.

_____

_____

_____

## 3. Plan the evaluation project by establishing the benchmarking team, defining a budget, and setting timelines.

Form the team using personnel actually doing the task, other library personnel, and people from other departments, or external colleagues.

| Member name | Title | Extension | Reason to be on team/Skills |
|---|---|---|---|
|  |  |  |  |
|  |  |  |  |
|  |  |  |  |
|  |  |  |  |

Develop a responsibility chart to assign responsibilities, as discussed in Chapter 12.

| Process          Responsible party → | Team member A | Team member B | Team member C | Team member D |
|---|---|---|---|---|
| 1. Identify the measure or measures to be benchmarked and start the planning process. | | | | |
| 2. Establish management commitment to the benchmarking process. | | | | |
| 3. Identify and establish the benchmarking team. | | | | |
| 4. Identify, define, and understand the metrics to be benchmarked. | | | | |
| 5. Use existing surveys to collect data. | | | | |
| 6. Analyze and present the data | | | | |
| 7. Identify areas for improvement and report your results. | | | | |
| 8. Collect the data from benchmarking partners if you need to: Identify partners | | | | |
|      Develop questionnaire | | | | |
|      Administer questionnaire | | | | |
|      Follow up and edit responses | | | | |
| 9. Analyze and present the data | | | | |
| 10. Identify areas for improvement and report your results. | | | | |
| 11. Continue to conduct benchmarking studies for comparative purposes over time. | | | | |

R - Responsible for carrying out the task. Every task must have an R.
C - Consults to the R person for the task.
A - Assists the R person with the task.
I - Is informed about the status of the work.

With the team, develop a Gantt chart for the planned activities. See Chapter 12 for an explanation. Below is a sample Gantt chart for a three-month plan. Extend the chart for longer projects.

| Months → | 1 | | | | 2 | | | | 3 | | | |
|---|---|---|---|---|---|---|---|---|---|---|---|---|
| Weeks → | 1 | 2 | 3 | 4 | 5 | 6 | 7 | 8 | 9 | 10 | 11 | 12 |
| 1. Identify the measure or measures to be benchmarked and start the planning process. | X | | | | | | | | | | | |
| 2. Establish management commitment to the benchmarking process. | X | | | | | | | | | | | |
| 3. Identify and establish the benchmarking team. | | X | | | | | | | | | | |
| 4. Identify, define, and understand the metrics to be benchmarked. | | X | X | | | | | | | | | |
| 5. Use existing surveys to collect data. | | | | X | X | X | | | | | | |
| 6. Analyze and present the data | | | | | | | X | | | | | |
| 7. Identify areas for improvement and report your results. | | | | | | | | X | | | | |
| *It would be a longer project if you had to collect data.* | | | | | | | | | | | | |
| 8. Collect the data from benchmarking partners if you need to: Identify partners | | | | X | X | X | | | | | | |
| Develop questionnaire | | | | X | X | X | | | | | | |
| Administer questionnaire | | | | | | | X | X | X | | | |
| Follow up and edit responses | | | | | | | | | X | X | | |
| 9. Analyze and present the data | | | | | | | | | | | X | |
| 10. Identify areas for improvement and report your results. | | | | | | | | | | | | X |
| 11. Continue to conduct benchmarking studies for comparative purposes over time. | | | | | | | | | | | | X |

Plan a budget by referring to the "Budget Planning" tool in Chapter 12. List the details of the types of expenses this evaluation project will incur.

## 4. Identify, define, and understand the metrics to be benchmarked.

After analyzing your reason for doing the study, identify measures that demonstrate quality in the areas you studying. If your study is large, you will have a long list. Develop definitions as you go along. You will use this list to develop a questionnaire, if you are doing one or you may find an appropriate question in established surveys such as the ARL, AAHSL, or MLA surveys.

| Service area | Measure | Definition |
|---|---|---|
| 1 | 1.1 | |
| | 1.2 | |
| | 1.3 | |
| 2 | 2.1 | |
| | 2.2 | |
| | 2.3 | |

And so forth . . .

## 5. Use existing surveys or plan to collect data to identify benchmarking partners.

Analyze existing surveys. Decide whether existing surveys meet your needs for performance benchmarking. Note here strategies for presentation of the existing data to see if it will meet your needs.

_____

_____

_____

_____

If the existing surveys do not meet your needs, your team will need to identify and contact benchmarking partners. Assign team members to work on these aspects of partner identification and contact.

_____

_____

_____

_____

Create a list of criteria for an ideal benchmarking partner, such as parameters of size, subject emphasis, location, or recommendation or reputation.

_____

_____

Decide which measures are most important and at what level for these measures potential partners should be.

Measure _____

Level _____

_____

Identify a selection of potential benchmarking partners through tools such as the MLA Benchmarking Network survey, library and association directories, and listserv announcements.

_____

_____

With a preliminary survey, ask potential partners about their institutional size and their ability or willingness to answer a lengthy survey.

_____

_____

Potential partners are analyzed using the ideal partner profiles.

_____

_____

Select benchmarking partner(s).

_____

_____

Contact the selected partner(s).

_____

_____

Gain acceptance from selected partner(s).

_____

_____

Be courteous and notify those you have not selected.

_____

_____

## 6. Collect the data from benchmarking partners if necessary.

Develop and administer a survey of the selected partners' performance. Note here the major steps in development and administration, using techniques from Chapter 10.

Develop survey.

_____

_____

Test survey in-house with a willing partner.

_____

_____

Administer survey.

_____

_____

Analyze, follow-up on unclear answers and edit.

_____

_____

### 7. Analyze and present the data.

If you are using existing data, the team can analyze the results and determine which are significant for your purposes. Based on the results, determine how to present the data to management and staff. Note here any ideas you have. See Chapters 10 and 12 for analysis and presentation ideas.

_____

_____

_____

### 8. Identify areas for improvement and report your results.

Using the data analysis lists, identify areas for improvement and areas of excellence.

_____

_____

_____

Present a report of the team's improvement plans to management and staff. Use the Evaluation Report Template as a guide, as found in Chapter 11 and on the CD-ROM in the Chapter 11 folder.

_____

_____

### 9. Continue to conduct benchmarking studies for comparative purposes over time.

Recycle the benchmarking process and repeat it on a periodic basis in other areas of your library.

# WORKBOOK FOR PROCESS BENCHMARKING

## A. PLANNING THE STUDY—PRE-BENCHMARKING

### 1. Identify the measure to be benchmarked and start the planning process.

Using previous performance benchmarking projects, customer surveys, or management directives, discuss with staff and supervisors which process to benchmark. Capture some ideas here.

_____

_____

_____

### 2. Establish management commitment to the benchmarking process.

Discuss with your supervisors the resources it will take to do the study and get a commitment to start with the project. Note here some of the issues discussed.

_____

_____

_____

### 3. Plan the Evaluation project by establishing the benchmarking team, defining a budget, and setting timelines.

Form the team using personnel actually doing the task, other library personnel, and people from other departments, or external colleagues.

| Member name | Title | Extension | Reason to be on team/Skills |
|---|---|---|---|
|  |  |  |  |
|  |  |  |  |
|  |  |  |  |
|  |  |  |  |

Develop a responsibility chart to assign responsibilities, as discussed in Chapter 12.

| Process           Responsible Party → | Team member A | Team member B | Team member C | Team member D |
|---|---|---|---|---|
| 1. Identify the measure to be benchmarked and start the planning process. | | | | |
| 2. Establish management commitment to the benchmarking process. | | | | |
| 3. Identify and establish the benchmarking team. | | | | |
| 4. Define and understand the process to be benchmarked. | | | | |
| 5. Identify metrics and collect process data | | | | |
| 6. Identify, rank, and implement internal process improvements. | | | | |
| 7. Identify and contact benchmarking partners. | | | | |
| 8. Collect process data from benchmarking partners. | | | | |
| 9. Analyze benchmarking partners' process data and compare against internal process data. | | | | |
| 10. Conduct site visits or interviews and reanalyze data. | | | | |
| 11. Present results, implement improvements, and monitor results. | | | | |
| 12. Continue to conduct benchmarking of this process and recycle the benchmarking process for other areas or processes. | | | | |

R - Responsible for carrying out the task. Every task must have an R.
C - Consults to the R person for the task.
A - Assists the R person with the task.
I - Is informed about the status of the work.

Develop a Gantt chart for the planned activities. See Chapter 12 for an explanation. Below is a sample three-month Gantt chart for the team to fill in. Extend for longer projects.

| Months → | 1 | | | | 2 | | | | 3 | | | |
|---|---|---|---|---|---|---|---|---|---|---|---|---|
| Weeks → | 1 | 2 | 3 | 4 | 5 | 6 | 7 | 8 | 9 | 10 | 11 | 12 |
| *Planning the study—pre–benchmarking* | | | | | | | | | | | | |
| 1.  Identify the measure to be benchmarked and start the planning process. | | | | | | | | | | | | |
| 2.  Establish management commitment to the benchmarking process. | | | | | | | | | | | | |
| 3.  Identify and establish the benchmarking team. | | | | | | | | | | | | |
| 4.  Define and understand the process to be benchmarked. | | | | | | | | | | | | |
| 5.  Identify metrics and collect process data | | | | | | | | | | | | |
| 6.  Identify, rank, and implement internal process improvements. | | | | | | | | | | | | |
| 7.  Identify and contact benchmarking partners. | | | | | | | | | | | | |
| *Collecting and analyzing information—benchmarking* | | | | | | | | | | | | |
| 8.  Collect process data from benchmarking partners. | | | | | | | | | | | | |
| 9.  Analyze benchmarking partners process data and compare against internal process data. | | | | | | | | | | | | |
| 10. Conduct site visits or interviews and reanalyze data. | | | | | | | | | | | | |
| *Reporting, adapting improvements, and monitoring results—post-benchmarking* | | | | | | | | | | | | |
| 11. Present results, implement improvements, and monitor results. | | | | | | | | | | | | |
| 12. Continue to conduct benchmarking of this process and recycle the benchmarking process for other areas or processes. | | | | | | | | | | | | |

Plan a budget by referring to the "Budget Planning" tool in Chapter 12. List the details of the types of expenses this evaluation project will incur.

_____

_____

## 4. Define and understand the process to be benchmarked.

Using flowcharts and descriptive steps, describe the process in detail. Allow time for revisions and corrections. Note here what needs to be done, which team members will do it, and by when.

Task          Team member(s)          Date due

## 5. Identify metrics and collect process data.

As the process is being described in Step 4, watch for measures of quality. Note present measures and look for new ones.

Task          Measure          Level

## 6. Identify, rank, and implement internal process improvements.

Analyze any problems in the current process and correct any that can be corrected without too much change. List here any that will benefit from comparing with others.

Task     Correction identified    Benefit from comparison

## 7. Identify and contact benchmarking partners.

Create a list of criteria for an ideal benchmarking partner.

_____

_____

Decide which metrics are most important and at what level potential partners should be.

_____

_____

Identify a selection of potential benchmarking partners through tools such as the MLA Benchmarking Network survey, library and association directories, and listserv announcements.

_____

_____

Survey potential partners about their performance level for the process that is being benchmarked.

_____

_____

Potential partners are analyzed using the ideal partner profiles.

_____

_____

Select benchmarking partner(s).

_____

_____

Contact the selected partner(s).

_____

_____

Gain acceptance from selected partner(s).

_____

_____

## B. COLLECTING AND ANALYZING INFORMATION— BENCHMARKING

### 8. Collect process data from benchmarking partners.

Using insight gained from your own process, develop and administer a survey of the selected partners' process.

Develop survey based on your internal survey.

_____

_____

Have site visit partners fill out the survey.

_____

_____

### 9. Analyze benchmarking partners' process data and compare against internal process data.

Compare data from partners with your own in preparation for interviews or site visits.

_____

_____

### 10. Conduct site visits or interviews and reanalyze data.

Collect data using the methods and tools decided on. These could include an additional questionnaire, telephone or personal interview, or a site visit with direct observation. Use tools found in Chapter 10.

_____

_____

Debrief each team or team member that collects these data.

_____

_____

Combine all data collected and analyze for the final report and decisions.

_____

_____

Check for errors and inaccuracies and follow up and correct.

_____

_____

Identify gaps in performance levels between your own and the benchmarking partners' processes.

_____

_____

Identify causes for the performance gaps.

_____

_____

Rank identified causes of performance gaps based on how much they contribute to the gap.

_____

_____

## C. REPORTING, ADAPTING IMPROVEMENTS, AND MONITORING RESULTS—POSTBENCHMARKING

### 11. Present results, implement improvements and monitor results.

Based on the ranked list of causes for the performance gaps, improvement opportunities are identified and goals set for implementation.

_____

_____

The findings are communicated to all affected parts of the organization.

_____

_____

Acceptance for implementing the improvements is gained and a plan for implementation of the improvements is developed.

_____

_____

The improvement plan is implemented and the progress monitored.

A measurement plan to assess improvements is developed and carried out.

The final reports from the benchmarking study are written. Use the Evaluation Report Template as a guide, as found in Chapter 11 and on the CD-ROM in the Chapter 11 folder.

How will you announce your decisions to your stakeholders? _____

Who will compile the project reports? _____

Who will write the executive summaries _____

How and to whom will you distribute the final information? _____

## 12. Continue to conduct benchmarking of this process and recycle the benchmarking process for other areas or processes.

Recycle the benchmarking process and repeat it on a periodic basis in other areas of your library.

# REFERENCES

American Productivity & Quality Center. "The Center." American Productivity & Quality Center. Available: www.apqc.org/portal/apqc/site?path=root (accessed April 3, 2006).

Andersen, B., and P-G. Pettersen. 1996. *The Benchmarking Handbook: Step-by-Step Instructions*. New York: Chapman & Hall.

"Benchmarking Code of Conduct; Guidelines and Ethics for Benchmarkers." APQC (last updated 2004). Available: www.apqc.org/portal/apqc/site/generic2?path=/site/benchmarking/code_of_conduct.jhtml (accessed April 3, 2006).

Buchanan, H. S., and J. G. Marshall. 1996. "Benchmarking Reference Services: Step-by-Step." *Medical Reference Services Quarterly*, 15 no. 1: 1–13.

Byrd, G. D., and J. Shedlock. 2003. "The Association of Academic Health Sciences Libraries Annual Statistics: An Exploratory Twenty-Five-Year Trend Analysis. Journal of Medical Library Association, 91, no. 2: 186–202.

CHLA/ABSC Benchmarking Task Force, Canadian Health Libraries Association/Association des bibliothèques de la santé du Canada. 1998. *CHLA/ABSC Benchmarking Tool Kit*. Toronto: Canadian Health Libraries Association/Association des bibliothèques de la santé du Canada.

Dudden, R. F., K. Corcoran, J. Kaplan, J. Magouirk, D. C. Rand, and B. T. Smith. 2006a. "The Medical Library Association Benchmarking Network: Development and Implementation." *Journal of the Medical Library Association*, 94, no. 2: 107–117.

Dudden, R. F., K. Corcoran, J. Kaplan, J. Magouirk, D. C. Rand, and B. T. Smith. 2006b. "The Medical Library Association Benchmarking Network: Results." *Journal of the Medical Library Association*, 94, no. 2: 118–129.

Fulda, P. O., and R. K. Satterthwaite. 2004. "Proceedings, 103rd Annual Meeting Medical Library Association, Inc. San Diego, California May 2–7, 2003." *Journal of the Medical Library Association*, 92, no. 1: 117–124.

Fulda, P. O., and R. K. Satterthwaite. 2003. "Proceedings, 102nd Annual Meeting Medical Library Association, Inc. Dallas, Texas May 17–23, 2002." *Journal of the Medical Library Association*, 91, no. 1: 103–136.

Goodall, D. L. 1988. "Performance Measurement: A Historical Perspective." *Journal of Librarianship*, 20, no. 2: 128–144.

Goodwin, C. 1999. "Report on a Benchmarking Project." *National Network*, 24, no. 2: 16–17.

Harris, L. 2000. "Report from Down Under: Results of a Benchmarking Project." *National Network*, 24, no. 4: 8–9.

Henczel, S. 2002. "Benchmarking – Measuring and Comparing for Continuous Improvement." *Information Outlook*, 6, no. 7: 12–20.

Management Information Services. University of Virginia Library. "Benchmarking Team Reports." Management Information Services, University of Virginia Library, Charlottesville, VA (last updated July 18, 2002). Available: www.lib.virginia.edu/mis/benchmarking/ (accessed March 29, 2006).

Muir, H. J. 1994. *Collecting & Analyzing Benchmarking Data: A Librarian's Guide*. Cincinnati, OH: Library Benchmarking International.

OCLC Online Computer Library Center. "Libraries: How They Stack Up." OCLC Online Computer Library Center. Available: http://digitalarchive.oclc.org/request?id%3Doclcnum%3A53042543 (accessed 2007).

Peischl, T. M. 1995. "Benchmarking: A Process for Improvement." *Library of Administration and Management*, 9: 99–101.

Poling, N. 2002. "Ahead or Behind the Curve." *Information Outlook,* 6, no. 7: 22–25.

Shedlock, J., and G. D. Byrd. 2003. "The Association of Academic Health Sciences Libraries Annual Statistics: A Thematic History." *Journal of the Medical Library Association*, 91, no. 2: 178–185.

Silcox, B. P., and P. Deutsch. 2003. "From Data to Outcomes: Assessment Activities at the NIST Research Library." *Information Outlook*, 7, no. 10: 24–25, 27–31.

Spendolini, M. J. 2000. *The Benchmarking Book*. 2nd edition. New York: McGraw-Hill.

Todd-Smith, B., and L. G. Markwell. 2002. "The Value of Hospital Library Benchmarking: An Overview and Annotated References." *Medical Reference Services Quarterly*, 21, no. 3: 85–95.

Wilson, F., and J. S. Town. 2006. "Benchmarking and Library Quality Maturity." *Performance Measurement and Metrics*, 7, no. 2: 75–82.

White, L. S. 2002. "The University of Virginia Library's Experiment with Benchmarking." *Virginia Libraries*, 48, no. 4: 17–25.

# METHOD 4: LIBRARY PERFORMANCE STANDARDS

## WHAT ARE PERFORMANCE STANDARDS?

There are three broad types of standards: technical, performance, and accreditation. Performance and accreditation standards are used for evaluation. Technical standards are needed for industry and manufacturing so that various products can work together, such as the standardization of the size of a lightbulb socket enabling you to buy any brand of bulb.

In libraries, technical standards exist for such things as interlibrary loan transactions and cataloging rules and machine-readable cataloging (MARC) records. These standards facilitate the transfer of data among libraries so that they can work together. Libraries are becoming more and more involved in computer standards and data transmission standards as they participate in more cooperative automation projects. The library and information science section of the American National Standards Institute (ANSI), known as Z39, has set many of the standards necessary for data transfer, including the federated search properties of the Z39.50 standard as well as the OpenURL standard Z39.88. Since technology is now changing at such a rapid pace, technology standards development processes also have changed. While these types of standards are not the focus of this chapter and are not particularly relevant to program evaluation, librarians do need to be aware of technical standards when evaluating products to buy and systems to participate in.

Performance standards are written for libraries of a certain type usually by the association that supports those libraries, such as the Medical Library Association (MLA) or the Association of College and Research Libraries (ACRL). Standards development has a rich history that is not without controversy. Current initiatives are discussed below. State and regional associations also write standards to address regional issues. Associations can write standards for general administration or for specific services in the libraries they represent. Some groups write guidelines instead of standards. What is the difference between a standard and a guideline? Must you follow one but not the other? This debate is still

**Definition: A Standard or a Guideline?**

Standard: Something that can be used as a model or example to be followed, such as a practice or a product, which is widely recognized or employed or established by authority or by the custom, especially because of its excellence; an acknowledged measure of comparison for quantitative or qualitative value; a criterion.

Guideline: A statement or other indication of policy or procedure by which to determine a course of action.

controversial, and the politics and semantics of the words have a lot to do with enforcement. Associations tend not to enforce their standards, since this is very costly. When linked to accreditation programs, surveys are carried out to judge whether the standards are met. The result is that the survey instrument itself becomes controversial, requiring careful training of the surveyor to use the instrument. Rather than be "forced" to comply, some prefer to adopt guidelines, while others who need justification for improvement prefer standards and inspections.

Accreditation standards apply to the institution the library serves. These include educational accreditation standards on all levels of hospitals and other institutions. Colleges and universities have regional accreditation bodies. Medical schools respond to directives from the Association of American Medical Colleges (AAMC). Medical residency training programs are accredited by the Accreditation Council for Graduate Medical Education (ACGME). Hospitals are accredited by the Joint Commission on the Accreditation of Healthcare Organizations (JCAHO). These agencies are important to libraries because they often contain clauses about libraries and library services. The standards help define the culture of the organization and how that culture could or should use information, information that is often provided by a library. In studying the standards, the library can determine how its services "impact" the attainment of a good rating from the accrediting body. Evaluating the impact or outcome of library services is covered in Chapter 8. Knowing the standards that are part of your organizational setting will help in deciding what to measure.

In this chapter, following the introductory material, there are two workbooks specific to hospital libraries that can be used to broadly evaluate library activities and programs in order to see if they can be applied to your situation:

- Workbook for using library performance standards: Use for library program evaluation—asking key questions using the text of the MLA 2004 *Hospital Library Standards*.
- Workbook for using accreditation standards: Use to assess library quality and institutional quality—a combined commentary on the integration of the library program into key provisions of the JCAHO standards.

They are available on the CD-ROM in the Chapter 7 folder, in Word format for easy editing for a contextual and systematic review of your library service. It is hoped that librarians in other settings will see parallels to their own environment.

# SPECIFIC STANDARDS PROGRAMS

Quote: How should *Charting the Future* be used? The foreword states:

"This report is intended to sensitize decision-makers to the unique strategic and operational roles that the AHC (Academic Health Center) library currently plays and could play in the future of ensuring the success of the institution. It is focused on the areas that can make a significant difference to the bottom line, to faculty and student recruitment and retention, to excellent patient care, to research competitiveness, and to community initiatives" (AAHSL, accessed: 2006).

The ACRL has an active program of writing guidelines and standards. Its latest overarching standard, "Standards for Libraries in Higher Education," was published in 2004 (ACRL College and Research Libraries Task Force, 2004). Other guidelines and standards on their Web site include documents for distance learning library services, information literacy competency standards for higher education, and guidelines for media resources in academic libraries.

In 1987 the Association of Academic Health Sciences Libraries (AAHSL) and the MLA produced the report *Challenge to Action*, which, while not officially a set of standards, has been very helpful in demonstrating to administrators what to expect from an academic health center library (AAHSL/MLA, 1987). Recently the AAHSL published the report *Building on Success; Charting the Future of Knowledge Management within the Academic Health Center*, which updates *Challenge to Action* and introduces technological, economic, and social changes since 1987 (AAHSL, accessed: 2006). The examples of success or suggestions for future collaborations suggest the critical areas in which libraries and librarians provide the most value to the organization.

While the AAHLS Report and the ACRL Standards do not seem to relate to the operations of a small special library, reading them can give the librarian ideas about the trends and concerns of these influential libraries. Step-by-step service analogies are not always appropriate, but the types of services offered by these libraries will be expected of the special library when these students become practitioners in a few years. Whether in a business library with recent college graduates or a hospital medical library with recently graduated doctors or nurses, these librarians need to keep up with the services provided at the schools and colleges.

Standards for hospital libraries have been continuously influenced by and intertwined with library standards of the JCAHO. The Hospital Libraries Section (HLS) of the MLA and its precursors have a history of publishing standards for hospital libraries that can be traced back to the 1953, the most recent updated in 2004. JCAHO accredits 20,000 health-care organizations. It has been in existence since 1951, and in 1978 it included a hospital library standard, based on work by MLA committees (Foster, 1979). At the time, the JCAHO standards were functionally focused on the workings of the various individual hospital departments. Each hospital was surveyed periodically and each department visited. During this time there were many anecdotal reports of libraries being both rigorously surveyed and totally ignored—and all variations in between. The MLA Hospital Library Standards and Practices Committee described the controversies and challenges of the JCAHO library standard in a guide to assist librarians "to participate in an institution-wide effort, to upgrade management practices, and to demonstrate the need for, and effectiveness of, library services in their hospitals" (Topper, et al., 1980: 212). Since these first JCAHO standards, the MLA and the HLS have responded to the changes in direction by publishing standards that enhance and interpret the JCAHO standards.

The MLA Hospital Library Standards and Practices Committee developed the 1984 *Minimum Standards for Health Sciences Libraries in Hospitals* to enhance the minimal descriptive text of the 1978 JCAHO standards (Hospital Library Standards and Practices Committee, 1984). In addition to qualitative descriptions of services, there was also a section describing various quantifiers based on hospital size. While controversial, it was used successfully by the Connecticut Association of Health Sciences Librarians in a program to have the standards accepted and used by that state's continuing medical education program (Gluck and Hassig, 2001).

In 1994, under a program called Agenda for Change, the JCAHO revised its accreditation philosophy and focused on mission and institutionwide functions versus individual department standards. While these first standards removed the requirement to have a physical library, by 1997, owing to effort by MLA representatives, the standards were modified to acknowledge the role of the professional librarian in assisting the organization in the application of knowledge-based information (KBI) in a variety of settings. The JCAHO library standards today are similar to these. They are part of the information management (IM) section. Figure 7.1 lists the IM section that refers to library service, IM.5.10, and four "Elements of Performance" that give some specific details about what it means. Several key papers on the JCAHO program guided hospital librarians in this major program shift.

In 1994 the MLA responded to the new JCAHO standards by developing *Standards for Hospital Libraries* again to complement and expand the JCAHO standards. This document includes a reference sheet that links the MLA standards to the JCAHO standards. The 1994 MLA standards were qualitative and contained no recommendations based on quantity. There had been no surveys done of the practices of hospital librarians on which to base any recommendations as to quantity. The Canadian Health Libraries Association/Association des bibliothèques de la santé du Canada wrote the *Standards for Library and Information Ser-*

---

**Reference: Key Papers on the JCAHO Program**

Four key papers listed in the references (Dalrymple and Scherrer, 1998; Schardt, 1998; Doyle, 1999; Glitz, et al., 1998) discuss the issues of the JCAHO standards in the 1990s, as well as two (Fuller, et al., 1999; Shearer, et al., 2002) that have excellent summaries of the opportunities the new standards present.

---

**On the CD-ROM: Librarian's Guide to a JCAHO Accreditation Survey**

Found in the Chapter 7 folder: an excellent overview of the Shared Visions-New Pathways program of the JCAHO, by Margaret Bandy, AHIP, MLA member liaison to the JCAHO, 2003–2006, April 2004. www.mlanet.org/resources/jcaho.html

*vices in Canadian Healthcare Facilities* in 1995 and have recently published a revision in 2006 (CHLA/ABSC, 1995; CHLA/ABSC Task Force, accessed: 2006).

The JCAHO developed a new initiative called "Shared Visions-New Pathways," introduced in 2004 to be fully implemented by 2006. As Margaret Bandy, then the MLA member liaison to the JCAHO, interprets the change, "The 'Shared Vision' is that health care organizations are dedicated to providing safe, high-quality care. JCAHO shares this vision, so it is providing an accreditation process to support a health care organization's quality and safety efforts. 'New Pathways' represents a new set of approaches or pathways to the accreditation process that will support the shared visions" (Bandy, accessed: 2006).

As with the 1994 major revisions, librarians can find the provision of knowledge-based information (KBI) is mentioned in many chapters of the accreditation manual. Enumerated by Connie Schardt in 1998 and Margaret Bandy in 2004, the inclusion of KBI in many areas shows how the librarian can collaborate with many departments to be an essential part of an organization that delivers "safe, high-quality care" (Schardt, 1998; Bandy, accessed: 2006).

Dalrymple and Scherrer suggest that the "JCAHO stipulates indicators of quality for information management: timeliness and accessibility, accuracy, security and ease of access, use of aggregate and comparative information for improvement, efficiency, collaboration, and sharing" (Dalrymple and Scherrer, 1998: 13). The 2002 (revised in 2004) MLA *Standards for Hospital Libraries* was written again to complement the JCAHO ideas of KBI integration into the health-care setting. The abstract of the MLA standards states:

> "The standards define the role of the medical librarian and the links between knowledge-based information and other functions such as patient care, patient education, performance improvement, and education. In addition, the standards address the development and implementation of the knowledge-based information needs assessment and plans, the promotion and publicity of the knowledge-based information services, and the physical space and staffing requirements" (*Standards for Hospital Libraries 2002 with 2004 Revisions*, 2005).

**On the CD-ROM: MLA Standards**

Found in the Chapter 7 folder: The 2002 MLA *Standards for Hospital Libraries* were revised in 2004 and are available with permission on the CD-ROM in various formats.

As libraries move into the fast-changing digital age, evidence of quality and meeting the needs of the user become the hallmark for standards.

# CONTROVERSIES

When using standards or guidelines, you need to be aware of the controversies involved in their development and use so that when you use them, you will be prepared to answer such questions. Baker and Lancaster developed five major questions that outline the controversies (Baker and Lancaster, 1991).

1. Should standards be qualitative or quantitative?
2. Should standards be based on the best thinking of the profession or on the best empirical research?
3. Should standards be set at minimum or optimal levels of adequacy?
4. Should standards define inputs or outputs or both?
5. How can standards be written to allow for the diversity of individual libraries?

## SHOULD STANDARDS BE QUALITATIVE OR QUANTITATIVE?

The hospital library standards are an example of how the pendulum swings between qualitative and quantitative. There were quantitative measures in 1953 and 1984, with only qualitative measures in 1970 and 1994, while in 2002 (revised 2004), the measures were qualitative with a quantitative formula for staffing. Development of quantitative standards has always been hindered by two major factors: the lack of data on the activities of the libraries involved and, as noted in Number 5, the diversity of the individual libraries. At the same time there are studies that indicate library directors are more likely to use quantitative than qualitative measurements.

It takes, on average, about two years of volunteer time to develop an association standards document. Data are available today from the AAHSL survey or the MLA Benchmarking Network survey, but including these data in a standards document is difficult given the rapid rate of change libraries are experiencing. "Reference questions answered" has been a yardstick measure of service for decades, but now the library user is doing his or her own searches and librarians are conducting educational classes. A number could be incorporated today only to have the service revolutionized within a short period of time by some new technological advance. Work could be done in the future to match the survey questions more directly to the qualitative standards. Using qualitative standards in combination with the surveys would allow directors to use a description of services with service numbers for like-sized institutions.

## SHOULD STANDARDS BE BASED ON THE BEST THINKING OF THE PROFESSION OR ON THE BEST EMPIRICAL RESEARCH?

When a decision is made to revise a standard or write a new standard, who does it? It is hoped that the "best thinkers" in the profession would be involved and that they would act free of prejudice or bias. Or is it better to use statistical reports of best current practices if they can be found and interpreted? The answer to this question is, a combination of both. During the two years of work on any standard, the committee needs to bring in any studies and expertise needed but at the same time use the thinking and expertise of the practicing librarians on the committee.

## SHOULD STANDARDS BE SET AT MINIMUM OR OPTIMAL LEVELS OF ADEQUACY?

If a standard is quantitative and is set at a minimum level, would an administrator require an outstanding department to reduce its services to meet the low standard? This sounds absurd, but it could happen. Anecdotally, one hospital librarian told me that her administrator did not want the library services and collection to be more than the 50% of their benchmark hospital. This would save them money. The 1984 MLA hospital library standards were titled with the word minimum. Today the trend is moving away from quantitative standards, so this is not such an issue, but it could crop up at any time. Performance improvement programs and benchmarking programs strive for excellence, not adequacy, the former of which has been interpreted as reaching the 75% mark, the 50% mark being average. The MLA Benchmarking Network survey results report the average as well as the 75%, or third-quartile, mark. If quantitative standards are developed, it might be best to report various levels of adequacy rather than just the average.

## SHOULD QUANTITATIVE STANDARDS DEFINE INPUTS OR OUTPUTS OR BOTH?

If a standard is quantitative, should inputs such as financial resources and staff or outputs such as circulation and reference questions be defined? Even with the trend toward qualitative standards, this question could come up. Differing levels of inputs (funding) and service (outputs) can mean different things. If you have good funding but low service levels when compared with a published standard, does this mean you are inefficient or that each service you count is a more intensive service than what others count? In your environment, maybe reference questions take twice as long as in a different library with a comparable reference staff. In today's environment that is emphasizing outcomes measures, as described in Chapter 8, using input and output standards may not be useful.

## HOW CAN STANDARDS BE WRITTEN TO ALLOW FOR THE DIVERSITY OF INDIVIDUAL LIBRARIES?

Even within the major types of libraries (public, university, special, or school), each group has a very diverse population of libraries. Even if segmenting into small groups, such as hospital libraries, the diversity is great. The 1984 *Minimum Standards for Health Sciences Libraries in Hospitals* attempted to describe categories of hospital libraries, but even those did not cover all types and were controversial (Hospital Library Standards and Practices Committee, 1984). The trend toward qualitative standards has allowed libraries to adapt the standards to their own situation. Today, it is common to write qualitative standards and then try to coordinate input and output measures from surveys against statistically similar libraries. This allows diverse libraries to use the same set of standards.

## OTHER ISSUES

Other problems with standards development and use include definitions; library size; obsolescence owing to lack of updates, lack of enforcement, lack of research on whether the standards are being used; and the need for intensive efforts by associations to educate members about the standards in the first place. With all these problems, why have standards at all? Accreditation standards that are subscribed to by institutions to assure their customers that they run a quality service, such as for colleges or hospitals, are very important to institutional administrators. These institutions pay to be accredited and expect to comply with an inspection. Having strong library standards as part of these institutional standards gives the library some leverage. These standards, however, often do not provide enough detail to sufficiently explain library operations to administrators. Association standards such as those by MLA and ACRL are written for a somewhat homogeneous group to explain further what a quality library, or service within the library, is. The association membership feels strongly enough about having standards to have written them.

# THE MLA STANDARDS FOR HOSPITAL LIBRARIES

Despite controversies, the standards or perhaps guidelines available today can by used for evaluation. The MLA standards program is based on strategic work the association did in the 1980s. It requires that any standards developed "incorporate the best of current practice and accommodate future change" as well as "be useful and feasible" (Miller, 1985: 393). Reading the two main resources for managing a health science library (noted in margin) will allow you to manage with excellence and above the standard. Neither is appropriate to use, however, to help you discuss what a quality library is with your supervisor. Many special libraries and certainly hospital libraries report to supervisors who know very little about how their libraries are run. They rely on the librarian to teach them the basics and describe a quality service. As Flower (1978: 296) states,

> "Right from the beginning we must realize that librarians are the only ones who really understand libraries. Or, to put it the other way around, we must begin discussing hospital libraries by grasping the fact that no one we deal with in any hospital will understand much of what we are talking about. They will think they do, but there is an unspoken difference in concept which shadows every discussion of information services between librarians and hospital personnel, at all levels."

Using the standards to educate the administration is a very effective strategy. The two workbooks in this chapter can be used to discuss the programs of the library with your administration. You can relate each section to the plans and programs of your own library. Baker and Lancaster are of the opinion that qualitative standards cannot be used for numerical evaluation, and that is true (Baker and Lancaster, 1991). But qualitative standards do reflect current practices and a point-by-point review of them can demonstrate services and programs that are lacking or that are exemplary. While not a "formal" evaluation, a point-by-point comparison can be made and used to communicate with your supervisor. A written report could be made using the Evaluation Report Template, as found in Chapter 11 and on the CD-ROM in the Chapter 11 folder, as a guide to how to structure your report. A review of standards can also help with development of a

---

**Reference: Managing Based on Current Practice**

The eight-volume *Current Practice in Health Sciences Librarianship* describes in detail how to manage a library. The *Medical Library Association Guide to Managing Health Care Libraries* is 371-page overview of the essential topics of management. (Bunting and MLA, 2001; Holst, et al., 2000).

departmental strategic plan. As you are writing it, you can refer to the standards for support for certain parts. The Logic Model, as described in Chapter 8, can be used as a planning tool. The ideas of strategic planning are briefly covered in Chapter 9.

# THE JCAHO ACCREDITION STANDARDS

The standards written by the Joint Commission on Accreditation of Healthcare Organizations are both a frustration and an opportunity for hospital librarians. In the section above, the interaction between the MLA standards for hospital libraries and the JCAHO standards was described. Complying with the standards is a critical component for all hospitals in the competitive environment, and there is a significant institutional effort to do so. The current JCAHO standard and its elements of performance that apply directly to hospital libraries are listed in Figure 7.1.

---

**Figure 7.1 Standard IM.5.10 Elements of Performance for the Hospital Library from the Information Management Chapter of the *JCAHO Comprehensive Accreditation Manual for Hospitals***

*IM.5.10*
Knowledge-based information resources are readily available, current, and authoritative.

*Elements of Performance for IM. 5.10:*

EP1. Library services are provided by cooperative or contractual arrangements with other institutions, if not available on site.

EP2. The hospital provides access to knowledge-based information resources needed by staff in any of the following forms: print, electronic, Internet, or audio. CAMH Footnote: Examples of knowledge-based information resources include current texts; periodicals; indexes; abstracts; reports; documents; databases; directories; discussion lists; successful practices; equipment and maintenance user manuals; standards; protocols; practice guidelines; clinical trials and other resources.

EP3. Knowledge-based information resources are available to clinical/service staff, through electronic means, after-hours access to an in-house collection, or other methods.

EP4. The hospital has a process for providing access to knowledge-based information resources when electronic systems are unavailable. (JCAHO, 2006b)

Before 1994, each hospital department had its own standard. It defined most of their operations and relied extensively on policy and procedure manuals. Every two years, a survey team employed and trained by the JCAHO, usually a physician, a nurse, and an administrator, would inspect the hospital based on a department-by-department physical survey. The hospital would start preparing for the visit a year in advance and dedicate many management personnel during the three-day inspection tour. The hospital received a score and a list of areas where improvements should be made. From 1977 to 1994, the library standards called for up-to-date resources and good policies and procedures. Shearer, Seymour and Capitani (2002: 27) describe well the atmosphere at the time: "JCAHO visiting teams came and went, after glancing quickly into libraries and at the librarians who had, by then, absorbed the collective anxiety of the institution concerning the visit. At this point in the development of hospital librarianship, the JCAHO was viewed favorably, as a proponent for the existence of hospital libraries."

The MLA Hospital Libraries Section and the MLA worked to help hospital libraries with the transition. Reports of survey visits were published and listed on the Web, such as the one by Schardt in the *National Network*, which reflects the transition problems around the 1994 change (Schardt, 1995). Even after the 1994 changes, it is still an uneven process.

In a process ending in 1994, the standards were extensively reorganized and rewritten. Areas of the hospital were defined and task forces convened to write the new standards. The MLA was able to get representatives on the Information Management Task Force, which included representatives from information systems, medical or health records, the patient business office, and more. The competition for attention among the various constituencies was strong. The fact that the hospital library got a standard at all was considered a winning situation. But since the standards for library services were relaxed and no longer specifically call for a physical library, some hospital librarians have given up on the JCAHO as a source of support for a continued library service in a hospital. Others, however, see the JCAHO concept of "Shared Visions-New Pathways" as an opportunity to show the value of the library service in supporting all hospital activities through efficient provision of knowledge-based information. The library can no longer be viewed as a passive responder for provision of information when asked, but instead must take on more proactive roles on the information management team of the hospital. Even if the library is not part of the survey, the librarian can work behind the scenes and be sure that they are involved in KBI provision on all levels possible. While this whole discussion is specific to hospital accreditation standards, the concepts reviewed can be applicable to libraries in other organizations that have accreditation standards.

This should not be considered unusual, since the concept of integration of the library's roles was first introduced in the Matheson Report of 1982, presenting the concept of the Integrated Advanced Information Management System (IAIMS) (Matheson and Cooper, 1982). Jacqueline Doyle reports an excellent comparison between the IAIMS and the JCAHO. Among her list of connections and new roles, Doyle writes, "IAIMS goals and JCAHO standards will require a new set of skills, knowledge, interpersonal and informal network connections, even new job descriptions and reporting structures for librarians. IAIMS goals and JCAHO standards have potential for elevating and demonstrating the value a professional librarian adds to the organization" (Doyle, 1999: 385).

The librarian has the opportunity to support the hospital's accreditation efforts in all departments and get involved in the institutional JCAHO effort. Figure 7.2 lists some specific ways to do this.

---

**Figure 7.2   Strategies for Involvement in the Institutional JCAHO Effort**

- Stay informed by reading articles by other librarians about the JCAHO.
- Do periodic needs assessments and document them.
- Be involved in the institutional performance improvement program and use the techniques to evaluate library programs and services.
- Participate or offer to participate in committees dealing with JCAHO issues and information systems issues.
- Using the literature, the JCAHO *Comprehensive Accreditation Manual for Hospitals (CAMH)*, or the Workbook for Accreditation Standards provided below, investigate which hospital functions appear to use KBI. Coordinate with those areas on provision of appropriate services.
- Provide current awareness services on the subject of the JCAHO to appropriate administrators.

---

The JCAHO's main objective, and the vision it wants to share with all accredited hospitals ("Shared Visions–New Pathways"), is quality patient care using assessment of need and quality improvement. These two evaluation concepts are covered in detail in Chapters 4 and 5. Librarians should strive to be part of any

**Reference: Literature Needed to Comply with the Standards**

The *Comprehensive Accreditation Manual for Hospitals: The Official Handbook (CAMH)* (JCAHO, 2006b) is a massive, annual two-volume set that lists all the provisions for compliance. Larger institutions may sub-scribe to a site wide Portable Document Format (PDF) online version, and there may be a CD-ROM included with the print version. There is also a smaller version (446 pages) that can be purchased for key department heads (JCAHO, 2006a).

JCAHO hospitalwide quality improvement program for their own department as well as supporting other departments. Oversight of the JCAHO accreditation process is usually assigned to one hospital administrator. In larger hospitals it may be that person's only job. Library needs assessment should be done routinely and reported to this group. The traditional library role of acquiring and distributing information can assist the JCAHO team in acquiring the literature needed to comply with the survey.

The JCAHO program can be used to evaluate your library service in a way that will mean something to your administration. There is nothing specific in the standards to "prescribe" what a library service will do or purchase, except in the four elements of performance for IM5.10. We know that libraries do more than that. The workbook below is a compilation of the thoughts and ideas of experts in the field. You could and probably should review the *CAMH*, but reading it to the depth that these experts did might take a lot of effort. The comments in the workbook could be reviewed in conjunction with the manual, and they give you a starting reference point to a complicated process. This review might bring up ideas for new services or for evaluation projects involving needs assessment, quality improvement, or benchmarking.

You could also report to your supervisor and perhaps the JCAHO coordinator on how the library complies with IM5.10 and its elements of performance. While not a formal evaluation process, you could write a report that used the Evaluation Report Template, found in Chapter 11. Some of the parts would have to be adapted, but the template does give you a format to start with. The same could be true of reporting your activities integrating the library into the JCAHO quality programs, as discussed below.

# WORKBOOK FOR LIBRARY PERFORMANCE STANDARDS

## USING THE MLA 2004 STANDARDS FOR HOSPITAL LIBRARIES

This workbook uses parts of the 2004 MLA *Standards for Hospital Libraries*. A full version of these standards is available on the CD-ROM in the Chapter 7 folder in various formats. There is a copy of this workbook on the CD-ROM folder that will allow you to edit the questions. Perhaps you would add some questions or insert answers to discuss issues with your supervisor.

Three standards contain an evaluation checklist to use for an evaluation of your program or to discuss issues with your supervisor. To develop the list of key questions, these three checklists that were developed by the standards committees were combined and compared. A chart was created that grouped the broad areas of library management. The comparison showed that the emphasis differed between the three standards and the 2004 MLA *Standards for Hospital Libraries*. This led to a slight reordering of the MLA standards to reflect the combined emphasis of the four standards.

Including the ACRL standards gives an interesting perspective about the services and expands the view of the smaller medical library. By combining the various checklists and questions from each set of standards, key questions were developed for each standards area. While the following standards do apply to hospital libraries, the key concepts and questions could be used for any small special library.

### Organization and Administration

STANDARD 1:

The library serves as the primary department responsible for developing systems and services to meet the knowledge-based information (KBI) needs of the organization.

The library shall have its own budget, and the medical librarian, as a department head, shall report to the senior management of the organization.

*Key Questions:*

1. Is the library a separate department?
2. Does the library director report to a member of the senior management team?

---

**Reference: Standards That Include an Evaluation Checklist**

- MLA *Standards for Hospital Libraries*, 1994 (Standards Committee, accessed: 2006)
- *Standards for Library and Information Services in Canadian Healthcare Facilities*, 1995 (CHLA/ABSC Task Force, 1995)
- Association of College & Research Libraries' *Standards and Guidelines*, 2004 (ACRL, accessed: 2007)

3. Are the relationships, responsibilities, accountabilities, and reporting lines clearly delineated, efficient, and effective?
4. Are there written policies and procedures?

(see additional administrative questions under resources below.)

## Planning, Needs Assessment, and Outcomes Assessment

STANDARD 6:

The librarian provides evidence of an ongoing assessment of the knowledge-based information needs of the organization and the development and implementation of a plan to provide appropriate resources and services to meet those identified needs.

*Key Questions:*

1. Does the library have a vision and mission statement coordinated with the mission of the institution?
2. Does the library have a strategic plan with goals and objectives?
3. Is the strategic plan reviewed periodically?
4. Does the library carry out a periodic assessment of the knowledge-based information needs of its customers?
5. Are there processes in place for the ongoing evaluation and improvement of the library services, collections, and programs?
6. Does the library inform its community of the results of assessments and evaluations?

## Communication and Cooperation

STANDARD 4:

The librarian, as the key KBI professional in the organization, is an active member of the information management team(s).

STANDARD 5:

There is evidence to demonstrate effective connections between KBI and:

- patient care
- patient education
- the performance improvement and patient safety functions
- the educational functions for hospital and medical staff
- other appropriate functions

*Key Questions:*

A. Internal Communication
1. Is the library involved in facilitywide planning, decision making, and problem solving?
2. Is the library represented on management teams, especially those involved in performance improvement?
3. Does the library have a system of liaisons or advisory groups with representation from various departments to advise on policies and services?
4. Does the library communicate regularly with its customers?
B. External Communication (not included in the MLA standard but included in some of the others and seemed to fit here)
1. Is the library a member of the National Network of Libraries of Medicine?
2. Is the library a member of a local consortium or statewide group?
3. Does the library staff participate in local, regional, or national professional associations?
4. Where there is participation in cooperative ventures or consortia, are there documented agreements in place?

## Resource Management: Financial
STANDARD 1:
The library shall have its own budget.
  *Key Questions:*

1. Is there a separate budget for the library, developed and managed by the medical librarian?
2. Is there a financial plan for the library integrated with the library strategic plan?
3. Is the budget developed and reviewed on an annual basis?
4. Is the budget sufficient to provide the resources and services required to meet the client needs?
5. Are there provisions made to ensure the availability of adequate funding for capital expenses and special projects or programs?
6. Is the budget reviewed and amended whenever there is a significant change in programs and services provided by the library and/or facility?

### Resource Management: Staffing

STANDARD 2:

KBI systems and services are directed by a qualified librarian. AHIP membership is preferred.

STANDARD 3:

Library staffing formula. (This feature of the MLA standards is a figure that relates staff size to total hospital FTE and medical staff. Other standards use a more qualitative approach.)

*Key Questions:*

1. Does a qualified medical librarian manage the library?
2. Is there adequate professional, technical, and clerical staff to meet service goals and objectives? Has the Library Staffing Formula been evaluated?
3. Is there a written position description for each staff member?
4. Are there regular written performance evaluations for each staff member?
5. Is there a staff development program for the library staff?
6. When client needs do not warrant the services of a librarian on a full-time basis, are appropriate arrangements in place to provide access to a librarian?
7. Where a librarian is not available on a full-time basis, are staff appropriately trained and qualified to ensure access to and maintenance of library resources?
8. Do the staff have the necessary qualifications and skills to meet service goals and objectives?

### Resource Management: Collection

STANDARD 6:

The library has a current and authoritative collection of print, electronic, and multimedia resources for the timely provision of knowledge-based information. There is a plan to provide access to knowledge-based information during times when electronic systems are unavailable.

*Key Questions:*

1. Does the library have a current and authoritative collection of print, electronic, and multimedia resources?
2. Is there a system for selecting and evaluating information resources in any format for incorporation into the physical or virtual collection?
3. Is there a written collection development policy that is

used to make decisions about the acquisition, retention, and use of print, electronic, and media resources?

4. Does the written collection development policy include a specific list of the various types of recommended print, electronic, and multimedia resources that are included or excluded in the collection?
5. Are there collection evaluation procedures in place?
6. Does the library use consortium purchasing and licensing agreements to improve its collection?
7. Are appropriate arrangements in place to provide access to information outside the scope of the library, using interlibrary loan networks and document delivery services?

## Information Service Provision and Promotion

STANDARD 7:
The library actively promotes KBI services and resources to all user groups, and provides documented evidence thereof.
  *Key Questions:*

1. Does the library offer an appropriate range of information services to support its mission and goals?
2. Can the library list its information services so they can be evaluated against other lists of traditional and emerging services?
3. Are the information services that are provided regularly monitored and evaluated?
4. Does the medical librarian market library information services?
5. Is there a list of marketing tools used to promote library services?

## Education and Training

STANDARD 5:
The library provides education for hospital and medical staff on information management and use of information technology and in the identification of print and/or electronic resources for further individualized learning on topics presented in educational sessions.
  *Key Questions:*

1. Does the library provide formal and informal opportunities for education and instruction?
2. Are the educational opportunities marketed to users?
3. Are the library services integrated into other educational services of the hospital?

## Legal and Ethical Responsibilities

STANDARD 8:

All KBI functions are performed in compliance with applicable federal, state, and local laws and regulations.

*Key Questions:*

1. Are all library services and functions performed in compliance with applicable federal, state, and local laws and regulations?
2. Is there a clear statement of the legal and ethical responsibilities of the library staff?
3. Are there written policies relating to the protection of the privacy and confidentiality of library staff and clients and to intellectual freedom, censorship, and access to information?

## Access to Services and Collections

STANDARD 9:

KBI resources are available to clinical staff 24 hours a day, 7 days a week.

STANDARD 6:

Resources, technology, and services that must be provided include:

- convenient access to expert searching
- a catalog or database and taxonomy to efficiently locate materials
- a plan to provide access to knowledge-based information during times when electronic systems are unavailable.

*Key Questions:*

A. Access to Collections via Location Tools
   1. Is the collection accessible to all employees, and the medical staff, and other appropriate customers using standard catalogs, databases, lists, Web sites, and taxonomy to efficiently locate materials?
B. Remote or Physical Access to Collections and Services
   1. Are resources available to clinical staff 24 hours a day, 7 days a week?
   2. Does the library maintain regular hours of access consistent with reasonable demand?
   3. Is there remote access to resources and services?
   4. Are there enough print resources to provide for safe

patient care if the electronic resources should become unavailable?

## Facilities and Technology

STANDARD 10:
The physical library will be large enough to accommodate the library staff; the in-house collection; an appropriate amount and selection of personal computers and other information technology hardware; and seating for an appropriate number of users. A separate office will be provided for at least the professional library staff.

*Key Questions:*

1. Are the facilities pleasant, functional, and for library use only?
2. Is the space sufficient to accommodate the library's collections and services as well as to allow for future growth?
3. Is the space sufficient to meet clients' needs?
4. Does the professional staff have a private office to meet with customers confidentially to discuss patient care questions?
5. Are there technological resources to support the delivery of information to staff and clients?
6. Are technological resources available to support the effective management and operation of library services?
7. Are new information technologies and their application to library management and services assessed on a regular basis?

# WORKBOOK FOR ACCREDITATION STANDARDS

## USING THE JCAHO ACCREDITATION STANDARDS TO ASSESS LIBRARY AND INSTITUTIONAL QUALITY

Just as in the hospital library standards compared in the first workbook, comparing the suggestions made in the library literature in an organized way reveals a list of activities your library operation could perform or be involved in. These activities might point you towards the new and expanding information roles listed in Figure 7.2. By reviewing this list with your supervisor, or communicating with the central hospital JCAHO office, you can show the quality of your library and its essential involvement in the quality of patient care. It is this quality patient care that the hospital is striving for by participating in the JCAHO and its "Shared Visions-New Pathways."

This workbook combines comments from the literature on the key provisions of the JCAHO standards where libraries and librarians can be involved. Not every standard number is listed, just those pointed out by the six authors (Bandy, accessed 2006; Doyle, 1999; Gluck, 2004; Kronenfeld and Doyle, 2003; Rand and Gluck, 2001; and Schardt, 1998) that were reviewed. The comments by the authors are referenced with only the first author's name. This workbook is available as a Word document on the CD-ROM in the Chapter 7 folder. Figure 7.3 contains a list of acronyms that are used by the JCAHO.

| Figure 7.3   **JCAHO Acronyms** | |
|---|---|
| *CAMH* | *Comprehensive Accreditation Manual for Hospitals* |
| EP | elements of performance |
| IM | information management standard |
| JCAHO | Joint Commission on Accreditation of Healthcare Organizations |
| KBI | knowledge-based Information |
| ORYX | a measurement requirement that integrates outcomes and other performance measurement data into the accreditation process |
| PFA | priority focus areas |
| PFP | priority focus process |
| PPR | periodic performance review |

### The Management of Information Standard (IM)

*IM Overview*

The goal of the information management function is to support decision making to improve patient outcomes . . . assure patient safety . . . improve performance (Bandy, accessed: 2006). A hospital's provision of care, treatment, and services is a complex endeavor that is highly dependent on information. This includes information about the science of care, treatment, and services (Bandy, accessed: 2006).

Managing information is an active, planned activity (Bandy, accessed: 2006).

To achieve a vision for effectively and continuously improving information management in health-care organizations, the following are critical:

- Ensuring timely and easy access to complete information throughout the organization
- Accessing and using external knowledge bases . . . to pursue opportunities for improvement
- The hospital plans and designs information management processes to meet internal and external information needs (Bandy, accessed: 2006).

Hospital librarians should be knowledgeable with the whole IM chapter, including the standards, intents, and common type 1 recommendations of the IM Plan (Rand, 2001).

### IM.1.10 The hospital plans and designs information management processes to meet internal and external information needs.

EP 5: The hospital has an ongoing process to assess the needs of the hospital, departments, and individuals for knowledge-based information.

Elements of Performance (EPs) for IM.1.10 state, "The hospital bases its information management processes on a thorough analysis of internal and external information needs." IM.1.10 outlines all of the components of needs analysis that should be used for knowledge-based information (KBI) as well as the other standards (Bandy, accessed: 2006).

### IM.2.10 Information privacy and confidentiality are maintained.

### IM.2.20 Information security, including data integrity, is maintained.

### IM.2.30 Continuity of information is maintained.

Hospital librarians should be knowledgeable with the whole IM chapter: the security and confidentiality issues such as firewalls, remote authentication, HIPAA compliance, Internet vs. Intranet vs. Extranet applications (Rand, 2001).

### IM.3.10 The hospital has processes in place to effectively manage information, including the capturing, reporting, processing, storing, retrieving, disseminating, and displaying of clinical/service and non-clinical data and information.

While this technical standard for clinical/service and non-clinical data and information, as opposed to knowledge-based information (KBI), has ten EPs, reading through this and understanding the complexity of the field can inform the librarian so that she can volunteer her expertise on committees. This expertise might address these four EPs:

- Information technology industry standards or hospital policies relating to uniform data definitions and data display
- Standardization of abbreviations, acronyms, and symbols that are not to be used throughout the hospital.
- Minimum data sets, terminology, definitions, classifications, vocabulary, and nomenclature, including abbreviations, acronyms, and symbols, are standardized throughout the hospital.
- Dissemination of data and information is timely and accurate.

Hospital librarians should be knowledgeable about the aggregate data sources that are used by their own institution for internal and external comparisons, benchmarking, and the chosen ORYX indicators (ORYX is a database project of the JCAHO) (Rand, 2001).

Organizational information (patient-specific, knowledge-based, financial/organizational, and comparative) should be linked or at least linkable within the organization and, externally, among organizations. But networking is not as technically simple as it at first appears. Barriers to connectivity exist and may include the conflict between ease of access and security, interdepartmental competition, and clashing of professional cultures and value systems, but they can be overcome (JCAHO and IAIMS concepts) (Doyle, 1999).

Hospitals have deeply entrenched and distinct information systems that are at first inflexible and not amenable to integration or external linkages. (JCAHO and IAIMS concepts) (Doyle, 1999) Some hospitals, especially those not affiliated with medical schools, may not have recognized the need for integration of information systems and structures, and if they have, the barriers are seen as too great, too costly, and too overwhelming to overcome (JCAHO and IAIMS concepts) (Doyle, 1999).

## IM.4.10 The information management system provides information for use in decision making.

Standard IM.4.10 addresses information-based decision making: The information management system provides information for use in decision making. The rationale for this standard states, "Clinical and strategic decision making depends on information from multiple sources, including the patient record, knowledge-based information, comparative data/information, and aggregate data/information" (Bandy, accessed: 2006).

Hospital librarians can participate in planning teams and educational activities that relate to any of these four types of information (Rand, 2001).

### IM.5.10 Knowledge-based information resources are readily available, current, and authoritative. (Previously IM.9)

JCAHO defines knowledge-based information as "a collection of stored facts, models, and information that can be used for designing and redesigning processes and for problem solving. In the context of this manual, knowledge-based information is found in the clinical, scientific, and management literature" (Bandy, accessed: 2006). (CAMH footnote and definition) (JCAHO, 2006) The rationale for the standards delineates the purposes for ready access to KBI for all hospital practitioners and staff. These purposes include maintenance of competence, clinical and management decision making, patient and family information, performance improvement and patient safety, and educational and research needs (Bandy, accessed: 2006).

The organization's manager of knowledge-based information (the librarian) has the potential to become a key component, or focal point, of the organization's information systems (JCAHO and IAIMS concepts) (Doyle, 1999).

Librarians are finding opportunities to work with other health and information professionals, such as the directors of health information management services (formerly known as medical or health records), information systems or services, and quality management (JCAHO and IAIMS concepts) (Doyle, 1999).

Hospital librarians may need to become a catalyst for change within their organizations (JCAHO and IAIMS concepts) (Doyle, 1999).

EP1. Library services are provided by cooperative or contractual arrangements with other institutions, if not available on site (JCAHO, 2006b).

EP2. The hospital provides access to knowledge-based information resources needed by staff in any of the following forms: print, electronic, Internet, or audio. CAMH Footnote: Examples of knowledge-based information resources include current texts; periodicals; indexes; abstracts; reports; documents; databases; directories; discussion lists; successful practices; equipment and maintenance user manuals; standards; protocols; practice guidelines; clinical trials and other resources (JCAHO, 2006b).

EP3. Knowledge-based information resources are available to clinical/service staff, through electronic means, after-hours access to an in-house collection, or other methods (JCAHO, 2006b).

New information systems and technologies can be used together to support clinical, educational, administrative, and research or continuous improvement activities (JCAHO and IAIMS concepts) (Doyle, 1999).

EP4. The hospital has a process for providing access to knowledge-based information resources when electronic systems are unavailable (CAMH) (JCAHO, 2006b).

These authors propose a model that uses the JCAHO standard and intent to provide needed KBI services. The technologies (systems and structures) put in place by the librarian will enable hospital staff to efficiently and effectively access and use KBI to accomplish the standards set forth by the JCAHO. One just has to know how to leverage his or her assets to make that apparent to hospital administrators.

The following building blocks for the ideal hospital library portal are based on the JCAHO's emphasis on "systems, resources, and services" that meet specific institutional information needs. The following steps, which are not new to hospital librarians but may be now accomplished using different electronic technologies, are recommended:

- Conduct a needs assessment and environmental scan in order to identify the key KBI users and their needs.
- Identify and acquire or contract for KBI resources that will best meet identified needs.
- Develop the organization's KBI Web portal to provide access to selected electronic resources and to complement appropriate print resources and mediated services already available in the library.
- Modify existing or establish a new array of library services, including mediated searching, document delivery, and training in the use of the portal and the resources it links to.
- Market and promote the newly developed library portal and its services.
- Evaluate the efficacy and use of the system in a continuous quality improvement process (Kronenfeld and Doyle, 2003).

New Internet, Intranet, and Web technologies enable the librarian to offer integration solutions to previously incompatible systems and platforms (JCAHO and IAIMS concepts) (Doyle, 1999).

IM.9 (now IM 5.10) states, "The hospital provides systems, resources, and services to meet its needs for knowledge-based information in patient care, education, research, and management." The intent for this standard states that: "Appropriate knowledge-based information is acquired, assembled, and transmitted to users. Knowledge-based information management consists of systems, resources, and services to:

- help health professionals acquire and maintain the knowledge and skills they need to care for patients
- support clinical and management decision making
- support performance improvement
- satisfy research-related needs
- educate patients and families

The emphasis is first on the provision of "systems, resources and services" rather than on the physical facility (that is, the library) that provides these services, and second on the specific activities in the hospital where KBI can have the most impact on its operation. In other words, the Joint Commission's focus is on what the *function* of the library is, and not on its physical attributes, how it achieves those functions, or who is in charge of them. In the same way, the Joint Commission Standards do not require a hospital to have a medical records department but demand that a function exists to create, process, and store patient-specific information appropriately (Kronenfeld and Doyle, 2003).

### IM.6.10–60 The hospital has a complete and accurate medical record for patients assessed.

IM 6 is an example of possible linkages between KBI resources and other information and data resources (Rand, 2001).

The new electronic health record (EHR) initiative calls for linkages from the EHR to a decision support system to KBI resources. The librarian's role here is expanding, as is the technology. There is a need for involvement so that while the health-care provider is looking at a patient record, they can seamlessly find evidence for diagnosis or treatment in the medical literature or KBI. In an integrated information environment, all parties involved in information management should communicate with each other (Shortliffe, 2005).

### OTHER STANDARDS AREAS WHERE THE USE OF KNOWLEDGE-BASED INFORMATION CAN BE PROMOTED

### NR.1–3—Nursing

The overview of the Nursing standard states, "The nurse executive also ensures the quality of nursing standards of patient care, treatment, and services and practice by incorporating current nursing research findings, nationally recognized professional standards, and other literature into the policies and procedures governing the provision of nursing care, treatment, and services." Librarians can improve their services to nurses and provide the research and literature that is mentioned in this standard (Bandy, accessed: 2006).

## EC—Management of the Environment of Care

This chapter deals with maintaining a safe and healthy working environment and is applicable to health sciences libraries, as well as to all departments and professionals within the hospital. The commission requires that all employees take responsibility for maintaining a safe and healthy working environment. While there are no specific standards in this Environment of Care section directly related to knowledge-based information, the library has an opportunity to keep appropriate staff aware of current trends, regulations, and other information in these fields, which include safety, infection control, security, facilities, and much more (Schardt, 1998).

## HR—Management of Human Resources

The HR standards can be used in two ways, as noted below. One is to be sure the competencies of medical librarians are current and their new roles reflected in the job descriptions. The other way is to be a KBI resource in the staff education arena and in developing other competency descriptions.

## HR.3.10 Competence to perform job responsibilities is assessed, demonstrated, and maintained.

## HR.2.30 Ongoing education, including in-services, training, and other activities, maintains and improves competence.

The goal of this chapter is to identify and provide the right number of competent staff necessary to meet the needs of patients served by the hospital (Schardt, 1998).

Are the competencies for hospital librarian developed by hospital HR personnel and librarians based on the Special Libraries Association publication, *Competencies for Special Librarians of the 21st Century* (Abels, accessed: 2006) or do job descriptions for librarian(s) require or prefer membership in MLA's certification program, the *Academy of Health Information Professionals?* (Rand, 2001)

IAIMS goals and JCAHO standards will require a new set of skills, knowledge, interpersonal, and informal network connections, even new job descriptions and reporting structures for librarians (JCAHO and IAIMS concepts) (Doyle, 1999).

IAIMS goals and JCAHO standards have potential for elevating and demonstrating the value a professional librarian adds to the organization. (JCAHO and IAIMS concepts) (Doyle, 1999) Is there an annual *professional development* budget for library staff? The Intent Statement for Standard HR.3 (in the 2001 standards) said, "Whenever feasible or possible, supervisors provide the staff with the support and encouragement needed to participate in professional associations and continuing education activities within or outside the hospital. Through formal and informal interaction with peers and colleagues from other hospitals and settings, staff competence improves" (Rand, 2001).

The 2001 HR standard addressed "the issue of maintaining competence through regular and on-going education. The specific examples used to identify in-service and training include formal classes, meetings, audiovisuals, and journal articles. Librarians can expand their role as educators and provide support and coordination for a wide variety of in-service programs within the hospital" (Schardt, 1998).

While the new standard, HR.2.30, does not have this detail or any rationale statement, its EPs address specific types of training and the use of needs assessment to identify training needs. Is there an *orientation* to the KBI resources (i.e., Library) of your institution for physicians, nurses, and other clinical and non-clinical staff appropriate to need? How is it documented? (Rand, 2001)

Does the library provide additional *training* besides basic orientation? To whom? How is it documented? Is it a part of the competencies for any staff, for example, House Staff? (Rand, 2001)

## IC—Surveillance, Prevention, and Control of Infection

This chapter is as applicable to health sciences libraries as it is to all departments and professionals within the hospital. The commission requires that all employees take responsibility for maintaining a safe and healthy working environment. While there are no specific standards directly related to knowledge-based information, the library has an opportunity to keep appropriate staff aware of current trends, regulations, and other information in these fields (Schardt, 1998).

The hospital uses a coordinated process to reduce the risks of hospital-acquired infections in patients and health-care workers. EP#1 states, "The hospital's infection control process is based on sound epidemiologic principles and evidence-based information on reducing nosocomial infection" (2004, no longer in EP#1 in 2005) (Bandy, accessed: 2006).

The hospital takes action to prevent or reduce the risk of nosocomial infections in patients, staff, and those who come into the hospital. Strategies for risk reduction include the statement that "the strategies are consistent with current scientific knowledge, accepted practice guidelines" (EP#2) (2004, not longer in EP#2 in 2005) (Bandy, accessed: 2006).

While direct reference to the literature is no longer found in the IC standard, careful reading of various parts of the standard shows that to accomplish these programs, access to KBI is essential. Library services can help practitioners discover the most current practice guidelines, and IC9.10 states that adequate resources, including KBI resources, we assume, need to be supplied to the programs by the leadership.

**LD—(Leadership) Overview: A hospital's leaders provide the framework for planning, directing, coordinating, providing, and improving care, treatment, and services to respond to community and patient needs and improve health-care outcomes.**

The Leadership standard has 31 parts in 5 sections covering governance, management, improving safety and quality of care, use of clinical practice guidelines, and teaching and coaching staff. As with other hospitalwide standards, a careful reading can suggest roles and services a librarian can evaluate.

The "Leadership" chapter identifies the leaders within the organization and provides a framework within which they should operate. Librarians may be included in this group if they are department managers; however, leadership is not necessarily limited to department managers and hospital administrators. According to the JCAHO, leadership is what individuals provide collectively and personally in the hospital and can be carried out by any number of staff. As part of the hospital staff, the librarian should be involved in hospitalwide activities that may not immediately require the resources or services of the library. Nevertheless, the potential will always be there to promote knowledge-based services and resources (Schardt, 1998).

**LD Overview: Teaching and coaching staff. To realize the hospital's vision and values, leaders are involved in teaching and coaching staff; thus, staff education is an essential leadership function.**

LD.1.9.1 (previously) indicated that leaders are responsible for implementing programs that promote job-related advancement and educational goals. Hospital librarians can assist organizational leaders in meeting this standard, by providing and promoting knowledge-based services and resources needed by staff who are studying for certification, advanced degrees, and other educational programs (Schardt, 1998).

### LD.2.20 Each organizational program, service, site, or department has effective leadership.

LD standards list the important functions of a department manager throughout the section. The library manager should be engaged in the types of activities that the JCAHO implies are essential for leadership. These responsibilities should be reflected in position descriptions. (The list previously included the following which can now be found throughout the 31 sections.)

- integrating department services with the primary functions of the hospital
- continuously assessing and improving the department's performance
- developing policies and procedures
- providing training and continuing education for all staff
- recommending space allocations and other resources
- participating in selecting outside resources needed for services (Schardt, 1998).

### LD.4.10 The leaders set expectations, plan, and manage processes to measure, assess, and improve the hospital's governance, management, clinical, and support activities.

An example of this might be developing a digital library of full text resources on practice guidelines, benchmark data, evidence based healthcare, regulatory and legal manuals, and other information needed by hospital leaders (Rand, 2001).

### LD.4.20 New or modified services or processes are designed well.

EP4 states that one of the design elements is "Current knowledge when available and relevant (for example, practice guidelines, successful practices, information from relevant literature and clinical standards)." Those leaders involved in this process could be helped by having good library service (Bandy, accessed: 2006).

### LD.4.50 The leaders set performance improvement priorities and identify how the hospital adjusts priorities in response to unusual or urgent events.

LD.4.50 states that leaders should understand the approaches to and methods of performance improvement. Understanding of these issues comes through education, which can include a variety of settings and formats including reading the literature. As evidence of compliance, the JCAHO specifically lists information from literature references. Hospital librarians can help the hospital administration meet this standard by developing current awareness services that focus on updating and evaluating current information on performance improvement (Schardt, 1998).

### LD.5.10 The hospital considers clinical practice guidelines when designing or improving processes, as appropriate.

Creating a pathfinder or Web page bibliography on sources of practice guidelines, evidence-based health care, or authoritative clinical/organizational benchmark data (Rand, 2001).

Creating an alert service for new guidelines or quality data resources (Rand, 2001).

Mounting the institution's accepted guidelines, Care Maps, and so forth, on the institutional Intranet (Rand, 2001).

### MM.8.10—The hospital evaluates its medication management system.

EP2—The hospital identifies opportunities for improvement by routinely evaluating the literature for new technologies or successful practices that have been demonstrated to enhance safety in other organizations to determine if it can improve its own medication management system (Bandy, accessed: 2006).

### PC.6.10—(Patient Care) The patient receives education and training specific to the patient's needs and as appropriate to the care, treatment, and services provided.

PC.6.10 requires hospitals to plan and coordinate activities and resources to educate patients and their families. Parts of this plan call for information and education to be provided at levels and formats that can easily be comprehended by patients and their families. In addition to identifying educational materials, librarians can be involved in programs that address the issue of appropriate reading levels and language. One such project may be assisting with readability assessments for patient education materials to ensure that material can be comprehended by an appropriate community reading level.

PC.6.10 states that the hospital should identify and provide the educational resources required to achieve its educational objectives. Clearly, this standard could be used in supporting the development or enhancement of patient education collections, providing appropriate databases such as Health Reference Center, and working with staff to provide access to other resources for educating patients and their families. It is important to note that the JCAHO does not assign the responsibility of educating patients and their families to any one specific department or profession. The overview of the chapter states the JCAHO's position. "While the standards in this chapter recommend a systematic approach to education, they do not require any specific structure, such as an education department, a patient education committee, or the employment of an educator" (Schardt, 1998).

The current PC6.10 has 3 EPs, all of which could be programs a library service could assist with:

1. Education provided is appropriate to the patient's needs.
2. The assessment of learning needs addresses cultural and religious beliefs, emotional barriers, desire and motivation to learn, physical or cognitive limitations, and barriers to communication as appropriate.
3. As appropriate to the patient's condition and assessed needs and the hospital's scope of services, the patient is educated about the following:
   - The plan for care, treatment, and services
   - Basic health practices and safety
   - The safe and effective use of medications
   - Nutrition interventions, modified diets, or oral health
   - Safe and effective use of medical equipment or supplies when provided by the hospital
   - Understanding pain, the risk for pain, the importance of effective pain management, the pain assessment process, and methods for pain management
   - Habilitation or rehabilitation techniques to help them reach the maximum independence possible

## PC.6.30 The patient receives education and training specific to the patient's abilities as appropriate to the care, treatment, and services provided by the hospital.

Understand how patient's learning needs are assessed including consideration of cultural, religious, and language issues (Rand, 2001).

- Know what methodologies and formats are currently utilized or could be available for education related to medications, medical equipment, drug-food interactions, nutrition, rehabilitation techniques, pain management, and community resources (Rand, 2001).
- Provide library resources, policies and procedures that support patient education, which may be supplemental to

what the library and library staff manage/provide in the realm of general consumer health information (Rand, 2001).

- Know how patient education is documented by multiple clinical disciplines in the medical record (whether print or electronic), what policies, procedures, quality measures, or patient satisfaction indicators about education are in place within the institution (Rand, 2001).

The current PC6.30 has 4 EPs, all of which could be programs a library service could assist with:

1. Education provided is appropriate to the patient's abilities.
2. Education is coordinated among the disciplines providing care, treatment, and services.
3. The content is presented in an understandable manner.
4. Teaching methods accommodate various learning styles.

## PC.15.10–30 Discharge or transfer planning

The previous standards in this area (PE1.7) required that patients be informed about access to additional resources in the community. Librarians can use this standard to become involved in community- or hospital-based information and referral services. Libraries can bring to local coalitions their specialized resources, training, and experience in organizing databases and resources for patients and their families (Schardt, 1998).

## PI—Improving Organizational Performance

The goal of this chapter focuses on the continuous improvement of patient health outcomes. By way of illustrating the practical application of these standards to health care, the JCAHO uses the preface of each chapter to follow the scenario of a little girl hospitalized after a serious automobile accident. Here, the respiratory department works with the child and compares her therapy response with results reported in the research literature. The child's individual response that is reported in the medical record (patient-specific data), the research literature (knowledge-based information), and an internal database of similar cases (aggregate data) are then compared to identify opportunities for improving patient care.

This chapter calls for a planned and systematic approach to process design and performance measurement, assessment, and improvement. Most hospitals have adopted a formalized plan for identifying and improving processes within the hospital. At Rowan

Regional Medical Center, the process is called the PDCA cycle, (plan-do-check-act). At Duke University Medical Center, it is called FADE (focus, analyze, develop, and execute) (Schardt, 1998). (PDCA is covered in detail in Chapter 5.)

### PI Overview: Disciplines across the hospital work collaboratively to plan and implement improvement activities.

Process improvement activities are collaborative and interdisciplinary. As staff members of the hospital, librarians may have the opportunity to participate on process improvement teams while simultaneously demonstrating the value of knowledge-based information services (Schardt, 1998).

### PI Leadership responsibility: LD.4.20 New or modified services or processes are designed well.

This standard has enormous impact for the library. It places a premium on good process design. The JCAHO explains that good process design should be clinically sound and up-to-date, meaning that the current literature should be reviewed before developing the next process. The JCAHO outlines four questions that should be addressed when designing a new process, service, or function:

1. Is it consistent with the mission of the hospital?
2. What do you and your customers expect from it?
3. What do the scientific and professional experts say about the design of it?
4. What information is available about the performance of similar processes?

The message of this standard is that every process improvement activity resulting in the redesign of a service or function should be preceded by a consultation of the published literature to review expert opinion as part of the redesign process. And the librarian is uniquely situated to filter the published literature for these expert opinions (Schardt, 2001).

### PI.2.10 Data are systematically aggregated and analyzed.

EP4 states, "Data are analyzed and compared internally over time and externally with other sources of information when available." Examples of external sources of information include recent scientific, clinical, and management literature (Bandy, accessed: 2006).

PI.2.10 addresses the need to assess organizational performance and requires the hospital to compare performance data about its processes with information from up-to-date sources. Your assessment should look at three levels of data from the hospital:

1. aggregate data (how it compares with itself over time),
2. knowledge-based data (how it compares with external sources of scientific and other up-to-date information), and
3. comparative data (how it compares with other hospitals).

The JCAHO defines external sources as recent, scientific, clinical, and management literature and well-formulated practice guidelines or parameters. This definition is familiar to hospital librarians because it is part of the definition of knowledge-based information from the "Management of Information" chapter. The "Improving Organizational Performance" chapter is a critically important chapter for the hospital and the hospital library. It clearly supports access to knowledge-based information as an essential part of the improvement process. The library has a crucial role to play in meeting this standard by ensuring that knowledge-based information services and resources be readily available to all hospital groups working on improving organizational performance (Schardt, 1998).

## Sentinel Events

The "Sentinel Event" chapter states that to be credible, a root cause analysis must "include consideration of any relevant literature" (Bandy, accessed: 2006).

In the root cause analysis process, many questions will arise that could be answered through the literature, yet a substantial proportion of these questions may never be articulated to the library staff. The presence of a librarian in the group performing the root cause analysis can help to identify, and fill, these needs for information. This is analogous to the role of the clinical librarian (Rand, 2001).

## National Patient Safety Goals (NPSG), 2006 Overview

"The goals highlight problematic areas in health care and describe evidence and expert-based consensus to solutions to these problems. Recognizing that sound system design is intrinsic to the delivery of safe, high-quality health care, the goals generally focus on system-wide solutions, wherever possible."

The proposed goals in 2004 used these statements:

Achieve and maintain an organization-wide culture of safety.

Use external, expert information when designing new or modifying existing processes to improve patient safety and reduce risks of sentinel events.

Increase awareness of and access to relevant patient safety literature and advisories for all organization leaders and staff (Gluck, 2004).

### NPSG—7 Goal areas

- Improve the accuracy of patient identification.
- Improve the effectiveness of communication among caregivers.
- Improve the safety of using medications.
- Reduce the risk of health care–associated infections.
- Accurately and completely reconcile medications across the continuum of care.
- Reduce the risk of patient harm resulting from falls.
- Institute the Universal Protocol to prevent "Wrong site, wrong procedure, wrong person" surgery

While the national patient safety goal areas have changed in 2006, the following recommendations by Rand (2001), Gluck (2004), and Zipperer and Sykes (2004) are still useful:

- This can be done most effectively if you are a member of the work groups or committees overseeing patient safety or medication safety.
- Learn what their biggest concerns are. If the group is just being formed, bring attention to the Medication Safety Assessment of the Institute for Safe Medication Practices (ISMP), which may be of help in determining where to start and on which issues to focus.
- Learn which goals are the most problematic and which safety-related processes the group plans to develop or re-design. Find ways in which other hospitals have met them. You can do this by searching the archives of relevant discussion lists, posting your own question to those lists, and searching PubMed or the Internet.
- Learn whether your state is pursuing any patient safety initiatives. One source for information is the National Academy for State Health Policy (www.nashp.org).
- Provide access to end-user resources, such as drug interactions, adverse effects, drug safety in pregnancy, and so forth. Teach others to use these resources effectively, so that searching is not a cumbersome process and is more likely to be used at the point of care. Make those resources available 24/7.

- Collaborate with the hospital pharmacy and coordinate your resources. Librarians and pharmacists in my own institution regularly consult with each other when faced with difficult pharmaceutical searches.
- Meet with key staff in patient safety, such as quality improvement officers and risk managers, to assess their specific information needs. In larger institutions, responsibility for the various safety issues may be assigned to different individuals. Learn who is doing what.
- While representatives of nursing, Quality Assurance, risk management, and pharmacy are central to the process, patient safety involves everyone.
- Keep the library in the radar of the group so that members are more likely to consult with you when concerns arise in other areas of their work.
- Work with your hospital's Institutional Review Board (IRB). Following the death of a patient enrolled in a clinical trial at Johns Hopkins, the importance of expert searching of the medical literature became clear.
- Participate, if possible, in clinical rounds. This will help you to become more tuned in to the safety-related concerns of the direct caregivers.
- Safe practices (and specifically, the root cause analysis itself) demand a review of the pertinent clinical (or other relevant) literature so that decision makers are looking at the problem in light of current knowledge.
- Those developing or refining procedures will benefit from learning how other hospitals have dealt with the same problems.
- Librarians can develop Web sites with links to the most useful safety-related information resources, with annotations to clarify the complex relationships among them.
- By means of current awareness services, librarians can proactively gather the most relevant current literature and route it to the appropriate individuals in the organization.

# REFERENCES

Abels, E., R. Jones, J. Latham, D. Magnoni, and J. G. Marshall. 2003. *Competencies for Information Professionals of the 21st Century.* Special Committee on Competencies for Special Librarians. Special Library Association. Available: www.slaorg/content/learn/comp2003/index.cfm (accessed September 21, 2006).

ACRL College and Research Libraries Task Force. 2004. "Standards for Libraries in Higher Education: The Final, Approved Standard." *College & Research Libraries News*, 65, no. 9: 534–543.

Association of Academic Health Sciences Libraries (AAHSL) Charting the Future Task Force. 2003. *Building on Success; Charting the Future of Knowledge Management within the Academic Health Center*. Seattle, WA: Association of Academic Health Sciences Libraries, 2003. Available: www.aahsl.org/document/CTFprint.pdf (accessed December 18, 2006).

Association of Academic Health Sciences Library Directors & Medical Library Association Joint Task Force. 1987. *Challenge to Action: Planning and Evaluation Guidelines for Academic Health Sciences Libraries*. Chicago, IL: Association of Academic Health Sciences Library Directors, Medical Library Association.

Association of College & Research Libraries. American Library Association. "Standards & Guidelines." Association of College & Research Libraries. American Library Association (last updated January 16, 2007). Available: www.ala.org/ala/acrl/acrlstandards/standardsguidelines.htm (accessed January 20, 2007).

Baker, S. L., and F. W. Lancaster. 1991. "The Relevance of Standards to the Evaluation of Library Services." In *The Measurement and Evaluation of Library Services*. 2nd edition. Arlington, VA: Information Resources Press.

Bandy, M. "Librarian's Guide to a JCAHO Accreditation Survey." Medical Library Association (last updated April 2004). Available: www.mlanet.org/resources/jcaho.html (accessed January 10, 2006).

Bunting, A., and the Association of Medical Libraries. 2001. *Current Practice in Health Sciences Librarianship*. Revised and expanded edition of the Handbook of Medical Library Practice, 4th edition. Metuchen, NJ: Scarecrow Press.

CHLA/ABSC Task Force on Standards for Library & Information Services in Canadian Healthcare Facilities. CHLA/ABSC Task Force on Hospital Library Standards. "Standards for Library and Information Services in Canadian Healthcare Facilities 2006." Canadian Health Libraries Association/Association des Bibliothèques de la Santé du Canada (last updated May 31, 2006). Available: www.chla-absc.ca/task/standards.html (accessed December 15, 2006).

CHLA/ABSC Task Force on Standards for Library & Information Services in Canadian Healthcare Facilities. CHLA/ABSC Task Force on Hospital Library Standards. 1995. *Standards for Library & Information Services in Canadian Healthcare Facilities*. 2nd edition. Toronto: Canadian Health Libraries Association/Association des Bibliothèques de la Santé du Canada.

Dalrymple, P. W., and C. S. Scherrer. 1998. "Tools for Improvement: A Systematic Analysis and Guide to Accreditation by the JCAHO." *Bulletin of the Medical Library Association*, 86, no. 1: 10–16.

Doyle, J. D. 1999. "IAIMS and JCAHO: Implications for Hospital Librarians. Integrated Academic Information Management Systems. Joint Commission on Accreditation of Healthcare Organizations." *Bulletin of the Medical Library Association*, 87, no. 4: 383–386.

Flower, M. A. 1978. "Toward Hospital Library Standards in Canada." *Bulletin of the Medical Library Association*, 66, no. 3: 296–301.

Foster, E. C. 1979. "Library Development and the Joint Commission on Accreditation of Hospitals Standards." *Bulletin of the Medical Library Association*, 67, no. 2: 226–231.

Fuller, S. S., D. S. Ketchell, P. Tarczy-Hornoch, and D. Masuda. 1999. "Integrating Knowledge Resources at the Point of Care: Opportunities for Librarians." *Bulletin of the Medical Library Association*, 87, no. 4: 393–403.

Glitz, B., V. Flack, I. M. Lovas, and P. Newell. 1998. "Hospital Library Service and the Changes in National Standards." *Bulletin of the Medical Library Association*, 86, no. 1: 77–87.

Gluck, J. C. 2004. "Running with the Squirrels: Supporting JCAHO Accreditation Activities." *National Network*, 29, no. 2: 21.

Gluck, J. C., and R. A. Hassig. 2001. "Raising the Bar: The Importance of Hospital Library Standards in the Continuing Medical Education Accreditation Process." *Bulletin of the Medical Library Association*, 89, no. 3: 272–276.

Gluck, J. C., R. A. Hassig, L. Balogh, M. Bandy, J. D. Doyle, M. R. Kronenfeld, K. L. Lindner, K. Murray, J. Petersen, and D. C. Rand. 2002. "Standards for Hospital Libraries 2002." *Journal of the Medical Library Association*, 90, no. 4: 465–472.

Hassig, R. A., L. Balogh, M. Bandy, J. D. Doyle, J. C. Gluck, K. L. Lindner, B. Reich, and D. Varner. 2005. "Standards for Hospital Libraries 2002 with 2004 revisions." *Journal of the Medical Library Association*, 93, no. 2: 282–283.

Holst, R., S. A. Phillips, K. M. Bensing, and the Medical Library Association. 2000. *The Medical Library Association Guide to Managing Health Care Libraries*. New York: Neal-Schuman Publishers.

Hospital Library Standards and Practices Committee. Medical Library Association. 1984. *Minimum Standards for Health Sciences Libraries in Hospitals*. Chicago: Medical Library Association.

Joint Commission on Accreditation of Healthcare Organizations. 2006a. *Comprehensive Accreditation Manual for Hospitals: The Official Handbook*. Oakbrook Terrace, IL: Joint Commission on Accreditation of Healthcare Organizations.

Joint Commission on Accreditation of Healthcare Organizations. 2006b. *Hospital Accreditation Standards 2006: Accreditation Policies, Standards, Elements of Performance*. Oakbrook Terrace, IL: Joint Commission Resources.

Kronenfeld, M., and J. D. Doyle. 2003. "From MEDLINE Gatekeeper to KBI Portal: A New Model for Hospital Libraries." *Journal of Hospital Librarianship*, 3, no. 2: 1–18.

Matheson, N. W., and J. A. Cooper. 1982. "Academic Information in the Academic Health Sciences Center: Roles for the Library in Information Management." *Journal of Medical Education*, 57, no. 10: 1–93.

Miller, J. K. 1985. "President's Page. MLA Standards." *Bulletin of the Medical Library Association*, 73, no. 4: 393–394.

Rand, D. C., and J. C. Gluck. 2001. "Proactive Roles for Librarians in the JCAHO Accreditation Process." *Journal of Hospital Librarianship*, 1, no. 1: 25–40.

Schardt, C. M. 1998. "Going Beyond Information Management: Using the Comprehensive Accreditation Manual for Hospitals to Promote Knowledge-Based Information Services." *Bulletin of the Medical Library Association*, 86, no. 4: 504–507.

Schardt, C. 1995. "JCAHO & Information Management: Complying with the Standards, Realizing the Vision." *National Network*, 20, no. 1: 30–31.

Scherrer, C. S., and S. Jacobson. 2002. "New Measures for New Roles: Defining and Measuring the Current Practices of Health Sciences Librarians." *Journal of the Medical Library Association*, 90, no. 2: 164–172.

Shearer, B. S., A. Seymour, and C. Capitani. 2002. "Bringing the Best of Medical Librarianship to the Patient Team." *Journal of the Medical Library Association*, 90, no. 1: 22–31.

Shortliffe, E. H. 2005. "Strategic Action in Health Information Technology: Why the Obvious Has Taken So Long." *Health Affairs*, 24, no. 5: 1222–1233.

Standards Committee. Hospital Libraries Section. Medical Library Association. 1994. *Standards for Hospital Libraries*. Chicago: Medical Library Association. Available: www.mlanet.org/archive/hospital/ (accessed December 15, 2006).

"Standards for Hospital Libraries 2002 with 2004 revisions." 2005. *National Network*, 29, no. 3: 11–17.

Topper, J. M., J. Bradley, R. F. Dudden, B. A. Epstein, J. A. Lambremont, and T. R. Putney, Jr. 1980. "JCAHO Accreditation and the Hospital Library: A Guide for Librarians." *Bulletin of the Medical Library Association*, 68, no. 2: 212–219.

Zipperer, L., and I. Sykes. 2004. "The Role of Librarians in Patient Safety: Gaps and Strengths in the Current Culture." *Journal of the Medical Library Association*, 92, no. 4: 498–500.

# 8 METHOD 5: OUTCOME MEASUREMENT

The emphasis on outcome measurement in libraries could be considered "new." It requires a change of paradigm. As discussed in Chapter 3, the culture of assessment requires a shift from measuring inputs and outputs to measuring outcomes and impacts on the customer. Management of services has become more customer focused than process focused. In the paradigm shift brought on by the age of the Internet, many are asking, "What is a library?" These people include librarians as well as those who use libraries and those who fund libraries. Do you believe the library is a collection of books, journals, and written materials that is stored efficiently so the items in it can be retrieved? Then you would want to evaluate for efficiency. Do you believe as John Cotton Dana, Denver's first city librarian, said in 1889, "The worth of a library is in its use?" If so, you would want to report the library's outputs, the number of books circulated, the number of questions answered, how many teenagers attended an after-school technology club, how the library is "used." Do you see the library as a social institution that impacts and changes the lives of the people who use it and the community in which they live? Do you see the library as a tool and not an end in itself, a tool that when used by staff adds value to the bottom line and the vision, mission, and values of the larger organization? Then you would want to measure an outcome for the people who use a library service:

- Teenagers who participate in a technology club get better grades in school.
- College students that take information literacy courses write better essays.
- Professional staff that use library services save personal time they can use for other work.
- Physicians order fewer expensive tests after requesting a literature search from the library.

"It's best to remember that value is priceless, but impacts leave a measurable change in the shape of things" (Urquhart, accessed: 2006)

The new paradigm requires us to assess the economic and social value our libraries deliver to our patrons as well as be able to show that use of library services changed the personal, academic, or professional success of an individual. The outcome of the library service may affect the individual who is the customer. The next step is to see the impact of that person's change on those around him or her. What is the value of the change, and was there a benefit?

- Teenagers who participate in a technology club get better grades in school
  - AND influence their family at home by talking about technology, and maybe the family will start using computers.
- College students who take information literacy courses write better essays
  - AND when they graduate will do better in business because they have better writing skills.
- Professional staff who use library services save personal time they can use for other work
  - AND with their improved productivity can contribute more to the company's profits.
- Physicians order fewer expensive tests after requesting a literature search from the library
  - AND by ordering the more specific test not only save the patient money but also perhaps provide better diagnosis and save the patient's life.

> **Definition: Outcome, Impact, Value and Benefit (Poll, 2003)**
>
> *Outcome:*
>    the consequence, visible or practical result or effect of an event or activity.
> *Impact:*
>    the effect or influence of one person, thing, or action on another.
> *Value:*
>    the importance or preciousness of something, the perception of actual or potential benefit.
> *Benefit:*
>    the helpful or useful effect that something has.
> *Library Outcomes:*
>    the eventual result of using library services, the influence the use had, and its significance to the user.

# WHAT IS OUTCOME MEASUREMENT?

These terms, *outcome, impact, value, and benefit,* are sometimes used interchangeably, but they do have subtle differences. Be sure that the word you select to use means the same thing to all involved in the discussion. As an example, a library program might be shown to have the *outcome* that more parents read to their children in the evening after attending programs at the public library on the importance of the activity. But the *impact* of the change could be that the children do better in school in the early grades. This then has *value* to the community and the family, or the impact or outcome has *benefit* to the corporation, the community, or the individual.

Impacts and outcomes can be described in a pretty dramatic way. Proving the outcome and impact has generally been left to large, well-funded studies of the type a librarian in a small library setting would be unable to perform. So the question for this chapter is: What can you, the practicing librarian, do to evaluate or assess the outcomes or impacts of your library service?

This chapter was developed to give you some background on

the major initiatives to measure outcomes and impacts. Understanding the terminology and who the experts are can help you keep up with new developments. Then five ideas are presented that could be accomplished by the librarian working in a small setting. These are strategies that could be incorporated into the culture of assessment that you are developing. Each is described, and a workbook is provided for three of them, in print and on the CD-ROM in the Chapter 8 folder.

The first section describes two ideas taken from the literature for reporting outcomes. The first idea is to report outcomes by doing a quantitative survey that counts outcomes. This is based on a funded program, Counting on Results (CoR). The next idea is based on a report in the literature that uses the techniques of another study funded by the Medical Library Association that uses taxonomies to categorize the library's contributions to the institution.

The next section, using published studies to describe outcomes, has two parts. The first strategy is to understand evidence-based librarianship and be able to interpret and describe to your supervisor published studies of outcomes resulting from the use of information. The second strategy is to understand published studies of cost outcomes that could be used to discuss value, benefit, or worth. Looking into these two strategies will help if you should attempt to do your own outcomes study.

The third section describes the fifth strategy for evaluation, which is to use what is called the Logic Model to plan for outcomes measurement. Defined as a self-contained description of the components of the program, the Logic Model is a planning document that starts with describing the desired outcome and then works backward to delineate the goals and activities that will produce the outcome. While seemingly a complicated approach, it is one that is advocated throughout government and not-for-profit programs. To recap:

- Taking ideas from the published literature
  - Using surveys to count outcomes
  - Using taxonomies to categorize contributions to the institution
- Using published studies to describe outcomes
  - Studies of outcomes as a result of using information
  - Studies of cost outcomes
- Using the Logic Model for planning outcomes measurement

If this is your first foray into the world of outcomes measurement, you may well ask: Where did this idea come from? This

"We believe that libraries have a profound impact on individuals, institutions, and communities. How can we engineer a measurement system that will verify our intuition?" (Rudd, 2000)

**Reference: Seminal Outcomes Manuals and Tool Kits**

United Way of America: *Measuring Program Outcomes: A Practical Approach*, 1996. The Outcome Measurement Resource Network provides resources for member agencies, with many examples of evaluation projects and techniques (United Way of America, accessed: 2006).

The W. K. Kellogg Foundation: *W. K. Kellogg Foundation Evaluation Handbook*, 1998; *Logic Model Development Guide*, 2004. Both publications can be ordered on the Web at no cost for one copy. The Evaluation Toolkit provides explanations and tools for all kinds of evaluation (W. K. Kellogg Foundation, accessed: 2006).

theory has been influenced by political and philosophical changes in government, social service, and philanthropy. Those administering social programs, whether funded by the government or philanthropy, are now being asked to prove that the money they received has produced a change in the lives of the people who used the program. This stance began when the U.S. federal government enacted the Government Performance and Results Act (GPRA) of 1993, which implemented regulations requiring most government agencies to justify their existence in real terms by describing the outcome of the funded program. Nongovernment agencies soon followed suit. If a program says it will change the lives of a certain population group, how does it prove it actually did? The GPRA required that all federal agencies develop objective, quantifiable, and measurable goals and report to Congress each year how well those goals were achieved (Government Performance and Results Act of 1993, accessed: 2006). The influence of the law spread to local governments and philanthropic organizations. Several organizations developed seminal programs, documents, and tool kits that have been influential. Leaders such as the W. K. Kellogg Foundation promote a culture of assessment. The following statement demonstrates this:

"Evaluation is sometimes seen as an intrusive requirement that takes time away from the "real" work of programming. However, we have learned that effective evaluation provides program practitioners with valuable information that leads to more effective programs.... Together we can move evaluation from being a stand-alone monitoring process to an integrated and valuable part of program planning and delivery" (W. K. Kellogg Foundation, accessed 2006).

The Kellogg Foundation was the first to describe and promote the Logic Model. The model asks the program developer to determine what the outcomes will be during the planning phase of a program. As the program progresses, the Logic Model can be used to monitor the program through evaluation to see if the program is on-track and to fine-tune the program as it goes along (W. K. Kellogg Foundation, 2004).

In the library world, the Institute of Museum and Library Services (IMLS) manages the Library Services and Technology Act (LSTA), which provides federal funding for libraries across the country. To assist libraries with the requirements for outcomes measurement, they funded researchers to come up with techniques for outcomes measurement for public libraries. In another library-related government effort, the National Library of Medicine (NLM) funded the Outreach Evaluation Resource Center (OERC), located at the National Network of Libraries of Medicine (NN/LM), Pacific Northwest Region, in Seattle, Washington. (Outreach Evaluation Resource Center, accessed: 2006). Public, academic, or medical librarians as well as health educators can be funded by the NLM or the NN/LM to conduct programs to improve access to health information. The OERC provides assistance in developing well-planned evaluation approaches to help target and measure outreach success. They have adopted the Logic Model as the preferred way to measure the outcomes of their funded programs. In the following section, these and other programs are described by library type.

# INITIATIVES BY LIBRARY TYPE

## PUBLIC LIBRARIES

"IMLS defines outcomes as benefits to people: specifically, achievements or changes in skill, knowledge, attitude, behavior, condition, or life status for program participants." (Institute of Museum and Library Services, accessed: 2006).

Public libraries are following this outcomes definition. Public librarians have lately stepped forward to provide excellent resources in explaining to various library groups the techniques of outcomes measurement. Durrance and Fisher, in their book *How Libraries and Librarians Help: A Guide to Identifying User-Centered Outcomes* (Durrance, et al., 2005), point out that political pressures are very strong for public libraries to prove their worth in competition for tax dollars. Their program at the Information Schools of the University of Washington and the University of Michigan has developed Web-based tools that assist and challenge librarians to design their own studies. In essence, librarians need be involved locally in outcome measurements, since one size does not fit all. The program advocates thinking about the outcomes from the point of view of the program participant as opposed to what library employees want. You need to ask, "What is it that the customers get out of it?" (Durrance, et al., 2005; Durrance and Fisher, 2003) In another IMLS-funded program, an interdisciplinary team at the Indiana University-Purdue University Indianapolis developed an extensive Web-based course on this topic called *Shaping Outcomes*.

---

**Reference: Outcomes Measures Tool Kits and Publications—Shaping Outcomes**

Shaping Outcomes: Making a Difference in Museums and Libraries

From Indiana University-Purdue University Indianapolis and the Institute for Museum and Library Services.

Primary researchers: Elizabeth Kryder-Reid

Products: Web-Based Course: Shaping Outcomes. (Indiana University Purdue University Indianapolis and Kryder-Reid, accessed: 2007)

**Reference: Outcomes Measures Tool Kits and Publications—IBEC**

IBEC: Information Behavior in Everyday Context, helping maximize the impact of information in communities.

From: the Information Schools of the University of Washington and the University of Michigan.

Primary researchers: Joan C. Durrance and Karen E. Fisher

Products: Book: *How Libraries and Librarians Help* (2005), the Web-based Outcomes Toolkit, version 2.0. and articles (Durrance, et al., 2005; Durrance and Fisher, accessed: 2006; Durrance and Fisher, 2003).

**Reference: Outcomes Measures Tool Kits and Publications—CoR**

Counting on Results (CoR) (Colorado State Library Library Research Service and University of Denver College of Education Library and Information Science Program, accessed: 2006)

From: Colorado State Library Library Research Service and University of Denver College of Education Library and Information Science Program.

Primary researchers: Nicolle Steffen and Keith Lance

Products: Web site, PowerPoint, and journal articles (Steffen and Lance, 2002; Steffen, et al., 2002; Lance, accessed: 2006)

The Public Library Association has added to its PLA Results Series a 2006 book by Rhea J. Rubin titled *Demonstrating Results: Using Outcomes Measurement in Your Library* (Rubin, 2006). This excellent monograph follows the Durrance and Fisher model and has step-by step instructions and 14 work forms to copy and use for your own evaluation plan. Another comprehensive work aimed at public libraries is Joseph R. Matthew's 2004 book *Measuring for Results: The Dimensions of Public Library Effectiveness* (Matthews, 2004). The author gives a very broad overview of evaluation methods with some reference to outcomes measures. He feels that most traditional input and output measure have little to do with outcomes. Even so, he has an extensive appendix of inputs, processes, and outputs to measure. This book could be very useful as a reference for any type of library.

In another IMLS-funded program, the CoR program has created several articles and a Web site (Colorado State Library Library Research Service and University of Denver College of Education Library and Information Science Program, accessed: 2006; Steffen and Lance, 2002; Steffen, et al., 2002; Lance, accessed: 2006). While the previously mentioned programs are generally qualitative in nature, the COR program, while asking qualitative questions, takes a more statistical approach to outcomes measurement. The researchers developed postcard questionnaires and tested them on 45 libraries in 20 states. Besides this statistical approach, there is also a place on the postcards for user feedback that can be used as anecdotes. The CoR questionnaires are on their Web site along with the results of the surveys done in 2001. The program is an example of quantifying questions that are qualitative in nature.

## ACADEMIC LIBRARIES

In the academic arena, pressures are mounting from accrediting agencies and funding sources to link library services to student learning outcomes. The key book with methods for academic libraries is Hernon and Dugan's *An Action Plan for Outcomes Assessment in Your Library* (Hernon and Dugan, 2002). College and university administrations are working on definitions of "student learning outcomes" to supplement their usual outputs such as graduation rates, retention rates, transfer rates, and employment rates for a graduating class. Hernon and Dugan suggest that "student learning outcomes are concerned with attributes and abilities, both cognitive and affective, which reflect how the student experiences at the institution supported their development as individuals" (Dugan and Hernon, 2002: 377). The authors define outcomes assessment, as a process that seeks to document how libraries contribute to the learning process, and in the case of universities, to the research process.

This is an extremely complicated issue because academic librarians are compelled to work with educators to define first what general student outcomes *are* and then how access to librarians and library resources helps those outcomes. Just as the IMLS has a list of attributes to be expected from a personal change, academic libraries now have their list for students, which takes the form of a set of questions. Possible questions were posed by the Association of College and Research Libraries (ACRL) Task Force on Academic Library Outcomes Assessment:

- Is the academic performance of students improved through their contact with the library?
- By using the library, do students improve their chances of having a successful career?
- Are undergraduates who used the library more likely to succeed in graduate school?
- Does the library's bibliographic instruction program result in a high level of "information literacy" among students?
- As a result of collaboration with the library's staff, are faculty members more likely to view use of the library as an integral part of their courses?
- Are students who use the library more likely to lead fuller and more satisfying lives?

The Task Force admits that questions like these are difficult to answer but takes the position that the most important outcomes for academic libraries are the future life changes of the library users (Association of College and Research Libraries, accessed: 2006).

The Association of Research Libraries (ARL), as part of its New Measures Initiative, has identified four areas to investigate outcomes: learning outcomes, research outcomes, institutional outcomes, and personal control or electronic service quality issues (Kyrillidou, 2002).

The New Measures Initiative Web site has links to the latest work in each of these areas (Association of Research Libraries, accessed: 2006). Another project, the Higher Education Outcomes (HEO) Research Review, which looks at institutional outcomes, will have an influence on these issues with its charge to investigate "strategies for assessing the library's value to the community and to explore the library's impact on learning, teaching, and research" (Association of Research Libraries New Measures Initiative, accessed: 2006).

## SPECIAL LIBRARIES

In the special and medical library arena, most of the major work has been done in the area of "value." While the new paradigm of outcomes evaluation situates the public library as a social institution, the special library has a completely different circumstance. A research library certainly has no goal to change the life of an employee who uses the library. The goal instead might be to make that employee more productive for the company itself. In that way, some outcomes might change lives, but the bottom line is still the defining factor. The Special Libraries Association (SLA) has concentrated on publications on how the library or librarian adds value to the corporation or contributes to the bottom line. Some SLA publications are:

- *President's Task Force on the Value of the Information Professional*, 1987 (Special Libraries Association, 1987)
- *Special Libraries: Increasing the Information Edge*, 1993 (Griffiths and King, 1993)
- *The Impact of the Special Library on Corporate Decision-Making*, 1993 (Marshall, 1993)
- *Valuating Information Intangibles: Measuring the Bottom Line Contribution of Librarians and Information Professionals*, 2000 (Portugal, 2000)

The most recent book is Joseph R. Matthews's *The Bottom Line: Determining and Communicating the Value of the Special Library* (Matthews, 2002). Matthews points out that the biggest outcome is to show a return on investment or cost benefit analysis. While he talks about outcomes on human activity, he does not have any concrete strategies to find them. This book is, however, a useful tool to review the many strategies one might use to talk about the value of a library.

## MEDICAL LIBRARIES

Medical libraries in some settings have programs that teach the general public or specific groups of health-care providers about health information resources available to them. Often called outreach, these programs usually go outside the library to the community to educate people. These programs are more like public library programs because they focus on the individual's personal improvement. The programs mentioned above, and specifically the Outreach Evaluation Resource Center (OERC) funded by the National Library of Medicine (NLM), have developed templates and guides for outcomes assessment based on the IMLS definition. Libraries in academic medical centers follow the trends men-

**Reference: Outcomes Measures Tool Kits and Publications—OERC**

Outreach Evaluation Resource Center (OERC) (accessed 2006).
   From: the National Network of Libraries of Medicine (NNLM)
   Primary researchers: Catherine Burroughs, Susan Barnes, Maryanne Blake, Betsy Kelly, and Cynthia Olney
   Products: Book, Web document and online supplements: *Measuring the Difference: Guide to Planning and Evaluating Health Information Outreach,* 2000. Course materials: *Measuring Your Impact: Using Evaluation to Demonstrate Value,* 2006. (Burroughs and Wood, accessed: 2006; Olney, et al., accessed: 2006a, 2006b, 2006c; Barnes, et al., accessed: 2006).

tioned above for academic libraries and for special libraries. The Association of Academic Health Sciences Libraries (AAHSL) works closely with the ARL on its New Measurements Initiatives. One of the AAHSL's communication initiatives was the publication in 2003 of the 28-page document *Building on Success; Charting the Future of Knowledge Management within the Academic Health Center* [Association of Academic Health Sciences Libraries (AAHSL) Charting the Future Task Force, accessed: 2006]. The document outlines the library's role in knowledge management in clinical practice, education, research, and community service. In each section, challenges, successful practices, opportunities, and outcomes are reviewed. This is an important document to review when looking to the future and how the academic health sciences library can interact with its parent institution.

Medical libraries in health-care institutions have other issues for outcomes too. As a special library that serves professionals who care for people, the medical library needs to show that having a librarian and library service impacts the outcomes of patient care as well as the bottom line. Quality patient care is a concern of the health-care industry and the Joint Commission on Accreditation of Healthcare Organizations (JCAHO), as covered in Chapter 7. Healing people in a cost-effective and efficient manner and preventing them from being harmed or dying are the goals of quality in health-care. These are serious outcomes because people's very existence hangs in the balance. Health-care institutions typically have well over 50 different professions and services that contribute to this goal, and therefore they are very complex organizations. This makes it difficult to track specific causes and effects. Whether a doctor, nurse, social worker, physical therapist, dietitian, accountant, pharmacist, food service worker, janitor or, of course, a librarian, all employees contribute to the ultimate goal. The library is in competition with all these services to prove they should be funded because they make significant contributions to this quality patient care.

The Medical Library Association funded a study to consider the value of medical libraries, and the resulting publication is titled "Identifying and Communicating the Contributions of Library and Information Services in Hospitals and Academic Medical Centers" (Abels, et al., 2004). The authors address one of the problems of outcomes research, the vocabulary or taxonomy involved in reporting outcomes to the administration. Using their survey method, they report a taxonomy to communicate the contributions of a library.

There are many experts working on the problems involved in measuring and reporting outcomes, whether in traditional library services or electronic services, and in many types of libraries. How to easily measure and describe library program impact on people's lives and communities is still in development. Durrance and Fisher (published under her maiden name, Pettigrew) list a number of factors that have converged to facilitate the development of tools to measure outcomes:

- an increased realization that tools are inadequate
- pressure on governmental agencies for more accountability
- growth in scholarship that focuses on impact
- the availability of funding for such ventures
- the willingness of agencies and groups, including libraries, to experiment with new evaluation approaches (Durrance and Pettigrew, accessed: 2005)

# TAKING IDEAS FROM THE PUBLISHED LITERATURE

While there is little chance a librarian in a small setting can do one of these extensive studies alone, you could volunteer to participate in a large study if asked. You can usually find the resources to do a small study and report it. Friedman postulates that small studies can be as informative and useful as large ones, if not more. He calls them "smallball" studies, using a sports metaphor—in baseball, "smallball" is a strategy of winning games by scoring single runs in multiple innings, as opposed to "powerball," a strategy designed to produce large numbers of runs in a relatively small number of innings. (Friedman, 2005). If you do a "small research project," you should always consider reporting the results in the literature, (Dudden, 2003: 5).

No matter what you call evaluation projects, most librarians can do one even in such a complicated area as outcomes measurement. Combining the results of your "small" study with an explanation of the large published studies is an effective way to present your findings. By reviewing published studies, you may get ideas on how to adapt some of their ideas to your "small" situation. The two ideas described below, using surveys to count outcomes and using taxonomies to categorize contributions to the institution, can all be scaled to evaluate one service or one area of the library. All the small studies that you perform can be combined over time to get a larger picture as you develop your culture of assessment. These articles can give you ideas about how to organize and report your evaluation and connect it to your planning documents and your institutions' priorities. These two sections do not have corresponding workbooks as other methodologies in the book do. If you use either of these ideas, you would use a variety of evaluation strategies found elsewhere in the book.

## USING SURVEYS TO COUNT OUTCOMES

The IMLS-funded program Counting on Results (CoR) developed a method to survey outcomes and count them. Working with public libraries, these researchers recruited 45 libraries in 20 states to participate in the project. They developed six questionnaires that addressed most of the 13 "service responses" that had been developed in the Public Library Association's book, *The New Planning for Results: A Streamlined Approach* (Nelson and PLA, 2001). These questions were sent out in postcard form for the survey. The postcards are available on the Web. The results of this survey are also reported online and in print (Colorado State Library Library Research Service, and University of Denver College of Education Library and Information Science program, accessed: 2006; Steffen and Lance, 2002; Steffen, et al., 2002).

The six service responses used by the CoR project are listed here. In your efforts to redefine your library to have a culture of assessment, this list may give you an idea of how you might define a service response for your library.

- *Basic literacy:* A library that offers basic literacy service addresses the need to read and to perform other essential daily tasks.
- *Business and career information:* A library that offers business and career information service addresses a need for information related to business, careers, work, entrepreneurship, personal finances, and obtaining employment.
- *Commons:* A library that provides a commons environment helps address the need of people to meet and interact with others in their community and to participate in public discourse about community issues.
- *General information:* A library that offers general information helps meet the need for information and answers to questions on a broad array of topics related to work, school, and personal life.
- *Information literacy:* A library that provides information literacy service helps address the need for skills related to finding, evaluating, and using information effectively.

- *Local history and genealogy:* A library that offers local history and genealogy service addresses the desire of community residents to know and better understand personal or community heritage.

You have decided to do a small survey to measure an outcome or benefit to your customers. Not many people come into the library anymore, since they use the library's e-resources at their desk. The library space is in need of minor renovation, but before anything is done, you want to know if your customers think the library as a place is a benefit to them. The library as place is a "service response," part of your mission and a response to the needs of your customers, but how does having that space affect their life and work? Using the IMLS definition of an outcome, how will having a space for customers in the library, or "the library as place," benefit your customers in relation to their "achievements" or changes in their "skill, knowledge, attitude, behavior, condition, or life status." You discover in the literature that one of CoR's six service responses as listed above is "Commons: the library as place." On its Web site, you find the list of questions from CoR's questionnaire on the library as place, as shown in Figure 8.1.

---

**Figure 8.1   CoR's "The Library as a Place" Questions**

The Library as a Place (Commons) (Colorado State Library Library Research Service and University of Denver College of Education Library and Information Science Program, accessed 2006)
How has having the library as a place helped you?
Mark (X) all of the following that apply:

As a result of my recent use of the library, I...
- ❏   Met a friend or co-worker.
- ❏   Made a new friend.
- ❏   Learned about new books, videos, music, and so forth.
- ❏   Completed or made progress on schoolwork.
- ❏   Learned about or was referred to another community organization.
- ❏   Had a quiet comfortable place to think, read, write, or study.
- ❏   Took a break at the library coffee shop or café.
- ❏   Enjoyed a lecture, concert, film, or other public event.
- ❏   Attended or participated in a public meeting.
- ❏   Visited a library-sponsored chat room on the Web.
- ❏   Other—please specify:

Using the CoR questionnaire could be a starting point to develop questions for your type of library. Working with a focus group on the subject of library as place could help develop questions. For a special or medical library, the library as place questions could be revised to include this list:

- Met a friend or coworker to work quietly on a project.
- Scanned print journals for new articles.
- Learned about new books.
- Had a quiet comfortable place to think, read, write, or study.
- Took a break with a cup of coffee from the coffee cart.

By working with a group of libraries, your end result might be more meaningful, since a larger group would be surveyed. Like the CoR project, individual library and demographic results also could be reported. With the use of e-mail, a group of like libraries could cooperate and develop some "service response" questions. For example, a group of hospital librarians could use the recent Medical Library Association's "Standards for Hospital Libraries" (*Standards for Hospital Libraries 2002 with 2004 Revisions*, 2005), as described in Chapter 7, to develop a list of service responses particular to hospital libraries. From this list, they could develop a questionnaire that addresses a particular service response.

## USING TAXONOMIES TO CATEGORIZE CONTRIBUTIONS TO THE INSTITUTION

Much of this discussion about outcomes has been based on the concept that well-planned and evaluated social programs make a difference in people's lives.

The effective library as a social construct, as discussed in Chapter 2, has come to be included in this discussion. As mentioned above, the IMLS describes an outcome as a benefit to people through achievements or changes in skill, knowledge, attitude, behavior, condition, or life status (Institute of Museum and Library Services, accessed: 2006). From successes in these individual changes, there are impacts on community and civic life. For special libraries, outcomes of a library service can benefit the individual in somewhat the same way, but the purpose of seeing changes in the individual in the workplace is to have a positive impact on the corporation. How to connect to that impact is the problem.

Theresa Cuddy used the study sponsored by the Medical Library Association called *The Value of Library and Information Services in Hospitals and Academic Health Sciences Centers*. The first part of the MLA study surveyed librarians and health-care administrators to develop a taxonomy of the contributions of library and information services (LIS) in hospitals and academic health sciences centers. By surveying librarians and health-care administrators, the authors developed a shared vocabulary or taxonomy to use to enhance communication between libraries and the management of the institution or company they work for. (Abels, et al., 2002, 2004) In her study, Cuddy (2005) gathered a critical incident survey taken over two years. She asked a simple question at the point of service: "We like to continuously validate and keep records of the contributions that the Health Sciences Library makes to the hospital and/or patient care. Can you please take a moment and write how the information you received helped yourself and ultimately the hospital?" Cuddy reported her findings by linking the responses to contributions' taxonomy developed in the MLA study. She was also able to demonstrate a table that linked anecdotal statements from the survey. Using the taxonomy from the study, found in a Word Document on the CD-ROM in the Chapter 8 folder, you could do an evaluation using any of the methods outlined in this book and communicate your results to the administration by linking them to the shared vocabulary of the taxonomy, as Cuddy did. While this is a health-care environment study, there may be other taxonomies developed for business in general or for general management that libraries in other environments could use.

# USING PUBLISHED STUDIES TO DESCRIBE OUTCOMES

Most special libraries work closely with professionals who use published evidence to support their decisions when performing the jobs assigned to them. Why not use published evidence to support the job that libraries and librarians do? This is known as evidence-based librarianship, and it takes its cue from evidence-based medicine (EBM), a movement that teaches healthcare practitioners to formulate questions and use effective literature searching to find evidence for medical issues. The idea is that with the explosion of literature in medicine it takes specific training in search and statistical techniques to find the "best" evidence for a treatment or diagnosis. Evidence-based librarianship is covered in Chapter 9 in more detail. The proponents believe librarians should change their professional focus from managing by the example of other programs to managing by applying the results of research studies that show through evidence that service strategies are effective in helping the library customer.

Many studies reported in the library literature are supported by grant funds and performed by librarians specializing in evaluation research. It is very unlikely that a librarian in a small-library setting could do the kind of research study that connects library services to secondary or long term outcomes, as described above. While small studies can be done and can be effective, the practicing librarian can also report on the large studies others have performed in a way that benefits his or her own library.

While each library is operating in a different context, we can draw parallels. Small special libraries serve professionals who use their professional experience to enhance a corporation's performance. Whether an engineer in a firm that needs to make a profit or a doctor or nurse in a hospital that needs to provide quality patient care, these professionals need information to continue to do their jobs competently on a daily basis. The information itself may be completely different for each person, but the information-seeking behavior cuts across professional lines. By locating outcomes-based research in the literature, you may be able to propose that these outcomes studies are applicable to your own situation.

In special libraries in a corporate setting, the approach of using cost and time savings to show the value or worth of the library service to the corporation has been researched and discussed. Using the theories of cost-benefit analysis or return on investment, the studies have been done to describe cost savings in libraries. In-press studies in Florida, led by José-Marie Griffiths, are developing Web-based tools, such as a return-on-investment calculator, for use in public libraries. Studying the literature in this area would help you decide if it was an approach you wanted to take to discuss library outcomes with the administration.

## STUDIES OF OUTCOMES AS A RESULT OF USING INFORMATION OR AN INFORMATION SERVICE

In studying outcomes, it is apparent that when information is requested from a library service and used for the reason it was requested, there can be an immediate impact and/or a long-term impact. Joanne Gard Marshall, who has conducted several groundbreaking studies into information impact, gives an excellent summary of some of her work in her 2000 *Library Journal* article (Marshall, 2000). Called "Determining Our Worth, Communicating Our Value," Marshall lays out the results she found in professionals' business activities after they used information provided by a library. In business and government, she found that professionals' use of libraries enabled them to:

- Proceed to the next step on a project or task
- Decide on a course of action
- Exploit new business opportunities
- Save time
- Avoid loss of funds
- Have the ability to meet a deadline or deal with an unexpected emergency
- Have the ability to improve or approve a procedure, policy, or plan
- Work toward prevention of conflict with the government agency or with another jurisdiction

In her well-known and often-cited Rochester study, Marshall (1992) found that physicians who were provided with a literature search by a librarian reported that this information contributed to changes in their patient care decisions. The percentage of physicians that reported changes in various patient care decisions was the end result of the study. Urquhart reports five studies that were based on Marshall's methodology (Urquhart, 2004). In a study of her own based in part on Marshall's methodology, Urquhart also studies physicians who do their own searches (Urquhart, 1995, 1996).

These studies are included in a recent systematic review by Weightman, "The Value and Impact of Information Provided through Library Services for Patient Care: A Systematic Review" (Weightman, 2005). In this systematic review, which located a potential pool of about 320 papers, the author rigorously examined the quality of 85 studies and reported comparable percentages in 13 studies that she considered of higher quality. From these studies, she could report the percentage ranges shown in Figure 8.2, where they are compared with Marshall and Urquhart.

| Figure 8.2 Percentage of Change in Patient Care Decisions after Using Library Services | | | |
| --- | --- | --- | --- |
| Affect of librarian-mediated literature search on patient care | Weightman (2005) | Marshall (1992) | Urquhart (1995) |
| General impact on clinical care | 37-97% | 97% | 79% |
| Handled case differently (definitely/probably) | 25-75% | | 25% |
| Affected choice of diagnosis | 10-31% | 29% | 31% |
| Affected choice of medical tests | 20-51% | 51% | 22% |
| Affected choice of treatment or drugs | 27-45% | 45% | |
| Altered diagnosis and treatment/management | 25-57% | | 32% |
| Reduced length of stay in the hospital | 10-19% | 19% | |
| Affected advice to patients | 47-72% | 72% | |
| Resulted in important changes in care/alternative therapies/referral | 11-54% | | 35% |
| Resulted in avoidance of adverse medical consequences, including: | | | |
| Hospital admission | | 12% | |
| Hospital-acquired infection | | 8% | |
| Surgery | | 21% | |
| Additional tests or procedures | | 49% | |
| Additional outpatient visits | | 26% | |
| Patient mortality or loss of life | | 19% | |

There is very little chance a librarian working in a small-library setting would be able to replicate these extensive studies. It is hoped that new studies will be funded and carried out in the future. You can, however, take some time to study them and present them to your administrator as "evidence" that libraries do have an "impact" on the business at hand and the "products" the company makes. In the area of health care, that "product" is quality patient care.

The workbook for this section, found at the end of the chapter and on the CD-ROM in the Chapter 8 folder, will assist you in a review of the literature. Part of the process is to understand the principles of evidence-based librarianship (EBL). The workbook proposes you develop a form to report the results of studies of outcomes that you locate. You can use the form to analyze the article and report to your supervisor the data in a consistent format. If your supervisor is unfamiliar with the ideas of EBL, this form will generate discussion that will educate him or her about these studies, which show value and how that value applies to your situation. Figure 8.3 is a demonstration of the use of such a form.

| Figure 8.3 | Report of Evidence of Library Outcomes from the Literature | |
| --- | --- | --- |
| Journal citation | Urquhart C.J., and J.B. Hepworth. "Comparing and Using Assessments of the Value of Information to Clinical Decision-making." *Bull. Med. Libr. Assoc.* 84 no. 4 (October 1996): 482–489.<br>Urquhart C., and J. Hepworth. "The Value of Information Supplied to Clinicians by Health Libraries: Devising an Outcomes-Based Assessment of the Contribution of Libraries to Clinical Decision-making." *Health Libr Rev.* 12, no. 3. (September 1995): 201–213. | |
| Methodology | Clinicians at 11 hospitals library sites were asked to describe the purposes for which they needed information, the steps they took to obtain it, and to assess the value of the information obtained from interlibrary loan requests, database searches, and end-user searches. There was a 46% to 69% response rate. | |
| Results: | Results show that information obtained from a library service did assist in personal clinical decision making. It also might continue to do so in the future. The kinds of decisions were most supported that were identified. The information impacted the following activities by the listed percentage. | |
| | General impact on clinical care | 79% |
| | Handled case differently (definitely/probably) | 25% |
| | Affected diagnosis | 31% |
| | Affected choice of medical tests | 22% |
| | Altered diagnosis and treatment/management | 32% |
| | Resulted in important changes in care/alternative therapies/referral | 35% |

*(continued)*

| Figure 8.3 | Report of Evidence of Library Outcomes from the Literature (Continued) |
|---|---|
| Copies of | interesting tables Table 3: Library customer's clinical decision making. <br><br> **Table 3** <br> Impact of information on clinical decision-making (library group) <br><br> The information would (or did) help in...    Frequency of mention (percentage of response) N = 486*) <br><br> one or more category of clinical decision-making   79% <br> recognition of abnormal or normal condition   36% <br> identification/evaluation of alternative therapies   35% <br> improved quality of life for patient and/or family   33% <br> confirmation of proposed therapy   32% <br> differential diagnosis   31% <br> minimization of risks of treatment   27% <br> audit or standards of care   26% <br> revision of treatment plan   25% <br> choice of diagnostic test   22% <br> legal or ethical issues   16% <br><br> **89% (321/361) of clinicians indicated that at least one category of clinical decision-making would be affected. 125 respondents were in clinically related posts but had no direct patient responsibilities.** <br><br> * Total number of responses = 486 (of which 361 were clinicians). % response is calculated on the response for the category. <br><br> (Used with permission from Urquhart, C. J., and J. B. Hepworth. 1996. "Comparing and Using Assessments of the Value of Information to Clinical Decision-Making." *Bulletin of the Medical Library Association* 84, no. 4: 482–489. |
| Conclusions | The value of the information provided by the library can be identified and categorized. The results suggest library services could be better targeted to customers' changing needs. The authors have developed a tool kit to help libraries evaluate these changes. Health information professionals need to understand the changes and dilemmas in patient care delivery. They then can understand what competencies they need to develop to meet the information needs of the health-care staff. |
| Relevance to our situation | After reading this article we will attempt to locate the tool kit mentioned. We will attempt to use it to survey our customers. If any changes in information use are noted, we will try to adjust our services. <br> One change in practice already noted in our reference questions is that customers are asking more for articles that meet the criteria for evidence-based medicine. We will discuss taking courses in this area to improve our skills. |

Combining this idea of reporting the literature with an alternative way of reporting results, described in Chapter 11, two other examples of reporting these published outcomes can be found, on the Web, by the Public Library Association and the Medical Library Association. Both programs use a PowerPoint presentation to report the facts and their meanings. Developed by Keith Lance and the Public Library Association, and called *Making It Count @ your library* ®, the PLA slide show is on the Web (Lance, accessed: 2006). The MLA presentation and its bibliography are on the Web and are also available on the CD-ROM in the Chapter 8 folder. Called *Myths and Truths about Library Services*, the presentation describes studies, gives the facts, and interprets their meaning (Bandy, et al., 2007).

## STUDIES OF COST OUTCOMES

In their book *Special Libraries: Increasing the Information Edge*, Griffiths and King take the approach that professionals have a communication pattern and libraries play a role in supporting that communication. They state that "professionals who use information extensively and effectively are more successful than those who do not. Furthermore, substantially greater benefits are achieved from information provided through organization libraries" (Griffiths and King, 1993: 1). From the studies they review, they document that the professionals who make effective use of information and libraries have an "information edge" when it comes to individual, corporate, or societal success.

In their chapter, "Impact of Special Library Services," they report impact in terms of dollars. First they looked at how much time a professional spent acquiring material from a library and reading it (annually: 118.6 hours). The authors postulate that a professional's time is a scarce resource and professionals choose to spend it in ways that are most beneficial to themselves and their organizations. Then you could conclude that what professionals spend their time on has a value equal to the hours they spend doing it. Therefore, acquiring and reading professional literature has a value of 118.6 hours annually. Multiply that by their salary, as demonstrated in Figure 8.4 and you can say that, with 2006 dollars, the professional assigns a monetary value of $6,517 to the acquiring and reading of professional literature. The authors state that the average cost of a library per professional is between $556 and $1,390 in 2006 dollars. (There is a 39% inflation factor between the 1993 and 2006 figures.) As demonstrated in the figure, this is a value ratio of between 11.72 to 1 and 4.68 to 1. The authors state, "Clearly, the value [of the service], expressed this way, far exceeds the total cost of the library."

| | 1993 | 2006 |
|---|---|---|
| Figure 8.4    The Value Professionals Give to Information Provided by a Library Service Compared with the Cost of That Service Per Professional | | |
| Time spent acquiring and reading information from a library annually | 118.5 hours | 118.5 hours |
| Hourly wage including fringe benefits | $40 | $55 |
| Monetary value the professional gives to information provided by a library service | $4,740 | $6,517 |
| Cost of a library per professional: least expensive | $400 | $556 |
| Cost of a library per professional: most expensive | $1,000 | $1,390 |
| Ratio: the value assigned by professionals to acquiring and reading literature to the cost of a library service: least expensive | 11.85 : 1 | 11.72 : 1 |
| Ratio: the value assigned by professionals to acquiring and reading literature to the cost of a library service: most expensive | 4.74 : 1 | 4.68 : 1 |
| (Adapted from information in Griffiths and King, 1993) | | |

In the second part of the chapter, the authors state that they believe that the strongest evidence of the usefulness or worth of a library service is in the examination of what it would cost professionals to acquire library-provided information if there were no library. They calculate the value of 13 specific services in terms of the amount of time and money a user would have to expend to obtain the same results as using a library service. For example, to obtain a document without access to interlibrary loan (ILL) services, a professional would have to spend 2.3 hours of his/her time, 0.7 hours of someone else's time, and $32 for various charges. In 1993 dollars, this added up to $138 per use compared with $28.32 if they were to use a library service ($18.79 library costs plus $9.53 for the user's costs).

Matthews calls this a "relative" value, the value of a product if the service did not exist (Matthews, 2002: 93). So if your ILL service processed 1,500 requests for your users this year, the relative value of this service at $138 per use would be $207,000. Since the library's actual interlibrary loan costs are $28,185 and the user costs are $14,295 (total: $42,480), it would cost the institution 20 times as much to not have this library service, and you can say that you saved the institution $164,520. This would be a demonstration of a cost-benefit analysis.

Using the 1993 value of service figures found in Griffiths and King's research and adjusting them for inflation for 2006, you can construct a table showing how much return your corporation received for its investment in the library. Figure 8.5 is an adaptation of Matthews's table, with specific numbers for the author's library for 1993 and 2006. The differences reflect changes in service levels due to the advent of e-journals and end-user searching. The numbers in the traditional services went down, while new ones have gone up. In this example, it was decided to value the retrieval of an e-journal article by a professional in the same way as a photocopied article from a print collection was. This and the advent of end-user searching almost double the return on investment. At the same time, this table does not reflect all services, such as quick reference and library educational programs. If you are having trouble getting through to your administrator in relation to communicating your value, this kind of tactic might work. A return on an investment of 8.4:1 is impressive. Providing services valued at over $4 million dollars on a $500,000 budget could give you some credibility.

While these numbers may seem amazing, the studies collated by Griffiths and King were taken from large professional studies. As they state in their final sentence, "It seems abundantly clear that library services pay for themselves by orders of magnitude" (Griffith and King, 1993: 174).

**Figure 8.5 The Value Professionals Give to Information Provided by a Library Service, Multiplied by the Number of Services, Compared with the Total Library Budget**

| Selected library services: National Jewish Medical and Research Center Tucker Medical Library | Value per service 1993 | Number of library services 1993 | Total value of library service 1993 dollars | Value per service 2006 (inflation increase 39%) | Number of library services 2006 | Total value of library service 2006 dollars |
|---|---|---|---|---|---|---|
| Interlibrary loans borrowed for a client | $143 | 2,392 | $342,056 | $199 | 368 | $73,147 |
| Item circulated to a client from the collection | $51 | 1,128 | $57,528 | $72 | 609 | $43,587 |
| Reference questions answered for clients | $45 | 350 | $15,750 | $63 | 274 | $17,139 |
| Use of online databases by the client | $17 | —- | —- | $23 | 49,113 | $1,138,012 |
| Photocopies made by clients or PDFs downloaded | $29 | 22,000 | $638,000 | $41 | 71,821 | $2,922,059 |
| Total value for library services | | | $1,053,334 | | | $4,193,944 |
| | | | 1993 dollars | | | 2006 dollars |
| Total library budget | | | $225,000 | | | $500,000 |
| Return on investment | | 4.6 : 1 | | | 8.4 : 1 | |

(Table format adapted from Matthews, 2002)

"Logic models establish the relationship between an intervention and desired results by describing the theory and assumptions underlying the provision of services. They may also guide the selection of data for monitoring and improving services. A basic logic model identifies the activities; resources or inputs; and output, outcome, and impact measures associated with an intervention or program" (Abels, et al., 2004: 50).

# THE LOGIC MODEL

To use another baseball analogy, the W. K. Kellogg Foundation guide cites Yogi Berra, the oft-quoted Yankee's manager: "If you don't know where you are going, how are you going to get there?" The Logic Model allows you to figure out where you are going by:

- Clarifing your program goals by listing the broadest first and working backward from there
- Working more effectively with your team by writing down and discussing not only the broad goals but also the specific program details that will lead to them
- Promoting success by team discussion of assumptions and beliefs that are core to the project and often not stated
- Allowing one system to be used for program design, planning, implementation, and evaluation
- Pointing out places in the process where evaluation can occur so that you not only adjust your plans but also report successes or problems

This model, while not called strategic planning, can be used in any planning effort you may choose to start including strategic planning. The ideas of strategic planning are briefly covered in Chapter 9. A logic model is a graphical representation of the relationship among resources, activities, and results, or, as they are also called, inputs, processes, outputs, and outcomes. These are the same measures discussed in Chapter 3. A logic model can be described and discussed when talking about planning, program management, evaluation, or communication and will allow you to project the results or outcomes that are expected. This systematic way of organizing your thoughts about a program, either in the planning stage or in the evaluation stage, gives you the framework for planning and evaluation to use throughout a project. It can be applied to an existing system as an evaluation tool. The basic frame of a logic model is demonstrated in Figure 8.6. When you actually start to write a model, you start at the end and move to the front. You plan backward and implement forward. At any point in your process you can evaluate what is happening.

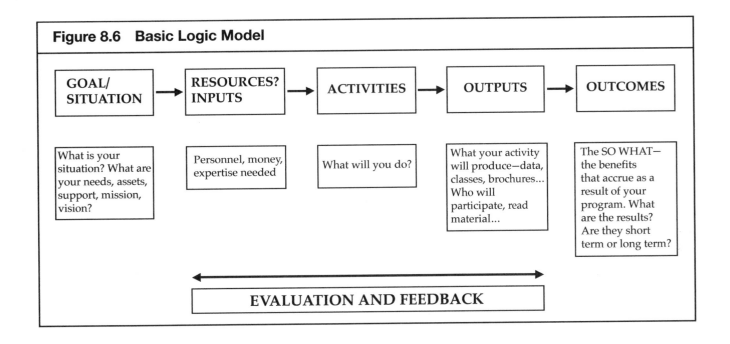

Figure 8.6  Basic Logic Model

| GOAL/ SITUATION | RESOURCES? INPUTS | ACTIVITIES | OUTPUTS | OUTCOMES |
|---|---|---|---|---|
| What is your situation? What are your needs, assets, support, mission, vision? | Personnel, money, expertise needed | What will you do? | What your activity will produce—data, classes, brochures... Who will participate, read material... | The SO WHAT— the benefits that accrue as a result of your program. What are the results? Are they short term or long term? |

**EVALUATION AND FEEDBACK**

The University of Wisconsin-Extension Program Web-based course discusses a more complicated but thorough model, which can be found on its Web site. At the beginning of the model, the course recommends discussing your "situation"—your needs, problems, and stakeholders. Then go over your "priorities," your mission, values, and environment and your intended outcomes. The course also emphasizes that outcomes are short term, medium term, and long term, and these are described and evaluated differently. It recommend that you analyze assumptions and external factors. Evaluation can be done at any point in their model. There are many free resources on the Internet that are based on the W. K. Kellogg Foundation's Logic Model. It is recommended that you take the time before you start to review these resources, especially the University of Wisconsin-Extension Program Web-based course. All expand on the explanations given here and include usable work sheets.

To begin to understand how you can "show" an outcome of your library service, start small. Choose one program and fill out a logic model for that program. Then do another and another. Then perhaps merge them into a plan for your library service that includes outcomes for the whole library. But, do not try to take care of the whole library at once. It would be overwhelming.

A logic model should be used when first starting a project, but it can be applied to a project that already exists. If you are just starting your project, here are the steps recommended by the three resources listed in the previous margin notes, Web Resources on Outcomes and Impact Methods.

## A. DETERMINE THE PROBLEM TO BE SOLVED

### Step 1: Determine the purpose of your logic model.

Who is asking you to do the model? Is it required by your administration? Are you applying for a grant that requires one? Have you undertaken a planning project? As the manager of the library, have you decided to evaluate one of your programs? This review will help you decide whom to involve and what your timeline is.

### Step 2: Involve others.

Gather a team. The logic model is based on the idea that everything is related and part of a system. To look at the system as a whole, all people who are involved in the system need to be involved in defining the model. Look for staff members who are performing the tasks, stakeholders who are funding the project, and even end users who might benefit from the project. Chapter 11 has a section on working with teams.

### Step 3: Decide on the scope of the logic model.

The purpose of developing the model will guide how much detail is in the model. How will the model be used and by whom? Decide with the team how much detail is needed. For example, if you are planning a PDCA (plan-do-check-act) evaluation of the technical system of sending overdue notices, the logic model might take up only a few lines, where as a planning and evaluation project of a reference service might be several pages long.

### Step 4: Understand the problem and the environment surrounding it and set priorities.

You and your team need to take the time to carefully define the problem and its environment. Make a statement that fully and succinctly describes the situation. This situation statement will guide the rest of the development of the model. To start, you could do some brainstorming with a SWOT analysis—analyze the strengths, weaknesses, opportunities, and threats that surround the problem. Using this technique is described in Chapter 12, and there is an example on the CD-ROM in the Chapter 12 folder. As you write the situation statement, remember that it is about the problem itself. It is not about how you are going to solve the problem and it is not about stating a customer need as a problem. Your statement should be short and succinct, perhaps 400–500 words, and avoid using jargon. Have it reviewed by others

---

**On the CD-ROM: SWOT Analysis**

Found in the Chapter 12 folder: SWOT Analysis Med Lib.doc and SWOT Analysis - NNLM.doc

A SWOT (strengths, weaknesses, opportunities, and threats) analysis is a type of environmental scan. It is an analysis and evaluation of key internal and external conditions to develop an understanding of the current environment that may affect how the organization functions. An explanation and two examples are on the CD-ROM.

for clarity. According to University of Wisconsin-Extension, your statement should cover these points:

- Describe the problem.
- Ask why it is a problem and what causes it.
- State whose problem it is, which stakeholders are involved, and in what way.
- Mention who has a stake in the problem or who cares about it.
- Mention existing research or studies you have found that describe or address the problem.

After you have written your statement, you can set some priorities. This would involve talking with your team and various stakeholders to determine that the stated problem is one you want to solve. Maybe you may have found it is *not* something you want to tackle at this time. Does solving the problem align with your library and/or institutional mission and values? Do you have the expertise and/or resources to work on this problem? What has already been done? Who outside your team can help you set priorities? From these priorities, you will be able to identify the desired outcomes of a program.

### Step 5: Find out what else has been done to solve this problem by doing a literature search.

Discuss with the team any solutions that may have been found and decide if they can be applied to your situation. Report back what has been found.

### B. START WRITING YOUR LOGIC MODEL
### Step 6: Write your outcomes.

Start at the end and move backward. Plan backward, implement forward. Start by reading your statement and discussing what outcomes you want to see happen. These are not activities or outputs but, as defined by the IMLS, actual benefits to people: specifically, achievements or changes in skill, knowledge, attitude, behavior, condition, or life status.

The University of Wisconsin-Extension Web-based course lists four attributes of outcomes and provides a worksheet on its Web site. Are the desired outcomes:

- Important? Does the end outcome represent important change or improvement valued by participant and key stakeholders?

- Reasonable? Are the outcomes connected in logical order and connected to the program activities?
- Realistic? Is the outcome achievable given local resources?
- Without any possible negative effects? What else might happen?

Outcomes can be divided into short-term, medium-term, and long-term. They are interdependent and form an ongoing chain. Figure 8.7 shows some of the personal attributes that a program may affect and thereby produce a change in the lives of people or organizations or communities. How do libraries and librarians help? The table compares two sources of ideas for categorizing outcomes.

| Figure 8.7  Types of Outcomes from Different Sources | | | |
| --- | --- | --- | --- |
| Durrance (Durrance, et al., 2005) (The IMLS definition is in bold) | University of Wisconsin-Extension Web-Based Course (University of Wisconsin-Extension, accessed: 2006a) | | |
| The changes in peoples lives: | Short-term outcomes: Changes in learning | Medium-term outcomes: Changes in action | Long-term outcomes: Changes in conditions |
| **Knowledge** gains (for example, wide ranging, individually focused, including knowledge of the community, knowledge needed to pass the GED, and so forth) | Knowledge | Practice | Economic |
| Learning gains (for example, increased interest in learning, active participation in learning, **achievement**, and so forth) | | | |
| **Skill** levels (for example, increased technological literacy, communication and social skills, and so forth) | Skills | Decision making | |
| Status changes or changes in **condition** (for example, decided to return to school, got a job, become a citizen, increased participation as a citizen) | Aspirations | Policies | Environmental |
| Progress toward a goal | Motivations | | |
| **Attitudes** (for example, negative to positive) | Attitudes | | |
| Social networks (for example, increased social and community connections) | Opinions | Social Action | Civic |
| Personal efficacy (for example, **behavior**, self-esteem, confidence building, a changed outlook on life, future prospects or **life status**, feelings of accomplishment and hope) | Awareness | Behavior | Social |
| Increased access to information | | | |
| Time (for example, time saved) | | | |

### Step 7: Work back along the Logic Model.

*Outputs:*

Now that you have your outcomes written down, you can decide what outputs might cause those outcomes to happen. What levels of programs and services can the library provide to change a person's life or work in the important, specific ways identified by your team? Here some brainstorming might be good, with no idea considered too outlandish. These could be traditional services or new ones. The program outlined below is a technological program intended to increase attendance at library educational programs. One of the major outputs would be to show an increase in library customers taking courses.

*Activities:*

What activities will be necessary to achieve the outputs? You have already discussed some ideas about programs that will produce outputs. Now you need to determine what activities will accomplish these outputs. Activities are the program elements, such as activities to promote the use of the new technology. In this column you would include plans for promotion of the program or purchase of equipment.

*Resources:*

What resources will be needed to carry out the activities? The major resource would be the money to buy the equipment and the staff time involved to set it up, as well as administrative support.

In the example below, a logic model is developed to plan, communicate, and evaluate the purchase of a portable WiFi (wireless fidelity) computer classroom. Figure 8.10 below demonstrates a logic model that is filled out using the plans from the project. First the outcomes were written, and then the outputs, activities, and resources in the front of the model were filled in.

### C. PLAN THE EVALUATION

Use the various sections of the Logic Model to plan an evaluation of various parts of the program. The framework you have developed to carry out your program will help you find the points in the program to evaluate. As you start your evaluation plan, as indicated in steps 8–14, fill out the Evaluation Plan Worksheet as you go along. Figure 8.8 shows a worksheet where you can relate the various steps in a flow from the activity being done to achieve an outcome to the people involved, to the measurable indicators, to the number you expect to achieve to the methodology of collecting the data and finally to the analysis methods. Figure 8.10 below shows the work sheet filled out using the example. The Evaluation Plan Work Sheet shown in Figure 8.8 is just one format. The University of Wisconsin-Extension Web-based course (accessed 2006a) has a complementary evaluation plan worksheet in Module 1, Section 7, page 19: "Using Logic Models in Evaluation: Indicators and Measures." You could develop your own worksheet to combine parts of each.

**Figure 8.8   Evaluation Plan Work Sheet 1**

| Step 7 | Step 8 | Step 11 | Step 11 | Step 12 | Step 12 | Step 14 |
|--------|--------|---------|---------|---------|---------|---------|
| Activity | Affects whom | Indicator | Target | Data source or methodology | Data collection frequency | Data analysis methods |
| What is done to achieve outcome | People involved in or influenced by activity | Measurable result of activity | Specific desired result | Origin of indicator measurements | Date, time, and intervals | Organize, examine, learn from the data. |

(From Barnes, Blake, and Kelly, accessed: 2006. Used with permission. Available on the CD-ROM in the Chapter 8 folder.)

As indicated in Figure 8.5, you can see that you can evaluate at any point. You can evaluate during the situation statement development (Step 4) and do a needs assessment, as described in Chapter 4. You could do a process evaluation, as described in Chapter 5, and look at the activities to see if they are performing well. You can evaluate the short-term outcomes by surveying the people using the program, as demonstrated in Durrance's work.

By building the Logic Model first, you will have a well-designed program that lends itself to evaluation. You will be able to see the ideal point in time when an evaluation can be carried out. The model gives you a clear picture of what your program is intended to achieve, and that achievement can be the basis of your evaluation.

### Step 8: Focus the evaluation.

The logic model clarifies the parts of the program and what each part plans to accomplish. This makes it easier to choose a part to focus on. Keep the evaluation simple: ask only what you need to know about that one part.

### Step 9: List the resources you have or will need.

Develop a management plan for the evaluation part of the logic model. This would include managing the staff involved, the time needed and any costs involved in doing the evaluation, for example, a budget. What tools do you have, and what expertise do you need? Do you have staff expertise in-house or access to expertise in another department? Often quality departments have statisticians who can help. Can you gain the expertise yourself, for example, by taking an Excel course? If you have to pay someone for development of the questions or analysis of the data, do you have the budget? If not, do a smaller evaluation.

Work with your team on a timeline in the form of a Gantt Chart and assign responsibilities using a responsibility chart. Both of these tools are described in Chapter 12. Draw up a budget using the resources listed under "Budget Planning" in Chapter 12 and on the CD-ROM in the Chapter 12 folder. Determine how much time and money you can spend. If your resources constrict the scope of your evaluation, explain this in your report.

### Step 10: Develop your question(s).

Which statement in the model are you planning to evaluate? Ask a few good questions, questions that are clear and to the point. You might not have the resources to ask a lot of questions, so be efficient with the ones you have. Remember to focus. Chapter 10 covers more principles of question writing.

If you are doing a process evaluation, you might ask:

- Who have been the customers of the program? Are they the ones we planned to target?
- What resources are you currently using? Do you need more?
- Is the program following the plan? If not, why not? Should there be adjustments in the model?

If you are doing an outcomes evaluation, you might ask:

- What difference does the program make to the users?
- Who has benefited the most?

- Has the user learned more about the subject because of the program?

## Step 11: Decide on your indicators.

What will indicate that the outcome (or process improvement) has been achieved? What measurement means the outcome happened? An indicator provides evidence that certain results have or have not been achieved. An indicator should be specific, observable, measurable, useful, practical, adequate, and in some cases, culturally appropriate. An indicator demonstrates a characteristic or measures a change. It gives you evidence that what you planned to happen did happen. It can also show the progress a program is making toward achieving a specified outcome. Indicators can come from any of the five senses. For example, if you have chosen observation as your methodology, the indicators will be a description of what you see or feel. An indicator can be quantitative (How many people attended a course?) or qualitative (The library customer said in the focus group that the course was the right length). Work hard on refining the indicators and their meaning and involve as many stakeholders in the process as you can. The University of Wisconsin-Extension Web-based course (accessed 2006a) has an excellent explanation of indicators in Module 1, Section 7: "Using Logic Models in Evaluation: Indicators and Measures," which includes helpful work sheets.

## Step 12: Determine which data collection method best suits the question.

Determine the source of the data, the method and instrumentation to collect the data, the sample necessary to use, and the timing of the collection. Data collection is covered in more detail in Chapter 10. You can also use the *Data Collection Methodologies Review* from the NNLM, as found on the CD-ROM in the Chapter 8 folder. Your data can be collected from various sources of information, such as existing information (documents, reports, records including photographs, and databases), people (participants or nonparticipants, staff, partners, administrators), or surveys and observations (using techniques such as observations, surveys, focus groups, interviews, or case studies).

## Step 13: Analyze the information.

Using tools and information from Chapters 10 and 12, analyze the results and make determinations and statements about the results. Depending on what type of evaluation you are doing, refer to other chapters in the book. Using charts and graphs, you and your team can look at the quantitative data collected and see what the results are. If you also did qualitative evaluation, you will have anecdotes to accompany your figures. Discuss the data as a group and come to a consensus about what the data mean.

### Step 14: Communicate your findings.

Determine a communication plan, including determining to whom to send the findings, when, and in what format. With the team, write reports to various stakeholders using the communication techniques and tools mentioned in Chapters 11 and 12. In many cases, evaluation within an institution is not a required function, but doing an evaluation and reporting your findings to your supervisor is a good way of discussing the library program in general and with a person who probably does not know much about how libraries operate.

# REAL-LIFE EVALUATION: THE LOGIC MODEL

**Idea: Have a portable WiFi computer classroom to take library instruction to the user's workplace.**

*A. Determine What the Problem to Be Solved Is.*

*Step 1: Determine the purpose of your Logic Model.*

The first purpose of using the Logic Model is to see if it is feasible to plan for a portable WiFi computer classroom. If feasible, it will be used to plan this new program for the library and consider if it is the best way to use the funds available. The Logic Model will also be used as a template to discuss with and justify to the supervisor spending the available funds. If the plan is carried out, it will be used for evaluation.

*Step 2: Involve others.*

Others in the institution may want to use this portable classroom. To assist with the planning, a team is formed that includes personnel from education, marketing and public affairs as well as information systems. Library staff members include the manager and the library educator.

*Step 3: Decide on the scope of the Logic Model.*

The purpose of using the Logic Model is for planning, communication and evaluation. The planning will allow the team to see the steps required and permissions necessary to accomplish the task and set the stage for evaluation and communication.

*Step 4: Understand the problem and the environment surrounding it and set priorities.*

The SWOT analysis is done:

### Figure 8.9  Sample SWOT Analysis

| | |
|---|---|
| *Strengths* (internal; positive statements about your library):<br>Allow more opportunity for library education for customers.<br>Give the library a larger technological presence.<br>Get the library out of its space. | *Opportunities* (external; services you are not providing perhaps discovered in a needs assessment):<br>Connect the library to customers in their work setting.<br>Customize educational programs for each user group. |
| *Weaknesses* (internal; what is lacking in your library):<br>It is hard to get attendance at regularly scheduled education courses, owing to the work schedules of the customers.<br>It may be too technical and difficult for the library staff to manage the technology.<br>It may become technologically obsolete too soon. | *Threats* (external; adverse factors in the environment):<br>There may be another, more appropriate department to run such a service.<br>Information Systems Department may not support the idea or the extra work required on their part. |

*Situation Statement:*

Library customers have a hard time attending library education courses, owing to the fixed schedule. Library courses may not be specific to their needs. The institution has a fixed computer classroom that is not very near work sites. Since the scheduled classes are open to all levels of customers, it is hard to customize them.

It is a problem for the library system that not enough customers know how to use the resources available. It is a problem for the customers that they do not know what resources are available that might help them in their job.

The customers have a stake in the problem because when doing scientific study, they need to use the library resources. If they don't know how the new electronic products work and what is available, their job productivity may suffer. The library has an obligation to educate the user.

*Priorities:*

In the changing paradigm of library service, it is important to educate library customers on new services. This program is in line with the mission of the library to provide access to the most technologically advanced library resources and to educate customers in their use.

*Step 5: Find out what else has been done to solve this problem by doing a literature search.*

A search is done in various databases, and several articles are found on different levels describing this type of program and listing its successes. One personal comment talks about the lack of library staff support for the technology.

*B. Start Writing Your Logic Model.*

*Step 6: Write your outcomes.*

Outcomes on three levels are brainstormed by the team and written down. Not every type of outcome is developed. The example in Figure 8.9 shows the Logic Model developed. In the figure, it is fully filled in, but the outcomes are written first, followed by the activities and resources needed to achieve those outcomes.

*Step 7: Work backward along the Logic Model.*

The front part of the Logic Model, inputs, activities, and outputs, is filled out. See an example in Figure 8.9.

| Figure 8.10 Work Sheet for Steps 6 and 7 | | | | | |
|---|---|---|---|---|---|
| Resources | Activities | Outputs | Short-term outcomes Changes in learning: | Medium-term outcomes Changes in action: | Long-term outcomes Changes in conditions: |
| Administrative support Money: to purchase equipment Staff: to teach the classes IS Dept.: to support the computer equipment | Hold classes using the portable classroom. | Increase in number of students taking courses overall | Knowledge: With a portable classroom, more scientists and health-care workers attend library courses and learn more about the intricacies of searching the various library resources. | Practice: By learning to access library systems better, doctors will reduce the costs of patient care and scientists will apply for and get more grants. | Economic: Patient care costs will go down because health-care workers use information resources. Grant revenue will go up. |

*(continued)*

| Resources | Activities | Outputs | Short-term outcomes Changes in learning: | Medium-term outcomes Changes in action: | Long-term outcomes Changes in conditions: |
|---|---|---|---|---|---|
| Staff time, contacts in departments | Contact departments and divisions to offer the services of the portable classroom to teach about accessing e-journals efficiently. | Increase in number of different departments that attend courses | Skills: Increased attendance will allow more scientists and health-care workers to increase their skills in searching by learning about advanced techniques. | Decision making: By learning to access library systems better, doctors will maker better decisions resulting in better patient care. | Environmental: Customers will learn to use electronic information and use less paper. |
| Staff time | Promote efficient use of library-supplied journals and resources. | Library customers download more journal PDFs than before the class. | Awareness: Increased access to information: Scientists and health-care workers will use the available resources more often and be able to access them more frequently. | Behavior: Scientists and health-care workers will be able to use the new information technologies in their work. | Social: Better science will be practiced. Patients who are treated at our hospital will have an influence for the better in their home and community. |
| Staff time | Develop specialized subject courses for departmental classes. | Increase the number of classes given in departments. | Motivations: The courses brought to them with the portable classroom will increase the motivation of scientists and health-care workers to schedule and participate in library courses because of the bond established in the classroom setting when they are with their peers rather than a group of unrelated library users. Attitudes: The health-care worker will become more accepting of the new technologies of information seeking by seeing how easy it is to have a portable classroom. Learning: Scientists and health-care workers will be open to learning about library information resources. Time saved: Bringing the classroom to the workplace will save workers time. Scientists and health-care workers will become faster at locating information and save time. They will be more accepting of asking librarians difficult questions, thereby saving themselves time. | | |

**Figure 8.10    Work Sheet for Steps 6 and 7 (Continued)**

*C. Plan the Evaluation.*
*Step 8: Focus the evaluation.*
The evaluation will focus on the outcome:
The courses brought to them with the portable classroom will increase the motivation of scientists and healthcare workers to find and use library resources.
*Step 9: List the resources you have or need.*

- Staff time to develop a questionnaire with the team to be administered via e-mail or telephone interview
- Staff time to administer a questionnaire by someone other than the instructor
- List of students who took courses in the stationary classroom and those who took courses using the portable classroom in a department
- The e-mail questionnaire and interviews will go out one month and six months after several course offerings.

*Step 10: Develop question(s).*
Questions will focus on whether the students in each group downloaded more electronic journal PDFs and more resources after the course. Questions will also be asked about the class dynamics among the students and the atmosphere of the room.
*Step 11: Decide on your indicators.*
The questions will be measured by the differences in the statements between the two groups being asked the questions—those who took the course in the stationary classroom and those who used the portable classroom.
*Step 12: Determine which data collection method best suits the question.*
Telephone interviews will be used. Personal interviews would be too time consuming. The goal will be to sample between 7 and 12 students who had participated in each type of course in the last six months. The questions would be asked one month and six months after attendance at the course.
See an example of the Evaluation Plan Work Sheet partially filled out in Figure 8.10.

| Figure 8.11 | Evaluation Plan Work Sheet 2 | | | | | |
|---|---|---|---|---|---|---|
| Step 7 | Step 8 | Step 11 | Step 11 | Step 12 | Step 12 | Step 14 |
| Activity | Affects whom | Indicator | Target | Data source or methodology | Data collection frequency | Data analysis methods |
| What is done to achieve outcome | People involved in or influenced by activity | Measurable result of activity | Specific desired result | Origin of indicator measurements | Date, time, and intervals | Organize, examine, learn from the data. |
| Held classes in departments using the portable classroom on the subject of accessing electronic journals | Departmental personnel and researchers | Retrieved more electronic journal PDFs than students taking the course in the stationary classroom | Retrieved two PDFs a week more than before the class | E-mail survey and telephone interviews of the two groups of students | One week after the class and six months after the class | Enter data in spread-sheet and make charts. |

(From Barnes, Blake, and Kelly, accessed: 2006. Used with permission. Available on the CD-ROM in the Chapter 8 folder.)

*Step 13: Analyze the information.*
The quantitative answers about the use of the resources will be entered into a spreadsheet. The quantitative statements will be categorized and evaluated. The answers will be reviewed and evaluated by the team. Conclusions will be drawn from the difference in outcomes between the two methods.

*Step 14: Communicate your findings.*
A report will be written comparing the statements of the two groups. The Evaluation Report Template, as found in Chapter 11 and on the CD-ROM in the Chapter 11 folder can be used and modified to write the various reports. Reports will go to the librarian's supervisor, the team members from the other departments, and the library staff. Data might be used to advertise the service in a flyer or on the library Web site.

# WORKBOOK FOR DESCRIBING PUBLISHED STUDIES OF OUTCOME MEASUREMENT

**STEP 1: DEVELOP A WAY TO REVIEW THE LITERATURE.**

Subscribe to and read primary library journals.

Auto-alert from a database search

RSS feed from library blogs

Library listserv monitoring

Other

**STEP 2: TAKE THE TIME TO READ AND UNDERSTAND THE POINTS MADE BY THE AUTHOR(S).**

List the outcomes reported.

Study the conclusions

**STEP 3: TAKE THE TIME TO STUDY THE QUALITY OF THE EVIDENCE USING EVIDENCE-BASED LIBRARIANSHIP METHODS.**

This list prompts you in the attributes of good practice for survey design, as used by the authors as recommended by Weightman (2005). Also recommended is Weightman's more extensive study of identifying evidence. (Weightman, et al., accessed: 2006).

Good sampling technique: 100% or truly random sample?

Not a preselected sample potentially causing bias?

Anonymous responses?

Researchers are independent of the library to ensure objectivity and anonymity?

_____

_____

Survey asked about a current specific use of library services, or customers were asked to request information and assess its value? These methods avoid bias from "recall" errors? (See Chapter 10 for more on survey design.)

_____

_____

## STEP 4: UNDERSTAND THE ATTITUDE OF YOUR SUPERVISOR AND ADMINISTRATION ABOUT PUBLISHED RESEARCH REPORTS.

Discuss with them some of the principles of evidence-based research. Educate them on the value of EBL through these discussions. Write down some notes on the situation at your library.

_____

_____

## Step 5: Prepare a report form to report new evidence-based articles to your supervisor. Use the report form to consistently report new evidence.

This report form will be adjusted for local requirements. See Figure 8.3 for an example of the template filled out. The reader can use the template to fill out this form in the Word document found on the CD-ROM in the Chapter 8 folder. The template below is an example.

| Report of Evidence of Library Outcomes from the Recent Literature | |
| --- | --- |
| Journal citation | |
| Methodology | |
| Results | |
| Copies of interesting tables | |
| Conclusions | |
| Relevance to our situation | |

# WORKBOOK FOR COST OUTCOMES

## STEP 1: DEVELOP A WAY TO REVIEW THE LITERATURE TO FIND COST STUDIES.

Subscribe to and read primary library journals.

Auto-alert from a database search

RSS feed from library blogs

Library listserv monitoring

Other

## STEP 2: READ ARTICLES FROM THE LITERATURE ON COST-BENEFIT ANALYSIS AND RETURN ON INVESTMENT TO FULLY UNDERSTAND THESE METHODS.

Keep up-to-date on the controversies involved.

## Step 3: Take the time to read and understand the development of costs and value made by the author(s) in the cost studies you find.

List the ways the author has assigned a price, cost, or value to the activities being reviewed.

Develop spreadsheets that outline the costs involved to be sure you understand how the results were arrived at. These are often complicated.

## STEP 4: UNDERSTAND THE ATTITUDE OF YOUR SUPERVISOR AND ADMINISTRATION ABOUT COST-BENEFIT ANALYSIS AND RETURN ON INVESTMENT.

Discuss with them some of the principles of cost-benefit analysis and return on investment. Find out what their attitude and that of the institution is. Write down some notes on the situation at your library.

### Step 5. Prepare a report form to translate the costs from the articles you find using your own data.

Any report form will be adjusted for local requirements. Figure 8.5 is an example of the developed form. The reader can use the template to fill out this form in the Word document found on the CD-ROM in the Chapter 8 folder. The template below is an example.

| Report of Library Value and Cost from the Recent Literature | |
|---|---|
| Journal citation | |
| Methodology of study | |
| Sample of results | |
| Copies of interesting tables | |
| Conclusions | |
| Relevance to our situation | |

Table of Value and Cost Using the Data from the Local Library

| Selected library services: (a sample) | Value per service from study | Value per service for current year (inflation increase ## %) | Number of library services current year | Total value of library service current year dollars |
|---|---|---|---|---|
| Interlibrary loans borrowed for a client | | | | |
| Item circulated to a client from the collection | | | | |
| Reference questions answered for clients | | | | |
| Use of online databases by the client | | | | |
| Photocopies made by clients or PDFs downloaded | | | | |
| Total value for library services | | | | Value |
| | | | | |
| Total library budget | | | | Budget |
| Return on investment | | | | Ratio: Value / Budget to 1 |

# WORKBOOK FOR THE LOGIC MODEL

## A. DETERMINE THE PROBLEM TO BE SOLVED
### Step 1: Determine the purpose of your Logic Model.

Who is asking you to do the model?

_____

_____

Why are they asking you to do it? Why is it required?

_____

_____

Is evaluation of the program a major requirement?

_____

_____

Write a succinct statement of purpose to discuss with your team.

_____

_____

_____

### Step 2: Involve others.

Gather a team.

| Member name | Title | Extension | Reason to be on team /Skills |
|---|---|---|---|
|  |  |  |  |
|  |  |  |  |
|  |  |  |  |
|  |  |  |  |

### Step 3: Decide on the scope of the Logic Model.

How will the model be used and by whom?

_____

_____

With your team, discuss and write down the scope of the Logic Model.

_____

_____

### Step 4: Understand the problem and the environment surrounding it and set priorities.

With your team, develop a SWOT analysis. Use brainstorming techniques, if appropriate.

| Strengths (internal; positive statements about your library): | Weaknesses (internal; what is lacking in your library): |
|---|---|
| Opportunities (external; services you are not doing perhaps discovered in a needs assessment): | Threats (external; adverse factors in the environment): |

Outline the problem statement using these five parts:

Describe the problem.

_____

_____

Ask why it is a problem and what causes it.

_____

_____

State whose problem it is.

_____

_____

Mention who has a stake in the problem or who cares about it.

_____

_____

Mention existing research or studies you have found that describe or address the problem.

_____

_____

Write the problem statement, keeping it short (400–500 words) and succinct, and avoid using jargon.

_____

_____

_____

_____

Ask others outside the team to review it for clarity.

_____

_____

Set priorities.

_____

_____

Does solving this problem align with your library and/or institutional mission and values?

_____

_____

Do you have the expertise and/or resources to work on this problem?

_____

_____

### Step 5: Find out what else has been done to solve this problem by doing a literature search.

Have team members do a literature search and review the literature for possible solutions to the problem defined in the situation statement.

_____

_____

Report back on what has been found.

_____

_____

### B. Start Writing Your Logic Model
### Step 6: Write your outcomes. "Plan backward, Implement forward."

Using the table below, start with long-term outcomes and move to the short-term. See examples that have been filled out in Figures 8.7 and 8.8. (On the CD-ROM in the Chapter 8 folder, you will find a template for the full Logic Model in the Word document called NNLM-Logic-Model-Worksheet.doc)

| Short-term outcomes: | Medium-term outcomes: | Long-term outcomes: |
|---|---|---|
| Changes in learning | Changes in action | Changes in conditions |
| How would individuals who took advantage of your program have benefited in relation to achievements or changes in skill, knowledge, attitude, behavior, condition, or life status? | What would be a change in the actions of the system that would be caused by people participating in your program? | What would be the biggest impacts on the conditions of society or your institution of the changes in the systems that might have been caused by changes in individuals who took advantage of your program? |
|  |  |  |
|  |  |  |
|  |  |  |
|  |  |  |

## Step 7: Work back along the Logic Model.

Add three columns to the left of the table you have developed above and fill in the sections on outputs, activities, and resources. If possible, turn the table so it is in landscape view across the page. See sample work sheet below.

| Resources | Activities | Outputs | Short-term outcomes: | Medium-term outcomes: | Long-term outcomes: |
|---|---|---|---|---|---|
|  |  |  | Changes in learning | Changes in action | Changes in conditions |
| Personnel, money, expertise needed. | What will you do? | What your activity will produce—data, classes, brochures, and so forth. Who will participate, read material . . . | How would individuals who took advantage of your program have benefited in relation to achievements or changes in skill, knowledge, attitude, behavior, condition, or life status? | What would be a change in the actions of the system that would be caused by people participating in your program? | What would be the biggest impacts on the conditions of society or your institution of the changes in the systems that might have been caused by by changes in individuals who took advantage of your program? |
|  |  |  |  |  |  |
|  |  |  |  |  |  |

## C. PLAN THE EVALUATION

Fill out the Evaluation Plan Work Sheet as you work through Steps 8–14. As you do each step, come back to this form and fill in the information.

| Step 7 | Step 8 | Step 11 | Step 11 | Step 12 | Step 12 | Step 14 |
|---|---|---|---|---|---|---|
| Activity | Affects whom | Indicator | Target | Data source or methodology | Data collection frequency | Data analysis methods |
| What is done to achieve outcome | People involved in or influenced by activity | Measurable result of activity | Specific desired result | Origin of indicator measurements | Date, time, and intervals | Organize, examine, learn from the data |
|  |  |  |  |  |  |  |
|  |  |  |  |  |  |  |

(From Barnes, Blake, and Kelly, accessed: 2006. Used with permission. Available on the CD-ROM in the Chapter 8 folder.)

### Step 8: Focus the evaluation.

For what purpose will the evaluation be used? Keep the evaluation straightforward and simple: What do you need to know and who needs to know it.

_____

_____

Determine who the target of the evaluation is.

_____

_____

Are you going to evaluate the whole program or just part of it?

_____

_____

### Step 9: Determine the resources you have or need.

List the resources you need to carry out the project. Examples are filled in but can be changed. With the team, create a responsibility chart listing all the tasks that need to be done and who will be doing them. Which staff members have the time and expertise? (See Chapter 12 for more on responsibility charts and examples in Chapters 4 and 6.)

_____

_____

_____

Using the task list, create a timeline employing a Gantt chart. (See Chapter 12 for more on Gantt charts and examples in Chapters 4 and 6.)

_____

_____

_____

With some idea of how much time it will take, calculate a budget to see what the expenses will be. See Chapter 12 under "Budget Planning" for a list of the items that can be included in an evaluation project.

_____

_____

_____

## Step 10: Develop your question(s).

What do you want to know? What do you see in the model that will help you shape your question? Write down a number of questions to test and debate using the techniques found in Chapter 10.

Question 1:

_____

_____

_____

Question 2:

_____

_____

_____

Question 3:

_____

_____

_____

Question 4:

_____

_____

_____

Prioritize your questions. Do not try to do too much. Remember the focus. Who wants to know what?

_____

_____

_____

### Step 11: Decide on your indicators.

Develop your indicators using the Indicator Review Work Sheet and other resources available online in the University of Wisconsin-Extension Web-based course (accessed 2006a).

Questions to ask while filling out the form:

What will indicate that the outcome (or process) has been achieved?

_____

_____

What measurement means the outcome happened?

_____

_____

Rate each indicator with these qualities on the form.

Specific?

_____

Observable?

_____

Measurable?

_____

Useful?

_____

Practical?

_____

Adequate?

_____

Culturally appropriate?

_____

### Step 12: Determine which data collection method best suits the question and the indicators.

Before you start filling out the Evaluation Plan Work Sheet, evaluate the various methodologies to see what the strengths and weaknesses are of different data collection methods in your context. Look at the Data Collection Methodologies Review from the NNLM as a reference for this activity to identify issues in choosing a methodology. It can be found on the CD-ROM in the Chapter 8 folder in the document named NNLM-DataCollectionMethodsRev.doc.

| Methodology | Strengths | Weaknesses |
|---|---|---|
| Focus groups | | |
| Interviews | | |
| Observation | | |
| Surveys | | |
| Follow-up interviews | | |
| Other methods | | |

### Step 13: Analyze the information.

Using the descriptions in Chapter 10 and tools from Chapters 11 and 12, analyze the results and make determinations.

_____

_____

Using charts and graphs, you and your team can look at the quantitative data collected and see what the results are.

_____

_____

If you also did qualitative evaluation, you will have stories to accompany your anecdotes.

Discuss the data as a group and come to a consensus about what the data mean.

### Step 14: Communicate your findings.

With the team, write reports to various stakeholders using the communication techniques and tools mentioned in Chapters 11 and 12. Use the Evaluation Report Template, as found in Chapter 11 and on the CD-ROM in the Chapter 11 folder, as a guide. Note the alternative reporting method from the CoR study. Make a communication plan.

How will you announce your results to your users and other stakeholders? _____

_____

Who will compile the project reports? _____

_____

Who will write the executive summaries? _____

_____

How will you distribute the final information? List the reports
you plan to make: _____

_____

# REFERENCES

Abels, E. G., K. W. Cogdill, and L. Zach. 2004. "Identifying and Communicating the Contributions of Library and Information Services in Hospitals and Academic Health Sciences Centers." *Journal of the Medical Library Association*, 92, no. 1: 46–55.

Abels, E. G, K. W. Cogdill, and L. Zach. 2002. "The Contributions of Library and Information Services to Hospitals and Academic Health Sciences Centers: A Preliminary Taxonomy." *Journal of the Medical Library Association*, 90, no. 3: 276–284.

Association of Academic Health Sciences Libraries (AAHSL) Charting the Future Task Force. 2003. *Building on Success: Charting the Future of Knowledge Management within the Academic Health Center*. Seattle, WA: Association of Academic Health Sciences Libraries. Available: www.aahsl.org/document/CTFprint.pdf (accessed December 18, 2006).

Association of College and Research Libraries. "Task Force on Academic Library Outcomes Assessment Report." Association of College and Research Libraries (last updated June 27, 1998). Available: www.ala.org/ala/acrl/acrlpubs/whitepapers/taskforceacademic.htm (accessed July 7, 2006).

Association of Research Libraries. "ARL New Measures Initiatives." Association of Research Libraries. Available: www.arl.org/stats/newmeas/index.html (accessed July 10, 2006).

Association of Research Libraries New Measures Initiative. "Higher Education Outcomes (HEO) Research Review." Association of Research Libraries. Available: www.arl.org/stats/newmeas/outcomes/heo.html (accessed July 10, 2006).

Bandy, M., J. Garcia, S. Weldon, K. K. Wells, and the Colorado Council of Medical Librarians (CCML) Advocacy Committee. 2006. *Myths and TRUTHS about Library Services*. Chicago, IL: Medical Library Association. Available: www.mlanet.org/resources/vital/index.html (accessed January 15, 2007).

Barnes, S., M. Blake, and B. Kelly. "Measuring Your Impact: Using Evaluation to Demonstrate Value." National Network of Libraries of Medicine (last updated May 30, 2006). Available: http://nnlm.gov/evaluation/workshops/measuring_your_impact/impact-slides.ppt (accessed July 31, 2006).

Burroughs, C. M., and F. B. Wood. "Measuring the Difference: Guide to Planning and Evaluating Health Information Outreach." Seattle, WA, and Bethesda, MD: National Network of Libraries of Medicine Pacific Northwest Region. National Library of Medicine, 2000. Available: http://nnlm.gov/evaluation/guide/index.html (accessed June 6, 2006).

Colorado State Library Library Research Service, University of Denver College of Education Library and Information Science Program. "Counting on Results." Available: www.lrs.org/CoR.asp (accessed July 12, 2006).

Cuddy, T. M. 2005. "Value of Hospital Libraries: The Fuld Campus Study." *Journal of the Medical Library Association*, 93, no. 4: 446–449.

Dudden, R. F. 2003. "The Importance of Small Research Projects: The Impact of Full Text Online Journals on Journal Use Surveys." *National Network*, 27, no. 4: 5–7.

Dugan, R. E., and P. Hernon. 2002. "Outcomes Assessment: Not Synonymous with Inputs and Outputs." *Journal of Academic Librarianship*, 28, no. 6: 376–380.

Durrance, J. C., and K. E. Fisher. 2003. "Determining How Libraries and Librarians Help." Library Trends, 51, no. 4: 541–570.

Durrance, J. C., and K. E. Fisher. "Outcomes Toolkit 2.0." Ann Arbor, MI and Seattle, WA: University of Michigan and University of Washington (last updated 2002). Available: http://ibec.ischool.washington.edu/default1024.aspx?subCat=Outcome%20Toolkit&cat=Tools%20and%20Resources (accessed June 12, 2006).

Durrance, J. C., K. E. Fisher, and M. B. Hinton. 2005. *How Libraries and Librarians Help: A Guide to Identifying User-Centered Outcomes*. Chicago: American Library Association.

Durrance, J. C., and K. E. Pettigrew. 2001. "Toward Context-Centered Methods for Evaluating Public Library Networked Community Information Initiatives." *First Monday*, 6, no. 4: unpaged. Available: http://firstmonday.org/issues/issue6_4/durrance/index.html (accessed November 22, 2005).

Friedman, C. P. 2005. "'Smallball' Evaluation: A Prescription for Studying Community-Based Information Interventions." *Journal of the Medical Library Association*, 93, no. 4 Supplement: S43-S48.

"Government Performance Results Act of 1993." Available: www.whitehouse.gov/OMB/mgmt-gpra/gplaw2m.html (accessed July 12, 2006).

Griffiths, J-M., and D. W. King. 1993. *Special Libraries: Increasing the Information Edge*. Washington, DC: Special Libraries Association.

Hernon, P., and R. E. Dugan. 2002. *An Action Plan for Outcomes Assessment in Your Library*. Chicago: American Library Association.

Indiana University Purdue University Indianapolis. Institute for Museum and Library Services and E. Kryder-Reid. "Shaping Outcomes: Making a Difference in Museums and Libraries." Indiana University Purdue University Indianapolis. Institute for Museum and Library Services (last updated 2006). Available: www.shapingoutcomes.org/course/index.htm (accessed January 4, 2007).

Institute of Museum and Library Services. "Outcome-Based Evaluation Overview: New Directives, New Directions: Documenting Outcomes in IMLS Grants to Libraries and Museums." Institute of Museum and Library Services. Available: www.imls.gov/applicants/basics.shtm (accessed July 7, 2006).

Kyrillidou, M. 2002. "From Input and Output Measures to Quality and Outcome Measures, or, from the User in the Life of the Library to the Library in the Life of the User." *Journal of Academic Librarianship*, 28, no. 1/2: 42–46.

Lance, K. C. "Making it Count @ Your library." Public Library Association. Available: www.pla.org/ala/pla/plaissues/smartestcardcampaign/toolkit/lance.ppt (accessed August 12, 2006).

Marshall, J. G. 2000. "Determining Our Worth, Communicating Our Value." *Library Journal*, 125, no. 19: 28–30.

Marshall, J. G. 1993. *The Impact of the Special Library on Corporate Decision-Making*. Washington, DC: Special Libraries Association.

Marshall, J. G. 1992. "The Impact of the Hospital Library on Clinical Decision Making: The Rochester Study." *Bulletin of the Medical Library Association*, 80, no. 2: 169–178.

Matthews, J. R. 2004. *Measuring for Results: The Dimensions of Public Library Effectiveness*. Westport, CT: Libraries Unlimited.

Matthews, J. R. 2002. *The Bottom Line: Determining and Communicating the Value of the Special Library*. Westport, CT: Libraries Unlimited.

Nelson, S. S., and the Public Library Association. 2001. *The New Planning for Results: a Streamlined Approach*. Chicago: American Library Association.

Olney, C., S. Barnes, and the National Network of Libraries of Medicine (U.S.). Pacific Northwest Region. "Collecting and Analyzing Evaluation Data; Booklet 3." National Network of Libraries of Medicine Pacific Northwest Region; National Library of Medicine (last updated: June 12, 2006a). Available: http://nnlm.gov/evaluation/guide/index.html (accessed July 6, 2006).

Olney, C., S. Barnes, and the National Network of Libraries of Medicine (U.S.). Pacific Northwest Region. "Getting Started With Community-Based Outreach; Booklet 1." National Network of Libraries of Medicine Pacific Northwest Region; National Library of Medicine (last updated: June 12, 2006b). Available: http://nnlm.gov/evaluation/guide/index.html (accessed July 6, 2006).

Olney, C., S. Barnes, and National Network of Libraries of Medicine (U.S.). Pacific Northwest Region. "Including Evaluation in Outreach Project Planning: Booklet 2." National Network of Libraries of Medicine Pacific Northwest Region; National Library of Medicine (last updated June 12, 2006c). Available: http://nnlm.gov/evaluation/guide/index.html (accessed July 6, 2006).

Outreach Evaluation Resource Center (OERC). "National Network of Libraries of Medicine, Pacific Northwest Region and the National Library of Medicine" (last updated August 22, 2006). Available: http://nnlm.gov/evaluation/ (accessed August 30, 2006).

Poll, R. 2003. "Measuring Impact and Outcome of Libraries." *Performance Measurement & Metrics*, 4, no. 1: 2–12.

Portugal, F. H. 2000. *Valuating Information Intangibles: Measuring the Bottom Line Contribution of Librarians and Information Professionals*. Washington, DC: Special Libraries Association.

Rubin, R. J. 2006. *Demonstrating Results: Using Outcome Measurement in Your Library*. Chicago: American Library Association.

Rudd, P. D. 2000. "Documenting the Difference: Demonstrating the Value of Libraries through Outcome Measurement." In *Perspectives on Outcome Based Evaluation for Libraries and Museums*, edited by B. Sheppard. Washington, DC: Institute of Museum and Library Services. Available: www.imls.gov/pdf/pubobe.pdf

Special Libraries Association. 1987. *President's Task Force on the Value of the Information Professional: Special Libraries Association, 78th Annual Conference, Anaheim, California, June 10, 1987*. Revised edition. Washington, DC: Special Libraries Association.

"Standards for Hospital Libraries 2002 with 2004 revisions." 2005. National Network, 29, no. 3: 11–17.

Steffen, N. O., and K. C. Lance. 2002. "Who's Doing What: Outcome-Based Evaluation and Demographics in the Counting on Results Project." *Public Libraries*, 41, no. 5: 271–276, 278–279.

Steffen, N. O., K. C. Lance, and R. Logan. 2002. "Time to Tell the Whole Story: Outcome-Based Evaluation and the Counting on Results Project." *Public Libraries*, 41, no. 4: 222–228.

United Way of America. 1996. *Measuring Program Outcomes: A Practical Approach*. Alexandria, VA: United Way of America.

United Way of America. "Outcome Measurement Resource Network." United Way of America. Available: http://national.unitedway.org/outcomes/ (accessed July 12, 2006).

University of Wisconsin-Extension. "Enhancing Program Performance with Logic Models." University of Wisconsin (last updated 2002a). Available: www.uwex.edu/ces/lmcourse/ (accessed August 1, 2006).

University of Wisconsin-Extension. "Logic Model." University of Wisconsin (last updated 2002b). Available: www.uwex.edu/ces/pdande/evaluation/evallogicmodel.html (accessed August 1, 2006).

Urquhart, C. "Assessing Impact: Let Us Count the Ways?" (Last updated 2005). Available: www.cilip.org.uk/publications/updatemagazine/archive/archive2005/december/urquhartdecupdate.htm (accessed December 15, 2006).

Urquhart, C. 2004. "How Do I Measure the Impact of My Service? (Guideline) (Special Topic D)." In *Evidence-Based Practice for Information Professionals: A Handbook*, edited by A. Booth and A. Brice. London: Facet Publishing.

Urquhart, C. J, and J. B. Hepworth. 1996. "Comparing and Using Assessments of the Value of Information to Clinical Decision-Making." *Bulletin of the Medical Library Association*, 84, no. 4: 482–489.

Urquhart, C., and J. Hepworth. 1995. "The Value of Information Supplied to Clinicians by Health Libraries: Devising an Outcomes-Based Assessment of the Contribution of Libraries to Clinical Decision-Making." *Health Libraries Review*, 12, no. 3: 201–213.

Weightman, A. L. 2005. "The Value and Impact of Information Provided through Library Services for Patient Care: A Systematic Review." *Health Information and Libraries Journal*, 22, no. 1: 4–25.

Weightman, A. L., M. K. Mann, L. Sander, and R. L. Turley. *Health Evidence Bulletins Wales. A Systematic Approach to Identifying the Evidence. Project Methodology 5*. University of Wales College of Medicine (last updated January 2004). Available: http://hebw.cf.ac.uk/projectmethod/title.htm (accessed August 11, 2006).

W. K. Kellogg Foundation. "Evaluation Toolkit." W. K. Kellogg Foundation. Available: www.wkkf.org/default.aspx?tabid=75&CID=281&NID=61& LanguageID=0 (accessed July 12, 2006).

W. K. Kellogg Foundation. 2004. *Logic Model Development Guide*. Battle Creek, MI: W. K. Kellogg Foundation.

W. K. Kellogg Foundation. 1998. *W. K. Kellogg Foundation Evaluation Handbook*. Battle Creek, MI: W. K. Kellogg Foundation.

# 9 OTHER SYSTEMS FOR QUALITY IMPROVEMENT AND EVALUATION

The principles of evaluation, assessment, and quality described so far are often combined into a companywide system. The system is named, and all employees are required to follow its principles. There is usually a companywide training program to teach people the principles.

Many of these systems are based on the idea of a business guru who has written a best-selling book. As such they appear to be fads, and book and articles opposing them appear over time. The objective of these systems is to produce a quality product that makes a profit, or, in the case of not-for-profits, to give quality service and programs to their customers. Even if your company does not have such a plan, you can learn about quality management from most of these systems. The purpose of this chapter is to bring these to your attention for further study if you think they could be useful to your work on creating a culture of assessment.

The principles of total quality management (TQM) can be seen in these various management systems. The management practices of TQM are meant to exist throughout the organization to ensure that the organization consistently meets or exceeds customer expectations. The focus of TQM is on *processes*—their measurement and continuous improvement. As you read through these descriptions below, you will see where meeting customer expectations, process measurement, and continuous improvement are present in all these systems, whatever they are called.

How these systems relate to library management has been reviewed by James Wiser in his recent article, "Kaizen Meets Dewey: Applying the Principles of the Toyota Way in Your Library" (Wiser, 2005). He makes seven recommendations in which he matches many of the quality initiatives mentioned below to library administration:

- Base your management decisions on a long-term philosophy, even at the expense of short-term financial goals.
- Grow leaders who thoroughly understand the work, live the philosophy, and teach it to others; develop exceptional people and teams who follow your company's philosophy.

**Reference: Principles of TQM**

TQM originated with W. Edwards Deming's "quality points" and "quality work" done in Japan, as described in Chapter 5. The culture of assessment discussed in Chapter 2 has TQM principles at its core.

- Standardized tasks are the foundation of continuous improvement and employee empowerment.
- Use only reliable, thoroughly tested technology that serves your people.
- Respect your extended network of partners by challenging them and helping them improve.
- Make decisions slowly by consensus, thoroughly considering all options; implement decisions quickly.
- Become a learning organization through relentless reflection.

Library quality systems and philosophies also have evolved over time. The three systems briefly discussed here all have aspects of evaluation, assessment, and quality. All of them are being instituted at libraries across the country and around the world. They are mentioned here so you can follow them in the literature as you develop your culture of assessment.

# BUSINESS MANAGEMENT SYSTEMS

## BALANCED SCORECARD

### Definition:

The balanced scorecard is a strategic management system that gives managers a comprehensive, multidimensional view of the company's performance. It uses certain performance measures that have been chosen by management as indicators of success. It balances these measures by looking systematically at them through four perspectives: financial, customer, internal processes, and learning and growth.

### Use:

The balanced scorecard is used as a management system to ensure both quality and financial success.

### Comments:

The balanced scorecard (BSC) was created by Robert S. Kaplan and David Norton with an article in the *Harvard Business Review* in 1992 and later in several books and articles (1992, 1993, 1996, 1996, 2001, 2006). Previous performance measurement systems tended to focus on past financial performance and did not always link performance measures to areas for strategic improvement and quality. In Chapter 2 the discussion of models of organizational effectiveness is related to the BSC in that it encourages managers to look at more than one dimension of the company. The BSC looks at four perspectives:

- Financial perspective—how are we seen by stakeholders?
- Customer perspective—how do our customers see us?
- Internal business processes—how can we do things better?
- Innovation and learning—how can we continue to improve and look for innovation?

The balanced scorecard translates the mission and goals of an organization into a set of objectives, measures, and targets within the four perspectives. Long-term and short-term actions are balanced and tied to the strategic vision. The resulting reports provide feedback and allow adjustment of strategy if needed.

Several libraries have started using the BSC. The University of Virginia Library has an excellent Web page listing each of its metrics, their results, and a bibliography. To implement the BSC, they recommend studying Kaplan and Norton's work and then reading what is available in the library literature. James Self assesses some of its negative and positive features:

- Provides only a snapshot, not a three-dimensional picture
- Reveals problems, not solutions
- Encourages clarity and focus
- Brings innovation and recognition
- Institutionalizes assessment

The balanced scorecard allows for the development of a culture of assessment that can track progress toward strategic goals and recognize emerging issues. A set of library articles can be found in the references below (Claggett and Eklund, 2005; Cribb and Hogan, accessed: 2006; Poll, 2001; Self, 2003a, 2003b; Willis, 2004).

## FIVE SS

### Definition:

The Five Ss are the five Japanese words: *seiri, seiton, seiso, seiketsu,* and *shitsuke.* They stand for organization, orderliness, cleanliness, standardized cleanup, and discipline, respectively. The theory is that with a tidy, disciplined environment, you can see many of the things that need further attention.

> **Resources on the Web:
> Balanced Scorecard at the
> University of Virginia Library**
>
> Available: www.lib.
> virginia.edu/bsc/index.html
> (1) Last Updated: September
> 25, 2006. Last Accessed:
> October 10, 2006.

**Use:**

The Five Ss are seen as the stating point for other continuous improvement plans that may be implemented such as Lean (see below). It fosters efficiency, maintenance, and continuous improvement in all areas of the company.

**Comments:**

The Five Ss provide a foundation for other quality activities. It seems simple to clean up things and keep them clean. And cleaning up things is certainly a start for any kind of quality improvement. The changes required by implementing the Five Ss can be controversial and resisted, but most staff accept the idea when the workplace becomes more pleasant and fluid. The five Ss are:

- Seiri —organization = structurize, and sort out: Look for things that are not necessary and eliminate them or put them away. Put things in order. Keep what is needed and remove what is not needed
- Seiton—orderliness = straighten, and systematically arrange: Arrange the essential things that are left so that they can be quickly and easily found or reached and put away.
- Seiso—cleanliness = scrub, sanitize, make spic and span: Keep all tools and the environment clean.
- Seiketsu—standardize cleanup = systematize, standardize: Have cleaning and checking for untidy things be part of the routine. Maintain a pleasant and quality environment. Purity. Perpetual cleaning.
- Shitsuke—discipline = standardize, self-discipline: Constantly monitor the previous four steps and improve on them. Be committed.

**GEMBA VISITS**

**Definition:**

A Gemba visit is an actual visit to the place where the work is carried out. *Gemba* as a business term that comes from the Japanese word that means "the place where the truth is found"; it now means the place where the work is carried out. That could be a manufacturing floor, a place where products are developed (a lab and design table), or a place where services are provided (like the reference desk).

### Use:

This is an evaluation technique where you go to the place where the work is done and, in an unscripted way, use all your senses to gather and process data to understand problems and opportunities.

### Comments:

Many of the business management systems described here are large and cost many thousands of dollars to implement. Masaaki Imai, the quality expert who writes about Kaizen, has written *Gemba Kaizen: A Commonsense Low-Cost Approach to Management* (Imai, 1997). He believes that companies can achieve phenomenal business success by doing many "little things" exceedingly well. By observing while the product is being made or the service provided, the manager can improve processes or increase capabilities. By going to where the customer is, such as in the library at a circulation desk, the customer may be observed asking for various services. These needs may never be mentioned in a more structured setting of a focus group, interview, or survey. Gemba has been described as the place where value is added. Basically it encourages managers to go where the work is done and not just read reports.

## KAIZEN

### Definition:

Kaizen is said to come from two Japanese words: *kai* meaning "change," and *zen* meaning "for the better or good," and it is therefore synonymous with improvement. In management, it has come to mean continuous incremental improvement to eliminate waste in a process, and it involves everyone, managers and workers.

### Use:

Kaizen is used as the team-based comprehensive improvement system that focuses efforts on eliminating waste in work processes, reducing setup time, and elevating customer satisfaction. It is usually broadly deployed across the businesses, processes, and functional work units of a company.

### Comments:

Imai first publicized Kaizen in his 1986 book, *Kaizen: The Key to Japan's Competitive Success* (Imai, 1986). A contemporary of W. Edwards Deming, Imai wrote about how Kaizen worked in Japan. All levels of the company participate in Kaizen. It operates on the PDCA cycle as described in Chapter 5. It can also start with the 5 Ss. It operates on three principles:

- Look at process *and* results, not results only.
- See the big picture, not just the narrow view; use systemic thinking.
- Be nonjudgmental and nonblaming because blaming wastes time and energy.

James Wiser's article mentioned above goes over many of the Kaizen principles and relates them to library management.

## LEAN

### Definition:

Lean manufacturing, or often referred to as just "Lean," is a business philosophy that focuses on enhancing quality, cost, delivery, and people. Its techniques expose waste and make continuous improvement possible.

### Use:

Lean is used in companies as the overarching philosophy that drives many performance improvement techniques, the core of which is to eliminate waste. By eliminating waste, quality is improved and production time and cost are reduced.

### Comments:

As with many of these systems, the name was popularized by a book, in this case *Lean thinking: banish waste and create wealth in your corporation*, by James Womack and Daniel Jones (1996). In Lean, the seven types of waste are classified into three groups: people, (processing, waiting, motion), quantity (inventory, transportation, overproduction), and quality (defects in inspection).

While one source listed over 30 tools to use in implementing Lean, the main three are flow, pull, and mistake proofing. But before you can use these tools, first you must define value and map the steps in the production process. The Lean process follows these steps:

- Specify value: Define value from the customer's perspective and express it in terms of a specific product.
- Map the value stream: Map all of the steps, value added and nonvalue added, that bring a product or service to the customer.
- Establish flow: Chart the continuous movement of products, services, and information from end to end through the process. Use the PDCA method, covered in Chapter

<table>
<tr><td>

**Real-Life Evaluation: The Implementation of Lean**

In 2001, our organization adopted the Toyota Production System as its management method. All departments were challenged to identify their main products, flow, and processes. Medical library staff received instruction on lean principles and began to apply these to all library operations. Staff suggestions are the basis for improvements in our processes. Initially, the medical library reorganized space using 5Ss concepts. Value stream mapping was used to analyze key products and process flows, identify value-added components, eliminate waste, decrease turnaround time, and reduce errors or defects. High volume library processes including document delivery, new book processing, and electronic journal access were the first studied. Ongoing improvement strategies include developing standard work, measuring performance in all processes, maintaining shared agreements, and trying out improvement ideas in rapid plan, do, study, act (PDSA) cycles. To conclude, all staff participates in evaluating library processes, measuring cycle times and process steps through direct observation. Management gains are evaluated according to reductions in time, travel, and inventory required for any given process. Lean is a journey and our processes continue to evolve, change, and improve.

</td></tr>
</table>

5, to streamline processes so that products flow into production without interruption.

- Implement pull: Nothing is done upstream until the customer downstream signals the need. Product pull means that customer demand drives production and products are made "just-in-time," rather than "just-in-case."
- Work to perfection: Completely eliminate waste so that all activities create value for the customer. Also called mistake proofing, this is a system of continuous improvement. Once a process is so streamlined, mistakes cannot happen. (Adapted from "Establishing a Framework for Organizational Transformation in Healthcare: Performance Solutions," accessed: 2006).

When a company adopts Lean manufacturing, usually all departments take part, not just manufacturing. Adapting the Lean methods to a library situation can be challenging. If you find yourself part of an institution that has plans to adopt the Lean process, you might consider asking around on listservs for others who have been through the same process. Susan Schweinsberg Long, library director of the Medical Library at Virginia Mason Medical Center, in Seattle, Washington, reported her experiences with Lean at the 2006 MLA Annual Meeting. Her paper *"Using Lean Methodologies to Gain Efficiencies in High-volume Library Processes"* reported on her experiences with the corporate implementation of Lean and how the use of Lean tools, methodologies, and concepts enhanced the delivery of knowledge-based information in the organization. The abstract of her talk is reprinted with permission in the margin.

## LEARNING ORGANIZATION

### Definition:

A learning organization is capable of transforming itself through continuous adaptation and improvement by acquiring new knowledge, skills, or behaviors. Employees working in teams are encouraged to think critically and to take risks with new ideas in a supportive environment.

### Use:

A learning organization management philosophy encourages continuous individual learning in a management atmosphere where knowledge is shared and the culture supports learning. The new knowledge, skills, abilities, or attitudes are applied to improve product or service quality.

## Comments:

The idea of the learning organization comes from Peter Senge's book *The Fifth Discipline: The Art and Practice of the Learning Organization*, revised in 2006 (Senge, 2006). Senge also heads an organization, the Society for Organizational Learning (SoL), which has a Web site with extensive resources (Society for Organizational Learning, accessed: 2006). The main idea behind a learning organization is that we as individuals and groups of individuals (teams) shape the world we see. In our technical society, people often do not see the big picture or the system in which the product or service operates. Applying the theories of the learning organization encourages teams to share a common vision, question the views they hold, and learn how to adapt and improve, as individuals and groups. The learning organization encourages practicing these five main disciplines (list adapted from the SoL Web site):

- Personal Mastery: This discipline requires the individual to understand the relationship between their personal vision and aspiration and their personal reality. The theory is that there is always a tension between these, like a rubber band, that allows people to make better choices and achieve their vision.
- Mental Models: This is the discipline of reflection and inquiry skills. It encourages the individual to be aware of attitudes and perceptions that influence thought and interaction. Through continuous reflection and questioning, people become more capable in making decisions and taking actions. They make fewer leaps to counterproductive conclusions and assumptions.
- Shared Vision: This collective discipline focuses on the project or company's mutual purpose. The team develops shared images of the future they seek to create as well as commitment to shared principles and values.
- Team Learning: This discipline transforms teams using techniques of team building and skillful discussion so that with their collective thinking they can mobilize their energies and abilities. The team becomes greater than the sum of individual members' talents.
- Systems Thinking: This discipline teaches people to better understand interdependency and change and to deal more effectively with the forces that shape the consequences of our actions. Systems theory, which addresses the behavior of feedback and complexity is taught to help

people see how to change systems more effectively and how to act more in tune with the larger processes of the natural and economic world.

Some libraries have adapted the learning organization to their principles and teams. The ARL initiative for adopting a culture of assessment, as discussed in Chapter 2, incorporated this management philosophy. The work of Amos Lakos and Shelley Phipps discuss the principles as they apply to library management (Lakos and Phipps, 2004; Phipps, accessed: 2006; Phipps, 2001).

## SIX SIGMA

### Definition:

Six Sigma is a structured method for improving business processes using a method called DMAIC (define, measure, analyze, improve, and control). It is a management philosophy, a set of tools, and a methodology.

### Use:

Six Sigma is used as a business management system that maximizes quality through rigorous statistical approaches to problem solving designed to reduce variation and defects.

### Comments:

Started by Motorola and applied by General Electric, Six Sigma is credited with saving millions of dollars for these manufacturers. It is beginning to move into other industries, including health care and the service industries. As a management philosophy, it has become a broader business strategy for increasing process efficiency, raising customer satisfaction, protecting quality and improving the bottom line. Six Sigma requires serious management support and training in its techniques. There was one recent report in the United Kingdom about using Six Sigma in a library (Kumi and Morrow, 2006). The *iSix Sigma* Web site is a robust site with a dictionary and extensive content. It would be good a place to start for people interested in learning more about Six Sigma (www.isixsigma.com/).

## STRATEGIC PLANNING

### Definition:

Strategic planning determines where an organization is going over a period of time, a long-term plan to get there, how it is going to get there, and how it will know if it arrives.

---

**Definition: Six Sigma**

*Sigma* is the Greek letter or mathematical symbol that, in statistics, stands for "standard deviation." Six Sigma identifies and prevents defects in manufacturing and service-related processes using total quality tools to improve a process so that the tolerances for the process for failure are at or better than six standard deviations, a rate of 3.4 parts per million or 99.9997%. In many organizations, it simply means a measure of quality that strives for near perfection.

**Reference: Strategic planning in the library literature:**

Matthews, J. R. 2005. *Strategic Planning and Management for Lbrary Managers*. Westport, CT: Libraries Unlimited.
Three articles stand out as giving insight into the process of strategic planning in libraries:
Wilson, S. 2005. "Saint Paul's Strategic Plan." *Library Journal*, 130, no. 15: 34–37. Key points: overview of the steps taken to start a plan at a large public library; discussion of the political process; discussion of the process of writing of a request for proposal to have the plan written.
Ladwig, J. P. 2005. "Assess the State of Your Strategic Plan." *Library Administration and Management*, 19, no. 2: 90–93. Key point: discusses how to find out what you already have and use it to your advantage.
Kuntz, J. J., et al. 2003. "Staff-Driven Strategic Planning: Learning from the Past, Embracing the Future." *Journal of the Medical Library Association*, 91, no. 1: 79–83. Key points: short but detailed account of the process at the Health Science Center Libraries at the University of Florida; discusses the tangible products and intangible benefits of the process; lists lessons learned and recommendations for the next planning process.

## Use:

Strategic planning is used to guide an organization into the future by first articulating what that future might be (vision) and making plans to be part of that future.

## Comments:

Strategic decisions or issues within the plan follow these guidelines:

- Define the institution's relationship to its environment, including assumptions and risks. Usually this involves running a SWOT analysis. (See Chapter 12 and on the CD-ROM in the Chapter 12 folder.)
- Generally take the whole organization as the unit of analysis.
- Depend on information input from a number of different areas.
- Provide direction for, and constraints on, administrative and operational activities throughout the institution.

The most common type of strategic planning is goals based. It starts with a focus on the organization's mission, vision, and/or values statements and establishes goals that work toward the mission, strategies to achieve the goals, and actions (who will do what and by when) to accomplish the goals. The mission states why the organization has been created. The values statement attempts to articulate the basic philosophy of the organization. The vision statement describes the organization and presents a picture of its most desirable future. The strategic planning process itself develops a sense of ownership of the plan by communicating the organization's purpose, goals and objectives to the organization's stakeholders. The Logic Model as a planning tool is covered in Chapter 8. It can be used as a strategic planning model (Greenfield, et al., accessed: 2007). You will find a set of mission statements and a SWOT analysis on the CD-ROM in the Chapter 2 and 12 folders.

In the culture of assessment, described in Chapter 2, an essential part of that culture is to have a plan. Most evaluation projects assess how well a specific part of the library is doing in relation to the overall goals and mission of the library. There are some recent publications on strategic planning in the library literature. Many libraries have posted their strategic plans on their Web sites.

# LIBRARY AND INFORMATION SYSTEMS

## EVIDENCE-BASED LIBRARIANSHIP

### Definition:

Evidence-based librarianship (EBL) involves applying results from rigorous research studies to professional practice to improve the quality of services to customers. It encourages librarians to read, interpret, and apply their own professional research literature.

### Use:

Evidence-based librarianship is a professional focus that encourages librarians to look for existing research in their profession and apply it to the management of their library. It is used to support decision making.

### Comments:

First used as a term in 1997, evidence-based librarianship grew out of the influence of learning about evidence-based medicine (EBM). In medical libraries in the 1990s, librarians were being asked to help formulate questions and use effective literature searching to find evidence for medical issues. Librarians in the Research Section of the Medical Library Association suggested these EBM principles could be applied to our own profession. Some of these EBL principles are:

- Improving practice by using evidence
- Using a variety of types of evidence, both quantitative and qualitative
- Rigorous searching for evidence to support decision making
- Valuing diverse authoritative research
- Appreciating all forms of information seeking and knowledge development
- Supporting evidence-based standards and protocols
- Supporting hierarchical levels or grading of evidence (Eldredge, 2000b)

Koufogiannakis and Crumley list six areas or domains where librarians will have opportunities to formulate questions to improve their practice (Koufogiannakis and Crumley, 2002).

- Reference/Enquiries—providing service and access to information that meets the needs of library users

> "EBL seeks to improve library practice by utilizing the best-available evidence combined with a pragmatic perspective developed from working experiences in librarianship" (Eldredge, 2000a: 291).

- Education—finding teaching methods and strategies to educate users about library resources and how to improve their research skills
- Collections—building a high-quality collection of print and electronic materials that is useful, cost-effective, and meets the users' needs
- Management—managing people and resources within an organization
- Information Access and Retrieval—creating better systems and methods for information retrieval and access
- Marketing/Promotion—promoting the profession, the library, and its services to both users and nonusers

Those involved in this evaluation method started holding conferences in 2003 and there are several continuing education courses and papers on the subject (Eldredge, 2000a, 2000b; Booth, 2002; Brice, et al., accessed: 2006; Morrison, 2006).

## INFORMATION AUDIT

### Definition:

An information audit is a systematic evaluation of information use, resources, and flows. It verifies information use in reference to both people and existing documents to establish the extent to which that information use is contributing to an organization's objectives (Henczel, 2000).

### Use:

An information audit provides an inventory of the information requirements of a company or the entity being evaluated, details of the tasks and/or activities that are required to support the company, and a rating of the information's strategic importance. This enables budgets to be prioritized, and access to resources and services to be customized, and it supplies tangible evidence of the business processes that are supported by each resource that is provided (Henczel, 2000).

### Comments:

The library literature is mixed in its opinion about the information audit in libraries, but several special librarians see it as a new role for librarians. The terminology is mixed because in the past *information audit* was used interchangeably with needs assessment or surveys. With the recent interest in knowledge management, experts in this field point to the "emerging recognition that sound information management practices form a solid foundation on which successful knowledge management strategies can be developed. Good information management is seen as the essential prerequisite to knowledge management yet many organizations are developing knowledge management strategies based on technical systems that disregard the information resources and the people who create the knowledge" (Henczel, 2000: 216).

Susan Henczel introduces and explains a seven-stage information audit model in her 2000 article and expands on it in her book (Henczel, 2001). While this list in the margin looks like any evaluation method, in this process there are differences. For example, under 4—data evaluation—the research would be identifying the problems that exist in the information transfer process, such as information hoarding, biased distribution of resources, gaps in the provision of resources, information overload issues, or lack of traceability, to name a few. Henczel also has a list of what an information audit can provide:

**Did You Know: A Seven-Stage Information Audit Model**

1. Planning
2. Data collection
3. Data analysis
4. Data evaluation
5. Communicating recommendations
6. Implementing recommendations
7. The Information audit as a continuum (Henczel, 2000)

- An inventory of information requirements
- Details of the tasks and/or activities the information is required to support
- A rating of the information's strategic importance
- Ability to prioritize budgets
- Access to resources and services to be customized
- Tangible evidence of the business processes that are supported by each resource that is provided
- A measure (albeit a "snapshot") of how well processes are currently supported (where we are now)
- What needs to happen in the information environment to enable the organization to be functioning at its optimal level (where we want to be)
  (Henczel, 2000)

If this audit were institutionwide and the librarian, or a significant member of the team, in charge of it, it would certainly be a new role for the librarian. If it were a departmental project, it would be a type of evaluation project. You can use the idea of an audit to count any part of the library. Merle Colglazier, the librarian at Bon Secours St. Mary's Hospital in Richmond, Virginia, did an extensive audit of his job duties, calling it a "job audit." While not a traditional evaluation technique, he was able to show how many hours it took to do the job and was able to add staff. A copy of his audit is on the CD-ROM in the Chapter 9 folder.

The information audit looks at the intersection of information and knowledge, and it has a great potential to be a useful tool in today's knowledge environment and knowledge economy. Some interesting opinions can be found in the literature. (Orna, 1999; DiMattia and Blumenstein, 2000; Dobson, 2002; Botha and Boon, 2003; De Stricker, 2004; Jones and Burwell, 2004).

## KNOWLEDGE MANAGEMENT (KM)

### Definition:

Knowledge management is a process of systematically and actively managing the knowledge and experiences of individual workers and groups within an organization and transforming the knowledge, information, and intellectual assets into enduring value.

### Use:

Knowledge management is used to identify, create, represent, and distribute knowledge for reuse, awareness, and learning across the organization.

### Comments:

Knowledge management is a major business buzzword, but it applies to libraries because libraries are in the knowledge business. Should we be involved in this? Is it a new role we could assume, or is it a new word for a role we have already occupied? The Wikipedia entry has a large bibliography, and there is even a book called *The Idiot's Guide to Knowledge Management*! Since knowledge is now seen as an asset and new technologies appear to be able to harness it, it is suggested that it will be a more significant management effort in the future. Knowledge management, or KM, attempts to bring together various ideas such as:

- Understanding knowledge
- Knowledge creation
- Knowledge architecture
- Intellectual capital
- Capturing tacit knowledge
- Knowledge codification
- System testing and deployment
- Enabling technologies: knowledge bases, expert systems, and Wikis
- Knowledge transfer and knowledge sharing
- The learning organization
- Communities of practice
- Knowledge transfer in the e-world
- Data mining—knowing the unknown

- Knowledge management tools and knowledge portals
- Ethical and legal issues of knowledge management
- Managing knowledge workers in the knowledge economy

As mentioned in the previous section on information audit, before you can manage knowledge, you have to understand it and know what is there. KM is a big industry now, and librarians as a group need to be more aware of what is happening in it.

# INFORMATION RESOURCES FOR OTHER EVALUATION SYSTEMS

As with subjects in Chapter 11, "*Skills for Communicating in Evaluation Projects,*" and Chapter 12, "*Tools for Improvement and Evaluation,*" there are books, articles, and Internet resources on all of these topics. Referencing each one to Web resources is not useful because of the changing nature of the Internet. All of these systems can be found in the literature and in search engines. The Internet is rich in information on all of these systems. Your public library may subscribe to business databases accessible from home or work. Larger systems will have federated search engines to search across the databases. A large number of educational institutions, corporations, and government agencies have tutorials and excellent information pages on these management systems. Many of the sites listed below are commercial and sell products and consultation services. To get you to buy their products, they offer a great deal of information for free. They are recommended because of the comprehensiveness of their content and are placed in order by most useful. No endorsement of their products is intended.

- *Mindtools.com* (www.mindtools.com/): This site lists many of these management tools and more under the headings of "Problem Solving" and "Decision Making." As a comprehensive management site, the articles on these tools are of good quality. There are more business topics covered on this site than just quality issues.
- *Syque Quality Toolbook* (http://syque.com/quality_tools/index.htm): This site is what the author, David Straker, calls a "knowledge-sharing site." Straker has put on the Web his out-of-print book *A Toolbook for Quality Im-*

*provement and Problem Solving*, as well as many other quality resources. His site is well organized, with information, illustrations, and step-by-step instructions.

- *The American Society for Quality* (www.asq.org/index.html): This society has a section called "Learn about Quality." The business systems are under: Organization-Wide Approaches—models and methods for getting your people on board and managing change.
- *Free Management Library* (www.managementhelp.org/): Put together by Authenticity Consulting, LLC, this site is being redesigned to become even more useful. There are many management topics mentioned and basic evaluation strategies. The language is written in plain English without a lot of management jargon.
- *Wikipedia* (http://en.wikipedia.org/): While sometimes the quality of the content of this free online encyclopedia is controversial, some of its entries are quite extensive with references and Web links to more extensive sites.

# REFERENCES

Booth, A. 2002. "From EBM to EBL: Two Steps Forward or One Step Back?" *Medical Reference Services Quarterly*, 21, no. 3: 51–64.

Botha, H., and J. A. Boon. 2003. "The Information Audit: Principles and Guidelines." *Libri*, 53, no. 1: 23–38.

Brice, A., N. Bexon, and A. Booth. "Evidence-Based Librarianship: A Case Study in the Social Sciences." World Library and Information Congress: 71st IFLA General Conference and Council, August 14–18, 2005, Oslo, Norway (last updated June 13, 2005). Available: www.ifla.org/IV/ifla71/papers/111e-Brice_Booth_Bexon.pdf (accessed October 10, 2006).

Claggett, L., and B. Eklund. 2005. "Create, Organize and Expedite a Strategic Plan: How to Use the Balanced Scorecard and the Stage-Gate Funnel." *Information Outlook*, 9, no. 3: 21–23.

Cribb, G., and C. Hogan. 2003. "Balanced Scorecard: Linking Strategic Planning to Measurement and Communication." *IATUL Proceedings*, no. 13: 1–8. Available: www.iatul.org/conference/proceedings/vol13/ (accessed December 15, 2006).

De Stricker, U. 2004. "Hunches and Lunches: Using the Information Audit to Understand Information Culture." *Searcher*, 12, no. 4: 57–61.

DiMattia, S. S., and L. Blumenstein. 2000. "In Search of the Information Audit: Essential Tool or Cumbersome Process?" *Library Journal*, 125, no. 4: 48–50.

Dobson, C. 2002. "Beyond the Information Audit: Checking the Health of an Organization's Information System." *Searcher*, 10, no. 7: 32–37.

Eldredge, J. D. 2000a. "Evidence-Based Librarianship: An Overview." *Bulletin of the Medical Library Association*, 88, no. 4: 289–302.

Eldredge, J. D. 2000b. "Evidence-Based Librarianship: Searching for the Needed EBL Evidence." *Medical Reference Services Quarterly*, 19, no. 3: 1–18.

"Establishing a Framework for Organizational Transformation in Healthcare: Performance Solutions." General Electric Company (last updated 2005). Available: www.gehealthcare.com/usen/service/performance_solutions/lean/docs/ps_transformation.pdf (accessed October 10, 2006).

Greenfield, V. A., V. L. Williams, and E. Eiseman. 2006. *Using Logic Models for Strategic Planning and Evaluation: Application to the National Center for Injury Prevention and Control*. Santa Monica, CA: Rand Corporation. Available: www.rand.org/pubs/technical_reports/TR370/ (accessed January 5, 2007).

Henczel, S. 2001. *The Information Audit: A Practical Guide*. München: K.G. Saur.

Henczel, S. 2000. "The Information Audit as a First Step towards Effective Knowledge Management: An Opportunity for the Special Librarian." *INSPEL*, 34, no. 3/4: 210–226.

Imai, M. 1997. *Gemba Kaizen: A Commonsense Low-Cost Approach to Management*. New York: McGraw-Hill.

Imai, M. 1986. *Kaizen: The Key to Japan's Competitive Success*. New York: McGraw-Hill.

Jones, R., and B. Burwell. 2004. "Information Audits: Building a Critical Process." *Searcher*, 12, no. 1: 50–55.

Kaplan, R. S., and D. P. Norton. 2006. *Alignment: Using the Balanced Scorecard to Create Corporate Synergies*. Boston, MA: Harvard Business School Press.

Kaplan, R. S., and D. P. Norton. 1993. "Putting the Balanced Scorecard to Work." *Harvard Business Review*, 71, no. 5: 134–141.

Kaplan, R. S., and D. P. Norton. 1992. "The Balanced Scorecard – Measures that Drive Performance." *Harvard Business Review*, 70, no. 1: 71–80.

Kaplan, R. S., and D. P. Norton. 1996. *The Balanced Scorecard: Translating Strategy into Action*. Boston, MA: Harvard Business School Press.

Kaplan, R. S., and D. P. Norton. 2001. *The Strategy-Focused Organization: How Balanced Scorecard Companies Thrive in the New Business Environment*. Boston, MA: Harvard Business School Press.

Kaplan, R. S., and D. P. Norton. 1996. "Using the Balanced Scorecard as a Strategic Management System." *Harvard Business Review*, 75, no. 1: 75–85.

Koufogiannakis, D., and E. T. Crumley. 2002. "Evidence-Based Librarianship." *Feliciter*, 48, no. 3: 112–114.

Kumi, S., and J. Morrow. 2006. "Improving Self Service the Six Sigma Way at Newcastle University Library." *Program*, 40, no. 2: 123–136.

Lakos, A., and S. Phipps. 2004. "Creating a Culture of Assessment: A Catalyst for Organizational Change." *Portal*, 4, no. 3: 345–361.

Morrison, H. 2006. "Evidence-Based Librarianship and Open Access." *Evidence Based Library and Information Practice*, 1, no. 2: 46–50.

Orna, E. 1999. *Practical Information Policies*. 2nd edition. Brookfield, VT: Gower.

Phipps, S. E. 2001. "Beyond Measuring Service Quality: Learning from the Voices of the Customers, the Staff, the Processes, and the Organization." *Library Trends*, 49, no. 4: 635–661.

Phipps, S. E. "Beyond Measuring Service Quality – Learning from the Voices of the Customers, the Staff, the Processes, and the Organization." (Last updated October 20–21, 2000.) Available: www.arl.org/libqual/events/oct2000msq/papers/Phipps/phipps.html (accessed September 20, 2006).

Poll, R. 2001. "Performance, Processes and Costs: Managing Service Quality with the Balanced Scorecard." *Library Trends*, 49, no. 4: 709–717.

Self, J. 2003a. "Using Data to Make Choices: the Balanced Scorecard at the University of Virginia Library." *ARL*, no. 230/231: 28–29.

Self, J. 2003b. "From Values to Metrics: Implementation of the Balanced Scorecard at a University Library." *Performance Measurement & Metrics*, 4, no. 2: 57–63.

Senge, P. M. 2006. *The Fifth Discipline: The Art and Practice of the Learning Organization*. Revised edition. New York: Doubleday/Currency.

"Society for Organizational Learning (SoL)." Available: www.solonline.org/ (accessed October 15, 2006).

Willis, A. 2004. "Using the Balanced Scorecard at the University of Virginia Library: An Interview with Jim Self and Lynda White." *Library Administration and Management*, 18, no. 2: 64–67.

Wiser, J. 2005. "Kaizen Meets Dewey: Applying the Principles of the Toyota Way in Your Library." *Information Outlook*, 9, no. 6: 27–28, 30, 32–34.

Womack, J. P., and D. T. Jones. 1996. *Lean Thinking: Banish Waste and Create Wealth in Your Corporation*. New York: Simon & Schuster.

# Part III

# Tools for Doing Evaluations

# 10 DATA COLLECTION AND ANALYSIS METHODS

When this book was envisioned, data collection methods were not at the forefront of the plans. The goal was to see what services the library's customers needed, communicate the value of the library to administrators, or test library systems for efficiency. The nuts and bolts of how to do this were not at the top of the list. The idea of planning an evaluation tends to jump right from posing the question to reporting the answer. Unfortunately, in the middle are a lot of methods that need to be learned and applied. The methods reviewed in this chapter can be applied to any of the evaluation projects covered in this book.

In the past, the field of evaluation used mostly structured data collection procedures, such as numeric surveys to provide quantitative data. Recently, more qualitative methods such as observation and interviews have been introduced. There is no single list of data collection methods. In some of the methodology chapters, informal methods of evaluation are described, based on the type of evaluation being conducted. These are secondary sources of information such as locally gathered statistics, national surveys, literature searches, previous needs assessments, or even comments from a suggestion box. This chapter discusses the more structured methods: surveys, focus groups, observational studies, and interviews. These methods use techniques in sampling and questionnaire design, which are covered in detail. At the end, is an overview of analyzing the results.

Choosing a method to complete your evaluation can be a major stumbling block. Should you do a survey or an interview or a focus group? Figure 10.1 lists some attributes to consider when selecting a method. Part of the problem is the skill set of the team set to carry out the project. The skills it takes to carry out a method can take valuable time to learn. By reading this chapter and two or three of the references, you should have enough information to develop your skill to a level where you can plan a small-scale evaluation project. If you were planning a major research project, more skill might be necessary, including hiring a consultant. But having learned the information in this book, you will be able to communicate with those who will be helping you. Your skills in data collection will improve over time as you work to establish a culture of assessment in your library, as described in Chapter 2.

---

**Figure 10.1   Choosing Your Evaluation Method**

---

The two categories of criteria to match your choice of research method to your evaluation plan or questionnaire are *meaningfulness* and *practicality*. Meaningfulness includes whether the method is goal related, able to be interpreted, timely, comparable, or appropriate. Practicality means affordability in terms of intrusiveness, ease, and cost.

*Meaningfulness:*

*Goal related:* This is most connected to evaluation of outcomes. Did the program meet its goals? Will the evaluation method show this?

*Able to be interpreted:* Can the results of the method chosen be communicated easily? Can a decision be made based on the results?

*Timely:* Will the method be able to return results within the timetable needed?

*Comparable:* Can the result be compared with other evaluations in the past or in the future?

*Appropriate:* Does the method have validity and reliability? *Validity:* Does the method measure what you wanted to know? Example: If you are measuring library non–use, can you use the fact that people do not have a library card as a "valid" measure of non–use? They may be using the library in another way. *Reliability:* Is the method being used the same way by all involved? If observation is being used, are all observers trained adequately so that their observations can reliably be compared?

*Practicality:*

*Intrusiveness:* How much does the method interfere with the normal functioning of the library, including staff and users?

*Ease:* Each method varies on the degree to which these factors are present: skills needed to do the method; availability of the information needed; time it will take to do; training; number of people involved; effort needed to analyze the results.

*Cost:* Personnel costs (internal and external) are the largest part of any method. Also potential costs include payment of participants, communications charges, supplies, printing, travel, and training. Each step in the evaluation plan can have costs associated with it.

---

(Adapted from Johnson, 1996)

# COLLECTING EVALUATION DATA

## SURVEYS

### Considerations for Your Survey Project

When you think of evaluation or assessment, usually the first thing that comes to mind is to go out and take a survey. Surveys can be used in many types of evaluation projects. Surveys can gather information from people about their beliefs, knowledge, opinions, attitudes, and backgrounds. You need to ask yourself: Is doing a survey the right method for the project at hand? Remind yourself of the purpose and objectives of the project. Is a survey really going to answer the question?

The decision to conduct a survey should involve the sponsor of the evaluation and the key stakeholders. Any method of evaluation has its costs, and because the sponsor will fund the project, the sponsor should understand why a survey is the data-gathering method of choice.

Now is the time to consider asking for help from experts. Be aware that you may not have the skills necessary to do an extensive survey using statistically valid methods, and it is always appropriate to ask for help from other personnel or colleagues who do. Your institution may even have a statistics department. The classic resources for survey development are the books by Dillman (2000) and Salant and Dillman (1994).

**Reference: Survey books**

Dillman, D. A. 2000. *Mail and Internet Surveys: The Tailored Design Method*. 2nd ed. New York: Wiley.
Salant P., and D. A. Dillman. 1994. *How to Conduct Your Own Survey*. New York: Wiley.

Whether you do an extensive survey or a more informal one, it is a professional responsibility to write up the results for publication. Your extensive survey results may be generalizable to other situations. While the results of an informal survey are not as generalizable, they may provide enough understanding of the situation to be useful to others in making a decision. Staying as close as possible to the methods outlined below will make the results as understandable and useful as you can afford. Look for other surveys in the literature that are generalizable to your situation. This can help you develop and modify your questions.

### Develop a Management Plan

The steps it takes to carry out a survey are detailed in Figure 10.2, adapted from Taylor–Powell, et al. (2000). They are detailed for a mail survey or an e-mail survey. Knowing these steps will help you make a management plan for the survey.

---

**Figure 10.2   Survey Procedure**

| Mail survey | Computer survey on commercial site |
|---|---|
| Complete the planning process. | Complete the planning process. |
| Decide if the survey is anonymous or confidential. | Decide if the survey is anonymous or confidential. |
| Develop the questionnaire. | Develop the questionnaire outline. |
| Pilot test the questionnaire. | Input the questionnaire on the commercial site. |
| Develop the cover letter. | Pilot test the questionnaire. |
| Develop advance notice material. | Develop the introductory e-mail. |
| Develop follow-up postcards. | Develop advance notice material. |
| Prepare mailing materials. | Develop follow-up e-mails. |
| Do advance notices. | Finish the questionnaire. |
| Finish the questionnaire. | Do advance notices via e-mail and paper. |
| Send 1st mailing. | Send 1st e-mail. |
| Track survey responses. | Track survey responses. |
| Send Follow-up postcard. | Send 2nd e-mail. |
| Send 2nd mailing. | Send final e-mail. |
| Send final mailing. | Process data. |
| Process data. | Analyze and interpret data. |
| Analyze and interpret data. | Write reports. |
| Write reports. | Communicate findings. |
| Communicate findings. | |

(Adapted from Taylor-Powell, et al., 2000)

---

- *Responsibilities:* Build your evaluation project team. Who is going to be included? Choose people who have skills or are willing to learn. It is important to decide early who is going to do what, even on a small project. Use the responsibility chart found in Chapter 12. You will save a lot of money by having a planning document that lists all the tasks, the timeline, the person responsible, and the resources needed.
- *Scheduling:* If you have a deadline, schedule backward from there. Develop a Gantt chart, as explained in Chapter 12. Many tasks overlap, and a Gantt chart will show you when your busier times will be.
- *Budgeting:* Web or e-mail surveys are now cheaper than mail surveys. Interviews have always been the most expensive. Some of the costs of a survey are outlined in Figure 10.3 from the American Statistical Association (ASA)

brochure, *How to Plan a Survey* (2004). As the ASA notes in the brochure, a good survey does not come cheaply! But if you are the one doing a small survey all by yourself, just be aware of the types of activities that will take up your time and materials. In Chapter 12 there is a more extensive overview of budget planning for the whole evaluation project, with an accompanying spreadsheet on the CD-ROM in the Chapter 12 folder.

---

**Figure 10.3   Activities That Affect Costs**

- Staff time spent planning and time spent with sponsors refining the data needs
- Sample selection and segmentation costs
- Pre-testing costs, which multiply if you need to test more than once
- For an interview survey, costs for hiring, training, and supervising the interviewers
- Interviewer labor costs and other costs needed for him or her
- Labor and materials for data entry and quality control of the data entry
- Cost of editing the final file and looking for inconsistencies
- Analyst cost and computer time for tabulating the data
- Labor and materials for the substantive analyses of the data and report preparation
- Incidental costs: telephone, postage, reproduction at all stages

---

### Determine Your Method of Distribution

How the survey is going to be administered will affect what is included in the questionnaire. There are several ways to administer a survey, and they all have implications for costs and results. Any of these methods could be appropriate, and none of them is better than the other. You can also combine techniques if that is appropriate to your situation. This list outlines various ways to administer a survey to attempt to maximize return.

- Surveys can be handed out and completed on the spot, ensuring a good response. The process should be quick if you are going to interrupt people on their way to doing something else.
- Surveys can be handed out and collected at a later date. This gives respondents more time to consider their answers but they may not return them.

- The questionnaire can be sent out in the mail. Be sure that the weight of the envelope complies with the lowest rate for mail, or cost could become prohibitive. Mail surveys generally have a poor response rate and require follow-up.

- You can send a questionnaire via e-mail and ask people to reply with their answers. This assumes your target group has e-mail and a level of technical ability to reply to the survey and then type the answers within the body of the e-mail. It is difficult to format e-mail for rating scales. People use different fonts, so a rating scale displayed in a line would not display the same way in everyone's e-mail. You could ask people to type in a number from a described scale. The replies might be confusing and hard to code because of the technology limitations. It might be best to limit e-mail reply surveys to answering a few simple narrative questions or just Yes/No questions. E-mail reply surveys are also not confidential, which may deter some respondents.

- You can use an online survey software product such as SurveyMonkey, Zoomerang, or InstantSurvey. You may have to pay to conduct a larger survey, but smaller surveys can often be done for free. You'll have to learn how to set up the survey on the screen and use the SurveyMonkey or other system. Understanding how the results are displayed also is important. Again, your population has to have access to and familiarity with the technology. E-mail notification with a link to the survey is the usual route, so your target group would have to have e-mail. Web-based forms are easier to fill out than are e-mail replies. You could do a flyer with tear-off tabs with the Web address for those without e-mail but access to a Web terminal. It is important to send your survey to a few testers to make sure all of the buttons and options work correctly and that they can even get into the survey.

- You can administer the survey questionnaire in person by appointment, as in an interview. This takes much longer, thereby increasing labor costs, but can achieve a good response rate. It can also allow for some clarification. Asking only the questions on the list would be considered a highly structured interview. Lack of interaction would not utilize the interview method to its fullest extent.

- The questionnaire can be administered by telephone, either by cold calling or by appointment.

## Plan the Questionnaire

Now that you have confirmed your purpose and planned your method of delivery, it is time to plan your questionnaire. This is a critical and time-consuming step. The actual details of question writing are covered below. There are issues in questionnaire planning no matter which method of survey distribution you decide on.

1. *Determine your total population*

After deciding what method of distribution you will use and while you are working on your questionnaire design, you'll need to define or describe your total population. It is essential to "locate" or "cover" this group so you know you can determine what resources are needed to survey this group. It is rare that you would be able to contact each member of the group or population. Most surveys are done using a sample. To survey a sample of your selected population, you need a "sampling frame." This is a definitive list from which you will draw your sample. Your sampling frame could be all members of the medical staff as listed in the directory on a certain date, or all allied health workers, or all managers, at the hospital based on lists from human resources obtained on a certain date. From this defined group, you will draw a sample to survey. Now is the time to consider the quality of the data in your frame or list. If you are doing a mail survey, do you have a good address list? If you are doing an e-mail survey, do all sample members have e-mail? These considerations in sampling apply to all evaluation methods.

2. *Determine your sample*

When you perform a survey, you rarely have the funds to survey the total population. If the number of your total population is small, you may choose to survey the whole group and then would not need to use a sample. It would depend on your budget. Usually you survey a sample of your population and generalize the results to the whole group. Choosing a sample is based on statistical probability. Whichever evaluation method you use, you will need to understand the methods of choosing a sample. Which kind of sample to use and how to choose one are discussed in this chapter in the separate section below. A correctly chosen sample will allow your results to be generalizable to other situations.

3. *Plan for quality*

The quality of the survey or evaluation depends on more than the quality of the questionnaire. But pretesting the questionnaire, as described below, is an essential part of quality checking. Here are a few places where you can check for quality.

*The actual survey:*

- Are the instructions clear and easy to follow?
- Is the survey too short or too long?
- Do the questions rely too much on memory, especially of things that happened too long ago?
- Are the questions too sensitive? Do they contain information of a personal nature?
- Are they understandable? Are the words unambiguous?
- Who is going to answer the questions? If it is mailed, will it be answered by the person you thought would answer it? How can you ensure that it is?
- Is your sample selected according to your specifications?
- Is the questionnaire formatted so that the results can be coded or transferred to your data analysis software easily and correctly?

*Post-processing of the survey*

- Will the people doing the coding be trained well, and will the coding be done correctly?
- Are the computer programs that are going to be used for analysis working properly, and do those assigned to analyze the data have the proper skills?

4. *Planning the analysis*

One recommendation is to make a draft report even before you start (Taylor-Powell, et al., 2000). It seems odd to think you know how the evaluation will turn out, but in most cases, the evaluator knows the system, program, or population being surveyed and can guess at the type of results. The results could be radically different from what you expected, and that might mean the survey was not very good or the survey planners were really out of touch. Writing a draft report helps you focus on what you need to find out and how it fits with your purpose. As you express the possible results, you will begin to see what form your data should take. You will see if you need frequencies or percentages or maybe just averages. Can you tabulate by hand, or will you need Excel or a more sophisticated program? Is your target population a good representation, or do you also need to divide your population into subgroups? What are your capabilities and resources in data calculation and formatting? As Taylor-Powell says, "Often our analysis abilities and resources determine what our survey looks like" (Taylor-Powell, et al., 2000).

5. *Planning to communicate*

Your management plan should include ideas and plans to communicate the results. These reports can be part of the timeline

**Reference: Focus groups in libraries**

Glitz, B. 1997. "The Focos Group Technique in Library Research: An Introduction." *Bulletin of the Medical Library Association*, 85, no. 4: 385–390.
Glitz, B., C. Hamasu, and H. Sandstrom. 2001. "The Focus Group: A Tool for Programme Planning, Assessment and Decision-Making—an American View." *Health Information and Libraries Journal*, 18, no. 1: 30–37.
Glitz, Beryl, and the Medical Library Association.1998. *Focus Groups for Libraries and Librarians*. New York: Forbes.
Higa-Moore, M. L., B. Bunnett, H. G. Mayo, and C. A. Olney. 2002. "Use of Focus Groups in a Library's Strategic Planning Process." *Journal of the Medical Library Association*, 90, no. 1: 86–92.
Johnson, Debra Wilcox. 1996. "Focus Groups." In *The Tell It! Manual: The Complete Program for Evaluating Library Performance*, edited by Douglas L. Zweizig, Debra Wilcox Johnson, Jane Robbins and American Library Association. Chicago, IL: American Library Association.

and can be done periodically according to the needs of the stakeholders. The usual method is a final report. To address different stakeholders, you can have different executive summaries for each type of stakeholder. Chapter 11 shows the Evaluation Report Template that can be used as guide. It is also available on the CD-ROM in the Chapter 11 folder. Communicating with the stakeholders on a periodic basis is important so they will know that the project is on track and when they can expect the results.

## FOCUS GROUPS

Focus groups are a form of qualitative research that can complement or replace surveys. While surveys can *quantify* people's opinions, focus groups can *articulate* their views, ideas, and opinions. Focus groups never decide on an issue or resolve conflicts; they only identify opinions. If you have a situation you wish to resolve, they are not a substitute for a working committee that might come up with a plan to solve a problem. Focus groups do not result in action. You can:

- Do a survey and then use a focus group to expand on problems brought out in the survey
- Use a focus group to discuss a topic and from this discussion, survey questions can be developed

Library customers usually have varied and strong opinions about information and its uses in their life and work. This context makes the results of using the focus group methodology in libraries particularly valuable. The basic methodology of focus groups is to bring together six to ten people to discuss a topic or question. It helps to offer them something in return for their time, such as lunch. A moderator is recruited. The moderator should be as neutral a party as possible, not closely involved with the question before the focus group. This person can be a library staff member from another department if you are in a large library. For smaller libraries, someone from human resources or the quality department may be willing to help. Also, the focus group members might not speak freely. The group usually meets for an hour or two and takes turns answering a pre-set list of open-ended questions. The moderator leads the group through the questions and keeps the group on topic. Another person, the recorder, documents the discussion by machine or by hand so long as all participants are informed that notes are being made. The moderator, and/or perhaps the recorder, transcribes the discussion. Then the transcription is analyzed, and trends and opinions are coded and pulled out. The responses to each question are analyzed and organized into topics and subtopics. The information is rearranged by these topics so that the researcher can see what was said about each issue and suggest from the conversions what the participants consider important. Using a focus group is a form of qualitative evaluation that has its own set of data analysis processes. These include reviewing the comments and categorizing and coding them. This is discussed briefly below.

The focus group meeting itself is short, perhaps 90 minutes or less, but the parts of the focus group process that take up the most time are the preparation and analysis. Deciding whom to invite to the focus group and getting them to the meeting can be very time consuming. After the meeting, transcribing the words needs to be part of the plan. Then time needs to be spent analyzing data that often does not lend itself easily to pattern recognition. See Figure 10.4 for a complete outline of the focus group process.

Focus groups have several benefits over other data-gathering techniques.

- They sometimes can be done more quickly than a survey and often using in-house personnel.
- Librarians often have the skills necessary to conduct focus group research without outside help.
- Since libraries have so many different types of users, the groups can be segmented by user type, which can often facilitate better discussions.
- It can be a relatively simple method for getting opinions from users, and the open-ended nature of focus groups helps you identify issues you might not think to ask about in a survey.

---

**Figure 10.4  Focus Group Procedure**

- Develop questions or script.
- Decide on a moderator and recorder.
- Recruit participants.
- Meet with group and discuss questions.
- Record discussions.
- Transcribe discussions.
- Code and classify responses.
- Analyze responses.
- Report findings.

## OBSERVATION

Sometimes called direct observation or unobtrusive observation, this evaluation technique can be simple if well planned. Watching what goes on is always informative, but using what you see as an evaluation technique takes a more systematic approach. It requires planning as to what is the purpose, whom you are observing, how it will be recorded and analyzed, and how it will be reported.

Observation is useful when you need or want direct information, such as visiting other libraries to see their physical setup. Observation is useful when you are trying to understand:

- An ongoing behavior, such as circulation or reference
- A situation, such as theft or vandalism
- A process, such as observing manager meetings or training sessions

Reviewing Web sites of other libraries using a plan and a systematic data collection form to see how they are arranged can be a form of observation where physical evidence can be readily seen. Sometimes a direct observation will work better, such as observing another librarian's class on the same subject as yours where other data collection methods and procedures may not be appropriate. As with every form of data collection, the question is: What do you really want know? Is this method, observation, the most appropriate method for the question? A recent article in the literature covers some of the issues and techniques involved in observation. Lynda Baker states, "Observation is a complex research method because it often requires the researcher to play a number of roles and to use a number of techniques, including her or his five senses, to collect data" (Baker, 2006: 172). Her article describes the types of roles a researcher can assume during an observational study and provides an overview of some of the characteristics unique to observational research, as well as validity and reliability and ethical issues.

The ethics of observing people with or without their consent or knowledge has to be taken into account. The observation or resulting reports cannot harm the people being observed. If you collect primary data by asking people questions or observing them, this is considered research with human subjects. You should check with your Institutional Review Board (IRB) for the protection of human subjects to see if you need approval. Another question about the observation method is whether or not those to whom you report will be seeing the information as credible because it lacks the authoritative punch of a survey. Choosing and training

---

**Warning: Primary research on human subjects:**

If you work in a hospital or research setting, your institution may have an Institutional Review Board, or IRB. An IRB is a group that has been formally designated to review and monitor biomedical research involving human subjects, in accordance with Food and Drug Administration (FDA) regulations. An IRB has the authority to approve, require modifications in (to secure approval), or disapprove research. This group review ensures protection of the rights and welfare of human research subjects. If you are planning a primary data-gathering project of hospital employees, they might be considered "human subjects," and their privacy and other issues may need to be protected. It is best to check to see if a review is necessary so as not to be stopped by regulations in the middle of the project. Of course, you also want to know that you are correctly protecting your subjects, and the IRB office can advise you on this. Once your data-gathering plans, or research protocols as they might call them, are decided on, the plans can be presented to the IRB.

your observers and systematically planning the structure of the project will help establish credibility.

There are two kinds of observations, structured and unstructured:

- In a structured observation, you are "looking for" something, a demonstration of a skill or a numerical quantity of what people are doing.
- In an unstructured observation, you are "looking at" something to gain insight into what is happening. This type of observation takes its lead from the field of anthropology. The results are more qualitative than quantitative. You can also look for what is *not* happening in a situation.

Zweizig and Johnson in the *TELL IT! Manual* list eight key elements in using observation as an evaluation method (Zweizig and Johnson, 1996).

1. *What you are trying to learn*: This is the usual first step in evaluation. Defining the purpose greatly increases your ability to collect useful data.
2. *Where you are going to make the observations*: Unlike other evaluation methods, observations are made in a specific place that needs to be defined. Remember that "space" may include non-physical manifestations such as the World Wide Web.
3. *When the observations will occur*: When you choose a time to observe you are in effect "sampling" the time from the 24-hour period or day or month or season. Choose times that are representative of the whole. Develop an observation schedule that reflects general library use, not just the busiest or slowest times.
4. *Who will make the observations*: It is usually best to have a team of trained observers. Choose observers who will not stand out from the crowd, and instruct them on the details that are important to you so that they do not overlook what may be the most salient events. For example, in a recent study of people's use of public library space, the researchers developed a "seating sweeps checklist" and walked through the library three times a day at different intervals to observe how people were using various spaces (Given and Leckie, 2003). The observers would need to agree on what to observe, for example: Would what people were wearing be important? If everyone had coats on the back of their chairs in the winter, how does this affect the use of the space? All

observers will need some training. Depending on your purpose, you can draw them from various groups, such as colleagues, volunteers, stakeholders, or program participants. You can do it yourself as long as your presence does not impact the actions of those under observation. Train observers in the use of forms and checklists, including the pretesting or piloting of the forms. With consistent training, the results can be recorded in a standard manner for easier analysis. See the discussion of pretesting below.

5. *How the observations will be made:* As the procedures are set up, they need to be pretested. The method of pretesting would be included in the final report.

6. *How the observations will be recorded:* Observation guides, recording sheets, or checklists will need to be developed and tested. You would use the same principles as you use with developing questionnaires. A standard method of recording would be detailed. A less structured method is to use field notes, leaving a wide left margin for later analysis. This method is harder to analyze but may yield more interesting details. Photographs or videos also can be used if you have made provisions to inform those under observation. A combination of any of these techniques can be developed, including a work sheet that includes checklists, scales, and space for notes.

7. *How the results will be analyzed:* As you develop your purpose and your checklists, always think about how you will analyze the results. If you need to know how much time someone spends doing a task, you will need to have a space for start time and end time and total time on the data collection sheet. Otherwise, you will not get this result.

8. *How to report the results:* From the very beginning, you should be thinking about how you will report the data and to whom. The observation method has a richness to it that can allow you to report numerical *and* descriptive anecdotal data.

To conclude, the observation method can be time consuming and thereby costly. As with all methods, it needs careful planning to gain maximum benefit. Those observed should be representative of the user population and the person observing must be trained and comfortable with the process. Team involvement is recommended but can add to the cost. Observation can be effectively combined with traditional interviews. See Figure 10.5 for an outline of the observation procedure.

---

**Figure 10.5   Observation Procedure**

---

- Develop the observation form with checklist and train personnel.
- Determine how many times the activity or population needs to be observed.
- Determine the time and place where the observation will take place.
- Decide who and how many people you are going to observe.
- Make the observations.

---

**Definition: Key Informant**

A key informant is a person who is selected on the basis of criteria such as knowledge, compatibility, age, experience, or reputation that provides information about their culture. They can contribute a knowledgeable perspective on the nature and scope of a social problem or a target population. They know the community as a whole, or the particular portion you are interested in. They can be professional persons, young or old, or from a variety of socioeconomic levels or ethnic groups.

## INTERVIEWS

Conducting an interview in person or on the telephone is an alternative method of evaluation. An in-person interview requires that good questions be developed, a time arranged, and an interviewer with good listening skills chosen. You can choose interviewees using sampling techniques, or you might consider using a key informant interview methodology in which a specific set of people are chosen, people who have a knowledgeable perspective on the nature and scope of the problem or question (Program Planning and Assessment, University of Illinois Extension, accessed: 2007). As with all studies, every question on the interview script should have a specific purpose, that is, what do you want to know? Using the principles discussed below in designing questionnaires is essential. Pretesting is a must. Variations of the one-on-one interview include the following:

- *Phone interviews:* The interviewer makes an appointment and interviews the person on the phone. The interviewer fills in the responses on the preset questionnaire but can still take advantage of the real-time interaction and is allowed to prompt the interviewee for clarification.
- *Online interviews:* These are conducted using Web-forms or just through e-mail. You could design your own Web forms or adapt an online survey software product such as SurveyMonkey, Zoomerang, or InstantSurvey, to be more like an interview. The questions would be mostly open-ended, unlike many survey questions, which require specific answers. Using either method, you would need preliminary communication, most likely by e-mail, to explain the structure and how to do the "interview." What would be lost in the immediacy of a face-to-face interview might be balanced by the time for reflection. You can also send a second e-mail for clarification of the re-

sponse. Another online modality called instant messaging, or IM for short, could be used. You get a transcript by saving what is typed, and you would save on long-distance telephone charges. You could also use Voice over Internet Protocol or VoIP, or computervideo conferencing for interviews.

- *Self-recorded audiotaped interviews:* Here the respondent is sent a list of questions or issues and asked to record responses at a specific time, perhaps following a class or after using a specific resource. Equipment would have to be available to lend out. It is an unusual, but workable, alternative.

If you select the interview method of evaluation, the interviewer is your best asset. Interviewers must be good, trained listeners and observers and not talk too much. It is also best if their age, race, appearance, and social demeanor were similar to the people being interviewed because people tend to speak more candidly to those who look and sound like themselves (Robbins, 1996). If this is not possible, the interviewer would have to be socially sensitive to the population being interviewed. If more than one interviewer is used, they will need to be trained together to make the interviews consistent. The interviewing section of Chapter 11 has communication tips on preparing for the interview, starting and conducting the interview, and follow-up after the interview. As with focus groups, plans for recording the interview should be prepared in advance. Taping the interview is a good method. Permission must be obtained beforehand, since it is unethical to tape people without it. Plans for transcription and coding also should be developed. Depending on circumstances, the whole interview does not need to be transcribed. Perhaps listening to it again and taking notes on predetermined categories would be enough.

Developing the interview questionnaire follows the same principles of good questionnaire design. As with a paper questionnaire, the interview can be of several types:

- *The standardized, open-ended interview:* This plan makes sure the exact set of questions are asked in the same way across a sample population by different interviewers. Analyzing the results may be clearer. With this plan, however, you might lose important, spontaneous, information.
- *The guided, structured interview:* This plan keeps the interaction focused while covering the same questions but allows individual experience to come out. But the inter-

viewer cannot get offtrack for long without losing some of the main reason for asking the questions.

- *The informal, conversational interview:* Here, the interviewer can respond quickly to individual differences and situational changes, but analysis for systematic information would take a great deal of time.

Using interviews instead of paper questionnaires can result in more understanding of an individual's experience and how that experience affected him or her. A bond can develop with the interviewee that may be beneficial in the future, especially with key informant interviews. You might choose this method when actually hearing the voice of the user appears to be important. A good interviewer or coder will make note of the changes in pitch and tone. That can tell you as much or more about a people's opinions than their words do. See Figure 10.6 for an outline of the interview procedure.

---

**Figure 10.6   Interview Procedure**

- Determine the purpose of the interview.
- Identify target interview issues.
- Determine the questions to be asked and produce an interview script.
- Determine the method to ask the questions, that is, in person, on the phone, via e-mail.
- Determine whom to ask or define your sample.
- Pretest the interview script.
- Select and train the interviewers.
- Prepare interview schedule.
- Obtain written permission at the beginning of each interview.
- Conduct the interviews.
- Code and analyze the notes or tapes.
- Interpret findings.
- Prepare reports.

# SAMPLING

Sampling, or using a sample to infer characteristics of a larger group, is a standard way to "estimate" what the larger group does or what their opinion is. Deciding on your sample depends on your population size, what you want to know, and your resources available. Your population size means all of those people in the group (population) who are affected by what you are evaluating and who share a certain set of characteristics, for example, a group where members are all at a certain place (employed by a company, live in a geographic area) at a certain time. For a survey of physician use of the hospital library, your population could be defined as all the active medical staff (population) who practice at Memorial Hospital (place) in January 2006 (time). If your population size is small, you may choose not to use a sample but instead survey the entire population (Taylor-Powell and University of Wisconsin-Extension, 1998).

There are two kinds of sampling techniques, both of which are discussed later in this chapter:

- probability sampling
- non-probability sampling

In probability sampling, every unit of the population has a chance of being selected. Statistically, you can generalize that the results are representative of the whole population. It requires random sampling and is more complicated and costly. If you choose to use non-probability sampling, you will not be able to infer that the whole group agrees with your results. The assumption is that there is an even distribution of characteristics within the population. Despite drawbacks, non-probability sampling methods can be useful when descriptive comments are desired. Also, non-probability sampling is quick, inexpensive, and convenient. In some circumstances, such as in applied social research, it is unfeasible or impractical to conduct probability sampling. Statisticians prefer to use probability sampling for almost all of their surveys, but they also use non-probability sampling for pretesting and some preliminary studies during the development stage of a survey.

- *Haphazard, or convenience, sampling:* A type of non-probability sample in which the sample is chosen based on convenience, such as choosing your friends to make up a sample of a specific age group. Another convenience sam-

---

**Definition: Sampling**

Sampling is a procedure by which to infer the characteristics of a large body of people (a population) by surveying only a few (the sample).

---

**Definition: Probability Sampling**

A method for drawing a sample from a population where each member of the population has a known probability of being selected in the sample. The chance of a unit being included in a sample can be calculated. Also called random sampling. Probability samples are more costly to obtain, but are more accurate.

---

**Definition: Non-probability Sampling**

A sample in which the probability of a population unit being chosen is unknown. The selection of population units is based in part on the judgment of the researcher or field interviewer. There are basic kinds: haphazard or convenience, quota, stratified, judgment, and snowball.

pling technique is volunteer sampling, where people in the sample volunteer their services for the study.

- *Quota sampling:* A sample similar to stratified sampling in which you first divide the population into classes (such as males and females) and then obtain a haphazard sample within each class or sample to adhere to certain proportions within each class.
- *Stratified sampling:* A sampling method in which the population is divided according to a common characteristic or attribute or subpopulations (strata) and a probability sampling is then conducted within each group.
- *Judgment sampling:* A type of non-probability sampling in which you make use of special expertise to select units for the study. This can used to obtain a balance of viewpoints or to select knowledgeable respondents.
- *Snowball sampling:* A type of non-probability sample where you start by sampling one person, then ask that person for the names of other people you might interview, then interview them and obtain referrals from them, and so on.

Whichever technique you use, you will need to choose a sample and be able to describe the results. Choosing the sample size has many factors, and as you determine what you want to know and who your population is, it might be best to consult with someone at your institution who has experience with surveys. Below is an overview of the types of considerations you will need to know about and perhaps discuss with your consultant.

Small populations show greater variability of the characteristics being observed, so you'll need a larger sample in proportion to the total population. Variability, also known as sampling error, always exists. To a certain extent, the bigger the population, the bigger the sample needed. Once you reach a certain level, however, an increase in population size no longer affects the sample size. These sample sizes reflect the number of obtained responses and not necessarily the number of surveys mailed or interviews planned. This number needs to be increased to compensate for non-response.

To select a sample size, you can use tables in standard statistical textbooks or find some on the Web using the search term "calculate sample size" in quotes, "sample size table" or "sample size" and "precision level." Taylor-Powell includes a table of recommended sample sizes for two different precision levels (Taylor-Powell and University of Wisconsin-Extension, 1998). These tables and calculators talk about precision in relation to confidence level and confidence interval. Figure 10.7 demonstrates what they look like.

| Figure 10.7 | Example of a Sample Size Table | |
|---|---|---|
| Size of population | Sample size for precision of: | |
| | ±5% | ±10% |
| 100 | 81 | 51 |
| 250 | 154 | 72 |
| 400 | 201 | 81 |
| 500 | 222 | 83 |
| 600 | 240 | 86 |
| 700 | 255 | 88 |
| 800 | 267 | 89 |
| 900 | 277 | 90 |
| 1,000 | 286 | 91 |
| 2,000 | 333 | 95 |
| 3,000 | 353 | 97 |
| 4,000 | 364 | 98 |
| (Combined from various published tables on the Internet) | | |

**Definition: Confidence Level and Confidence Interval**

The confidence level is the probability, based on statistics, that a number will be inside a corresponding confidence interval, an upper and lower limit. A measure of sampling error. A 95% confidence level for an estimate is that the estimate will be within the range, or confidence interval, 19 times out of 20.

If you use a confidence interval of 4, or 4%, and a confidence level of 95%, and 51% percent of your sample agrees with a question, you can be 95% sure that if you had asked the question of the entire target population, between 47% (51–4) and 55% (51+4) would have agreed.

The confidence interval, or margin of error, is the plus-or-minus figure usually reported in public opinion poll results. The confidence level tells you how "sure" you can be. It is expressed as a percentage and tells you how often the true percentage of the population who would agree lies within the confidence interval. The 95% confidence level means you can be 95% certain; the 99% confidence level means you can be 99% certain. Most surveys use the 95% confidence level.

There are three factors that may affect the confidence interval for a given confidence level: sample size, percentage of the response to the question, and population size.

The larger your sample, the more certain you can be that respondents' answers truly reflect the population. The relationship is not simply inversely proportional; for example, doubling the sample size does not halve the confidence interval. Using a sample size calculator or table is important because using a large sample size may cause you to oversample and waste time and money.

Your confidence interval also depends on the percentage of your sample that picks a particular answer. If 99% of your sample says Yes and 1% said No, the chances of error are remote, irrespective of sample size, however, if the percentages are 51% and 49%, the chances of error are much greater. It is easier to be sure of extreme answers than of middle-of-the-road ones.

How many people are there in the target population your sample represents? This may be the number of hospital employees, the number of allied health personnel, and so forth. Often you may not know the exact population size, such as in the MLA Benchmarking Network survey, where the exact number of hospital libraries in existence, even as MLA members, is unknown except through estimates. This is not a problem.

While it is true, as stated above, that the sample size required depends on the population size, a small error in the estimate of population size typically will not impact the results significantly. If you have errors in estimating total population size or you can get only an estimate, there might be errors in minimum required sample size, as seen on the table. As the total population size increases, however, sampling errors caused by this situation matter less and less. Be aware that the confidence interval calculations assume you have a genuine random sample of the relevant population. If your sample is not truly random, you cannot rely on the intervals. Nonrandom samples usually result from some flaw in the sampling procedure. An example of such a flaw is to only call people at home during the day and miss almost everyone who works. For most purposes, the nonworking population cannot be assumed to accurately represent the entire population (working and nonworking).

## PROBABILITY SAMPLING

If you have the resources to choose a probability sampling versus non-probability sampling, you have three main ways to determine your sample:

- simple random sample
- systematic sample
- stratified sample

In a simple random sample, every person in your sample frame has an equal chance of being chosen. Your list, or sample frame, must be an accurate representation of your population. There are two ways to pick a simple random sample: using a random number table or a random number generator. If the population is small, say, around 100, place the names or assigned numbers in a basket and draw out the slips. Write down the number or name drawn and replace those you draw and mix again. Ignore duplicate drawings and put them back in the basket.

To identify your sample in a large population, use a random number table. Using your list of people that you have identified as your total population or sampling frame, assign a number to each person. If you had 500 people, the list would be numbered 1 to 500. The sample size for a population of 500 is 83, according to the sample size table shown in Figure 10.7. You have decided to over sample and send out 100 surveys. You then generate 100 random numbers between 1 and 500 using a system of random number generation. If your numbers are 20, 40, 17, 44, 28, and so forth, you choose those numbered people to send the survey to.

You can use random number tables found in standard statistical textbooks or find some on the Web using the search term "random number table" in quotes. Taylor-Powell includes a random number table and describes a method for making your own random numbers (Taylor-Powell and University of Wisconsin-Extension, 1998). Or you can use the 'rand()' function in Excel. Also, you can find a "Random Number Generator" on the Web by searching for one. One Web site, Research Randomizer, v3.0, (www.randomizer.org/) allows you to download sets of randomly generated numbers in Microsoft Excel format. Executing the above example and importing a set of 100 random numbers from a frame of 500 to Excel takes less than two minutes.

The next type of random sample is a systematic sample. In this method you choose an interval, for example, the ratio of the total population size and the desired sample size, and you take every member at that interval. If you have chosen 4 as your interval, you chose the 4th member as your starting point; you would then include the 8th, 12th, 16th member, and so forth. Under certain circumstances, this method can be biased if your list is not randomized first, for example, if the list was generated in a way that presorted and categorized the contents in any way.

The third type of random sample is a stratified sample. In this type, you divide your population by selected characteristics and choose a random sample from each group. This could be by age, race, sex, geographic area, and so forth, but in a library it could be by employee type. If your combined full-time equivalent (FTE) and medical staff equaled 4,700, your potential sample could be 350. Figure 10.8 shows what your sample would be in each strata.

**Reference: Excel Random Number Generator**

To generate a random whole number in between 1 and 100, enter '=1+int(rand()*100)' into a cell. (If the '1+' is omitted, you get a random integer between 0 and 99.) 'Fill down' to fill 500 cells. 'Recalculate' to get a different list. Save the numbers by using the Edit command, 'copy special – values,' otherwise the numbers will change. If you use a random number generator, make sure that it produces numbers with an even, or uniform, distribution. The Excel rand() function satisfies this requirement. Do not use a random number generator with a Gaussian, or normal, distribution (these produce numbers with the familiar "bell curve" distribution).

| Subgroup | Medical staff | Medical residents | Nurses | Other allied health professionals | managers | Other workers | Total |
|---|---|---|---|---|---|---|---|
| Number of workers | 2,000 | 200 | 800 | 500 | 200 | 1,000 | 4,700 |
| % of total group | 43% | 4% | 17% | 11% | 4% | 21% | 100% |
| Sample size | 149 | 15 | 60 | 37 | 15 | 74 | 350 |

**Figure 10.8. Population and Stratified Sample of Hospital Workers/Potential Library Patrons**

(Adapted from Taylor-Powell and University of Wisconsin-Extension, 1998)

## NON-PROBABILITY SAMPLING

The second type of sampling is non-probability sampling. Sometimes it is not possible to do a probability sample, because of cost or because the population sample frame does not exist. When using a non-probability sample, you should not generalize your findings to the whole population. This type of sampling is not as cumbersome as random sampling, and it may give you enough information for your question.

There are three main types of non-probability sampling:

- Convenience or haphazard sample
- Quota sample
- Volunteer or self-selected sample

In a convenience or haphazard sample, you select participants as they become available until your planned sample is reached. For instance, you might ask one question of patrons at the reference desk, maybe 10 people a day for two weeks until you had 100 people answer the one question. A quota sample is a variation of this where you try to get a quota within your sample. So, if in your reference desk survey of 100 people, you want 40% to be members of the medical staff, you keep sampling until 40% represents that group. The last type of non-probability sampling is called a volunteer or self-selected sample. This is where you ask a large undifferentiated group to participate and you survey those who volunteer without regard to their characteristics. An example here might be putting out a call via e-mail for participants in a web-usability study.

To summarize, deciding on your sample depends on your population size, what you want to know and your resources available. But it also depends on your resources in relation to time and money. Can you afford to send out a large survey? To answer this question, decide on your precision level, 5% or 10%; calculate your sample size by using Figure 10.7, and then estimate the time required to collect, tabulate, and analyze the data from that sample size. If it costs too much, reduce the precision level until it is something you can afford that will still serve your purpose.

# QUESTIONNAIRE DESIGN

All of the data-gathering techniques above rely on asking good questions, questions that can give useful answers. The word *useful* implies you have a well-defined purpose for your study. While writing questions and designing your questionnaire, take your time; the effort is worth it. The principles of good question writing and design apply whether you are doing a paper, electronic or telephone survey, a focus group, interviews, or an observational study.

Review other questionnaires. Although published in 1990, Marshall's *Evaluation Instruments for Health Sciences Libraries: MLA DocKit #2*, provides good examples of questionnaires (Marshall and Medical Library Association, 1990). On page 10 in Burroughs and Woods's, *Measuring the Difference: Guide to Planning and Evaluating Health Information Outreach*, there is a list of articles from the *Bulletin of the Medical Library Association* that contain questionnaires (Burroughs and Wood, 2000). The bibliography of this book, found on the CD-ROM, has a section that lists articles that contain questionnaires. If possible, make use of or adapt the questions from these sources, since they have been tried and tested by other researchers.

Whether you write your own questions or adapt them from other sources, you should follow the evaluation methodology outlined in Chapters 4 through 8. The point is to not ask a question unless the answer will be of use to the purpose of the project. Collecting too much information is time consuming and expensive, so every question should reflect the purpose of the study. Items that are nice to know or ambiguous should be eliminated.

Using the tools in the previous chapters, such as Figure 4.2, a matrix for designing an instructional program needs assessment, or Figure 8.8, an evaluation plan work sheet, you can connect the purpose of each question to the purpose of the evaluation. The Logic Model as explained in Chapter 8 allows you to review the goals and purposes of the program being evaluated. Issues to consider as you work on writing your questions:

- Write down what you want to know and what you hope to achieve. What evidence do you need in order to show support for that purpose? Is the purpose clear? If not, back up to clarify the purpose.
- Check to see if the information you want is already available.
- Link the question to the goal or purpose. How will the information be used?
- View the questions from your respondent's eyes. Are they reasonable? Are there privacy issues? Can the respondent answer the question?
- How are you going to analyze the answer? Are you going to use frequencies, percentages, or narratives?

## KINDS OF INFORMATION

Questionnaires can elicit four kinds of information in many combinations (Taylor-Powell, et al., 1998). Be clear about the type of information you are trying to get. Otherwise, you may get opinions when you wanted knowledge or knowledge when you wanted opinions. The answer you get is only as good as the question you ask! Below are the four main kinds of information you can elicit from your questions:

- knowledge
- beliefs, attitudes, and opinions
- behaviors
- sttributes

*Knowledge:* What do people know? Is their knowledge accurate? What is their awareness level of your service?
  You might ask, for example:

- How many journal titles are accessible online to this institution's employees?
- Are you aware of the benefits of using Medical Subject Headings (MeSH) when searching MEDLINE on Ovid?
- Have you heard of, or used at another institution, any library services that our library is not offering?

*Beliefs, attitudes, and opinions:* What are people's thoughts or opinions? How do they perceive the situation? How do they feel about the subject?

For example:

- What is your opinion about keeping back volumes in print of journals that are available online?
- How do you believe the library should experiment with new technologies and try out new ideas?
- What do you think will be the biggest challenge the library will face in the next two years? five years? ten years?

*Behaviors:* What do people actually do, in the past, present, or future?

For example:

- Have you used the library's electronic journal collection?
- How many times have you visited the library in the last month? Year?
- Do you use the library's Web site?

*Attributes:* Who are the people answering the questions? What is their age, job, or education?

For example:

- Which department do you work in?
- What is your education level? High school, two-year college, four-year college, master's, doctorate?
- If you have an advanced degree, what is it and in what subject?

## WORDING OF THE QUESTIONS

When wording the questions, consider the people who are going to answer the question, the purpose of the questionnaire, and the order of the questions. Always pretest the questionnaire. Pretesting is covered below. Here are some tips [adapted from several sources (Taylor-Powell, et al., 1998; Englesgjerd and Larson, accessed: 2006; Frary, accessed: 2006; Lance and Johnson, 1996; "Designing a Questionnaire," 2004; Dillman, 2000]:

- *Keep it simple*, make it easy, and make it fun, if possible. Use language your customers will understand.
- *Use clear wording.* Does the word have a double meaning? Is it confusing? Are the words too simple or too com-

plicated for the level of the respondent? For most surveys, a 5th-grade reading level has been recommended ("Designing a Questionnaire," 2004). This can be tested using Microsoft Word's "readability statistics" measures found in the spell-checker utility.

- *Use simple wording and sentences.* Avoid the use of abbreviations, jargon, and foreign phrases. Does the term *OPAC* mean anything to the public?
- *Use short but complete sentences.* Be brief. Do not get so brief, however, that you are misunderstood.
- *Be specific.* The question, "What time of day do you use the library?" could be answered in a variety of ways, whereas a multiple-choice question with time segments would yield more comparable answers. What does *often* mean? Hourly, daily, weekly? If you are asking a quantitative question, use quantifiable language.
- *Avoid "double-barreled" questions.* Do not have two concepts or situations in the same question. A question such as "Do you use books and journals online?" can be answered Yes or No, but it does not give you the information you need to judge the use of books or journals. It would be better to divide it into two questions about this behavior. If the word *and* or *or* appears in a question, check to verify whether it is a double-barreled question.
- *Include all necessary information.* If you were to ask an opinion about the library mission statement, make sure to provide a copy, since the respondent may never have seen it.
- *Make the response categories clear and logical*, especially time periods. If you ask, "How many times did you check out materials last year?" do you mean in the last 12 months or last calendar year? Do you mean books or journals or audiovisuals?
- *Avoid questions that may be too precise.* The respondent may not have an accurate answer. Avoid asking the respondent to make calculations, for example: How many days did you visit the library in the last year?
- *Phrase personal or potentially incriminating questions in less objectionable ways.* Although it is hard to imagine that a library user would be asked an incriminating question (such as "Do you steal books?"), personal questions could include age, ethnic background or salary levels, if such demographics are important to the purpose of the survey. Using a range of ages allows the person to not be specific. Phrase your questions as unobtrusively as pos-

---

**Definition: Double-Barreled Question**

A double-barreled question combines two or more issues or attitudinal objects into a single question. Combining the two questions into one question makes it unclear which attitude is being measured, since each question may elicit a different attitude. If the word *and* or *or* appears in a question, check to verify whether it is a double-barreled question.

sible to avoid disturbing your participants and causing them to answer less than truthfully.

- *Do not use questions that are too demanding or time consuming.* If someone has to call another office to get the answer, it might not get answered. Ask questions that can be answered from memory. Most people will not spend the time to look up things unless either the survey is very important to them or they understand that the purpose of the survey is to gather data from many sources and are tolerant of the time it takes to do this.
- *Use mutually exclusive categories when asking for one answer.* If you asked a multiple-choice question where only one answer may be chosen and a person might want to choose more than one answer, it would be frustrating. Age ranges or time periods are examples of mutually exclusive categories, as long as they do not overlap. One example could be a list of courses and respondents could choose only one that they were interested in. Another example of what not to use for the one-choice answer is a question about how a customer heard about a library service when he or she may have heard from multiple sources. Using "check all that apply" would be more appropriate.
- *Avoid making assumptions.* If you start off with a question such as, "How often do you use the library?" you are assuming that respondents do use the library. It might be better to ask if they use the library first and then branch off to "How often?" or "Why not?"
- *Avoid bias in questions*, including language and question order. This would include questions where one would assume a kind of behavior. The question, "Which database do you search most often?" assumes that they do search. The people who do not search bias the answers by skipping the question. When you include only positive choices, the answers would be obviously biased. Using words loaded with positive or negative meanings not only can bias the results, but also this may give your audience the impression that you are scheming rather than trying to find out what they really think.

## TYPES OF QUESTIONS

There are two types of questions, open-ended and close-ended. For example:

"How many PDF copies of e-journals do you download for work in a month?"

Open-ended response (*specify number*):

_____

Close-ended response (circle one):
None  1–5    6–10   1–15    16–20    21–25    26 or more

In this example, the first question relied on the respondent to be more exact. He or she was not given the opportunity to give an estimate. In the second example, the respondent can estimate, but did the writer know enough about his or her users to give the right ranges? Maybe the users are downloading 100 PDFs a month, in which case "26 or more" is a poor estimate, at best.

## Open-Ended Questions

Open-ended questions give respondents the opportunity to give you their opinions and ideas. This kind of question requires the respondent to come up with ideas on the spot, so it can be difficult to answer. You might, however, be able to gather new ideas. You will get a wide variety of answers that will be difficult to analyze. Open-ended questions are used in focus groups in which participants are encouraged to discuss and develop together. In personal interviews, they are used to generate opinions rather than facts. Open-ended questions are time consuming and could lower the response rate on surveys. During pretesting, a completion-time estimate should be included as well as impressions of whether the tester thought the survey to be too brief or too long.

With open-ended questions, it is particularly important that the question be clear and easily understood. You want the respondent to think about the answer, not what the question means. The question should be neutral and not lead the respondent to an answer. Easier questions should come first. As in most ordering of questions, general topics precede personal or demographic questions. Put demographic questions at the end and ask for the minimum amount of absolutely essential information. You want the respondent to answer the core questions and address the important issues, not answer boring demographic questions or fill in background information. If respondents can begin by answering the core material, they will be more likely to complete long surveys and answer honestly.

Responses to open-ended questions can be useful in preliminary studies or pre-tests of the survey to find out what issues respondents consider to be important in the first place. You can use the responses to these questions to develop more specific, close-ended questions for a later survey. Figure 10–9 gives some examples of open-ended questions.

---

### Figure 10.9  Open-Ended Questions

*When asking about a literature search:*
- In what specific ways was this information helpful in your decision making?

*From user satisfaction surveys:*
- What do you like most about the library at present? Please be specific.
- What is the most valuable service the library provides for you?
- If you could change one thing in the health sciences library, what would it be?

---

## Close-Ended Questions

Close-ended questions give respondents a list of answers to choose from, whether it is just a Yes or No or a list of answers. These are harder for the question writer to construct but easier for the respondent to answer. The problem for the writer is to think of all the possible answers in creating an exhaustive list that has mutually exclusive terms. The respondent does not have to think as much but may be frustrated that his or her opinion is being ignored if some term is forgotten. The answers are easier to analyze and quantify, however. It is best to limit response possibilities to a range of 5 to 7. Allow respondents to skip questions that do not apply. These types of close-ended questions are covered here: single-choice questions (two-option responses, one best answer, rating scale, ordered choice, items in a series, paired comparisons, and matching) and multiple-choice questions (check all that apply, lists, and ranking), and the use of "other, please specify."

## Single-Choice Questions

- *Two-option responses*
  This is your basic Yes/No question that can also be phrased as Favor/Oppose, True/False, or Agree/Disagree. This may be appropriate but you do not get much information. It can be used to branch the survey, for example, "If No, go to question #6" (see Figure 10.10)

---

**Figure 10.10   Two-Option Responses**

- Do you download full-text journals from the Web?
  ____ Yes ____ No (If No, go to question #6)

- Do you use the library's online catalog?
  ____ Yes ____ No (If No, go to question #10)

---

- *One best answer*
  Allowing only one best answer tests respondents' knowledge or has them choose between definite products or services. It is an appropriate technique if all choices that answer the question are known. Only one best answer is allowed, and the choices are independent of one another, not part of a series, as demonstrated in Figure 10.11.

---

**Figure 10.11   One-Best-Answer Questions**

For an online search evaluation form:
Why did you request this search? (Choose only one.)

❑   Patient care

❑   Research

❑   Instruction/Education

❑   Management/Administration

❑   Class assignment

❑   Other (please specify) _____

---

**Definition: Likert Scale**

A Likert scale (pronounced 'lick-urt') is a multipoint rating scale using a range of response categories, such as strongly agree, agree, disagree, and strongly disagree, where respondents indicate their level of agreement with the statements to express a favorable or unfavorable attitude toward the concept being measured. Rensis Likert, who invented the scale in 1932, developed this type of response format using an attitudinal rating scale.

- Rating scale
Called a Likert scale, this type of question asks for a choice based on the opinion of the respondents. They offer their opinion based on a scale that is described. The number of points on the scale depends on how much differentiation is possible as well as the respondents' ability to answer. Offering an even or odd number of choices has some implications. An even number of choices avoids the "middle-of-the-road" selection and encourages the respondent to make a choice, but it can result in respondents' just adding a midpoint of their own if it is a paper survey. The even-numbered scale is used more in rating a product or service, while the odd-numbered scale may be better for measuring attitude, in which case it is useful to have a midpoint or "no opinion" option. In order to avoid respondents' agreeing with a set of statements without thinking clearly about each one, vary positive statements with negative statements.

One can use words or numbers or points on a scale between phrases like *strongly agree* and *strongly disagree*. Figure 10.12 gives some examples of words to use. If using words, no more than five choices is appropriate, while with numbers, you could go as high as ten. It is easier for people to process ten choices that are all numerical (for example, a scale of 1–10) than it is to process ten verbal choices (agree, disagree, and so forth). The phrasing of responses provided in an attitudinal scale can be tricky. The goal is to have a well-balanced range of descriptive words.

---

**Figure 10.12   Examples of Likert Scale Phrases**

- Strongly agree, agree, neutral, disagree, and strongly disagree (implies "total" agreement, versus using the term *somewhat*" as in the next example)
- Strongly agree, agree somewhat, neutral, disagree somewhat, strongly disagree
- Strongly unfavorable, generally unfavorable, neutral, generally favorable, strongly favorable
- Decreased, stayed the same, increased
- No help at all, slightly helpful, fairly helpful, very helpful
- Never, rarely, sometimes, often, always
- Poor, fair, good, excellent
- Very dissatisfied, somewhat dissatisfied, somewhat satisfied, very satisfied

There are several problems involved in the use of a mid-point in a Likert scale. It is better not to use "do not know," since this could mean the respondent really does not know, or it could mean that he or she did not understand the question or did not want to give an opinion. Other center-position terms might be *neutral, undecided, uncertain,* or *same.* The respondent's choice of the middle position, no matter what word you use, could have many reasons that confuse the results, such as reading difficulty, reluctance to answer, inapplicability, or just plain uncooperativeness or ignorance (Frary, accessed: 2006).

To avoid misinterpretations you can always suggest at the top of the page that respondents skip any questions they do not understand or do not want to answer. Another technique is to include a selection (or several selections) at the end of an even-numbered scale, such as "refuse to answer," "prefer not to answer," "not applicable," or "no knowledge of subject."

To analyze a Likert scale, one cannot use an average since adding the responses of agree and undecided makes no sense. The data collected are ordinal: they have an inherent order or sequence, but one cannot assume that the respondent means that the difference between agreeing and strongly agreeing is the same as between agreeing and being undecided. To summarize these data, use a median or a mode, not a mean. See explanations of these under data analysis below. Use a bar chart to display the findings. Likert scales are often represented in surveys as a matrix. Figure 10.13 provides an example of a matrix.

---

**Figure 10.13   Likert Scale Using a Matrix**

How would you rate the following services:

|  | Excellent | Good | Fair | Poor | Never used |
|---|---|---|---|---|---|
| Circulation of materials | 1 | 2 | 3 | 4 | x |
| Librarian-mediated literature searches | 1 | 2 | 3 | 4 | x |
| Current awareness services | 1 | 2 | 3 | 4 | x |
| Library Web site | 1 | 2 | 3 | 4 | x |
| Instructional workshops | 1 | 2 | 3 | 4 | x |
| Interlibrary loan | 1 | 2 | 3 | 4 | x |

- *Ordered choice*
  Using the same kind of words as in rating-scale questions, ordered-choice questions ask for a definite opinion. They also measure an attitude by asking someone to choose one answer in a range that reflects an opinion, which is not a rating. You are not being asked to decide if the service is good or poor, that is, to rate it, but whether, in your opinion and to what degree, the service met your needs. These are useful when the choices are well defined and the responses have a clear difference and are appropriate to the question. The negative and positive choices must be balanced. These responses could be averaged with a mean instead of a median because of their relationship to each other. In Figure 10.14, respondents are not rating the services but choosing an answer that reflects their experience.

---

**Figure 10.14   An Ordered Choice**

Circle the number that best describes your experience using the following library services:

|  | Never | Rarely | Often | Almost always |
|---|---|---|---|---|
| The library owns the books you need: | 1 | 2 | 3 | 4 |
| When you want to check out a book, it is on the shelf: | 1 | 2 | 3 | 4 |
| When you ask for assistance in the library, staff are helpful: | 1 | 2 | 3 | 4 |

---

- *Items in a series*
  When you use a rating scale or an ordered choice, you can often group questions together in a table or matrix so you do not have so many questions. But remember, in relation to the time it takes to complete the survey, the respondent will still have to think about each line of the matrix as if it were a separate question. But since several questions are combined in a matrix, the questionnaire may appear shorter. The matrix examples in Figures 10.13 and 10.14 are actually items in a series. They could be individual questions with a scale under each one. More and more, questionnaires are using this series format. The

availability of computerized surveys has probably influenced this trend.

- *Paired comparisons*
  Sometimes you want to compare different services or products or their use. You can set up a matrix where the respondent must choose the best answer from a pair of options. Figure 10.15 shows an example.

| **Figure 10.15   A Paired Comparison** |  |
| --- | --- |
| In comparing our present computer situation to future possibilities, which technology would you be likely to use more often? (Circle your choice.) | |
| Public access computer with Web access or | Wireless network access for your laptop |
| Public access computer with Web access or | Wired network access for your laptop |
| Public access computer with Web access or | Wireless network access for your personal digital assistant (PDA) |
| Public access computer with Web access or | Syncing ability for your PDA on the public access computers |

- *Matching*
  If you want to test someone's knowledge of a subject, you can ask him or her to match columns. Make sure that each item has one and only one match, otherwise you may cause the respondents to second-guess their answers and your results will not reflect what they know. This type of question is ideally given in a quick test before a class. Figure 10.16 is an example of matching.

| **Figure 10.16   Matching** |  |
| --- | --- |
| Match each database service to the content option by putting the correct lowercase letter from the right side into the blank: | |
| _____ PubMed MEDLINE | a.  Contains full-text articles |
| _____ ACP PIER | b.  Citation index with links to full-text articles |
| _____ MD Consult | c.  Contains subject monographs |
| _____ UpToDate | d.  Provides evidence levels |

## Multiple-Choice Questions

- *Check all that apply*
  This type of question, where you have a list and respondents can check as many as they want, is really a group of Yes/No questions. A caution here is that respondents tend to favor the answers at the top of the list. Also, keep the list short. Figure 10.17 is an example of "check all that apply."

---

**Figure 10.17   Check All That Apply**

Topic of survey: What do customers do with articles supplied to them from interlibrary loan?

Did you read the article? ____ Yes ____ No

If no, why not? (Check all that apply.)

❑  Did not arrive on time

❑  Did not contain the desired information

❑  Did not have time to read it

❑  Obtained desired information from another source

❑  Could neither read the language nor get it translated

❑  Received a poor photocopy

❑  Other (please specify) _____

---

- *Lists*
  Lists of questions are an alternative to the "check all that apply" format. The items in the list are not independent, but the respondent can still make more than one choice. The lists usually are adjectives and assess attitudes rather than choices. Figure 10.18 is an example of a multiple-choice list.

**Figure 10.18    Multiple-Choice List**

In a new library facility, which of these features would you use?

| | Would use | Would not use | Don't know |
|---|---|---|---|
| Library tables for studying | 1 | 2 | 3 |
| Study carrels for studying | 1 | 2 | 3 |
| Group study rooms | 1 | 2 | 3 |
| Public access computer with Web access | 1 | 2 | 3 |
| Wireless network for your laptop | 1 | 2 | 3 |
| A multipurpose library instructional room | 1 | 2 | 3 |

- *Ranking*
  In multiple-choice questions, respondents can be asked to rank the list in order of importance. The idea of "top choice" is different from a plain "check all that apply." Figure 10.19 is an example of ranking.

**Figure 10.19    Ranking**

Please indicate three primary areas in which you use MEDLINE search information.

Rank them so that your most common use is #1, second most common use is #2, and so on.

Please give no more than three answers.

Rank Order

__ Patient care

__ Education

__ Research/Testing

__ Management/Administration

__ Regulations

__ Other (please specify) _____

*Use of "Other, please specify"*
If you feel you cannot include the full range of possible answers, you can use "other, please specify." It protects you against leaving out an important choice. On the pretest (covered below), another choice you had not initially considered may become apparent and be able to be incorporated into the question. Or the opposite may happen in that you get so many different answers you may need to abandon the question or do a major restructuring of it. It also gives the respondent an opportunity to give his or her own response and relieves the frustration of not being able to choose anything. While this can be good, the text in the box will be difficult to analyze. Make sure you want to know this information, because too often this answer is never used. Plan to have a place to list these answers or a summary of them on your report. Otherwise, why bother to ask? For examples of "other, please specify" see Figures 10.11, 10.17, and 10.19.

## FORMAT OF THE QUESTIONNAIRE

Now that you have written simple, clear questions, how will you arrange them on the page? Each type of questionnaire calls for decisions about format. How long will it be, and therefore how long will it take to fill out? Will there be some white space on the page or screen? On an e-survey, how many questions will be on a page before you move to the next screen? If a paper questioning, will it be two-sided or in columns? Will there be sections, lines, boxes, shading? Will the answer of one question influence the next? These issues will need to be decided as you go along, and they can influence how people answer the questions. Some tips on formatting:

- *Include a brief introduction* explaining the purpose of the questionnaire. In a mailed questionnaire, include a cover letter. If your questionnaire pertains to a specific program, describe the program specifically and neutrally so the respondents know what program you are talking about.
- *Give clear instructions* with each question about how to fill it in. Repeat the instructions as often as you need to. Make sure the instructions are not confused with the questions, use a different typeface or bold formatting.
- *Order the questions* to help the respondent remember what happened. If the first questions get the respondent thinking about the topic, when another question on the topic

is asked, he or she will have improved recall. This is called a cognitive design technique.

- *The order of questions* can influence or bias the response. This is lessened by asking more general questions that lead into specific questions. A specific question can be skipped when a preceding question's answer makes it not applicable.

- *Address important questions first.* Arrange questions in a logical order, putting sensitive issues toward the end. Ask demographic questions at the end. You want the respondent to answer the core questions, not deal with boring demographic questions first. If your questionnaire has parts, use transitional statements to move to the next part.

- *Asking too many questions is a common mistake.* Respondents may answer superficially if the questionnaire takes a long time to complete. When pre-testing, record the time it takes a respondent to fill out the survey. Estimate how long your respondent population would tolerate answering questions. Compare the two numbers and adjust the number of questions accordingly.

- *Have a clear path on branching questions.* If your questionnaire has filters or screens, permitting skipping of groups of questions that do not apply, make sure it is clear where to go to answer the next question. In print, use arrows, boxes, or indentions to guide respondents. On the computer, the questionnaire will "branch" to the next appropriate question, but make sure it is a branch where respondents will not wonder what they would be answering if they had answered the branching question the other way. You can accomplish this by graying out nonapplicable questions so that they cannot be answered unless respondents goes back and change a previous answer.

- *Vary the question format* to encourage respondents to think about each of their responses and not just go through checking the "agree" boxes. At the same time, do not jump around from one type of question to another and then back again. The respondent might get confused or irritated.

- *Use a consistent style.* Online questionnaires do this for you, but do not change the color on every page or be too flashy. Do not use a mixture of check boxes and circles or vary whether Yes or No comes first. Instead, mix up the questions themselves so that some are negative and some are positive.

- *Use an easy-to-read typeface*, in print or on the computer. This information can be obtained from graphic designers or on the Web.
- *Do not have too many questions per page* on a computer survey or in print. In print do not turn a page in the middle of an instruction/question/answer combination.
- *Plan ahead for analysis* by numbering or coding each question and answer for easier tabulation.
- *Give the questionnaire a professional appearance.*
- *Include a thank-you at the end*, in print and on the computer.

## PRETESTING / PILOTING THE QUESTIONNAIRE

No matter what format you use, pretesting is *the most essential step* and should never be skipped. In your planning, time and resources should be allotted for this activity. With e-mail and Web communications, this could be accomplished in a short time for small questionnaires. If your project is large, this step will take some time. If you have time, a way to start a survey project is to hold a focus group on the topic and ask some of the open-ended questions you may be planning for your questionnaire. This discussion may bring up variations in language or interpretation you had not thought of, as well as content problems. A very preliminary questionnaire could be discussed in the group, and the give and take of the group may produce valuable information.

The "final" version of the questionnaire is then field-tested. The questionnaire is sent out to a group of people, and they are asked to actually take the questionnaire and comment on it. The method of sending it out should mimic what you are planning to do. So if it is a print questionnaire, mail it out. If it is an e-mail questionnaire, e-mail it. If it is a Web-based questionnaire, send the planned e-mail invitation to participate as a test as well. You could include a feedback form or some general guidelines for the critique as a whole as well as for the individual questions. But do not spend more time crafting the critique portion than for the questionnaire itself! The results of the pre-test can be tabulated if you have enough people in your test group to see what problem may arise with coding and analysis. This will also allow you to be sure the answer will relate to the study purpose.

While there are many ways of pretesting, there are three groups to potentially involve in process. It is best not to use library staff or the committee planning the survey, since they are too close to the process. Their comments might be skewed because they care so much about the subject. The three groups are questionnaire experts, library colleagues at other institutions, and and a small sample of the people you plan to question.

You can find statistical experts in a statistics department in your own institution or perhaps in your professional association. The Medical Library Association's Mentoring Service, available on the MLA Web site (www.mlanet.org/mentor/), has categories for research, benchmarking/needs assessment, and user surveys, among other subjects. Through your local or regional association, you could ask five or six colleagues to review your questionnaire. They certainly would be able to identify confusing questions. You already know to whom this questionnaire is directed, so you can choose people from the target population to pretest the questionnaire. Most will be happy to help. Include a cover letter (e-mail) thanking them for helping out, explaining the feedback form, and giving them a deadline. Figure 10.20 shows what problems you could look for and what could be mentioned in your feedback form.

---

**Figure 10.20    Potential Question Problems**

- Are questions confusing? Or can they be misinterpreted?

- Did you miss any questions or answer choices? Review your goals and purpose.

- Do close-ended questions include enough answers, or did you miss some? Is using "other, please specify" appropriate? Are the answer choices appropriate, meaningful, or correct?

- Did the reviewer see any bias?

- Was the questionnaire arranged to motivate the reviewer to finish it? Was it positive?

- How many minutes did it take to complete the questionnaire?

---

If there are major revisions, it may be necessary to pretest again. The pretests stand alone as a test, and the results cannot be combined with the main survey. After all this work, always go back to the beginning with each question. What is the purpose of the study? Will the information gathered from a particular question contribute to the study? What will the answer mean in relation to the purpose of the study?

## MAXIMIZING YOUR RETURN RATE

How the questionnaire is going to be administered will be part of your development planning and will affect what is in the questionnaire, such as length and inclusion of open-ended questions. The expected return rate, the number of surveys returned divided by the number sent out, should be discussed in the planning stages. There is no standard for a return rate but most authorities quote between 50% and 75% as a good return rate (Lance and Johnson, 1996). Also some populations have a lower rate of response, so this should be considered in your planning. If you need a 60% rate of return and you are using a sample of 95 for a population of 2,000 (see Figure 10.7), a 60% return would be 62 questionnaires. If you have decided that your population responds poorly at the 40% level, instead of sending out 95 questionnaires, you would oversample and send out 160. Forty percent of 160 is 64, which would give you the 60% return you required on the sample needed. Any findings would be qualified by an analysis of the return rate. A return rate far below what was expected may nullify your results.

Whether distributed as a survey or used in one of the other data collection modalities, there are various ways of attempting to get a good return rate. These can be divided into two parts; one is good questionnaire design and distribution, and the other is more of a "sales" approach.

### Good Questionnaire Design and Distribution

- Be respondent-friendly. Are the questions meaningful and important to the respondent? Did you explain why they were chosen or why the survey is important?
- Keep it short.
- List a person to contact if the respondent has questions.
- If appropriate, a little humor in the questions can keep the respondent's attention.
- Make the questionnaire interesting.
- Keep request for personal information at a minimum. Assure confidentiality.
- Have a return date that is reasonable. Decide on a close-out date after which you will not accept any responses.
- Plan a follow-up mailing or follow-up e-mail. Each contact results in a certain percentage of returns, so have a plan for several follow-up contacts.
- Oversample. If you want 75 responses from a given population, and can decide you might get a 75% response rate, send 100 surveys.
- Be sponsored by a legitimate authority.

### The "Sales" Approach

- Use press releases and announcements at meetings to make the population being surveyed aware of the survey.
- Establish trust by indicating clearly that the sponsor is legitimate and can do something with the results. Make the questionnaire appear important, indicating how the data will be used. State clearly why the task is important.
- Support group values. What is the value of participating? What is in it for them?
- Show respect for the respondent's time and effort. Show common courtesy.
- Say thank-you.
- Your cadence of questions has to hold their attention.
- For e-mail surveys, include instructions on how to reply.
- For Web-based surveys, make sure the URL is a hot link in the e-mail. Pretest it on yourself to be sure it is. Most e-mail now has the ability to click on a URL and go to the Web if the URL is formatted correctly in the e-mail.
- Your announcements have to be clever enough to entice the respondent to click on the link. On the screen, a little humor in the questions also can keep their attention.
- If the questionnaire is for a course or workshop, make sure the person is given time to fill it out.
- For paper surveys, the survey should be easy to return. Provide pre-addressed, stamped envelopes where necessary. Self-mailers have been known to increase return rates. You could also have a fax option.
- Give a reward or prize. Send a dollar or more in the envelope or place the respondent's name in a raffle. Providing tokens of appreciation in advance is often done, but you have to be careful not to make the tokens too large, since this could be a source of bias (Dillman, 2000).

# ANALYZING EVALUATION DATA

Data analysis can be many things. It can be as complicated as what you might find in a statistics textbook or as simple as saying, "After the data have been processed, generate and display the findings." What most librarians need is something toward the simpler end of the spectrum. It would be great if every library manager had taken a statistics course and became competent in the use of statistical practices. Credit is due to those individuals who did and do take such courses! But the reality is that most librarians took a research methods course in graduate school, perhaps one-third of which covered statistics. Often librarians get right up to the point of assessment and stop because they lack skills in data analysis.

There are two parts to this problem: performing the math itself and understanding and interpreting the results. Luckily we have computers, spreadsheets, and statistical programs to do the math. But to learn what to do with these programs, you have to understand what you are doing. Every librarian has access to Microsoft Excel, and this is a powerful tool that most of us use like a calculator. Beyond Excel, there are statistical programs such as SPSS and JMP that allow you to manipulate data as if you were a statistician. If you work for a research institution, you might be able to get a copy of one of those programs at an institutional license price.

Once you have the basic tools, you still need to understand how to use them and what they can produce. The details of learning Excel or JMP are beyond the scope of this book. Certainly if you want to use SPSS or JMP, you'll need to take courses in statistics and learn these programs in that context. These programs produce statistical reports that are most likely beyond the needs of the types of evaluation programs covered in this book. If you are lucky enough to have the skills to use these programs, you may be faced with another problem—the managers you are presenting to may not understand the statistics involved. So always remember you audience. A bar chart may be more meaningful to them than knowing what the confidence interval is.

There are courses, books, videos, and Web sites on how to use Excel. Check with your human resources or information systems departments to find out what courses and resources they recommend. Do not stop at the beginning level course; usually it is in the intermediate or advanced courses that you will find what you need for data analysis. As with the data collection section above, the University of Wisconsin-Extension has resource booklets that cover using Excel for data analysis. The Internet will help you find many calculation tools that can help both in setting up data collection and in analysis. Some of these resources are listed below in the "Information Resources" section.

*Statistics* can be a scary word for some, and *mathematics* is no different. *Statistics* has several different meanings. As a discipline, courses in statistics generally cover a range of techniques and procedures for analyzing data, interpreting data, displaying data, and making decisions based on data. In another usage, *statistic* in the singular is defined as a numerical quantity (such as the mean)

---

**Resources on the Web: Data Analysis with Excel:**

"Using Excel for Analyzing Survey Questionnaires." University of Wisconsin-Extension, 1998. "Using Graphics to Report Evaluation Results." University of Wisconsin-Extension, 2003. www.uwex.edu/ces/pdande/evaluation/evaldocs.html

A Word document is available on the CD-ROM in the Chapter 10 folder that links directly to all these resources.

calculated in a sample or in the popular use, it can be defined as any number that is calculated from raw data. In this book, the word *measure* is used synonymously with this second meaning of *statistic*, because most evaluation literature use that term. Whatever your reaction to the word, if you are going to create a culture of assessment, you will need to accept the fact that doing an evaluation involves working with numbers and get some training and skills in this area.

Since teaching a statistics course is also beyond the scope of this book, in the section below you are presented with a list of statistical terms and methods that are commonly used in data analysis for evaluation projects. The data you have collected from primary sources, that is, data you collected yourself, falls into two general categories, quantitative and qualitative. You may also have data that were collected from secondary sources, as covered in Chapter 4. Any evaluation project could have all three types of data, and they need to be integrated into the final analysis and report. Each one is analyzed differently, but the results need to relate to one another seamlessly in the final report.

Using the mathematical and content analysis techniques listed below, you will be able to work with your data to find an answer or result. In your evaluation plan, as questions are being developed, you will discuss how to analyze the answers. The data are collected and entered into Excel in a manner that will produce the planned analysis method, whether of percentages or averages. You and your team should look at it in various ways to see which display technique best answers the question for your stakeholders. A ranked report might be more understandable as a bar chart than a pie chart. The ranking might be from left to right or right to left. Which display helps your group understand what the results mean? Discuss these details with your group and develop a consensus. Five techniques are usually used to analyze and display data (Taylor-Powell and University of Wisconsin-Extension, 1996a):

1. frequencies, percentages, and measures of central tendency and variation
2. comparisons between groups
3. cross tabulation (creating a table of relationships between data)
4. correlation of data
5. analysis of trends

Except for cross tabulation, which requires higher-level statistical software, all of these techniques can be done using Excel. Quantitative or numerical data are gathered from surveys, tabulations of qualitative data, or secondary sources. These raw data are summarized or described in a clear and understandable way using the category of statistics called descriptive statistics. An excellent example from the literature using descriptive statistics is the report of a survey of the use of e-journals and databases written by Sandra De Groote and Josephine Dorsch (2003). They reported the results of the survey using numerical and graphical methods (percentages and bar graphs, respectively). They also included some qualitative statements, which gave narrative reasons why the user preferred to access journals online versus in print. Numerical approaches are more precise and objective. Graphical methods can identify patterns in the data. Since these two approaches complement each other, it is a good idea to use both. The authors also used correlation to compare searching and use of online journals. The correlation of the data gathered showed that the more individuals there were who searched MEDLINE, the more likely they were to access electronic journals.

The next level of complexity in analysis is called inferential statistics. The two main methods used in inferential statistics are estimation and hypothesis testing. You use statistical methods to make inferences or judgments about a larger population based on the data collected from a small sample drawn from the population. De Groote and Dorsch collected data from 188 staff members at an academic health center. Can you infer that the answers these people gave are representative of the total population of people working at all academic health centers? The authors do conclude that "the findings in this study confirm that a large percentage of users in an academic health sciences environment prefer online resources to print" (De Groote and Dorsch, 2003: 234). As a research study, this inference has been applied to the population. As an evaluation study, this inference might lead to a management decision about what system you might buy to improve access to online resources.

Another important issue is how to analyze qualitative data. These data are collected using focus groups, interviews, and observational studies. It may seem difficult to do so because of its variegated nature, but there is a way to analyze qualitative data. Ellen Taylor-Powell recommends a step-by step plan (Taylor-Powell and University of Wisconsin-Extension, 1996b):

- Get to know your data.
- Focus the analysis.
- Categorize the information.
- Identify patterns and connections with and between categories.
- Bring things together with interpretation.

In her monograph, which is definitely recommended reading, Taylor-Powell also gives some practical tips about how to do it and pitfalls to avoid.

Sally Thorne, in her article titled "Data Analysis in Qualitative Research," calls data analysis "the most complex and mysterious of all of the phases of a qualitative project" (Thorne, 2000: 68). She goes on to say, "In order to generate findings that transform raw data into new knowledge, a qualitative researcher must engage in active and demanding analytic processes throughout all phases of the research." Understanding how it is done also helps those reading to understand and interpret it. She also points out that explanations of the practices by authors often do not help when, for instance, they "claim that their conceptual categories 'emerged' from the data—almost as if they left the raw data out overnight and awoke to find that the data analysis fairies had organized the data into a coherent new structure that explained everything!" Fanciful as her description is, her article goes on to explain some of the analytic strategies specific to qualitative research. While the fairies may not do the work for you, most people who work with qualitative data report that it is a rewarding experience that enhances their professional experience with creative and analytical thinking.

Beyond this point, unless you are an expert yourself, if would be wise to consult a statistician. You may find help in your institution perhaps in the quality, statistics, or even biostatistics departments. The statistics you will be using are still pretty basic, so do not get talked into doing analyses that are complicated. If you did, would your stakeholder understand them? Also you have to understand what you are presenting. Just like in any profession, statisticians come in all kinds, so find someone who enjoys helping people at your level of expertise.

Where do you start? In this chapter, as in Chapters 9, 11, and 12, you are given a short synopsis of a set of techniques that are relatively simple. These techniques were chosen because they appear in many of the books and articles used as reference for this book. When dealing with data analysis, books on evaluation tend to range from those with long technical chapters to those with too brief overviews. While trying to avoid this imbalance, our approach is certainly aimed at beginners, so readers skilled in statistics will not find it useful. Following this list, the section on information resources gives you a set of Web sites that offer further explanation on and education in the subject.

# MATHEMATICAL TECHNIQUES

## MEASURES OF CENTRAL TENDENCY

A measure of central tendency is a single number or value that describes the typical, representative, or central score among a set of scores. It measures the location of the middle or the center of a distribution. The definition of *middle* or *center* is purposely left somewhat vague so that the term *central tendency* can refer to a wide variety of measures. The three measures of central tendency are the mode, median, and mean. The mean, or average, is the most commonly used measure of central tendency.

The mean is obtained by adding the scores and then dividing the sum by the number of scores. The mean is a good measure of central tendency for mostly symmetric distributions but can be misleading in skewed distributions, since it can be greatly influenced by scores at the extreme end of the spectrum, called outliers. Other statistics such as the median may be more informative for distributions that are especially skewed.

The median is the middle score in a distribution of scores that divides the distribution in half; half of the scores are above the median and half are below the median. The median is less sensitive to extreme scores than the mean, and this makes it a better measure than the mean for highly skewed distributions. The median is said to be robust, that is, less sensitive to outliers than the mean. The median income is usually more informative than the mean income, for example. When there is an odd number of data, the median is simply the middle number. For example, the median of 2, 4, and 7 is 4. When there is an even number of numbers, the median is the mean of the two middle numbers. Thus, the median of the numbers 2, 4, 7, 12 is $(4+7)/2 = 5.5$.

The mode is the most frequently occurring score in a distribution of scores. The advantage of the mode is that its meaning is obvious. Further, it is the only measure of central tendency that can be used with nominal data or a set of data, which consists of categories with no particular ordering, such as race. The mode is not the frequency of the most numerous score. It is the value of that score itself. It is not sensitive to extreme scores. The mode is greatly subject to sample fluctuations, and it should not be used as the only measure of central tendency. A further disadvantage of the mode is that many distributions have more than one mode. These distributions are called "multi modal." The mode is easily and quickly computed but not very useful; it does not give much information about the distribution.

## Example

- *Problem:* A hospital librarian believes the library's professional development and travel budget lines are too low. She decides to do a quick performance benchmarking review and see what the typical budget allocation is for a similarly sized hospital.
- *Data collection:* She locates the appropriate table for measure on the 2004 MLA Benchmarking Network survey (found on the CD-ROM in the Chapter 6 folder), as shown in Figure 10.21.
- *Data analysis:* Her hospital has 1,750 FTEs, so her performance falls in Range 4, as shown in the bolded row in Figure 10.21. She observes that the mean for the 34 libraries in her size range is $1,600 and the median is $1,500. From the fact that the mean is higher than the median, it can be inferred that the distribution of the budget numbers is skewed rather than symmetrical. If she could see the data, she would see that a small number of quite large budget allocations raised the mean without affecting the median. This is also evident, since this survey shows the maximum ($4,500) and minimum ($100) for her range. She can also view the average and median for all the 185 libraries responding. If her hospital has a quality program that uses the third quartile or 75% figure for its quality target, that figure also is available. For further analysis, since these data are two years old, using a consumer price index found on the Web, she finds that goods purchased in 2004 for $1,500 now would cost $1,601, with a two-year inflation rate of 6.7%.
- *Conclusion or recommendations made based on the data:* The librarian decides to show this chart to her supervisor and request a budget line for professional development and travel of $1,700. She bases her decision on the fact that her hospital FTE number (1,750) is at the higher end of the range and the inflation rate would apply to these available figures. The median of $1,500 for her size range would be $1,600 with inflation, and she asks for $100 more, since the hospital is at the higher end of the range.

**Figure 10.21 MLA Benchmarking Network Survey 2004—Expenditures—Professional Development and Travel by Number of Hospital FTEs**

| Number of hospital FTEs | Expenditures—professional development and travel | | | | | |
|---|---|---|---|---|---|---|
| | qualified answers | mean | median | third quartile | maximum | minimum |
| Range 1: 0 to 449 | 6 | 908 | 729 | 1,377 | 1,887 | 250 |
| Range 2: 450 to 824 | 11 | 1,453 | 1,747 | 2,500 | 2,661 | 150 |
| Range 3: 825 to 1,449 | 32 | 1,056 | 825 | 1,364 | 4,275 | 75 |
| **Range 4: 1,450 to 1,849** | **34** | **1,600** | **1,500** | **2,150** | **4,500** | **100** |
| Range 5: 1,850 to 2,699 | 36 | 1,566 | 1,000 | 2,000 | 6,700 | 106 |
| Range 6: 2,700 to 4,599 | 38 | 2,082 | 1,664 | 2,302 | 7,300 | 150 |
| Range 7: 4,600 to 7,799 | 21 | 2,258 | 2,300 | 2,652 | 8,532 | 500 |
| Range 8: 7,800 and up | 7 | 5,261 | 3,000 | 7,362 | 12,500 | 2,000 |
| All | 185 | 1,780 | 1,403 | 2,300 | 12,500 | 75 |

## VARIABILITY

Measures of variability describe the spread or dispersion of scores about a central value. These include the range, variance, and standard deviation.

The range of a sample or a data set is a measure of the spread or the dispersion of the observations. It is the numerical difference between the largest and the smallest observed value of some quantitative characteristic, and it is easy to calculate. A great deal of information is ignored when computing the range, since only the largest and smallest data values are considered; the remaining data are ignored. The range value of a data set is greatly influenced by the presence of just one unusually large or small value in the sample (outlier). The range is used to characterize the dispersion among the measures in a given population.

The variance is a measure of variability that statisticians use to characterize the dispersion among the measures in a data set. To calculate the variance of a data set, first calculate the mean of the scores, then measure the amount that each score deviates from the mean, and then square that deviation by multiplying it by itself. Numerically, the variance equals the average of the several squared deviations from the mean. It is the first step in calculating the standard deviation.

The standard deviation is the average deviation of scores from the mean. It also characterizes the dispersion among the measures in a given population. Numerically, the standard deviation is the square root of the variance. Unlike the variance, which is a somewhat abstract measure of variability, the standard deviation can be conceptualized as a distance along the scale of measurement. The more widely the values are spread out, the larger the standard deviation. The standard deviation has proven to be an extremely useful measure of spread in part because it is mathematically tractable. The standard deviation is used in inferential statistics.

## CORRELATION

Correlation, sometimes called the correlation coefficient, is an index of how strongly two variables are related to each other. It also indicates the direction (positive or negative) of the relationship. The computation of the correlation coefficient is most easily accomplished with the aid of a statistical calculator or program. Excel has a correlation function. The correlation coefficient may take any value between 1 and –1. The sign of the correlation coefficient (+ ,-) defines the direction of the relationship, either positive or negative. A positive correlation coefficient means that as the value of one variable increases, the value of the other variable increases; as one decreases, the other decreases. A negative correlation coefficient indicates that as one variable increases, the other decreases, and vice versa.

### Example

Jacoby, J., and N. P. O'Brien. 2005. "Assessing the Impact of Reference Services Provided to Undergraduate Students." *College & Research Libraries*, 66, no. 4: 324–340.
From the abstract:

- *Problem:* What is the impact of reference services on undergraduate students? Three outcomes were examined: (1) Do undergraduate students perceive the reference staff as being friendly and approachable? (2) Do they learn something during the course of the reference interaction? and (3) Do they feel more confident about their ability to find information after the reference interaction than they did before?
- *Data collection:* The study targeted undergraduates receiv-

ing non-directional reference assistance, yielding 69 survey responses and 5 follow-up interviews.

- *Data analysis:* The methodology of the analysis uses correlations to judge the relationships among the variables and provides a table of the correlations. This is a demonstration of the extensive use of correlations.
- *Conclusion or recommendations made based on the data:* Our findings suggest that reference services can play a significant role in helping students become confident, independent information seekers. Correlations between variables and a multiple regression model* further indicate that friendliness of the reference staff was one of the best predictors of students' confidence in their ability to find information on their own. These outcomes are particularly salient in a college and university environment, where building skills for independent information exploration is a primary goal (Jacoby and O'Brien, 2005).

*Regression is a class of statistical methods in which one dependent variable is related to one or more independent variables. A regression line is a line drawn through the points on a scatterplot to summarize the relationship among the variables being studied. Multiple regression aims to find a linear relationship between a response variable and several possible predictor variables.*

## RATIOS

A ratio is the relationship between two numbers or measurements, usually with the same units, like the ratio of the width of an object to its length. The ratio a:b is equivalent to the quotient a/b. It is expressed as the quotient of two numbers, or as two numbers separated by a colon (pronounced "to"). As a comparison it can be expressed as a fraction. For example, there is a ratio of three boys to two girls in a class (3/2, 3:2). Ratios can be expressed in words, fractions, decimals, or percents. For example, the ratio given when a team wins 4 out of 6 games can be said as 4:6 or four out of six or 4/6 or 66%.

### Example

Knievel, J. E., H. Wicht, and L. S. Connaway. 2006. "Use of Circulation Statistics and Interlibrary Loan Data in Collection Management." *College and Research Libraries,* 67, no. 1: 35–49.
   *From the abstract:*

- *Problem:* To assist with management decisions in relation to remote storage, preservation, and collection development.

- *Data collection:* This project utilizes three distinct sets of data from the UCB libraries. In all three sets, data are limited to books only and analyzed across subject areas, rather than title-by-title. The three data sets are: the entire collection of books owned by UCB; all the books that circulated at UCB from January 1998 through December 2002; and all the books that were requested via UCB's ILL department between January 1998 and December 2002.

- *Data analysis:* The data collected for this study yielded many valuable results that are too numerous to discuss in full in this paper. Based on previous studies reported in the literature, the elements selected for discussion are: Overall holdings; Average transactions per item; Percentage of items circulated in a given subject collection; and ratio comparing ILL requests with holdings in a subject area. Tables were displayed.

- *Comment on the results from the subject of sociology as demonstrated in Figure* 10.22:

   "Although it was not among the largest or smallest collections, sociology had very high transactions per item, percentage of the collection circulated, and ratio of holdings to interlibrary loan. This indicates that sociology is an extremely active collection in all ways. This is possibly due to the fact that sociology books are relevant to many subjects outside sociology" (Knievel, Wicht, and Connaway, 2006: 324). Perhaps the overall most important factor demonstrated by this study is the importance of combining different sources of data for collection development decisions.

- *Conclusion or recommendations made based on the data:* A sample of the conclusions: The results of this research have provided empirical data for collection management and remote storage decision making at UCB. The results also could be utilized for the development of qualitative assessments, such as interviews with faculty. The circulation statistics and ILL borrowing requests could be used to calculate the obsolescence of a book based on its publication date and the increase or decrease of the number of circulations during a five-year period (Knievel, Wicht, and Connaway, 2006).

| Figure 10.22 Statistics on Sociology Holdings |||||
| --- | --- | --- | --- | --- |
| Number of UCB Holdings in WorldCat by Subject |||||
| Rank | Subject | Holdings | | |
| 7 | Sociology | 43,437 | | |
| Average Number of Circulation Transactions per Item by Subject |||||
| Rank | Subject | Circulation Transactions | Circulating Items | Transactions per Item |
| 3 | Sociology | 106,724 | 17,809 | 6.0 |
| Percentage of Collection Circulated by Subject |||||
| Rank | Subject | Holdings | Circulating Items | % Items Circulated |
| 2 | Sociology | 43,437 | 17,809 | 41.0% |
| Holdings: ILL Ratio by Subject |||||
| Rank | Subject | Holdings | ILL Items | ILL Ratio |
| 6 | Sociology | 43,437 | 1,673 | 26.0:1 |

## PERCENTAGES

A percentage expresses information as a proportion of a whole. It is expressed as a proportion, a ratio, or a fraction as a whole number, by using 100 as the denominator. A number such as 45% (45 percent or 45 per cent) is shorthand for the fraction 45/100 or 0.45. The number of units with a certain characteristic are divided by the total number of units in the sample and multiplied by 100. For example, the percentage that represents 5 out of 20 boys is 5 divided by 20 x 100, which is 25%, 25 per cent means 25 in every 100 or 25/100. Common fractions or numbers expressed as decimals can also be expressed as percentages. Percentages are relatively easy to interpret. (1/2 = .50 = 50%; 1/4 = .25 = 25%; 3/4 = .75 = 75%; and so forth.)They are often used with frequency distributions.

### Example

The example from the literature, as described under "Ratios," is also an excellent example of the use of percentages.

## NUMERICAL COUNTS OR FREQUENCIES

Numerical counts or frequencies represent the number of times something occurs over time or how many responses fit into a category. It is sometimes called a frequency distribution. To calculate the frequency, one fixes a time interval or category, counts the number of occurrences of the event within that interval or category, and then divides this count by the length of the time interval or total in the category. It is an arrangement of a set of scores from lowest to highest that indicates the number of times each score was obtained. For example, a frequency distribution of a class of 45 students may indicate that 25 were male and 20 were females. It is usually a list, ordered by quantity, showing the number of times each value appears.

### Example

Example of a frequency by category:

- Twenty-five of the 55 medical libraries in Colorado and Wyoming are net lenders of interlibrary loans.
- In the annual total for 2005, 30 of the 123 participants in the library courses were physicians.

Example of a frequency by time:

- In a one-week checklist survey of the reference desk (hypothetical), there were 188 questions, which would average 4.7 per hour for the 40 hours the desk was staffed.
- In a one-week checklist survey of the reference desk (hypothetical), there were 188 questions, 125 of which occurred in the morning and 63 in the afternoon.

## RANK

Data are ranked when they are placed in order from largest to smallest. Rank is not an actual measure but a number created to indicate where one number stands in relation to other numbers. The actual differences in a ranked list are usually concealed, so it is best to explain the meaning of the rank. If you say "My library is ranked number 1," it is meaningless, but if you say, "My library is ranked number 1 among small medical libraries in the city in relation to number of square feet," it has some meaning to your audience.

# INFORMATION RESOURCES FOR DATA ANALYSIS

## FREE TEXTBOOKS ON THE WEB

*The Qualitative Research Web Page* by Don Ratcliff, Ph.D. (http://don.ratcliffs.net/qual/): This site contains Dr. Ratcliff's book and other writings and a resource page linking to other sites.

*Rice Virtual Lab in Statistics* (http://onlinestatbook.com/rvls.html): Includes HyperStat Online, an online statistics book with links to other statistics resources on the Web, as well as an extensive glossary.

*Statistics Every Writer Should Know* (www.robertniles.com/stats/): A simple guide to understanding basic statistics; for journalists and other writers who might not know math.

*SurfStat Australia* (www.anu.edu.au/nceph/surfstat/surfstat-home/surfstat.html): A textbook with many illustrations.

University of Wisconsin-Extension (www.uwex.edu/ces/pdande/evaluation/evaldocs.html): See the document on the CD-ROM in the Chapter 10 folder for hot links to these resources and others from the University of Wisconsin-Extension:

- *Analyzing Quantitative Data*, 1996
- *Analyzing Qualitative Data*, 2003
- *Using Excel for Analyzing Survey Questionnaires*, 1998
- *Using Graphics to Report Evaluation Results*, 2003

## RESOURCE LISTS

IFLA Statistics and Evaluation Section Useful Links Related to Statistics and Evaluation (www.ifla.org/VII/s22/statlinks.htm)

Internet Glossary of Statistical Terms (www.animatedsoftware.com/statglos/statglos.htm)

Library Research Service (http://lrs.org/): Sponsored by the Colorado State Library, this site has many resources for librarians, including Research Methods Resources page and a statistical tools and calculators page with a variety of useful calculators.

The Researching Librarian (www.researchinglibrarian.com/): This site is run by Beth Ashmore. It has extensive resources including databases, funding, journals, statistics, tools, current awareness, proceedings, and a site index, which lists links to all the sites listed on the site in alphabetical order.

# REFERENCES

Baker, L. M. 2006. "Observation: A Complex Research Method." *Library Trends*, 55, no. 1: 171–189.

Burroughs, C. M., and F. B. Wood. 2000. *Measuring the Difference: Guide to Planning and Evaluating Health Information Outreach*. Seattle, WA, Bethesda, MD: National Network of Libraries of Medicine Pacific Northwest Region. National Library of Medicine. Available: http://nnlm.gov/evaluation/guide/index.html (accessed June 6, 2006).

De Groote, S. L., and J. L. Dorsch. 2003. "Measuring Use Patterns of Online Journals and Databases." *Journal of the Medical Library Association*, 91, no. 2: 231–240.

"Designing a Questionnaire." 2004. In *What is a Survey?* edited by F. Scheuren. Alexandria, VA: American Statistical Association. Available: www.whatisasurvey.info/

Dillman, D. A. 2000. *Mail and Internet Surveys: The Tailored Design Method*. 2nd edition. New York: Wiley.

Englesgjerd, A., and C. Larson. "Needs Assessment Tutorial." Needs Assessment and Data Management Project Team, University of Arizona Library (last updated April 2000). Available: http://digital.library.arizona.edu/nadm/tutorial/index.htm (accessed December 15, 2006).

Frary, R. B. "A Brief Guide to Questionnaire Development." Test Scoring Services of Virginia Tech (last updated October 27, 2006). Available: www.testscoring.vt.edu/questionaire_dev.html (accessed December 18, 2006).

Given, L. M., and G. J. Leckie. 2003. "'Sweeping' the Library: Mapping the Social Activity Space of the Public Library." *Library & Information Science Research*, 25, no. 4: 365–385.

"How to Plan a Survey." 2004. In *What is a Survey?* edited by F. Scheuren. Alexandria, VA: American Statistical Association. Available: www.whatisasurvey.info/

Jacoby, J., and N. P. O'Brien. 2005. "Assessing the Impact of Reference Services Provided to Undergraduate Students." *College & Research Libraries*, 66, no. 4: 324–340.

Johnson, D. W. 1996. "Choosing an Evaluation Method." In *The TELL IT! Manual: The Complete Program for Evaluating Library Performance*, edited by D. L. Zweizig, D. W. Johnson, J. Robbins, and the American Library Association. Chicago, IL: American Library Association.

Knievel, J. E., H. Wicht, and L. S. Connaway. 2006. "Use of Circulation Statistics and Interlibrary Loan Data in Collection Management." *College & Research Libraries*, 67, no. 1: 35–49.

Lance, K. C., and D. W. Johnson. 1996. "Questionnaires." In *The TELL IT! Manual: The Complete Program for Evaluating Library Performance*, edited by D. L. Zweizig, D. W. Johnson, J. Robbins, and the American Library Association. Chicago, IL: American Library Association.

Marshall, J. G., and the Medical Library Association. 1990. *Evaluation Instruments for Health Sciences Libraries: MLA DocKit #2*. Chicago, IL: Medical Library Association.

Program Planning and Assessment, University of Illinois – Extension. "Key Informant Interviews." University of Illinois – Extension, Program Planning and Assessment. Available: http://ppa.aces.uiuc.edu/KeyInform.htm (accessed January 10, 2007).

Robbins, J. B. 1996. "Interviewing." In *The TELL IT! Manual: The Complete Program for Evaluating Library Performance*, edited by D. L. Zweizig, D. W. Johnson, J. Robbins, and the American Library Association. Chicago, IL: American Library Association.

Taylor-Powell, E., and University of Wisconsin – Extension. 1996a. *Analyzing Quantitative Data*. Madison, WI: University of Wisconsin – Extension. Cooperative Extension Service. Available: www.uwex.edu/ces/pdande/evaluation/evaldocs.html (accessed December 18, 2006).

Taylor-Powell, E., and University of Wisconsin – Extension. 1996b. *Analyzing Quantitative Data*. Madison, WI: University of Wisconsin – Extension. Cooperative Extension Service. *Available*: www.uwex.edu/ces/pdande/evaluation/evaldocs.html (accessed December 18, 2006).

Taylor-Powell, E., and University of Wisconsin – Extension. 1998. *Sampling*. Madison, WI: University of Wisconsin – Extension. Cooperative Extension Service. Available: www.uwex.edu/ces/pdande/evaluation/evaldocs.html (accessed December 18, 2006).

Taylor-Powell, E., C. Hermann, and the University of Wisconsin – Extension. 2000. *Cooperative Extension Service. Collecting Evaluation Data: Surveys*. Madison, WI: University of Wisconsin—Extension. Cooperative Extension Service. Available: www.uwex.edu/ces/pdande/evaluation/evaldocs.html (accessed December 18, 2006).

Taylor-Powell, E., M. G. Marshall, and University of Wisconsin – Extension. 1998. *Questionnaire Design: Asking Questions with a Purpose*. Madison, WI: University of Wisconsin – Extension. Cooperative Extension Service. Available: www.uwex.edu/ces/pdande/evaluation/evaldocs.html (accessed December 18, 2006).

Thorne, S. 2000. "Data Analysis in Qualitative Research." *Evidence-Based Nursing*, 3: 68–70.

Zweizig, D., and D. W. Johnson. 1996. "Observation." In *The TELL IT! Manual: The Complete Program for Evaluating Library Performance*, edited by D. L. Zweizig, D. W. Johnson, J. Robbins, and the American Library Association. Chicago, IL: American Library Association.

# 11 SKILLS FOR COMMUNICATING IN EVALUATION PROJECTS

Evaluation is all about communication. You listen to your staff about problems that need to be fixed. You hear complaints from library customers. You challenge the team to get the job done. You keep the staff or team informed via e-mail. You write reports to different stakeholders about the outcome of the evaluation. You present your findings orally to a budget committee to explain what you need. Just as you are motivated to learn about evaluation, you need to be motivated to learn to communicate effectively.

## WHAT IS GOOD COMMUNICATION?

Good business communication skills are considered a decisive factor in job success. This chapter gives you some brief tips on communication skills and allows you to assess your own skill level. You need to make an honest assessment of your skills and work to improve those you find lacking. These are some strategies to follow for improvement:

- Ask for help within your organization. The human resources department may provide courses in the various types of business communications or recommend outside firms.
- Take some courses offered by your corporation or local college or community center.
- Form mentor relationships with other managers or other librarians in your area to go over your learning needs. Use mentoring networks established by library associations such as the MLA or SLA.
- Read books. As a librarian you know there are a multitude of books on the subject. Ask for recommendations. One recommendation is *The Elements of Style* by Strunk and White, considered one of the most influential and best-known prescriptive treatments of English grammar and

usage in the United States. It details eight elementary rules of usage, ten elementary principles of composition, some few matters of form, and a list of commonly misused words and expressions. At 105 pages, this may be what you need, if you think you need help in this area (Strunk, White, and Angell, 2000).

- Search the Web. While there is too much information on the Web on communication alone, combining any of the topics discussed below with the term *business communications* will yield many informative and interesting sites. One excellent site is MindTools.com ("Essential Skills for Your Excellent Career!") (MindTools, accessed: 2006). This site provides free articles on most of these topics without requiring a registration. It has a free newsletter, and you can buy materials and take online courses.
- Join groups or clubs to improve your skills. Toastmasters International can give you great practice in public speaking (Toastmasters International, accessed: 2006). There are clubs or improvement groups for all of these skills.

The purpose of good business communication is to relay your message in a way that others understand it. You are the sender; you choose a channel of communication. The receiver receives the message. Does he or she understand it? The receiver will give you feedback that you need to understand. And all of this takes place in the context of a business culture, an ethnic culture, and a language that at times can be imprecise (Fowler, accessed; 2007b)! Librarians are trained in the reference interview, so perhaps they are a step ahead when it comes to understanding others. But we all know even that can be challenging. A reference librarian was once observed accepting a question on an immunological subject for a computerized search from a visiting Chinese scientist. What language were they speaking? English, Chinese, library science, computerese, or immunology? That communication was fraught with barriers to understanding. This is a list of the different components in the transfer of the information from one place to another:

- *The Sender:* Establish credibility. Display knowledge of the subject, the receiver, and the environment. Know your audience well enough so that your message is understood. Be complete, concise, accurate, and easily understandable.
- *The Message:* No matter what the channel chosen, the content is affected by the tone of the words, the organization of the material, the reasoning behind the argument, and

the sender's individual style. Our intellects allow us to reason with the receiver, whereas the emotional component of the message appeals to the person more subtly and has just as much ability to change minds and actions. If your message is disorganized, too long, or erroneous, it will be misunderstood.

- *The Channel:* Transmission can take place textually, verbally, or visually, and it can be both private and public, often at the same time. Many of the same principles apply whether you are giving a speech, a presentation to management, chatting in the hallway, talking on the phone, or writing an e-mail, letter, memo, or report.

- *The Receiver:* Whether your message is intended for 1 person or 100, you should know what reaction you want the receiver to have. Each individual who receives the message will be doing so within his or her own context and with his or her own set of ideas, feelings, influences, and time frames. These need to be considered by the sender before delivering the message.

- *The Feedback:* The receiver will send feedback, verbally and nonverbally. Is he or she looking at his or her watch? Maybe you should speed up. No response to an important e-mail? Maybe it was too long and detailed (or the receiver is on vacation or it got deleted as spam). A follow-up phone call may be in order. If you want your message understood, you have to find a way to determine that it was.

- *The Context:* The context of all of the above factors must be considered. If you get 40 spam e-mails a day and routinely delete them, are you likely to delete a message from the CEO's new secretary whose name you do not know if the subject line says, "Some assistance please?" Probably you would. If she had come to the library desk in person, her words in that context would not have been misunderstood. So watch your environments, both cultural and technological, and understand how they can impact the receiver's life.

There are barriers at every stage of the communication cycle; however, if you keep all these components in mind as you prepare your communication, you will be able to deliver your message more effectively. Whichever communication channel you decide to use to send the message, always think of your audience. What you want to say is less important than what you want them to hear.

# YOUR AUDIENCE

Thinking about your audience is the first thing to do when planning a communication, no matter what the channel. In an evaluation project, you will have many audiences. To start, your supervisor will need to hear that you want to do the evaluation and that you need his or her support. Your team needs to hear your reasons for doing the evaluation. Other stakeholders will need to come on board through good communication. Finally, your report needs to be understood so you can take action. And do not forget your responsibility to the profession to report your findings at meetings and in publications. All of these recipients of your communications are separate audiences in separate contexts. Gather some information before starting each communication. Here are some questions to ask:

- *Who is your audience?* This may sound easy, but it is not always so. Even in a roomful of librarians, people have different backgrounds, levels of experience, and even languages. Take some time to think about those backgrounds. Not only will their cultural references influence how they understand, but also their unique ideas and feelings will come into play.
- *How many audiences do you have?* List them. Are they all going to be at the same meeting or receiving the same report, or can you segment them and do different presentations or reports?
- *What does the audience already know about the subject?* As most special and medical librarians know, the managers who are influential in your budget allocation know very little about the issues of librarianship. Some background may be necessary. But these are busy people so do not overdo it. It is a fine balance.
- *What is your audience's purpose?* Did they come to learn a new skill or hear about the latest developments? Are they required to be there? Do they have to make a decision based on your presentation? You have asked for their time to read or listen, so you need to make your message clear and interesting. Tell them what your message is. Do not assume they are all up to speed.
- *What do they want?* Needs and wants are nuances, but see if you can see the differences in your audience. The receiver of the message may have some specific need when reading a report or listening to a presentation. This may

**Tip: Readability Levels**

In Microsoft Word you can set your preferences or options to display "readability statistics" when the "spelling and grammar" check finishes. Search "help" for readability statistics.

not be related to his or her purpose for being in the audience.

- *What is most important to them?* Likewise, what are they least likely to care about? Does your administrator care about saving time or managing risk? Talk to fellow managers and find out before you make assumptions.
- *What is their general reading level?* You still need to take readability level into account for all communications, even oral presentations. In general, you want to keep it as low as possible. An eighth-grade reading level or below is common except in very technical fields and some business settings. Your audience will read and remember writing that is easy and clear.

The idea is you have to know your audience so you can tailor your message to them so they can understand it. If you are giving a presentation or talking about the benefits of OpenURL technology, you would be giving a different speech to librarians than to the administrator who is going to give you the funds to purchase access to it. The skill to learn is to think more about what you want them to hear and understand than about what you want to say.

# EFFECTIVE WRITING

The process of evaluation requires good writing skills in every phase. Whether writing a proposal to perform the evaluation, sending a memo to the evaluation team, being on the team to craft good survey questions, or writing the final report to the administration and other stakeholders, good writing skills will be necessary to get the message across. "The single biggest problem with communication is the illusion that it has taken place," said George Bernard Shaw. This should make you think about the words you write down. As mentioned before, the tips given here are just an inventory to let you decide if you need some help with your writing skills. Books, courses, and Web sites will help you improve your skills in this area.

It is mostly practice, however, that will get you to the point where you consider yourself a skilled writer. Write reports to friends and colleagues and ask for their criticism. Find someone who knows how to write and ask if he or she can be your mentor. The ability to write clearly is important across all professions.

Your choice of words tells a lot about who you are and what is important to you.

To check on your proficiency, ask yourself the following questions:

- Did I take the time to prepare an outline of my message before actually writing it?
- Is my message clear, concise, and relevant?
- Did I consider my audience, or do I write the same way for everyone?
- Does it have a main statement, with smooth transitions, and a topic sentence for each paragraph?
- Did I use methods to provide variety and interest?
- Am I using proper grammar and language?
- Do I regularly use a thesaurus to add variety to my vocabulary, and have I stopped using trite words such as *very, great, exciting,* or *interesting*?
- Am I too wordy in my written communications, saying the same thing over and over but in different ways?
- Have my colleagues told me that my writing is inspirational and witty, as well as informative?
- What courses can I take, or to what professional journals can I subscribe, to enhance my written communication skills?

Review your writing for these qualities. You can judge whether you believe you are communicating effectively.

## STRUCTURE

Every good communication should have these three structural elements: an opening, a body, and a closing. Can you read your communication and identify these three parts? Take the time to outline the message. Many communications are remembered by the power of their opening and closing. Some people use stories, quotes, or jokes. Make sure you are good at humor if you choose to use it. Any joke or story has to have something to do with the business at hand, or it should be left out. Make sure you tell the story correctly, do not mess up the punch line, and make sure the story is appropriate for the audience.

- *Opening:* Begin with the real purpose of the communication. If you have a lot of background material, it can be discussed later. A strong, sharp opening allows the audience to quickly understand what the communication is about and choose whether to pay attention. Get to the point right away and respect your audience's time.

- *Body:* Here is where you communicate your background information, the facts and figures about the action you want your audience to take. Keep your facts and figures and any graphs or charts you might present to the point.
- *Closing:* Sum up your key points and state clearly what action you expect to be taken. Use headlines such as "Action Requested," "Deadlines," and "Next Steps."

## CLARITY

- *Choose the right words.* Use everyday, simple, clear words. Read the message aloud. How does it sound? Avoid formal or complex jargon. If you have to use jargon, define it.
- *Cut down on long words.* Read a memo or letter you have written recently and see how many three-syllable words you use and change them. For example, change *initiate* to *start* and *expedite* to *rush* and *utilize* to *use.* Your readers will thank you.
- *Use strong verbs.* They keep the reader interested. Instead of "We will hold a discussion on the topic," say, "We will discuss the topic."
- Avoid passive verbs. Do not say, "It was decided by the committee," when you can say, "The committee decided."
- *Do not try to impress with pretentious, inflated language.* Being understood the first time through is the most important element of writing for a business audience.
- *Balance your writing with long and short sentences.*
- *Try to keep each written communication about one topic.* Otherwise, it will be very lengthy and no one will know where to file it.
- *Respect your reader's time.* No one appreciates confusing, careless prose.

## CONSISTENCY

The following should be true of your content, style and design.

- Make sure your overall message does not change in the middle or from one memo to another.
- Do not change verb tenses or switch from first to third person and back again.
- Good writing is rewriting. No one gets it right the first time around.

## MEDIUM

Choose your medium. Is your message appropriate for that medium? The one to choose communicates your message accurately, creates high audience comprehension, and has a low cost monetarily and temporally. You have a choice from any one or combination of the written communication mediums, such as paper-based or e-mail memos, formal letters, annual reports, final reports, threefold flyers, bookmarks, press releases, or Web pages. It is unlikely you would use some of these in a library setting, but as you analyze what you are going to write and how you are going to state your message, the medium will dictate the style and design.

## RELEVANCY

Is your message relevant to the people you are sending it to? Do not send a memo or e-mail if you can imagine the receiver saying, "Why did she copy me on this?" This is another reason to have only one point to each message.

## THE RULE OF SEVEN PLUS OR MINUS TWO

According to psychologists, the human brain has a finite capacity to hold information in short-term memory. They have also determined that the brain retains information in "clusters," or groups of items, and these groups contain seven items, plus or minus two. So if you have ten points to make in the background section of your writing, it might be a good idea to drop or combine a few.

## THE PROCESS OF WRITING

Here are some questions that will guide you in your development before you start your outline and actual writing:

- Why write this text?
- Why write this text now?
- Who is the audience (or audiences)?
- How is this text going to be delivered?
- What else has been written on this subject before? Are you citing it?
- When is the deadline for this text?
- What is the format or medium of this text going to be?
- Is there a house style for this text?
- Are there questions of copyright or confidentiality?

As you write, edit, check, and proofread. Then proofread again.

## WRITING AN EVALUATION REPORT

Final evaluation reports have a certain set of parameters that describe the evaluation process in detail. Since evaluation is a type of research, it follows the standard research report format. Depending on the formality of the evaluation project, this template can be modified to fit the needs of the project. But leaving out any part should be carefully considered.

It is best to develop a report for archival purposes that follows this total outline and contains all the data that can be printed or put on a CD-ROM. This template shows you what to include in the large project report. From this archival report, smaller reports in the same general format, and often using the same words, are written for the various stakeholders of the evaluation. Each one should be complete but sometimes can refer to the archival report for review of data and other lengthy items. The template is printed here and available on the CD-ROM in the Chapter 11 folder. An excellent example of an evaluation report of a needs assessment is available on the CD-ROM in the Chapter 6 folder.

## EVALUATION REPORT TEMPLATE
### Title Page and Presentation

*Title page:* Have a proper title page with the name of the project, the dates of the project, and the date of the report. Include the name of the library and some of the key players, if appropriate.

*Presentation:* Begin by setting up a binder or portfolio. Tabs and sheet protectors could be used to show the labeled and dated material quickly to any requestor. Besides the narrative report described below, the binder should contain the following:

- Full descriptions of the evaluation methods
- Copies of questionnaires
- Copies of the data from the questionnaires before the analysis
- The statistical analysis
- The decisions made
- The changes requested

This report should be kept in the library to document the evaluation project for any survey activity, such as a visit from the JCAHO, or for any stakeholders to review if they choose to. If you feel that more than a few people will want to see the final archival report, you should prepare two or three copies to circulate. If the evaluation project generated different reports for different stakeholders, such as a benchmarking report, copies of the various reports should be included in the final archival report.

> **On the CD-ROM: Via Christi Needs Assessment Final Report and Appendices**
>
> In the Chapter 6 Folder: Via Christi Folder
>
> Thanks go to Via Christi's administration for giving permission for this final report and appendices to be placed on the CD-ROM. This is a hard-to-find kind of document and is a useful example for all small libraries of a comprehensive needs assessment project report.

### Section 1: Summary and Introduction

*Summary:* Sometimes called an executive summary, the summary presents an overview of the evaluation findings in a format that allows the administration to make important decisions effectively and efficiently. Remember that these are busy people and the more important they are, the less detail they want to know. Summaries are developed for different stakeholders and may be included here and/or at the end. If it were an executive summary, it would go at the beginning. Make this a short summary for people who would not be reading the whole report. Give the reasons why the evaluation was conducted and toward whom it is targeted, together with any conclusions and recommendations. The summary would include:

- What was evaluated
- The purposes of evaluation
- The audience interested in evaluation results
- Any limitations or restraints on the evaluation due to cost or time
- Major findings and recommendations

*Introduction:* Introduce the major sections of the report as well as the primary people involved in the project. Give a statement of the need or purpose of the report, including any relevant history and dates. Fully identify the project team and any support personnel. If a benchmarking report, identify the benchmarking partners. This may be specifically by name or generally by category. Discuss why the evaluation was conducted and what it was and was not intended to accomplish.

### Section 2: Background

*Background:* Describe any information that is needed to provide the reader with an understanding of the background for the analysis, such as who initiated it, why the process or outcome was chosen, and what it was meant to achieve. If a needs assessment, explain why it was done now. Include the library vision and mission that prompted the evaluation. Describe the customers, the inputs, and the outputs. Describe how your team was structured and the timelines involved. The depth of description will depend on how knowledgeable the intended audience is about the program. Try to achieve a balance between leaving things out and burdening the reader with too much detail.

## Section 3: Description of Evaluation Methods

*Methodolgy:* Review the methodology and any relevant technical information, such as how the data were collected and what evaluation tools were used. If appropriate, provide step-by-step descriptions of what was done. Include examples of instruments in an appendix. Cover these points:

- *Purposes of the evaluation.* Describe the purpose(s) of the analysis. This could be rephrased from the content of the planning document or Logic Model. Examples might be:
  - "The purpose of the study is to determine if there is a need for more instruction in using the OPAC."
  - "The purpose of the study is to assess the library's physical collection by comparing it with like libraries through benchmarking and comparing these results to a survey of users concerning their opinion about the collection."
- *Evaluation design.* Spell out any limitations of the analysis in relation to the interpretation and generalizability of the data. Also describe any problems with the reliability and validity of the instruments used in the analysis.
- *Data collection instruments used.* Describe the various methods you use to collect your data—questionnaires, interviews, site visits, and so forth. Discuss the questions you developed to do the evaluation.
- *Data collection procedures.* Describe the sample used and target population(s) included in the analysis and the size of the sample. Discuss how the instruments were used and the timelines involved. For a benchmarking report, discuss how partners were chosen for site visits or interviews. Describe how the metrics or indicators for your process or assessment were developed, with descriptions of any flowchart or fishbone diagrams that were done. Actual diagrams should be included in an appendix. Include an overview of the primary and secondary sources (as described in Chapter 4) you used to gather information employed in the process. Refer to details in an appendix containing the printed sources and the names of people interviewed, if appropriate.

## Section 4: Discussion of Results

*Results:* Spell out the findings from each part of the evaluation. Use graphics (charts, tables, and so on) to illustrate the information—but use them sparingly to increase their effectiveness. See Chapter 12 for explanations of charts and graphs. After presenting actual results with an explanation, present interpretations of their meaning. You could describe these parts of various sections of the evaluation:

- description of the participants of the evaluation
- the actual results, including the rate of return
- a discussion of the statistical analysis if appropriate
- interpretation of results in terms of stated goals and purpose
- explanation of the results
- strengths and weaknesses shown in the results
- unexpected results

In a benchmarking report, present your charts and graphs with your rank represented. Explain what your ranking means in relation to the process. Include only the important findings here and leave other findings to be listed in an appendix. Describe the findings of the quantitative data developed at the site visit or interview. This is your chance to explain how the enablers of practice affect a process and why they might be important in yours.

**Optional Section: Costs and Benefits**

It is a trend to look at the cost of evaluation. If you had a budget for the evaluation and the evaluation's purpose was to look for cost savings in the process or program, it would be a good idea to include some commentary here about this issue. Evaluation projects are not free. This section could cover:

- What was the method used to calculate costs and effects/benefits of the evaluation study?
- How were costs and benefits defined?
- List costs that were associated with the study and how costs were distributed (for example, start-up costs, operating costs).
- Were there any hidden costs that might affect future studies? For example, if there were many in-kind contributions that were not mentioned, it might be thought that a second study without these could be done for this budget?
- What benefits were associated with the evaluation study?
- Were there any unexpected benefits?

**Section 5: Conclusions and Recommendations**

*Conclusions:* This section and the summary are often the only parts of a report that are read. This attaches a lot of importance to this section. Conclusions and recommendations should be stated clearly and precisely. Present your main points in a list format for easy reading. Make sure that you get your main points across in the opening summary and in the conclusion.

Recommendations: Present recommendations based on the results reported in the previous section. Describe how they were prioritized and rated. Are you continuing, extending, modifying, or terminating the program? If doing a benchmarking report, present recommendations based on your best practices template and the gaps you found in your own process. Recommend specific improvements and indicate budgetary requirements. Include the time frame in which you will evaluate the changes made in the process.

### Section 6: Summary and References

*Summary:* Present a brief "easy-to-digest" synopsis of the report.
*References:* Lists the sources reviewed or consulted during the analysis.

### Alternative Approach to Evaluation Report Writing

After doing your extensive evaluation report, perhaps you are asked to give just the results and not all the details about the methodology. You should always finish your evaluation project with a formal report, even if no one will read it. Then if someone does take an interest in the future about how something came about, you have the report and methodology to explain it. But you have been asked to give a two-page written report or perhaps a ten-minute presentation. And you have all these FACTS to present! How boring! So how do you create excitement and present the facts?

Keith Lance, leader of the Counting on Results (CoR) project, discussed in Chapter 8, has come up with an interesting way of presenting results of outcomes that could be applied to most evaluation reports, written or in a PowerPoint presentation (Lance, accessed: 2006a; accessed: 2006b). He discusses this method and has posted the presentation on the Public Library Association Web site, "The Smartest Card. The Smartest Campaign Toolkit" on the sub page, Numbers You Can Use (www.ala.org/ala/pla/plaissues/smartestcardcampaign/toolkit/statistics.htm). Lance has developed a five-step process for using statistics gathered from outside sources or from surveys combined with anecdotes or stories gathered from your own library users. The PowerPoint presentation is called *Making It Count @ your library* ® (Lance, accessed: 2006a). His demonstration message is "Public libraries are for YOU! The library is what you want it to be." Figure 11.1 is an example of the presentation of one point.

1. Develop your message: What is known about your type of library?
2. State the outcome that demonstrates the message: How is the message demonstrated in terms of library programs?
3. List the facts: Data that back up the message.
4. The Sources: Where to find the data.
5. Your Story: How to communicate it.

| **Figure 11.1** | **Alternative Methods of Results Presentation** |
|---|---|
| Message | Public libraries are for YOU! The library is what you want it to be. |
| Outcomes | Public libraries will get you through times of no money... |
| | Public libraries generate a measurable return-on-investment in terms of community development. |
| | Public libraries change people's lives. |
| | Public libraries are gateways to the World Wide Web. |
| | Public libraries bridge the Digital Divide. |
| Facts | Of general library users: |
| | 74% read for pleasure. |
| | 56% learned about a skill, hobby, or other interest. |
| | 46% found info needed for school, work, or a community group. |
| | Counting on Results: |
| | Of all users for libraries that studied specific service responses: |
| | Library as place: 59% found quiet place to think, read, write, or study. |
| | Local history/genealogy: 53% made progress researching family histories. |
| | Basic literacy: 36% read to a child or helped a child choose a book. |
| Sources | Chief Officers of State Library Agencies, Member Profiles. Available: www.cosla.org |
| | Counting on Results: New Tools for Outcome-Based Evaluation of PLS. Available: www.lrs.org/CoR.asp. |
| | Knowing What Audiences Learn: Outcomes & Program Planning. Available: www.imls.gov/grants/current/ACM-03-fnl.pps |
| | Perspectives on Outcome-Based Evaluation for Libraries & Museums. Available: www.imls.gov/pubs/pdf/pubobe.pdf |
| Your story | Conduct an outcome-based evaluation of a specific program at your library. |
| | Conduct an annual user survey to give patrons the opportunity to identify how they have benefited from your library's services. |

In another example, in late 2006, the Medical Library Association updated its *Vital Pathways for Hospital Librarians* section of its Web site. (www.mlanet.org/resources/vital/index.html). It includes a PowerPoint presentation based on this idea of reporting. Titled *Myths and Truths about Library Services*, the presentation can be edited to suit your local situation (Bandy et al., accessed: 2007). Developed by the Colorado Council of Medical Librarians (CCML) Advocacy Committee and MLA, the presentation addresses the published outcomes from the literature, as discussed in Chapter 8. The slides attempt to use the presentation methodology described above to counter these issues quoted from the Web site: "What myths do your administrators believe? Do they think that patient care can remain high quality without library services? Do they believe everything is available for free on the Web, or that technology has replaced librarians? Perhaps they think that closing your library will save money. Counter these and other common myths with this presentation, which you can revise to meet your specific needs."

The PowerPoint presentation, its bibliography, and other communications resources can be found on the CD-ROM in the Chapter 8 folder.

# PRESENTATIONS

You have been asked to present your evaluation results to the vice–president of your organization. A colleague has heard about your work and invites you to present it to a professional group. You will be presenting on your feet! You will be standing in front of a group of people and making your point. Public speaking is a major fear for most people. But it is a skill that can be learned just as any other, and with skills, fear will recede.

## SHORT PRESENTATIONS

You may not think of it this way, but one type of public speaking occurs every day. Say you meet someone in the hall who asks you a complicated question. In an instant, you need to organize your thoughts and respond. Or say you are in a meeting and you are asked a question. Again, you pull together your thoughts and "present" the answer. At Toastmasters meetings, each member of the club gives a two-minute speech on a topic of the day to practice this skill. Another short speech discussed these days is the "elevator speech." Can you answer a question or describe what you do in the time it takes to travel a few floors on an elevator? If not, you better hope it will be a tall building!

If you happen to be in an elevator with the VP and he or she asks you about your benchmarking project, would you say, "We just finished, and it's *finally* over!" Hopefully not! Instead, you should draw attention and generate interest with just a few sentences. You can develop an elevator speech using these ideas:

- Develop a story about the results, not the activity. Have it pass a "So what?" test.
- Keep it simple, explicit, and, of course, brief.
- Practice out loud with friends and colleagues.

What you might say to that VP instead: "Thanks for asking! The benchmarking project showed the library's performance exceeded expectations in most areas of resources. We appear to have a reasonable number of journal subscriptions and books. But in the important area of computer equipment in the library, it indicated we could be doing a better job. We will be submitting a budget request in that area based on our findings."

## FORMAL PRESENTATIONS

You have worked hard on your evaluation projects and had many good ideas and results that can be applied to your library operation. You now need to develop your ability to express those ideas and get others to know that they are important. Whether you are presenting to your team or to a budget committee, good presentation skills will help get your point across. As with other skills, there are a multitude of resources in print and on the Web to draw upon, but the following tips will get you started on developing your presentations. The most important thing is to have fun doing the presentation and see it as an excellent opportunity to communicate the importance of your library.

### Before You Start

Do not just jump into writing your presentation. Think about the context and environment you are presenting in.

- *Know your audience.* Who are they and why are they attending? How many will be there? Are they going to be friendly? Will there be interaction with the audience? They are investing their time; are you going to make it worth it? With a smaller group, create rapport if you can. You will be tailoring your message to the audience so you need to understand their knowledge level and attitude toward your topic, as well as their needs and desires.

- *Know what type of talk you will be giving.* It could be a formal presentation, an informal chat, or a classroom situation. How much time have you been given? If you prepare a ten-minute talk and then discussion goes on for half an hour afterward, are you prepared for this? Has the purpose of the talk been clarified by those who asked you to give it? Are you presenting a new idea, or will the audience already know quite a bit about the topic?

- *Prepare early.* Do not leave your preparation to the last minute. You want to have time to develop your outline, and your visuals and to practice.

- *Plan your presentation based on its purpose.* Understand your purpose and role. Be concise, specific, practical, and relevant and clarify your objectives in giving the talk. Is your intention to persuade, motivate, or inform? Or are you teaching? Each purpose calls for a different approach and perhaps a different role. Sketch an outline of the compelling parts of your presentation; those are the parts that will solve the problem or advance the idea.

- *Research your topic.* While this seems obvious, make sure you are current and knowledgeable about what you are speaking on. If something comes up that you do not know about, be honest about your ignorance, but have a phrase ready, such as "I do not have that information right here, so I will get back to you on that."

- *Learn and use PowerPoint.* Computer-based presentation programs such as Microsoft PowerPoint accompany most presentations today. If you choose not to use PowerPoint, you might even explain why. You might prefer to just give people a handout. If you can think of only two or three slides to illustrate your point, maybe a handout would be better. Most sources on presenting give such facts as "55% of a presentation is visual." Even with only a few slides, it is a good idea to use PowerPoint and not skip it. Using PowerPoint to outline the speech is a wonderful technique for developing your ideas. While Word has an outlining feature, PowerPoint "controls" you as you put your ideas down and helps you emphasize the key points. Invest some time in learning to use PowerPoint because it has many features that are underutilized. Use the tutorial, take a course, or buy a book. Amazon lists over a thousand books on how to use PowerPoint. Most conference rooms have screens, and the institutional audiovisual service can usually supply a projector and often a laptop. PowerPoint tips are covered in a section below.

## Prepare Your Presentation

Now you can start to outline your speech. Unlike a written report that can be reread if necessary or an informal conversation where there are questions and feedback, a presentation is a one-shot effort to present your case. The presentation needs to follow a logical sequence and be condensed into a meaningful message. Here are some pointers to organize your ideas.

- *Place your topic in context.* Develop a theme using one sentence with no jargon in it. Brainstorm for the issues you want to address. Combine and consolidate them until you have a manageable number of points to address.
- *Develop an outline.* Most resources use the "tell them" structure:
  - Tell them what you are going to tell them (introduction).
  - Tell them the key points (main part).
  - Tell them what you have told them and conclude.
  While this has become formulaic, it can still be effective if it is not too obvious but instead hidden in your enthusiasm in giving the speech. Allocate an amount of time to each section. As an example, if you have 15 minutes:
  - Introduction: 3 minutes
  - Body of speech: 8 minutes—2 minutes each for 4 points
  - Conclusion: 4 minutes
- *Have an effective introduction.* Here is where you catch the attention and interest of the audience. Orient the audience to the purpose of the presentation and then review the outline briefly. Avoid using jargon and weak introductions such as jokes, apologies, or filler phrases. Establish rapport with your audience from the start. Set the tone and establish credibility.
- *Organize the main part of your presentation.* Prioritize your points and allocate time accordingly. Use the rule of three and have only three points per slide. Present your points in a logical order using chronological or other organizational elements, such as compare and contrast, problems and solutions, cause and effect, or simple to complex. Experiment with different logical orders by moving your slides around. Develop your transitions so you move smoothly from one point to the next. Make sure the rela-

**Tip: Rule of Three**

People tend to remember three things better than two or four. It may be psychological or just the rhythm and sound. Familiar examples come from all parts of life: Healthy, Wealthy, and Wise; Stop, Look, and Listen; Faith, Hope, and Charity.

tionships among elements are clear to the audience. After your outline and transitions are established, fill in gaps with your supporting details. Use examples, statistics, expert opinions, and anecdotes.

- *Develop your conclusion.* Some experts recommend doing this right after you work on your introduction. Then fill in the middle. Make sure you present a solid conclusion and do not just trail off at the end. Summarize your key points concisely, pointing out benefits or recommendations. State your conclusion. Be specific: Where are we; what does this mean; what are the next steps, actions, or options, and so forth.

## Practice your Presentation

This is very important. How you actually present depends on your personal style and experience as to whether you prefer to read the presentation, speak from notes, or speak from the slides. It is usually better not to memorize. Giving speeches is scary enough without worrying that your memory will fail. But it does depend on your style and experience. One technique using PowerPoint is to use the "Notes" feature under each slide. Put the oral part of your speech in there; then you can print out the slides in Note format. As you move from one page to another you advance your slides. If you use a separate written speech or notes, mark where you will advance the slides. Practice by yourself several times, standing up, reading aloud, and moving the slides on your computer. This is a rehearsal. Do not go too fast. Speak slowly and clearly and use gestures. Stand tall and be relaxed. Look up from your notes to a pretend audience. Write down the time on your paper or notes every few minutes so each section is timed. Most likely it will be too long. Go back and discard nonessential sentences and slides.

For a final practice, reserve a conference room and invite colleagues and staff to critique your presentation, both the content and the delivery style. Select people who might mimic your audience. Simulate the atmosphere where you will be presenting, including standing at a podium. Do not waste their time. Be accepting of their criticism. If many changes are recommended, consider doing the practice again. Remember, you started early! If you have the equipment, you can videotape yourself and do your own critique. Figure 11.2 gives you a checklist you can review to be sure all points have been covered.

---

**Figure 11.2   Presentation Checklist**

---

The Presentation:
- Does your introduction grab participants' attention and explain your objectives?
- Do you follow by clearly defining the points of the presentation?
- Are the main points in logical sequence?
- Do they flow well and have good transitions?
- Do the main points need support from visual aids?
- Does your closing summarize the presentation clearly and concisely?
- Is the conclusion strong?
- Have you tied the conclusion to the introduction?

---

The Delivery:
- Are you knowledgeable about the topic covered in your presentation?
- Do you have your notes or speech in order and pages numbered?
- Do you know where and how you will present?
- Have you visited the presentation site?
- Have you checked your visual aids to ensure they are working and you know how to use them?

---

Your Appearance:
- Make sure you are dressed and groomed appropriately and in keeping with the audience's expectations.
- Practice your speech standing (or sitting, if applicable), paying close attention to your body language and your posture, since the audience will assess both.

---

The Visual Aids:
- Are the visual aids easy to read and easy to understand?
- Are they tied to the points you are trying to communicate?
- Can they be easily seen from all areas of the room?

---

(Adapted from "Presentation Planning Checklist" by Kellie Fowler, 2007b)

---

### Before the Presentation

Sometime before the presentation, visit the room where the presentation will take place. Check out the actual place where you will be speaking and the equipment. Set out any prepared handouts.

- Print out your notes or speech and number the pages. Instead of stapling it and flipping the pages, slide the pages across or under as you finish reading them.

- If you have the opportunity, stand behind the podium or wherever you will be speaking from. Practice moving the pages.
- Make sure the podium is arranged so that you face your audience and can see both the slides on the computer monitor and your paper notes.
- Do you have water, a tissue, cough drops, and a pen?
- Are you going to the wallboard, and if so, do you have chalk or the proper markers?
- Are the lights adjusted properly, and if necessary, do you know how to adjust them? Microphones? If offered one, do not turn it down. The room may need it.
- If you have control over this, is your audience comfortable?
- Spiff up your personal appearance. Use the rest room and comb your hair, and so on.
- Do not over stimulate yourself with drinks such as coffee—or do if that is what you need.

## The Actual Presentation

As one person said, this is the moment of truth. Take several deep breaths. There are many tips below, but practice and experience are the best ways to make a better presentation, so taking a course or joining a club will be the best way to improve. Even if you are a confident speaker, these tips can act as a checklist.

- Review your rehearsed opening statement; do not improvise at the last moment.
- If the person who introduces you does not give your name and role, provide these yourself and say something like, "Although I am familiar to most of you, my name is . . . "
- Unless you are good at it, avoid making jokes.
- Use a natural rate of speech, neither too slow nor too fast, and use moderate gestures. Do not appear bored or too enthusiastic. Sound spontaneous, conversational, and moderately enthusiastic, but not hyper. Moderation in all things!
- Vary your volume and tone. Do not be afraid of silence. Have your friends tell you if you use a lot of "um"s or "ah"s and try to stop. This is hard to do but can be improved with practice.
- Monitor your behavior and be aware of possible annoying habits such as pacing or looking down.
- Make eye contact as much as you can.
- Use a laser pointer sparingly. Do not point it at the audience or swirl it around. Turn it on, point, and turn it off. The same is true if you use a cursor to point.

- Be prepared for possible interruptions such as cell phones, fire drills, and so forth. Do not lose your composure and try to take the interruptions in stride.
- Do not apologize for any part of your presentation. You have done your best, right?
- Do not criticize the place where you are, the city, the facilities, or the trip you may have taken to get there.
- Give credit where it is due and acknowledge people's efforts. Do it at the beginning or on the bottom of the slide if you are using data or figures from other sources.
- End with your prepared summary. Do not add anything at the last minute. It will appear unpracticed and the audience may go away with that impression.
- Do not run over your allotted time. If you cannot watch your time, have a colleague watch it for you and prompt you with a three-minute and one-minute warning.

## Handling Questions

In most situations, your talk does not end with your conclusion. A question-and-answer (Q&A) period at the end will influence your audience. It shows you know your subject and can respond under pressure. If announced during your speech, it will deflect interruptions and supplement the presentation with confident, informed responses. If a question is asked during the presentation, answer it immediately, since it might clarify a point. Or if it is a distraction from the points of the speech, say you will answer it at the end. Here are a few tips about handling a Q&A session:

- Try to anticipate questions: Think of the ten most likely questions and plan out your answers. Know what questions you will not answer. Have an appropriate response prepared such as "It is too early to make that decision; and I will get back to you."
- Understand the question. Always repeat it if you think the audience did not hear it. Paraphrase it if necessary.
- Maintain control of the exchanges. Let the questioner finish, unless he or she is vague and rambling. To focus the question, you could tactfully say something like "So, are you asking . . . ?" Avoid long discussions with one person. Suggest you meet after the session. Although this does not happen often in business situations, learn how to deflect hecklers or disruptive questions. One technique for this is to enlist aid from the audience.
- Do not rush to answer. Take a moment to think about it.
- Be honest: If you cannot answer the question, say so and

perhaps ask for clarification. Offer to get back to the questioner later after you have researched the answer. If appropriate, ask the audience to answer. Or suggest resources for the questioner to find the answer.

- Finish the answer by asking the questioner if he or she was satisfied with the answer. This encourages audience participation. Ask for a clarifying question, but if it goes on too long, suggest you meet later.
- Use the last question to summarize your conclusion and main point.

### Follow-up

Do not leave a meeting without knowing what is next. After the Q&A, ask, "So, what's the next step?" If there is no response, suggest a next step. Call for another meeting to discuss issues or, better yet, actions. Set a deadline for the next meeting.

### POWERPOINT TIPS

PowerPoint was originally written in 1987 to produce Mylar slides for a projector. It allowed speakers to distill their information in an organized way and intersperse their images and data tables throughout the presentation. Since about 2000, it has been used on the computer using a data projector, and the production of Mylar slides has all but ceased. According to Microsoft, more than 30 million PowerPoint presentations are made around the world every day. It is so pervasive that it is now being criticized as being tedious and causing all presentations to look alike. The templates provided by the software are very convenient but have become overused. Even though it is time consuming, try and find a template that is not common, find one on the Web, or have one made by an in-house illustration department. Some of the criticisms are:

- It is too linear. One slide doggedly follows another, and you do not see any tangential issues.
- The uniform formatting is tedious. Almost all slides are headlined with bullet points.
- The graphics are bland and predictable.
- It stifles creativity.

A major reason for PowerPoint's popularity is that if you have something complicated to present, it does allow you to easily and visually outline it. You can overcome the criticisms by using your creativity and learning the program's details. Your presentation should strike a balance between the bland bullets and the overdone sound and movement that also are possible. PowerPoint is usually only as boring as your talk, so work hard to give a good talk and a good PowerPoint presentation will follow. There are many how-to books to teach you PowerPoint as well as the tutorial within the program itself.

A talk with slides can never present as much detail as a written paper. Getting complicated, detailed information to the audience is a combination of three elements: the verbal presentation of the speaker based on his or her notes, the PowerPoint slides the audience will see, and the handouts for the audience to take away and study later.

Effective PowerPoint slides have these attributes:

- *Purpose and organization:*
  - The quality and number of slides should enhance, not distract from the purpose of the presentation.
  - Have a good reason for showing each slide.
  - The amount of time for each slide depends on its content, but estimates range from 30 seconds to 2 minutes. Its all in the timing. If you have a 10-minute presentation, are 10 slides enough? Maybe. But do not try for more than 20, or you will be going to fast.
  - For longer presentations, distribute an outline to help the audience follow along. PowerPoint has several printout options. Consider making a copy of your presentation to use for the handout and then removing some of the slides that do not reproduce well on paper or are transitional.
  - Vary your bulleted lists with graphics and pictures to increase interest.
- *Appearance:*
  - Use a plain font like Helvetica of substantial size (24 points or more).
  - Do not use more than three colors.
  - Make sure the audience quickly and easily understands what they see.
  - If you use an image with words that cannot be read, explain that it is a representation and that people do not need to read it.
- *Textual format:*
  - Make one key point per slide.
  - Organize material into natural categories and contrasts, such as problems and solutions, advantages versus disadvantages, costs and benefits.

- Use no more than six lines of text per slide and no more than seven words per line of text. Are they spending time reading and not listening?
- Avoid using several text slides in a row. Intersperse them with graphics.
  - *Graphic format:*
- A well-designed diagram or chart can often make your point more quickly and clearly than can words.
- Use no more than three curves on a line chart or graph.
- Do not use a page full of numbers.
- Translate complex numbers into representative pie charts or bar graphs.
- Use diagrams or models to present complex concepts.
- Do not distract the audience with fancy moving graphics and sound unless there is a point to be made.
- While you may be tempted to be very creative, do not substitute art for content.
  - *Presenting the slides:*
- Do not read the slides. While you are talking, the audience is reading the slides. They can read faster than you can talk and will become bored. Verbally highlight what is presented. Use more graphics than lists, if possible.
- Do not block the slides or have your back to the audience while looking at the slides.
- Know your equipment and environment and be prepared for the worst: How will you give your talk if you have no slides? Be prepared for this because it does happen.

# TEAMWORK

The purpose of working with teams on evaluation projects is that high-quality outcomes can be achieved when you work with people who have a wide range of skills and perspectives. Evaluation projects involve many constituencies, from the user to management and everyone in between. As with all business communications theories, there is a lot written on the theories of working in teams. Teams can be discussed from many angles, whether in terms of business leadership and control, behavioral and psychological issues, group dynamics, or employee training and participation.

In libraries, teams are being used more since the advent of total quality management philosophies of the 1990s. Some processes have become so complex that a team is necessary to handle them. In the recent case study on team effectiveness by Elaine R. Martin (Martin, 2006), library teams were studied and compared with a team framework theory developed by J. Richard Hackman (Hackman, 2002). In Martin's excellent study, characteristics of and barriers to team effectiveness are discussed. The positive and negative aspects of team structure, accountability, communication, teaming (becoming a team), the relationship to the larger organization, team leadership, coaching, training, and support systems are listed. As you develop your teams, a review of the benefits of teams in libraries and the problems that occurred will help in your process.

Teams develop naturally. From the psychological point of view, the most commonly quoted team dynamic is a model developed in the 1960s, "forming, storming, norming, and performing" and then "adjourning." By describing the stages a team goes through, this model helps team members communicate about what is happening at any given point. While there are different stages of team growth, there are also activities that need to be done to move ahead, such as establishing the purpose, getting to know one another, rules of behavior, work processes, and measures of effectiveness.

Teams are formed for a purpose. Sometimes they are functional and watch over a system, like a Web site or another interdisciplinary library function. Sometimes they are formed to solve a problem or improve a process or system. They could be formed from the bottom up by a group of concerned employees asking to solve a problem. Or a manager who sees a problem and asks the employees to solve it could form the team from the top down. Either way, teams often perform evaluations using the methods covered in this book. When you are gathering your team to carry out your planned evaluation, the structure and dynamics of the team need to be attended to.

## FORM THE TEAM AND GET TO KNOW ONE ANOTHER (FORMING)

Choose people who have some relationship with the purpose of the team. They should be able to contribute something unique, either by knowing the system under review or having skills the team needs to do the review. Each person should have a purpose on the team. Make sure everybody knows everyone's name. Introduce yourselves and have someone develop a roster with names, addresses, and so forth. Discuss what each person is good at and what resources they can bring to the project. Each team member has different abilities, and motivations and a different personality. Talk enough in the beginning to get these out in the open. This will help to avoid conflict later on. Meet in a comfortable room and, if possible, arrange food and drink. This may not seem important, but you are going to meet a lot and you do not want the team members to dread sitting in the chairs in a certain room.

## ESTABLISH THE PURPOSE AND OPERATING PROCEDURES (STORMING)

The next step is to establish that everyone has a shared understanding of the purpose of the team. If someone outside the team has called the team together, perhaps have him or her come to this part of the discussion. This could be considered a "vision" for the team, what they hope to accomplish. Why does the team exist? This discussion needs to be strong and participatory. All members should participate, and during the discussion, members will continue to get to know and appreciate one another.

After the purpose has been written down, develop some behavior and communication plans. Some things to consider:

- *Choose a leader*. If necessary, agree on how a leader will be chosen and choose someone. This person should have his or her role clearly defined.
- *Set ground rules for acceptable behavior*: Discuss such things as interruptions, sharing the floor, active listening and constructive feedback, being on time for meetings, not missing meetings, and following the task schedule.
- *Decision making*: Discuss how decisions will be made. Will it be by consensus or a majority rule? Would there be any exceptions?

## ESTABLISH A STRUCTURE (NORMING)

By this time the team should be coming together. They have a leader and have reviewed and understood the purpose. They should now determine a structure under which to operate. To do this, they might brainstorm to create ideas, plans, and tasks. Again, all these should be fully discussed by the team. Some of these might be:

- *Set lines of authority*: Make sure it is clear what authority the team has to carry out its plan.
- *Discuss other possible roles and responsibilities*: Brainstorm about what tasks may be needed and assign roles to team members. These could be:

- Leader/facilitator/coordinator:
  - Runs the meeting and keeps it on task
  - Keeps everyone involved
  - Reminds people of their agreed-on behavioral rules
  - Focuses the team on the task
  - Keeps the team from stalling by suggesting alternatives
  - Is neutral in most questions
  - Summarizes and clarifies decisions
- Communicator:
  - Communicates with stakeholders and keeps them informed of progress
  - Monitors that the team's direction and purpose are synchronized with the larger organization's mission and goals
- Recorder:
  - Schedules meetings and make arrangements for food and drink
  - Records discussion at meetings and circulates minutes
  - Keeps team roster and e-mail lists current
  - Keeps members current with revisions of team decisions and documents
- Data coordinator:
  - Skilled at data collection methods
  - Team leader for the data collection phase
  - Responsible for storage and display of data collected in the evaluations
- Reporter
  - Responsible for coordinating periodic and final reports

- *Develop a task list:* Have a discussion of what it will take to accomplish your purpose.
- *Set timelines:* Develop a Gantt chart (see Chapter 12) to see what tasks have to be done and when. Revise the task list as necessary.
- *Assign responsibilities for tasks:* Using the task list and Gantt chart, assign responsibilities.
- *Set future meeting times:* Decide how often to meet and stick to your schedule.
- *Develop measure of team progress:* Discuss early on what signals or measures will indicate the team is making progress or has accomplished its goals. Set a completion date, if appropriate.

## MAINTAIN PROGRESS AND DO THE WORK (PERFORMING)

All the plans are laid down, and now the work begins. The leader keeps team members on track by monitoring progress and team dynamics. At the same time the leader can become more participative. Team members are now more autonomous and have the skills and competency to make decisions without supervision. An effective team can function more as a unit and can operate without inappropriate conflict or direct supervision. The leader and team members can accomplish their jobs by:

- *Encouraging fair participation by all team members:* Make sure everyone is participating. Coach or mentor members that may be falling behind. Give others leadership opportunities, if possible.
- *Recognizing team members for their contributions:* Set up a system of rewards for a job well done. Do not leave anyone out. Praise one another. Share success stories.
- *Recognizing agreement:* Getting team members to agree is often difficult. If some major or even minor agreements are reached, recognize them as a positive example.
- *Managing conflict and social dynamics:* Monitor and give feedback often. Summarize hard problems and then let people think on their own and write down some solutions. Then discuss the solutions together and pool them on a flip chart.
- *Assess progress periodically:* Review the purpose or charge of the team and link it to the institution's mission and goals. Check on the previously agreed upon measures and report the progress (or lack of it) to the team.

## ENDING THE PROJECT (ADJOURNING)

Some functional teams do not end, but most evaluation or project teams do. If one assumes that the team has been formed to effect a change, there are certain tasks they should be sure to see finished. Even if the team is continuing, this list could be used on an annual basis. As the team ends its project, it should review its work and make sure these activities were done:

- Results are checked and matched to the original purpose of the team.
- Any small, unfinished tasks are assigned to be done.
- If there is a new process, it is documented and people are trained.
- The accomplishments of the team are reviewed to see if there are any areas to improve.

- The changes instituted by the team have been communicated to everyone who is affected by them.
- The team celebrates its efforts together with a lunch and makes sure their accomplishments are in the employee newspaper. Presentations are made to all interested parties.
- Team members acknowledge to one another that they did a good job, increased their skills, and established new and better relationships with their coworkers and fellow team members.

# LISTENING

What about when *you* are the audience? In the evaluation process, this will often be the case. You listen to others at meetings. You conduct interviews and need to listen to the interviewee. You need to hear what your stakeholders have to say and understand them. In any job you need to be a good listener to influence, persuade, and negotiate. These are also the skills needed in evaluation as well as general management. Start by analyzing your own communication style. You need to be self-aware to be a good listener or speaker or writer. By knowing your strengths and weaknesses, you can work to use them to overcome your weaknesses. You will be more ready to connect with others through active listening.

Paul Blodgett and Richard Harris point out the issues stopping us from listening well and then give us six tips for better listening (Blodgett, 1997; Harris, 1997). Everyone drifts when listening, they say. There are too many distractions in the environment and issues in your own life that can interfere. By understanding why you do not listen when you need to, you can catch yourself and bring your attention back. An accomplished listener is someone who is fully present. Some of these personal issues involved in listening are:

- *Partnership.* Good listening is not a one-way street. In a conversation, it takes time to establish a connection (and sometimes you never do). The partnership means reacting to the speaker, whether with a comment after a speech or stopping to really hear a customer when they make comments. Let your listening show because it will help you make a better connection.
- *Reviewing systematically.* Do not just keep listening with-

out checking to see that you understand. Test your assumptions of what you heard by restating the content. Stop processing the information for a minute and rephrase what was said. If you cannot do this out loud, do it in your mind or in your notes. Think of it as active understanding.

- *Effort.* Do not just sit there—participate! Put a little effort into listening. Not all speakers are dynamic or concise, clear, interesting, and relevant. Observation in conversations, or as an audience to a speaker, can include nonverbal clues of tone, gesture, or posture. Respond and paraphrase and practice enlarging your repertoire of appropriate responses. Do not just say "yeah" after every pause in the conversation.

- *Star events.* These are the emotional triggers that cause us to lose concentration. Do you hear something that makes you so defensive or irritated that you stop listening? Get to know what these are so you can control them. If you slip for a moment, bring yourself back by asking a question or paraphrasing. Try to reset your connection.

- *Empathy.* Listening is not just an intellectual exercise. We need to connect emotionally. You do not have to go overboard or even agree with the feelings expressed, but if feelings are expressed, you need to show empathy. Your listening-response repertoire needs to include phrases acknowledging emotions as well as ideas.

- *Neutralizing snap judgments.* We are all quick to judge others, how they look or speak or act. But being too quick to judge undermines your efforts to get needed information. You need to tolerate differences to be an effective listener.

- *Tenacity.* Mostly we are encouraged to be an active listener, but a tenacious listener relates to both the cognitive and emotional aspects of the message and looks for deeper meaning. He or she learns how to respond without interrupting, then grabs opportunities to engage the speaker so he or she can develop a mutual understanding on the topic being discussed.

So now you have a way to inventory your personal characteristics. The next step is to take specific actions to be a better listener. These steps are action oriented and less analytical. You must make a conscious decision to practice them.

- Let the other person finish speaking, and encourage him or her to go on. Do not interrupt. This is hard sometimes if you do not know the cadence of the speaker. Some people pause but are not finished, so be silent for a while after you think the person has stopped. Do not ask excessive questions or turn the topic to something else. Choose from your newly developed response repertoire and indicate you are following what is being said.

- Use your body language to demonstrate that you are listening. According to communication theory, only a small percentage of communication involves words. The largest component is body language, followed by sounds. As the listener, you want to encourage communication by using body language. That would include smiles, the sound of your voice, gestures, eye contact and your posture. All of these show you are paying attention.

- Focus on what the person is saying, not on your response. According to theory, you can listen six times as fast as a person can talk. So your attention may wander. Try listening with a purpose to stop the drift. Instead of thinking of your response, paraphrase what you are hearing. Catch yourself if you notice you are thinking of a response and reset your attention.

- Put your tendency to evaluate on hold. Try to keep an open mind. It is natural to stop listening to something we disagree with, especially if it is an emotionally charged subject. But even in a business setting, you can put your judgments aside and listen. If you want people to talk to you, you have to be willing to listen to their point of view.

- Try to see things from the speaker's perspective. Just as the speaker needs to know the audience's context, the listener needs to know the context of the speaker. Do you really know what the speaker means just from the words that are spoken? Probably not, because you would most likely react differently to the same exact words if they came from a different person.

- Let a speaker know you hear and understand. Again this is where you practice your response repertoire. Repeat back or summarize to ensure that you understand. Restate what you think you heard and ask, "Have I understood you correctly?" Feedback is a means to clearly demonstrate you are actively listening and to confirm the communication. Give feedback on content, meaning, and feelings and summarize the main message.

# INTERVIEWS

Interviewing is a communication skill used in evaluation to learn views and opinions. As a data-gathering technique in evaluation studies, it is covered in Chapter 10. There we talk about the types of channels for the interviews:

- In person
- On the phone
- Over the Internet using e-mail, chat, or open-ended surveys
- Self-recorded audiotaped interviews

We also covered the types of structured or unstructured interviews:

- Standardized, open-ended interview
- Guided or structured interview
- Informal, conversational interview

There is a procedure for setting up interviews found in Figure 10.6. The types of questions to ask at the various types of interviews also are covered in Chapter 10. What was not covered were some of the communication issues involved in the interview. As an interviewer, you will want to know about your audience and practice the good listening skills we have just covered. In the interview setting, there are a few specific communication issues to be considered. Your four parts involve preparation, starting the interview, the actual interview, and your immediate follow-up. Some of these things are good planning, good management, or just common sense or common politeness. Combined they make for a good interview.

## PREPARE FOR THE INTERVIEW

- *Make an appointment.* Call or e-mail for an appointment. Use the opportunity to explain your interview goals. This also allows interviewees to prepare if they want to. Schedule enough time for the interview, often more than one hour. Ask if you may record the interview so you can be prepared for the interviewee's preference.
- *Set up the room.* Decide where to have the interview. A neutral space such as a scheduled conference room, will deter distractions such as telephones and office noises. If you decide to use your office or the interviewee's office, consider how the context may impact his or her responses.

- *Bring the right equipment and test it.* If you decide to tape the interview, make sure your device works and you know how to use it. Have extra cassettes and batteries. Occasionally during the interview, verify that the tape recorder is working. You will also be taking notes, so bring two pencils (or pens) and paper. Use equipment you are comfortable with. You might consider a bottle of water and a snack bar for each of you.
- *Review your interview guide.* Before going to the interview, review your interview guide and other materials that affect the purpose of the interview. In an evaluation interview, there is usually an exact set of questions to follow so that the answers can be compared with those of other interviews being conducted for the project.

## START THE INTERVIEW

- *Be prompt.* Sorry, this may be obvious, but it does need to be mentioned. Tardiness implies that the interview is not important to you. If you have to be late, call.
- *Introduce yourself.* Give your name and position in the project and/or company. Make sure you are interviewing the person you thought you would be. Even if you know the person, explain your capacity in the interview. It is best not to interview people you know, but sometimes you will have no choice.
- *Explain your purpose.* Give a concise statement about the purpose of the interview and/or the evaluation. This should include the type of information you are looking for.
- *Address confidentiality.* Explain your plans for keeping the interview confidential. Talk about who will have access to the information and plans for analysis. If you plan to quote interviewees, get their permission or ask if you can contact them later for permission to quote them.
- *Discuss recording the interview.* Ask permission to record the interview. Do not turn on the tape player until you get this permission. If you did not get permission when you set up the interview, you could consider bringing someone to take notes. If so, introduce this individual. Explain that you will be taking notes also. If necessary, after you turn on the recorder, repeat your name and the interviewee's name and position.
- *Discuss the interview guide or format of the interview.* Explain how you plan to conduct the interview. You probably have a set list of questions, so state whether you will

be going down the list or maybe straying from it a little. Explain how questions from the interviewee will be handled, at once or at the end of the interview. This may be dictated by your evaluation plan, and specific explanatory words may be on your script.

- *Give a time frame.* In most cases the interview time is limited by the appointment, so be sure you have set up enough time to ask all the questions and allow the interviewee to express all of his or her opinions.
- *Exchange contact information.* Do this at the beginning because you may be rushed at the end. Provide your business card or perhaps a sheet of paper with contact information for the study coordinators as well as yourself. Ask the interviewee for full information if you do not have it, including the secretary's contact information, if appropriate. Ask the interviewee to call you if he or she wants to add anything later. Mention that you might be calling for clarification.
- *Ask if the interviewee has any questions.*

## TIPS ON HOW TO CONDUCT AN INTERVIEW

- *Follow your interview guide.* It is not necessary to start the questions right away. If you have time, some casual conversion may relax both of you. Ask one question at a time and be sure to ask all of them. Make transitions between the different topics. Make sure you understand the responses. Clarify and verify the answers. Control the interview and do not let the interviewee stray to another topic, give too long answers, or start asking too many questions.
- *Use your listening skills.* People will give you information when they believe you are listening. Use all the skills outlined above. Give the interviewee time to answer. Use phrases that encourage discussion.
- *Remain neutral.* Be accepting and friendly and as neutral as possible. Certainly do not argue or judge. No matter what your response, try not to show a strong emotional reaction.
- *Learn the art of subtle note taking.* If you suddenly take a note and look pleased, you may influence future answers.
- *Let the interviewee talk.* Interviewees should go at their own speed. They should be able to choose their own topics in their answers as long as they are not too far off the main topic.

- *Summarize.* As you close, give a short summary and discuss it with the interviewee to see if you understood the answers correctly.
- *Do not exceed the time limit.* If you need more time schedule another interview.
- *Thank the interviewee for his or her time.*

## IMMEDIATELY AFTER THE INTERVIEW

- *Write a thank-you note.*
- *Verify that your tape recorder worked.* If it malfunctioned, you will need to write down more in your notes before you forget everything that was said.
- *Review your notes.* As soon as you get back to your office, review your notes and fill in gaps. Clarify any writing that is unclear and fill out any abbreviations. Number the pages.
- *Add observations.* At the end of your notes, record any observations you had about the interview. You could comment on the demeanor of the interviewee, if there were any interruptions or other problems. You could do a preliminary review and highlight points of importance or state some conclusions. This will help in the transcription.

All these tips will give your set of interviews some consistency so the data you gather can be compared. The process will make it easier to categorize the responses and make final conclusions.

## BEING INTERVIEWED

Now that you have conducted an interview, maybe you will someday be on the other side: being interviewed. Most people know about being interviewed only when they are looking for a job. A multitude of resources on that subject exist in books, in journals, and on the Web. In the context of evaluation, why would you be interviewed? Maybe you have made some major changes as a result of your evaluation and you want them publicized in the employee newsletter. Or maybe you work in a library that deals with consumers and you want to get the word out to the public. You want to tell them how your consumer library changes lives, something you can talk about because of your outcomes research. Then you want to be interviewed by a "real" reporter, whether for print, radio, or television.

The Medical Library Association has an online publication on public relations called *Making a Difference; A Communications Toolkit* (2000). It has chapters on media relations, contacting the media, and being a spokesperson. While the intent of the publication is to advocate for and represent medical libraries, this information can be useful to those who finds themselves being interviewed by the media.

The purpose of mentioning this topic in an evaluation book is that having done all this work to conduct an evaluation, why not get the word out? These tips would be good for any communication that is verbal, including giving speeches or just talking in the hall. You are the spokesperson for your library (probably), or you know who is. One word of caution, however, is that if you work for a large organization, there is usually a media relations department or person and employees are not "allowed" to contact the media. Contact that individual and get permission for the interview and also help in contacting the media if that is what you want to do. He or she will probably be a big help.

If you have been asked for an interview, your goal is to get a "key message" across during the interview. This key message could be as simple as mentioning your company or hospital name and Web site. It could be more complicated, such as condensing the findings of your evaluation project. Work on these objectives before you go to the interview.

According to the MLA toolkit, a good spokesperson has the following qualities:

- willing
- available on short notice
- comfortable
- good at conversation
- able to translate technical information
- well-informed
- credible
- calm under pressure

That is a lot to practice!

As with any communication, you need to know your audience, who will be interviewing you, and the company they work for. Ask who their customers are and what their audience size is. What is their editorial position? What kind of person is your interviewer? The MLA toolkit lists various kinds, such as interrupter, hostile questioner, or know-nothing interviewer and gives tips on how to deal with them. You want your interview to go smoothly and not be overwhelmed by the personality of the interviewer.

If you should be in the position of being interviewed, review the MLA toolkit for more details about the process. The MLA has a public relations program and would appreciate knowing if its members are planning to give or have given, an interview to the press. They also might help you prepare, so contact them if you want some help.

## TELEPHONE COMMUNICATION

When doing evaluation projects, you will spend a lot of time on the phone. You will be calling team members, stakeholders, and consultants and possibly setting up interviews. People take the phone for granted because it is so much a part of daily life. The technologies of the phone have gotten very advanced, and there might be some features of your institution's system that you do not know exist and could be useful. There may be others, but these are the ones that may be useful in a project:

- Conferencing: Many modern phone systems allow you to conference with two or more people.
- Voicemail: You probably are used to the basics of voicemail, but do you forward voicemails with added messages? Is your answering message up to snuff? Do you use more than one out-of-the-office message for different purposes? Check all the added features.
- Group mails set to stored groups: This is a voicemail feature that allows you to store your team's addresses, compose a message, and send it to all of them. It is a slightly more personal alternative to group e-mails.

Today we also have cell phones, which may someday replace business landlines. They have their own set of features and are being combined with other technologies such as PDAs, MP3 music players, and cameras. The latest phone technology is Voice over IP, or VoIP, which allows you to place phone calls over the Internet, sometimes accompanied by video. If you have access to these technologies, you can become familiar with their set of capabilities and use them to your advantage as a communication channel.

Once you learn the technology of these channels of communication, you should use your other communication skills, such as good listening and polite but strong speech. You will want to make your phone conversations as effective as you can so as not to waste your time and that of the other person. *Etiquette* is often used to describe how to behave on the phone, in e-mail, or in person. Using proper etiquette in any given situation ensures the best results for effective communication. A Web search on "Telephone Etiquette" will produce many lists of what to do and not do. Here are a few highlights:

- *Identify yourself.* Whether making or receiving a call, always identify yourself. If you are making the call, explain the reason for your call. If you are receiving the call, also include your department or other identifying phrase.
- *Create a good first impression.* Answer promptly. Sound friendly. Ask the caller his or her name, if it has not been given. Lower your voice, if necessary. Speak clearly and slowly.
- *Respect others' time.* If making the call, ask, "Do you have a minute?" This is especially true if you intend to have a longer conversation. If the person is too busy, you can make arrangements for a telephone appointment. Keep the conversations to the point.
- *Ask before placing someone on hold.* Never keep a person on hold for more than 30 seconds. Say, "Thank-you for waiting," when you return.
- *Always leave your phone number if you ask others to call you back.* Do not count on the phone system to give them a number and do not expect them to call you back if they have to look up your number. Give the number slowly at the beginning and repeat it slowly at the end. Have you ever gotten a 90-second message with a phone number at the end that you could not hear and you have to replay the whole message? Spare others this annoyance.
- *Maintain a phone log to refer back to for valuable information.* This is a general good practice in all aspects of your work life, but in an evaluation project, it is good to keep a record of what is going on. Do not use sticky notes, because they get all over the place. Use a Day-Timer® or Franklin Covey® calendar or planning system or a dedicated notepad. Jot down notes during phone conversations. Write in-coming messages down in the same log. Note when the call was returned.
- *Listening is as essential on the phone as in person.* Using the same techniques as described in the listening section above, be an active listener and respond verbally. If necessary, recap at the end of the call, using your notes, and repeat any decisions or commitments on either side to be sure you are both "on the same page."
- *Use voice mail properly.* For people calling you, compose a concise and clear message. If your system allows it, ex-

plain early how they can skip the message and go straight to voicemail, especially if you have to have a long outgoing message. If you will be gone all day or more, activate a message that explains when you will be back. You can store several messages so you do not have to record over your carefully composed main message. Just record another message and activate it when you are out. Reactivate your main message when you get back. When leaving a message, be clear what you want callers to do, how you want them to respond and by when.

- *Try to return calls on the same day.* This is not always possible but it is the polite thing to do.
- *Last impressions.* Make sure the conversation is over and the caller's or your questions have all been answered. If you feel the conversation has gone on too long, you can offer to continue at another time.

# E-MAIL COMMUNICATION

As a communication channel, electronic mail has almost replaced the telephone and the U.S. Postal Service for many people. E-mail is great for many reasons:

- You do not get busy signals.
- Your written message may be more precise than your verbal one.
- It can be very fast, almost instantaneous.
- There are no long-distance charges.
- You can send pictures and attachments to discuss.
- It is an efficient way to communicate.

It has many technological problems, however, not the least of which is spam. You or your spam filter may delete legitimate messages. Your careful formatting may show up as plain text on the other end. Sometimes the e-mails never reach the receiver at all. Many people get so much e-mail they cannot cope with the volume. Others have secretaries who rightly intercept the e-mail, so your message might not get to where you intended it to go.

E-mail is an important communication channel in evaluation projects. You can communicate with your team to set up meetings or report progress. With their permission, you can send informal progress reports to your stakeholders. While talking on the phone to someone, this person can e-mail you a document to look at as part of the conversation. If you have a multilocation project, it cuts down on long-distance and postal charges. And as mentioned, you can even attempt to conduct a survey via e-mail. Just as with the telephone, there are some etiquette tips for e-mail that you should try to observe. As with any written communication, you will want to be clear and concise.

- *Before you write anything*, think of where you are in the process and what you are going to say; this could be true of any communication channel, but it just seems that e-mail is more prone to embarrassing mistakes and unfocused comments. Do not hurry just because the medium of communication is fast. Write important messages in your word-processing program and copy them over. Or write and save a draft that has no one in the "to" field so that you cannot accidentally send it before it is finished. Keep saving the draft as you would in word processing, because it is frustrating to lose a long or carefully worded e-mail in a sudden loss of Internet connectivity.
- *Any message you write may be seen by others.* Do not be informal and make comments you would not want others to see, especially your boss. Any e-mail can be forwarded to anyone.
- *E-mail is almost never confidential.* Read your company policy; any e-mail you send can likely be read by company officials and even subpoenaed in court.
- *Formatting issues.* You can see how any of the following formatting tips work by e-mailing a message to yourself. You can see what the subject line looks like and how the formatting turns out. Remember, however, that the recipient may have formatting turned off and will see only a plain-text message.
  - Use the subject line to grab a person's attention. Be clear what the message is about. Do not use words that you see in spam, such as "I need assistance" or "For your information." If it is an FYI, preface it with your department name. Be specific about yourself in the subject line so that people can see without opening your e-mail that you are a legitimate person, not a spammer.
  - Use your e-mail program options or preferences to be sure your name is being sent correctly in the "from" field. If the "from" field is not recognizable, the e-mail may be deleted as spam.

- Personalize the message by using the person's name in the message, if appropriate.
- Since e-mails have a time and date attached to them, there is no need to put this in the body.
- Always include a "full" signature. This would include your name, title, telephone and fax numbers, e-mail as well as postal address, and Web address. Some people include their company or department motto. If this formality does not work for you, have several signatures stored for various purposes. But always have one automatically attached that includes your title and phone number at least. Have you ever gotten an e-mail and wanted to call the person but you had to look up the phone number? It is unnecessary and annoying.
- Many people scan e-mails so use bolding and color for important points.
- When referencing a Web site in your e-mail, always use "http:// . . . " in the address so that the e-mail system transforms it into a hot link to the browser.
- Do not type in all caps or all lowercase letters. Using capitals is considered "shouting," and using all lowercase is just poor writing.
- Proofread your message and use the spell and grammar checker if available.
- For important e-mails, save a copy by sending a copy to yourself.
- *Writing style issues unique to e-mail:*
  - Be clear, useful, short, and to the point. Cover only one subject in an e-mail. This makes it easier for your recipient to respond.
  - Use short paragraphs in case the recipients have their formatting turned off and can see only text.
  - While informality is discouraged, e-mails can have a more relaxed, conversational tone than printed letters or reports.
  - Place any meeting announcements early in the e-mail.
  - The meat of the e-mail should be in the first paragraph. Sometimes people do not scroll beyond the first screen.
  - Put long explanations in attachments.
  - If giving a "call for action," be precise. Say exactly what response you expect from the reader(s), such as a phone call, a follow-up meeting, or a document you need.
- *When not to use e-mail:* Do not "spam" your readers with cute e-mails forwarded from others. This will cause people to ignore your messages. Reserve this habit for at home

with friends and family. Do not "discipline" people using e-mail. If you are having trouble with a team member do not deal with it via email. This is partly due to privacy issues and partly because the lack of emotion in the written word can be misinterpreted. Keep this activity for a face-to-face meeting or perhaps a telephone call.

- Respond in a timely manner: Check your e-mail at least once a day, preferably more. If you cannot give a detailed response within 24 hours, send an e-mail stating when you will get back to the sender. Often a phone call in response to an e-mail is appropriate. Always activate your out-of-the-office message if you are on vacation or away. On listservs, this message usually goes to the person posting the message and not the whole list, although that may happen.

# ASSERTIVENESS

Communication can be thought of as a technical skill or a personal skill, or both. E-mail and telephones skills may be technical. Listening and negotiating could be both. Being assertive seems mostly personal. It is included here because it has to do with the environment or context in which you are developing your evaluation plan. Being assertive falls in the middle of a continuum between being overly passive and overly aggressive. Communicating from either side of the continuum causes stress in your life and for the people you are communicating with. Being assertive has a lot to do with your overall effectiveness. According to many resources, a lack of assertiveness is related to stress. Being assertive actually relieves stress; improves your health, confidence, and performance; and allows you to use good judgment to make decisions, since you are not being overly passive or aggressive. Being assertive allows you to:

- Reduce misunderstanding
- Communicate your vision or goals more effectively
- Motivate others to accept an idea
- Produce meetings and projects that get the job done

But if assertiveness is so great, how come not everyone is on board? Reasons include low confidence, an overdone desire to please, or fear of what might happen if you rock the boat. As with all of the topics in this chapter, there are many books and Web resources that will expand on the tips below. Some of them will provide you with rating scales to see where you fall on this continuum. An honest self-assessment will allow you to see where you need to improve.

On the personal side of this skill, there are some things you need to take into account. Say a situation comes up where you need to talk with your supervisor about a problem with the budget. Some practical things to remember about presenting the problem in an assertive way are:

- Your fear is all in your mind. Ask yourself, "What is the worst thing that could happen if I present this factually?" You may see that this is a business problem that can be negotiated and does not really carry the risk of blame and punishment.
- What are your intentions for bringing up this problem? What is your motivation, opinion, or belief? Are you trying to solve the problem or just please others?
- Use clear, specific, open, and rational statements to explain the problem. Avoid making assumptions about what people already know. Do not send mixed messages.
- During the discussion, express disagreement if called for. Do not pretend to agree out of fear or the desire to avoid rocking the boat. Be polite and say something like, "I have an opinion I would like to put forward about this situation." Do not give in—negotiate.
- Do not agree to something you do not fully understand. Ask for clarification. After a more detailed explanation, you will feel better about saying Yes or No.

A specific technique to use when confronted with a problem where you need to be assertive is described in the *Relaxation & Stress Reduction Workbook* (Davis, et al., 2000) and reviewed at MindTools.com (accessed: 2006). Each time you use it, you will get better at being assertive. Eventually you will find yourself being assertive in everyday transactions. This technique is a six-step process, using *LADDER* as its mnemonic:

L: *Look* at your rights and what you want and understand your feelings about the situation. According to the book, you have legitimate emotional rights. They list 19, such as "You have a right to say "No" and "You have a right to negotiate for change," and so forth. Review these as you analyze the problem to identify your fears.

A: *Arrange* a meeting with the other person to discuss the situation. This gives you time to prepare your information and to discuss the problem. Sometimes, if you are experienced, a spontaneous discussion may be appropriate.

D: *Define* the problem specifically. Give objective, factual information and do not color it emotionally. Give the other person a chance to add his or her facts. This may help you see more fully what is going on.

D: *Describe* your feelings so that the other person fully understands how you feel about the situation. Since many situations are emotionally charged, you cannot ignore your feelings entirely. After presenting the facts and having a discussion of them, explain how you feel. Use "I" statements and do not point fingers.

E: *Express* what you want clearly and concisely. If you have a solution to suggest, politely put it forward in a direct and unambiguous way.

R: *Reinforce* your plan by explaining the mutual benefits of its adoption. After the facts and feelings and plans have been discussed, lay out the positive mutual benefits to your plan of action. If there are negative consequences of not taking action, lay them out carefully.

Assertiveness is a skill well worth learning. Where you reside on the continuum has a lot to do with your personal style. It is a skill to use when dealing with all people, not just your supervisor. Aggression or passivity can cause problems on any team or in any staff and can negatively affect the results you want. If you see this problem in others, if appropriate, advise them to learn more about assertiveness.

# NEGOTIATION AND PERSUASION

When reading about business communication skills, negotiation is always included. In an evaluation project, you may need to negotiate after the results are presented. If it is a big project, you may be negotiating with consultants. The subject of negotiation is so huge that it is a profession of its own. Professional negotiators negotiate labor contracts, mergers and acquisitions, and other major legal situations. In other aspects of your life, you may be negotiating to buy a house or a car, take out a loan, or get a raise. Just as with assertiveness, you will need to take a personal inventory and decide if you must improve your skills. You may feel you are always compromising so much that you are losing what is important to you. You may not even be participating in win-win situations if the atmosphere of your company is intimidating or dictatorial. A better understanding of the negotiation process may show you that you need to improve your skills.

Searching the literature for the purpose of learning about negotiating is difficult because most of the articles are about some specific negotiation or are too theoretical for the general manager. For librarians, articles focus around negotiating electronic licenses or better salaries. Searching the Web was not very useful. Searching the general management literature on the databases available at your public library may be the most rewarding. Most have tips about how to act in a negotiation process. They are varied and often circumstantial. Sometimes they are called "tricks." In a library setting, it is unlikely you will need to resort to tricks if you can gain confidence and learn some of the basics. The idea of a win-win negotiation is for both parties to come to an agreement where they both win on an acceptable number of points. It is acknowledged that when both parties walk away with a win, their relationship in the future will be better. The basic strategies for negotiating a win-win situation are:

- *Focus on your goal.* Have a clear understanding of what you want to accomplish. Know what your priorities are.
- *Identify the issues (yours and theirs).* Simplify the issues involved and do not mix up the personalities and the issues.
- *Gather information on both sides of the subject.* Support your position with data. Establish the benefits of doing things your way. Learn all you can about the other participant's background and position, strengths and weaknesses.
- *Plan.* Decide where you might compromise and what issues you will not yield on. Be prepared to trade.
- *Find supporters.* If the issue affects others in the department or company, enlist the support of others to help persuade the other side of the merits of your various points. Ask a mentor or trusted colleague for advice.
- *Acknowledge other points of view.* Listen to what the other side is saying and be open to new ideas.
- *Be willing to compromise.* A flexible attitude will help you see alternatives. While you may not get everything you hoped for, you may feel it is the first step toward getting what you want in the end.

While negotiation is a "discussion intended to induce an agreement," persuasion is an "inducement to act by argument, reasoning, or entreaty." In an excellent article in the *Harvard Business Review*, Jay Conger writes about the art of persuasion. In a negotiation process, whether formal or informal, your skills at persuasion need to be acknowledged. Conger (1998) points out four essential steps of persuasion:

- *Establish credibility.* Credibility comes from expertise and relationships. With a history of sound judgments and proven success, you can establish expertise. Your relationships should be marked by honesty and integrity and interest in the well being of others.
- *Frame for the common ground.* Identify the tangible benefits to all parties and have a solid understanding of the opposing point of view. Frame your statements to reflect that you and the others have something in common.
- *Provide evidence.* You need all the facts in a case, but facts are not necessarily going to persuade. Use language to supplement the facts by including stories, metaphors, and analogies to make your point.
- *Connect emotionally.* While you may think all decisions are based on reason, emotions are always in play. Try and get a sense of your audience's emotional state and match your presentation to it so they can better receive your message.

Communicating with others during your evaluation project is of great importance. All of the skills covered here come into play at some point during the process. A lot of communication suffers from a kind of inertia that sets in after time. The same e-mail, the same announcements appear over and over. To make yours more interesting, you could change your mood or tone, your pace or posture, the environment, or even your audience.

As you plan your communication, ask: Is it:

- Really necessary?
- Targeted?
- Timely?
- In the right language?
- Clear?
- Accurate?
- Short and to the point?
- Reasonable in tone?
- Covering what it should cover?
- Going to get a response?

If you have used this chapter as an inventory of your skills, perhaps you have found places where you would like to improve such as:

- Read and surf the Web.
- Join clubs.
- Reflect after each communication on what you have learned.
- Find a coach.

- Take courses.
- Practice.
- Observe others.
- Obtain feedback from your audience.

These communication skills will help you with your evaluation project and with most other parts of your career.

# REFERENCES

"Assertiveness – Getting What You Want, In a Fair Way." MindTools.com: Essential Skills for Your Excellent Career; Job Stress Management from Mind Tools (last updated 2007). Available: www.mindtools.com/stress/pp/Assertiveness.htm (accessed January 10, 2007).

Bandy, M., J. Garcia, S. Weldon, K. K. Wells, and the Colorado Council of Medical Librarians (CCML) Advocacy Committee. 2006. *Myths and TRUTHS about Library Services*. Chicago, IL: Medical Library Association. Available: www.mlanet.org/resources/vital/index.html (accessed January 15, 2007).

Blodgett, P. C. 1997. "Six Ways to Be a Better Listener. (Training 101: The Art of Listening)." *Training and Development*, 51, no. 7: 11–12.

Conger, J. A. 1998. "The Necessary Art of Persuasion." *Harvard Business Review*, 76, no. 3: 84–95.

Davis, M., E. R. Eshelman, and M. McKay. 2000. *The Relaxation & Stress Reduction Workbook*. 5th edition. Oakland, CA: New Harbinger Publications.

Fowler, K. "Introduction to Communication Skills: Why You Need to Get Your Message Across." MindTools.com: Essential Skills for Your Excellent Career. (last updated 2007a). Available: www.mindtools.com/CommSkll/CommunicationIntro.htm (accessed January 10, 2007).

Fowler, K. "Presentation Planning Checklist." MindTools.com: Essential Skills for Your Excellent Career (last updated 2007b). www.mindtools.com/CommSkll/PresentationPlanningChecklist.htm. (accessed January 10, 2007).

Hackman, J. R. 2002. *Leading Teams: Setting the Stage for Great Performances*. Boston, MA: Harvard Business School Press.

Harris, R. M. 1997. "Turn Listening Into a Powerful Presence. (Training 101: The Art of Listening)." *Training and Development*, 51, no. 7: 9–11.

Lance, K. C. *Making It Count @ Your Library*. Public Library Association. Available: www.pla.org/ala/pla/plaissues/smartestcardcampaign/toolkit/lance.ppt (accessed August 12, 2006a).

Lance, K. C. *Numbers You Can Use*. Public Library Association. Available: www.pla.org/ala/pla/plaissues/smartestcardcampaign/toolkit/statistics.htm (accessed August 12, 2006a).

Martin, E. R. 2006. "Team Effectiveness in Academic Medical Libraries: A Multiple Case Study." *Journal of the Medical Library Association*, 94, no. 3: 271–278.

Medical Library Association. 2000. *Making a Difference: A Communications Tool Kit*. Chicago, IL: Medical Library Association. Available: www.mlanet.org/publications/tool_kit/index.html (accessed December 15, 2006).

"MindTools.com: Essential Skills for Your Excellent Career." (Last Updated 2006). Available: www.mindtools.com (accessed August 25, 2006).

Strunk, W., E. B. White, and R. Angell. 2000. *The Elements of Style*. 4th edition. Needham Heights, MA: Allyn & Bacon.

"Toastmasters International." Available: www.toastmasters.org (accessed August 25, 2006).

# 12 TOOLS FOR IMPROVEMENT AND EVALUATION

Communicating the results of an evaluation study takes a certain set of skills. Chapter 11 discussed general communication principles, written and verbal. This chapter list tools that can be used in assessment and evaluation studies. These tools can be used during the study process, in analysis of the data, or in the final report.

The discipline of evaluation contains many unfamiliar terms and jargon. This book does have a glossary, but a small definition may not be enough for some of the tools and systems you might be working with. On the other hand, there are printed and Web resources where you can get expert information about these tools and systems. As a librarian, you may never have heard of many of these tools. The purpose of including them in this chapter with a brief overview is to bring them to your attention so if they could be applied to your project, you could do further research on the subject.

No one source was found that listed all tools and systems and described them in one place. The problem is:

- The readers of this book need to know something about these tools and systems.
- They may never use some of these tools and systems.
- The author is not enough of an expert on all these methods to fully describe each one.
- There are experts who have described these processes in books, in articles and on the web.
- Citing very specific Web pages about these tools and systems is not useful because they may be gone or outdated by the time someone reads this book.

Given these problems, the most useful resource for the readers of the book would be:

- A list of the tools with definitions, usage, and comments
- Followed by a list of general information resources to find more data on these tools and systems, including graphics and images

# TOOLS FOR QUALITY IMPROVEMENT PROJECTS

## 1. ACTIVITY NETWORK DIAGRAM/PERT CHART
### Definition:

An activity network diagram (AND), or PERT chart, is a diagram that depicts project tasks and their interrelationships, showing the critical path for a project as applied in a calendar. PERT is an acronym for Program Evaluation and Review Technique.

### Use:

While it is used to manage large projects, this tool could be a good starting point for any project. It is used to schedule, organize, and coordinate tasks within a project.

### Comments:

Sometimes a PERT chart is called a Critical Path Method (CPM). It helps you to see all parts and subparts of a project. By assigning time to each part, you can then lay out a time frame that is more realistic. A Gantt chart (see below) or an action plan in table form is a simplified version of a PERT chart.

The idea behind PERT charts is that most projects involve activities that are performed simultaneously, not in a straight line. If one of the simultaneous activities does not get done, it is helpful to know what steps will be delayed as a consequence. By putting each task in a network diagram, the activities also can be evaluated for estimated time and other attributes, such as cost and staff.

## 2. ACTION PLAN
### Definition:

An action plan is a table that depicts project activities with assigned responsibilities and due dates.

### Use:

Used to manage smaller projects, this tool can also schedule, organize, and coordinate tasks within a project but is not as complicated as a PERT chart.

### Comments:

An action plan table is a simple table in Word or Excel that lists the activity number and name, date due, responsible party, date completed, and other remarks or notes.

### 3. AFFINITY DIAGRAM
### Definition:

An affinity diagram is a way to organize facts, opinions, ideas, and issues into logical categories and natural groupings to aid in solving a complex problem.

### Use:

Used in teams or groups, affinity diagramming is a simple and effective technique for soliciting ideas and obtaining consensus on how information can be structured without using preordained categories. The final diagram shows relationships between the issue and the category.

### Comments:

It is a technique used as a continuation to a brainstorming session. It organizes facts and thoughts that may be uncertain. It can overcome set paradigms or established ideas. It shows which ideas need to be clarified. As a team activity it can build unity. The diagram can connect a large number of ideas into simple concepts.

### 4. BRAINSTORMING
### Definition:

Brainstorming is an organized approach for generating numerous ideas using the creative talent and experience of a group in a facilitated meeting environment.

### Use:

Brainstorming is used in: team building, process management, problem solving, project management and new service development.

### Comments:

There is a specific set of techniques to run a group brainstorming session:

- Clearly define the problem you want solved as you start the session.
- Stay focused on the problem.
- Do not criticize or evaluate any of the ideas during the session. Criticism stifles creativity and stops the free thinking necessary for a session.
- Be enthusiastic and uncritical as you get everyone to contribute and develop ideas.
- Include everyone in the group, even the quietest members.
- Have fun brainstorming. Welcome all ideas, from the practical ones to wildly impractical ones.

- Do not follow one train of thought for too long.
- Use one idea to create new ones.
- Use a flip chart and have one person write down ideas as they come up.
- Ideas can be studied and evaluated after the session using other tools.

## 5. BUDGET PLANNING
### Definition:

A budget plan outlines the project's need for resources based on the overall plan for the project. It is an action plan that summarizes the intended expenditures and sources of income for the project.

### Use:

A budget plan is used to control the expenses of a project and to be sure that costs do not get out of control. If plans or costs change, the budget needs to be adjusted. The existence of a budget can also explain why some things were not done due to lack of money.

### Comments:

Budgeting is a management skill most librarians have developed. Budgeting for an evaluation project is not that different, but you have to think up every item that might be included in the budget plan. The majority of the cost will be in staff time. Even if the project has no separate budget, it is best to attempt to keep track of the time spent on the project. This helps you understand how much it is really costing you to evaluate a program or process; the costs can get pretty high. It also allows you to explain the limitations of the project, since it would have cost too much to do it in a more time-consuming way. The list below is reproduced in the CD-ROM in the Chapter 12 folder as an Excel spreadsheet. You can use this spreadsheet to edit the items and create a budget. On Tab 2 of the spreadsheet there is an example of costing out staff time.

Budget Items to Consider

Note which costs are assigned from a real budget and which are in-kind or indirect costs.

Time—Labor costs

- For general planning:
  - Planning and meetings
  - Meeting with sponsors for refining the data needs

- Learning details of the methodologies chosen
- Research and reading time
- Consultants for training and data analysis
- For most methodologies:
  - Questionnaire or data intake form design
  - Sample selection and segmentation costs
  - Pretesting costs; multiplies if you need to test more than once
  - Substantive analyses of the data
  - Presenting the data to the team for analysis
  - Report preparation, writing, and presentations
  - Incentives for participation such as drawings or gifts
- Associated with a survey:
  - Data entry and quality control of the data entry
  - Editing the final file and looking for inconsistencies
  - Tabulating the data
- Associated with focus groups, observation, or interviews
  - Finding and contacting participants
  - Hiring, training, and supervising the moderators and recorders, observers or interviewers
  - Conducting the focus group meeting, observation, or interview
  - For focus groups, refreshments or lunch
- Associated with benchmarking:
  - Contacting and recruiting partners
  - Staff time on site visit including travel time
- Materials
  - Specialized computer programs
  - Computer time for tabulating the data
  - Interlibrary loan and article photocopying
  - Postage
  - Long-distance telephone
  - Printing or copying of surveys and report
  - Paper and toner
  - General office supplies
  - For benchmarking, site visit costs including travel and lodging
- Equipment
  - Work space
  - Computers
  - Access to the Internet for e-mail and Web surveys
  - Telephone
  - Copy machine
- Other

## 6. CAUSE AND EFFECT/FISH BONE DIAGRAM

**Definition:**

Cause and effect diagrams are just what they sound like. They use a fish-bone–shaped diagram to point to the real cause of a problem and rule out other issues that have no effect.

**Use:**

Used to analyze potential problems in new program objectives. The diagram processes problems for both positive and negative effects.

**Comments:**

The cause and effect diagram is constructed to identify and organize possible causes for a problem. It illustrates factors that really influence an outcome. As causes of a problem are discussed, fish bone diagrams cut down on complaints and irrelevant discussion. You can also see which areas lack data. It is a tool that effectively allows people to see the relationship between factors in the study of processes and situations. The diagram itself has lines angling off a central line to list the causes; these lines look like fish bones. For an example, see Figure 5.4 in Chapter 5.

## 7. CHECK SHEET

**Definition:**

A check sheet is a simple form used to collect data in a standardized way by making tally marks on the form to indicate the number of times something occurs.

**Use:**

A check sheet tabulates occurrences of certain events, such as reference transactions.

**Comments:**

A check sheet collects data for analysis in an efficient, graphical format. This could be as simple as listing items that might occur, or it might be a pictorial representation of a process where by a check is made where problems occur. It is important to identify clearly the process being examined as well the area or location from which the information is being collected; otherwise you will end up with erroneous information. For example, if you collected directional questions with the same mark as reference questions, the data would not be very meaningful. Decide how the information will be collected and the name of the person(s) to complete the sheet. A "tally mark" or stroke is the easiest way to record each instance. Total these at the end of each recording period. There is an example of a check sheet on the CD-ROM in the Chapter 12 folder.

## 8. CONTROL CHARTS

### Definition:

Control charts display the results of a process over time. They are used to determine if the process has variation and is in need of adjustment.

### Use:

Control charts are used to monitor processes. Control charts focus on acceptable limits of the process while run charts (see number 6, below) focus more on time patterns.

### Comments:

The control chart is a fundamental tool of statistical process control. It takes special software to construct, and usually the help of a statistician. It is used more in industry than in libraries. Depending on your project, it may still be a quality tool you want to use. It indicates the range of variability that is built into a system, and it helps determine whether or not a process is operating consistently or if a special cause has occurred to change the process mean or variance. The bounds of the control chart are marked by upper and lower control limits that are calculated by applying statistical formulas to data from the process.

## 9. COST ESTIMATION

### Definition:

Cost estimation helps gauge the tangible costs of a product, process, or project. The results are usually necessary to obtain some kind of approval or to make a decision. If you can show what is really going into a process financially, you will have ammunition for your argument to make a change.

### Use:

Cost estimation can be used to set priorities or look at resource requirements for a project.

### Comments:

There are two types of cost estimates, top down and bottom up. The top-down approach starts with an overall cost and divides out the components. Then you can see what each component actually costs, for example, titles held in a serials package. This type of analysis is often used in pursuit of ways to save money. Bottom-up analysis is used when you want to find out the cost of a total program. Here you figure out the various components of time and materials and perhaps facilities use. By adding them all together, you get the cost of the program. If a problem is identified and it costs more to fix it than it costs to replace or remove it, it might be better not to fix it.

## 10. FIVE WHYS
**Definition:**

The 5 whys is a simple system. You just ask, "Why?" five times in a row, as if you were a five-year-old.

**Use:**

The 5 whys can be used to identify the root cause of a problem in the process because the question why usually is asking for a cause.

**Comments**

To use the 5 whys, you write down the specific problem, describing it completely. Ask why the problem happens and write the answer down below the problem. Then ask why what you wrote next happens and continue to ask why at least five times. Even though it is called the five whys you can ask why more or fewer times until you are satisfied that you see the root cause for the problem. This technique can be used with the fishbone diagram. Using the case study from Chapter 5, you could start with the problem:

There is no use data for the journals we own.

> Why: The data we have are not combined.
> Why: The data come from different sources.
> Why: The systems are not integrated.
> Why: The systems are incompatible. The data are present in the various systems, but not combined.
> Why: We do not have enough personnel time.
> Why: All our paid workers have other jobs to do, but we could use volunteers or interns.

## 11. FLOWCHART
**Definition:**

Flowcharts are pictorial representations used to identify key steps in a process. By dividing the process into its various steps, flowcharts can be useful to identify the place where problems are likely to be found in the system.

## Use:

Flowcharts identify where problems are, and they can be used to plan stages of a project. Flowcharts can provide a form of documentation for a process.

## Comments:

Flowcharts can provide people with a common language when dealing with a project or process. Software packages are available to produce process flowcharts. For Windows, the programs are ABC Flowcharter, Corel Flow, and Visio. For the Macintosh, one program is Inspiration.

To produce a flowchart, you gather information on how the process flows by observing it or listening to someone describe it. Then you sketch out the flow. You then transfer the sketch to a computer software program and have someone familiar with the process check the chart for accuracy. Compare final flow with a best possible flow you might have seen in a benchmarking exercise, or you can simply analyze the flow to see where it can be made more efficient.

## 12. FORCE FIELD ANALYSIS

### Definition:

Force field analysis is a method of weighing pros and cons. It is a useful for looking at all the forces for and against a decision. The idea is to understand, and to make explicit, all the forces acting on a given issue, because they are not always obvious.

### Use:

The force field diagram is built on the idea that forces both drive and restrain change. These forces include persons, habits, customs, and attitudes. A force field diagram can be used at any level: personal, project, organizational, or network. In any level, the purpose is to visualize the forces that may work for and against a desired outcome.

### Comments:

A force field diagram visually demonstrates the driving forces and the restraining forces of a situation. The ideal is a system that is held in balance by the interaction of the two opposing sets of forces. Those seeking to promote change are the driving forces, and those attempting to maintain the status quo are the restraining forces. In order for any change in the equilibrium to occur, the driving forces must exceed the restraining forces, thus shifting the equilibrium. Force field analysis is a useful tool because it helps you weigh the importance of these factors and decide whether a plan is worth the effort of implementing. It can also be used in team-building projects when attempting to overcome resistance to change.

## 13. GANTT CHART

### Definition:

The Gantt chart is a project management tool that shows tasks over time. It is a graphical representation of the duration of tasks against the progression of time. It is easier to develop than a PERT chart and more graphic than an action plan.

### Use:

The Gantt chart is used for planning and scheduling projects and monitoring a project's progress. With it you can assess how long the project will take and the order in which the tasks need to be done.

### Comments:

By starting a grid with time across the top and tasks along the side, you can experiment and adjust the time frames it will take to complete the activities. It shows relationships between the task, such as which should be done first and which can be done at the same time. A Gantt chart allows you to note which tasks are dependent on other tasks. As you are monitoring a project, the Gantt chart can show you what has been achieved at any point in time. You can also take action on certain parts if the project gets off course. You can use Word tables or Excel to construct the charts, which can be automatically constructed using project management software. See examples in Chapters 4 and 6.

## 14. INTERRELATIONSHIP DIAGRAM

### Definition:

An interrelationship diagram is a graphical technique that allows team members to identify, analyze, and classify cause and effect relationships.

### Use:

Interrelationship diagrams are used to graphically depict relationships among topics, ideas, individuals, functions, or units. They can point out the factors in a situation that are driving many of the symptoms of an issue or problem.

**Comments:**

This technique starts with a box for the issue or question. Then all the elements involved in the issue are represented as circles or boxes around the issue. Arrows are drawn between all the boxes, showing the influence one element has on another or on the issue as a whole. The arrows can be identified as root causes (drivers) or key outcomes (results). The diagram may need to be redrawn several times, but it can show potential breakdowns in communication, delays in interaction, various checks and balances, and noncommunication. The technique allows people to look in multiple directions for causes and effects instead of merely seeing them in a linear way.

## 15. MATRIX DIAGRAM

### Definition:

A matrix diagram identifies and analyzes the presence and strength of relationships between two or more sets of information and rates them.

### Use:

A matrix diagram is used to compare two or more lists to understand the many-to-many relationships between them. If a list of activities is on one side of the matrix, the matrix can be expanded to include a Gantt chart for project management or a third set of information for comparison.

### Comments:

By listing one set of information on the side and another set on the top, you form a grid or matrix. In each cell of the matrix, a specially defined symbol is placed. Usually there are three different symbols, such as circles and squares and triangles, indicating a relationship between the two pieces of information. The resulting matrix can be visually analyzed or the symbols counted up. By seeing many or few symbols on the matrix, you can see patterns, problems, and areas of importance. It also allows you to see nonlinear relationships.

## 16. NOMINAL GROUP TECHNIQUE (MULTIVOTING)
### Definition:

The nominal group technique (NGT) is a structured method of collecting and organizing the thoughts of a group. It can be done in a way that prevents the originator of individual thoughts becoming known. This anonymity and the lack of interaction among the members of the group give it its name, since the team is only "nominally" interacting as a group.

### Use:

The nominal group technique is employed for problem solving by using a group to come to a consensus on an issue relatively quickly. It is a structured alternative to brainstorming that allows people to express ideas they may not feel comfortable saying out loud to their peers.

### Comments:

The nominal group technique promotes equal participation and commitment. It can eliminate peer pressure and control dominant members. It is a visible means of showing group consensus or lack of it. First the group silently and individually writes down their thoughts on the issue. All the thoughts are collected and written on a flip chart. The thoughts can be clustered but not discussed. This works best when the team members are quite knowledgeable about the subject. Then each person votes four to six times by putting hash marks by his or her top choices on the list. It is decided beforehand if members can give more than one vote to one thought. The votes are tallied, and the top-ranked thoughts are discussed. A second vote may be taken on the top-ranked items. Then the group can act on the top-ranked items.

## 17. PRIORITIZATION MATRIX
### Definition:

A prioritization matrix is a technique to achieve consensus about an issue. The matrix helps you rank problems or issues by various criteria of importance to decide which ones to work on first.

### Use:

A prioritization matrix is used to determine what the most pressing problems are. It can help you sort a list of items into order of importance. It can be used to prioritize complex or unclear issues that have multiple criteria. It employs numerical techniques, so it takes a little extra effort, but you can be more confident in your resulting rankings.

**Comments:**

This matrix is best done on a spreadsheet. You start with your set of problems that you want to prioritize, sometimes as a result of brainstorming. Then generate a set of criteria that will be meaningful to the quality of the decision. Make a matrix with the problems in the left column and the criteria across the top. The criteria can be weighted to give more importance to some areas. Data are put into the cells from various sources. In the next column the weighted score is calculated. The weighted scores are then sorted for priority. The math here can take some time, but it does allow you to compare different kinds of data. Look it up on the Web or in books to become more comfortable with the math, if necessary. Even with its complications, it is a useful tool.

## 18. PROCESS DECISION PROGRAM CHART

### Definition:

The process decision program chart identifies what might go wrong in a plan under development.

### Use:

The process decision program chart is used during the planning of a program to identify risks. It allows you to change the program to avoid the risk or to select possible countermeasures in case the problem should happen. It is especially useful when the plan is large and complex and the price of failure is high.

### Comments:

This type of assessment begins with a copy of the tree diagram developed for the proposed plan. The tree diagram should be articulated at least to the third level. Then you look at the third-level plans and brainstorm about what could go wrong. After a review of all possible problems, show only the significant problems as a fourth level linked to the tasks. Brainstorm possible countermeasures and add these as a fifth level. Decide which ones are practical. It is a proactive management strategy to include these identified risks and countermeasures in your tree diagram.

## 19. RESPONSIBILITY CHART

### Definition:

The responsibility chart defines the roles responsible for completion of the project, and summarizes the entire management process.

**Use:**

A responsibility chart is used to improve the distribution of work, to clarify understandings among team members and to build agreements. It helps you to determine who does what and who helps.

**Comments:**

To build a responsibility chart, first define the purpose of the project and write it at the top. Across the columns, list the people involved. Then, in the rows on the left, list the tasks to be done. In the matrix cells, assign the responsibilities you have decided on. There should be only one code per person per task. Common codes are:

R: Responsible for carrying out the task, or is accountable to see that the task is done. Every task must have an R.

C: Consults with the R person for the task. The two work collaboratively, and both have significant responsibility for doing the work.

A: Assists the R person with the task. Assisting means this person helps carry out the work but is not as involved in making decisions about what is to be done or how.

I: Is informed about the status of the work, including when it is done, but is not directly involved in planning or doing the work.

There could be other roles and responsibilities depending on the context of the project. See examples in Chapters 4 and 6.

## 20. SIX THINKING HATS

**Definition:**

The Six Thinking Hats technique was created by Edward de Bono and is used to explore different perspectives towards a complex situation or challenge. By putting on each hat, you see the problem or plan in different ways.

**Use**

Six Thinking Hats looks at the effects of a decision from a number of different points of view. You can use Six Thinking Hats in meetings or on your own.

**Comments:**

Each hat has a different color and a different style of thinking and emotional state. No one thinking style (or hat) is inherently "better" than another. A team needs all hats to consider all aspects of whatever issues it is facing. The hats help individuals deliberately adopt a variety of perspectives on a subject through role-playing.

The six hats and the perspectives they represent are:

- White—focuses on information available, objective facts, what is needed, how it can be obtained; white paper; neutrally presents the facts of the case.
- Green—creative thinking, possibilities and hypotheses, new ideas, vegetation; generates ideas on how the case could be handled.
- Yellow—logical positive view, looks for benefits, what is good, sunshine, optimism; evaluates the merits of the ideas and lists the benefits.
- Black—judgmental, critical, why something is wrong, logical negative view, stern judge wearing black robe; evaluates the merits of the ideas and lists the drawbacks.
- Red—emotions, feelings, intuition, hunches; presents views without explanation, justification; fire, warmth; gets everybody's gut feelings about the alternatives.
- Blue —overview, control of process, steps, other hats, chairperson, organizer, thinking about thinking, sky, cool; summarizes and adjourns the meeting.

## 21. SMART GOALS

### Definition:

SMART is an acronym for specific, measurable, attainable, results-oriented, and timely. SMART goals are more likely to be met and are more easily described than nonspecific, nonmeasurable, nonactionable goals.

### Use:

SMART goals are used for any planning activity and ensure that the goals you set will be able to be carried out.

### Comments:

SMART goals should be straightforward and emphasize what you want to happen.

- S—specific, significant, stretching
  - Are well defined.
  - Are not vague.

- Are clear to anyone who has a basic knowledge of the project
- Exactly what do you want?
- What needs to be done?
- Provide enough detail so that there is no confusion about what exactly you should be doing when the time comes to do it.
- Why is this important to do at this time? Give specific reasons and purposes, for benefits of accomplishing the goal.
- M—measurable, meaningful, motivational
  - Know if the goal is obtainable.
  - Quantify your goal.
  - How will you know when you reach your goal?
  - To determine if your goal is measurable, ask questions such as: How much? How many? How will I know when it is accomplished?
  - Establish concrete criteria for measuring progress toward the attainment of the goal so you can see the change occur.
- A—attainable, agreed upon, achievable, acceptable, action-oriented
  - Agreement with all the stakeholders what the goals should be, not set by someone outside the process.
  - Be honest with yourself and your team about what the team can reasonably accomplish, taking into consideration current responsibilities.
  - Can the objectives pertaining to the goal be carried out?
- R—results-oriented, realistic, relevant, reasonable, rewarding
  - Within the availability of resources, knowledge, and time.
  - Doable, real, and practical.
  - Is the goal possible to achieve?
  - Does the team have the skills, or can they learn the skills to accomplish the goal?
  - What might help or hinder the accomplishment of the goal?
  - A realistic project may push the skills and knowledge of the people working on it, but it should not break them.
  - Do not plan to do things if you are unlikely to follow through.
- T—timely, time-based, tangible, trackable
  - Enough time to achieve the goal.

- Not too much time, which can affect project performance.
- Associate a time frame with each goal.
- When should the goal be completed?

## 22. STRING DIAGRAM

### Definition:

A string diagram examines the physical movement in a process to see if it is efficient.

### Use:

A string diagram is used to analyze a process that involves significant physical movement to make movements easier and quicker. Movements may be of people, materials, or machines. It is also used to design the layout of a work area.

### Comments:

The basic diagram consists of a map of the work area with the actual movements drawn on top. The term *string diagram* comes from the way the diagram could be created on a board using pins and a piece of string. By seeing where people and things move, you can minimize the movement. A revision in the physical layout of the process could make a big difference in the efficiency of the task.

## 23. SWOT ANALYSIS (ENVIRONMENTAL SCAN)

### Definition:

SWOT analysis is an abbreviation used to denote an analysis of an organization's strengths, weaknesses, opportunities, and threats. The SWOT analysis is part of the internal/external assessment an organization conducts to analyze and evaluate internal conditions (strengths and weaknesses) and external factors (opportunities and threats) that affect the organization.

### Use:

A SWOT analysis is a tool used in strategic planning to look at the environment of the program for which the plan is being written. It can be used in an evaluation plan to see what issues might affect the evaluation.

### Comments:

To analyze the strengths, weaknesses, opportunities, and threats that surround a problem, start with a brainstorming session.

- Strengths are internal and are listed as positive statements about your library.
- Weaknesses also are internal and address what is lacking in your library.
- Opportunities come from the outside and refer to services and programs you are not doing that perhaps were discovered in a needs assessment.
- Threats also are from the outside and list adverse factors in the environment that may influence your library.

First, using a brainstorming session, list the strengths, weaknesses, opportunities, and threats that apply to your library situation. The National Network of Libraries of Medicine (NNLM) course presenters have gathered a list that came out of their classes, and it is available on the Web and on the CD-ROM in the Chapter 12 folder. Also, there is a second SWOT document with examples gathered from the Internet. Figure 12.1 is an example from a brainstorming session. Figure 12.2 matches the four areas in a matrix from a brainstorming session. Figure 12.3 is an example of how strategies might be developed in a library using the second step of a SWOT analysis.

| Figure 12.1   Results of a Brainstorming Session | |
|---|---|
| STRENGTHS (Internal):<br>Collection<br>Knowledgeable staff<br>Library as place | WEAKNESSES (Internal):<br>Less $$$ all the time<br>Perceived gaps in the collection<br>Library is in a bad or not easily accessed location |
| THREATS (External):<br>The Internet "has all the information for free"<br>The Internet is more convenient; don't have to go to the library<br>The Internet is more fun | OPPORTUNITIES (External):<br>Magnet status (in nursing) of hospital<br>Clinical librarianship; rounding; informationist<br>Electric medical records |

**Figure 12.2   SWOT Analysis Matrix**

|  | Strengths | Weaknesses |
|---|---|---|
| Opportunities | S-O strategies:<br>• Pursue opportunities that are a good fit to strengths.<br>• Use your internal strengths to take advantage of external opportunities. | W-O strategies:<br>• Overcome weaknesses to pursue opportunities.<br>• Improve internal weaknesses by taking advantage of external opportunities. |
| Threats | S-T strategies:<br>• Use strengths to reduce vulnerability to external threats.<br>• Use your strengths to avoid or reduce the impact of external threats. | W-T strategies:<br>• Establish a defensive plan to prevent weaknesses susceptible to external threats.<br>• Aim defensive tactics at reducing internal weaknesses and avoiding external threats. |

**Figure 12.3   Second Step of SWOT Analysis**

| | |
|---|---|
| S-O strategies:<br>Strength: Wide range of networked resources enabling access to evidence from home and from the workplace<br>Opportunity: Focus on clinical care and evidence-based practice<br>Strategy: The library could package various electronic resources that we already hold that support evidence-based practice and market them as a specialized service (maybe an "evidence gateway") to home and workplace users. | W-O strategies:<br>Weakness: Paper backup system in ILL is staff-intensive<br>Opportunity: Local group very active with participation in mentoring<br>Strategy: The library could arrange to visit several other libraries informally and see how they handle the paper flow in ILL. |
| S-T strategies:<br>Strength: Well-used library Web site<br>Threat: Internet and access to advanced information technology enabling potential users to bypass the library<br>Strategy: We could develop the library Web site to be more of a portal as an access point for users to access external resources. | W-T strategies:<br>Weakness: Lack of user involvement in service development<br>Threat: Rising costs of resources, in particular, journals<br>Strategy: We involve our users in a survey to assist in selecting and endorsing the library's choice of electronic journals. |

## 24. TREE DIAGRAM
### Definition:
The tree diagram shows a program or process with successive levels of detail.

### Use:
The tree diagram is used in planning to break down a task in a hierarchical manner. It can be translated into a PERT chart and used with a process decision program chart.

### Comments:
A key characteristic of the tree diagram is that it is a hierarchy. Each node on the tree has one predecessor or parent and one or more successor nodes, like children in a family tree. Each parent is completely described by its children. A tree diagram is written in a logical and systematic way, repeating the same process of analysis and breakdown with each node. It makes specific details clearer. To begin, define your objective. For the higher levels, use an affinity diagram to organize the plans. Using flip charts or sticky notes, organize the nodes. Confirm that your final list of actions consists of everything you need to accomplish the objective.

# TOOLS FOR DATA DISPLAY

## 1. BAR CHART (HISTOGRAM)
### Definition:
A bar chart is graphic display of data in the form of a bar showing the number of units or frequency in each category.

### Use:
A bar chart graphically summarizes and displays the differences between groups of data and plots the frequency with which different values of a given unit occur. Each bar represents the relative magnitude of the values.

### Comments:
Bar charts are relatively easy to create using the Chart Wizard in Excel. The data from the process being monitored are displayed graphically so the viewer can see if the variation is what is expected. Called distributions, the data can display in various ways

and the meaning is contextual. A bell-shaped curve occurs when the most frequent measurement appears at the center of distribution and less frequent measurements taper gradually at both ends. Other distributions are: two peaks, clifflike, saw-toothed, or skewed.

## 2. DATA POINTS

### Definition:

A data point is a single measurement in a set of data points that represent in descriptive form a set of facts. They are numerical descriptions of what we do and how well we do it.

### Use:

Data points are plotted in a graphic display. Sometimes they are called scatter diagrams because of the way dots appear to be scattered between the X and Y axes.

### Comments:

Data points can be words or numbers. There can be attribute data or variable data. Attribute data are the count of the occurrences of the attribute, such as yes or no, good or bad, or right or wrong, and so forth. Variable data are measured and plotted on a scale, representing such things as time, weight, length, or volume.

## 3. PARETO CHART

### Definition:

A Pareto chart is a bar chart where the bars are sorted into size order, with the highest bar on the left. They are sometimes called 80/20 charts because often the two bars on the left represent 80% of the units.

### Use:

Pareto charts are used to identify those factors that have the greatest cumulative effect on the system and screen out the less significant factors in an analysis. They can allow the user to set priorities and focus attention on a few important factors in a process.

### Comments:

Plotting frequency data in descending order creates a Pareto chart. When this is done, the most essential factors for the analysis are graphically apparent and in an orderly format. Typically, the chart is used to highlight problems or issues. The height of the bars implies priority. This shows not only the absolute priority of each bar, through its position in the chart, but also its relative priority through its height as compared with the other bars. Pareto charts may have different overall "shapes" just as bar charts do. A "spiky" or convex chart is the most useful where one or two bars on the left are significantly higher than the rest, usually adding up to 80% or more of the total. This makes it easier to decide where to act. The other shapes are plateau and convex curves. A plateau is where the bars are approximately the same height and no selection can be made. A convex curve, where the bars on the left are the same height, makes it difficult to tease out a definite problem.

## 4. PIE CHART

### Definition:

The pie chart is a way of showing data in the form of shares of a whole. It is so named because it looks like a pie.

### Use:

The pie chart is used to show proportions graphically.

### Comments:

A pie chart is a circular chart divided into sectors, illustrating relative magnitudes or frequencies. Together, the sectors create a full disk. It usually takes percentages as input data. Excel's Chart Wizard can make 3-d pie charts or charts where one part is exploded or separated from the rest. The values of a pie chart should number 2 and usually not more than 6. With more than 6, the pieces can get too small to see; if they are equal, the differences will be lost.

## 5. RADAR CHART

### Definition:

A radar chart graphically demonstrates the size of the gaps among five to ten organizational performance areas. The chart displays the important categories of performance and can show concentrations of strengths and weaknesses.

### Use:

A radar chart is useful for showing performance relative to other measurement sets, with crossing lines highlighting changes. It is useful when you want to look at several different factors all related to one item.

**Comments:**

In a radar chart, a point close to the center on any axis indicates a low value. A point near the edge is a high value. It can be described as a bar chart with the bars radiating from the center. The resulting radar chart will graphically show areas of relative strength and relative weakness, as well as depicting general overall performance as the ends of the "bars" move toward the outside. It allows a visual comparison among several quantitative or qualitative aspects of a situation.

## 6. RUN CHART

**Definition:**

A run chart displays the variation of data over time.

**Use:**

Run charts are used to analyze processes according to time or order. Run charts are useful in discovering patterns, trends, shifts or cycles that occur over time. A run chart focuses more on time patterns, while a control chart focuses more on acceptable limits of the process. It can be used to predict trends.

**Comments:**

Creating a run chart requires these four activities. Some type of process or operation must be available to take measurements for analysis.

- Gather data
  - Measure a process or operation over a period of time.
  - Collect the data in a chronological or sequential form.
  - You may start at any point and end at any point.
  - For best results, use 25 or more samples to get an accurate run chart.
- Organize the data.
  - Once the data have been placed in chronological or sequential form, divide them into two sets of values, x and y.
  - The values for x represent time, and the values for y represent the measurements taken from the process or operation.
- Chart the data.
  - You can plot the y values (data along the side) versus the x values (time along the bottom) using the Chart Wizard in Excel, or you can do it manually.

- Use an appropriate scale that will make the points on the graph visible.
- If there is no trend line, you can calculate an average and insert an average line.
- Interpret the data.
  After drawing the horizontal and vertical lines to segment data, interpret the data and draw any conclusions that will be beneficial to the process or operation. Some possible outcomes are:
  - Trends in the chart
  - Cyclical patterns in the data, such as seasonal trends
  - Observations from each time interval are consistent.

Cautions:

Run charts can be drawn in ways that misrepresent or distort reality. Trends can be buried if the time intervals are too frequent. If the Y values (data along the side) are too wide or narrow the data can be distorted.

## 7. SCATTER CHART
### Definition:

Scatter diagrams, or charts, are graphical tools that attempt to show the influence that one variable has on another. A diagram of this type usually displays points representing the observed value of one variable corresponding to the value of another variable.

### Use:

Scatter diagrams are used to study possible relationships between two variables. These diagrams cannot prove that one variable causes the other, but they do indicate the existence of a relationship, as well as the strength of that relationship.

### Comments:

The scatter diagram is used to test a theory that the two variables are related. The slope of the diagram indicates the type of relationship that exists. A strong relationship between the two variables is seen when most of the points fall along an imaginary straight or curved line with either a positive or negative slope. No relationship between the two variables is observed when the points are randomly scattered about the graph.

To construct a scatter diagram, collect and construct a data sheet of paired samples of data that you suspect to be related. Use the Excel Chart Wizard to construct a scatter diagram.

# ADDITIONAL INFORMATION RESOURCES

The tools listed in this chapter are mostly part of the quality improvement movement, covered in Chapter 5. In the literature, there is reference to the "first seven tools," which are used for qualitative measurement and the "second seven tools," which are used for management and planning. Figure 12.4 lists these.

| Figure 12.4   Tools for Quality Improvement | |
| --- | --- |
| First seven tools for quality improvement | Second seven tools for management and planning |
| Cause-effect diagram<br>Pareto chart<br>Check sheet<br>Scatter chart<br>Bar Chart and other graphs<br>Histogram<br>Control chart | Activity network<br>Affinity diagram<br>Interrelationship diagram<br>Matrix diagram<br>Prioritization matrix<br>Process decision program chart<br>Tree diagram |

Many of the resources consulted for this book did not fully describe these tools. The reader is referred to the publication *Memory Jogger II*. This small, 3.5 x 5.5 inch book, gives explanations of over 25 tools. It is available at Amazon for under $10, and the publisher's Web site lists quantity discounts as well as electronic versions. Since 1994, GOAL/QPC has published three in the series.

- Brassard, M., and D. Ritter. 1994. *The Memory Jogger II: A Desktop Guide of Tools for Continuous Improvement & Effective Planning.* Salem, NH: GOAL/QPC.
- Brassard, M. 1996. *The Memory Jogger Plus: Featuring the Seven Management and Planning Tools.* Rev. ed. Methuen, MA: GOAL/QPC.
- Brassard, M. 2000. *The Problem Solving Memory Jogger: Seven Steps to Improved Processes.* Salem, NH: GOAL/QPC.

In her chapter "Quality Improvement," pp. 55–73 of *The Medical Library Association Guide to Managing Health Care Librar-*

*ies* (R. Holst, et al., editors. Medical Library Association/Neal-Schuman Publishers, 2000), Nardina Mein lists several tools: cause and effect diagram, Pareto chart, run chart, flowchart, and story boarding. She also discusses team leading, which is covered in Chapter 11, and she does all this from the library point of view.

You can search the Web for all of these techniques, and you will find many examples of the charts and graphs and get step-by-step instructions. Searching for images also is useful. Many educational institutions have tutorials, and business and government agencies have excellent information pages on quality improvement and management planning. Many of the sites listed below are commercial and sell products and consultation services. To get you to buy their products, they offer a great deal of information for free. They are recommended because of the comprehensiveness of their content, with no endorsement of their products intended.

- Mindtools.com (www.mindtools.com/): Many of these tools and more are listed under the headings of "Problem Solving" and "Decision Making." This is a comprehensive management site, and the articles on these tools are very good. There is more information here than just quality issues.
- Syque Quality Toolbook (http://syque.com/quality_tools/index.htm): This site is what the author David Straker calls a "knowledge-sharing site." Straker has put his out-of-print book *A Toolbook for Quality Improvement and Problem Solving*, on the Web as well as many other quality resources. His well-organized Web site contains illustrations and step-by-step instructions.
- Free Management Library (www.managementhelp.org/): Developed and sponsored by Authenticity Consulting, LLC, the Free Management Library "provides easy-to-access, clutter-free, comprehensive resources regarding the leadership and management of yourself, other individuals, groups and organizations. Content is relevant to the vast majority of people, whether they are in large or small for-profit or nonprofit organizations." This site has an emphasis on nonprofit organizations. Each of the more than 600 entries has many links out to resources on the Internet.
- The American Society for Quality (www.asq.org/index.html): This society has a section called "Learn about Quality." While sometimes a little too technical, many of

the explanations are excellent and it is well worth exploring all the sections to see what they say:
- Basic Concepts—the first things you need to know about quality
- Quality Tools—the basics for gathering and analyzing information, for your own job or within your whole organization
- Organization-Wide Approaches—models and methods for getting your people on board and managing change
- People Create Quality—how to keep people working, individually and as teams, to embrace quality
- Using Data—putting numbers behind your quality efforts: how to apply measuring tools to your program and its performance
- Specific Applications—how real-world organizations make quality work
- Wikipedia (http://en.wikipedia.org/): While sometimes the quality of Wikipedia's content is controversial, some of its entries are quite extensive with references and Web links to more extensive sites.

# GLOSSARY OF TERMS

**Accountability**
The responsibility of program managers and staff to provide evidence to stakeholders and funding agencies that a program is effective and in conformance with its coverage, service, legal, and fiscal requirements.

**Accreditation**
A formal process by which a recognized body, usually a nongovernmental institution, assesses and recognizes that an organization meets applicable, predetermined standards.

**Action plan**
A tool that assists in defining and documenting the details of a series of planned activities that, when completed, will result in the accomplishment of a stated objective.

**Bar chart**
A graphic display of data in the form of several bars of varying lengths, which show the number of units (for example, frequency) in each category.

**Baseline**
An observation or value that represents the base level of a measurable quantity.

**Benchmarking**
1. A tool to measure and compare your library's performance or work processes with those of other libraries. 2. The ongoing comparison and review of one's own process, product, or service against the best-known similar activity, so that realistic goals can be set and effective strategies can be identified and implemented. 3. A continuous, systematic process for evaluating the products, services, and work processes of your organization and comparing to other organizations that are recognized as representing best practices for the purpose of organizational improvement.

**Best practice**
A way or method of accomplishing a business function or process that is considered to be superior to all other known methods.

**Brainstorming**
A group process used to generate a large number of ideas in a nonjudgmental environment.

### Cause and effect diagram
A tool that assists in identifying and displaying the factors (causes) that lead to an outcome (effect). It is used to group people's ideas about the causes of a particular problem in an orderly way. It is also known as a fishbone diagram because of the shape that it takes.

### Comparative data
Data that compare internal performance against others who perform the same process, usually in the form of an average.

### Confidence level; Confidence interval
The confidence level is the probability, based on statistics, that a number will be inside a corresponding confidence interval, an upper and lower limit. It is a measure of sampling error. A 95% confidence level for an estimate is that the estimate will be within the range, or confidence interval, 19 times out of 20. If you use a confidence interval of 4, or 4%, and a confidence level of 95%, and 51% percent of your sample agrees with a question, you can be 95% sure that if you had asked the question of the entire target population, between 47% (51–4) and 55% (51+4) would have agreed.

### Continuous quality improvement (CQI)
A management approach to improving and maintaining quality that emphasizes internally driven and relatively continuous assessments of potential causes of quality defects, followed by action aimed at either avoiding a decrease in quality or else correcting it in an early stage.

### Control chart
A graphic display of the results of a process over time and against established control limits. The dispersion of data points on the chart is used to determine whether the process is performing within prescribed limits and whether variations taking place are random or systematic.

### Cost-benefit analysis
A determination of the economic efficiency of a program through analysis of potential benefits accrued from the function or service in relation to its known cost.

### Critical success factor
Issues that are deemed so important to the organization that they must work in order for the organization to achieve its mission.

They come from specific industry characteristics, competitive strategies, environmental changes resulting from economic or technological trends, or from internal organizational needs.

### Culture of assessment
An organizational attitude that can be achieved by creating systems and structures that are based on continuous assessment and evaluation; a culture that is customer focused and uses assessment systematically.

### Customer satisfaction
Satisfying the needs and reasonable expectations of customers with an attitude that puts the needs of the customer first.

### Data
Information or a set of facts presented in descriptive form. Numerical descriptions of what we do and how well we do it.

### Data analysis
The process of systematically applying statistical and logical techniques to describe, summarize, and compare data.

### Data collection plan
A written document describing the specific procedures to be used to gather the evaluation data. The document describes who collects the information, when and where it is collected, and how it is obtained.

### Deductive reasoning
The process of reasoning from general principles to particular examples; a system of reasoning based on definitions and premises.

### Double-barreled question
A double-barreled question combines two or more issues or attitudinal objects in a single question. Combining the two questions into one question makes it unclear which attitude is being measured, since each question may elicit a different attitude. If the word *and* or *or* appears in a question, check to verify whether it is a double-barreled question.

### Effectiveness
The degree to which program objectives are achieved to maximize outcomes in relation to inputs. See Outcomes.

### Efficiency

The ratio of outputs (services produced) to inputs (resources used to produce the services). Increasing efficiency is a matter of achieving the same outputs with fewer resources or more outputs for the same amount of resources.

### Environmental scan

An analysis and evaluation of key internal and external conditions to develop an understanding of the current environment that may affect how the organization functions. Factors included in an environmental scan are usually strengths, weaknesses, opportunities, and threats.

### Evaluation

The systematic review of the missions, goals, objectives, action plans, performance measures, and operations of an organization or program using systematic methods for collecting, analyzing, and using information to answer basic questions about a program.

### Evaluation plan

A written document describing the overall approach or design that will be used to guide an evaluation. It includes what will be done, how it will be done, who will do it, when it will be done, why the evaluation is being conducted, and how the findings will likely be used.

### Evidence-based medicine

The practice of medicine or the use of health-care interventions guided by or based on supportive scientific evidence; also, the avoidance of those interventions shown by scientific evidence to be less efficacious or to be harmful.

### Executive summary

A nontechnical summary statement designed to provide a quick overview of the full-length report on which it is based.

### Flowchart

A graphical representation of the sequence of activities, steps, and decision points that occur in a particular, discrete process, such as registering a client in a clinic.

### Focus group

A client-oriented approach for collecting information where a group of people selected for their relevance to the evaluation meet to discuss and share ideas about the topic. By constructing descriptive summaries of views, experiences, insights, and ideas on the topic, the results of focus group discussions collect information on the in-depth feelings, perceptions, and observations from program participants.

### FOCUS-PDCA cycle
A problem solving methodology. The steps in FOCUS-PDCA are find, organize, clarify, understand, and select and plan, do, check, and act.

### Frequency distribution
The pattern that emerges out of a set of data.

### Gantt chart
A type of bar chart used in a process or for project planning and control that displays planned work targets for completion of work in relation to time. Typically, a Gantt chart shows the week, month, or quarter that each activity will be completed and sometimes the person or persons responsible for carrying out each activity.

### Gap analysis
An assessment of the difference between the present state, what the customer has, and the desired future state, what the customer needs.

### Generalizable
The degree to which sample results can be universally applied or representative of the population from which the sample was taken.

### Guideline
A statement or other indication of policy or procedure by which to determine a course of action.

### Histogram
A graphic display used to plot the frequency with which different values of a given variable occur. Histograms are used to examine existing patterns, identify the range of variables, and suggest a central tendency in variables; also known as a line graph.

### Impact
The effect or influence of one person, thing, or action on another; the part of a change in society that can be attributed uniquely to a specific program when the influence of other sources is con-

trolled, removed, or accounted for. It is often difficult or impossible to measure or to understand exactly how one program influences a very large, long-range, or broadly stated impact.

## Indicator
A specific, observable, and measurable characteristic, action, condition, or change that can be used to determine the degree of adherence to a standard or the level of quality achieved. A measure used to quantitatively assess how well a process is performing.

## Inductive reasoning
Drawing a general conclusion based on a limited set of observations; a system of reasoning based on observation and measurement.

## Informatics
A newer word for information science and technology, especially when computers are involved, that is concerned with the collection and organization of information (gathering, manipulating, storing, retrieving, and classifying recorded information) using computers and statistical methods. Bioinformatics: the information science of biology; Medical Informatics: the information science of the practice of medicine.

## Input
The resources needed to carry out a process or provide a service. Inputs are usually financial, physical structures such as buildings, supplies and equipment, personnel, and clients.

## Interview
An exchange of information using face-to-face or telephone communication to assess individual opinions and experiences.

## Key informants
Persons who are selected on the basis of criteria such as knowledge, compatibility, age, experience, or reputation and who provide information about their culture. They can contribute a knowledgeable perspective on the nature and scope of a social problem or a target population. They know the community as a whole or the particular portion you are interested in.

## Knowledge-based information (KBI) services
Systems, resources, and services to help health professionals acquire the knowledge and skills needed to maintain and improve competence; to support clinical, managerial, and business deci-

sion making; to support performance improvement and activities to reduce risk to patients; to provide needed information and education to patients and families; and to satisfy research-related needs. It is usually quality filtered or peer reviewed and based on accepted knowledge or current research.

**Library performance standards**
Something that is established by authority or by general consent to be a model or example; an explicit statement of expected quality. Standards represent performance specifications that, if attained, will lead to the highest possible quality in the system.

**Likert scale**
A Likert scale (pronounced 'lick-urt' or 'like-urt') is a multipoint rating scale using a range of response categories, such as strongly agree, agree, disagree, and strongly disagree, where respondents indicate their level of agreement with statements that express a favorable or unfavorable attitude toward the concept being measured.

**Logic model**
A systematic and visual way to present the perceived relationships among the resources you have to operate the program, the activities you plan to do, and the changes or results you hope to achieve. It shows how the parts of a program are logically related by showing the links among program objectives, program activities, expected program outcomes, and how those outcomes will be evaluated.

**Mean**
The sum of a set of measurements divided by the number of measurements.

**Measure**
A number assigned to an object or an event. Measures can be expressed as counts (45 visits), rates (10 visits/day), proportions (45 primary health-care visits/380 total visits = .118), percentages (12% of the visits made), or ratios (45 visits/4 health workers = 11.25).

**Measurement**
The act of gathering data in order to assess performance.

**Median**
The middle value when figures are arranged according to size.

**Mission statement**
A short, comprehensive statement of purpose to help focus activities, state priorities, and identify key audiences and purposes for an agency, program, or subprogram.

**Needs assessment**
A systematic process for determining discrepancies between optimal and actual performance of a service by reviewing the service needs of customers and stakeholders and then selecting interventions that allow the service to meet those needs in the fastest, most cost-effective manner.

**Objectives**
Statements describing the results to be achieved and the manner in which these results will be achieved.

**Outcome**
The consequence, visible or practical result or effect of an event or activity. Outcomes address the impact or benefit of a program in a broad sense, which can include the social context. Library outcomes are the eventual result of using library services, the influence the use had, and its significance to the user, such as a change in knowledge, and so forth.

**Outcome measures**
A type of performance measure that demonstrates the benefits to people: specifically, achievements or changes in skill, knowledge, attitude, behavior, condition, or life status for program participants. They assess the impact of a program on people and society (Institute of Museum and Library Services).

**Outlier**
A data point significantly above or below the rest of a set of related data points.

**Output**
The direct result of the interaction of inputs and processes in the system; the types and quantities of goods and services produced by an activity, project, or program.

**Pareto chart**
A graphic representation of the frequency with which certain events occur. It is a rank-order bar chart that displays the relative importance of variables in a data set and may be used to set priorities regarding opportunities for improvement.

**Performance**
The actual output and quality of work performed.

**Performance improvement**
Selecting and implementing actions to improve processes and their outcomes; also known as quality improvement.

**Population**
A statistical term used to describe the whole range of possibilities from which a measurement could be taken.

**Problem statement**
A concise description of a process in need of improvement, its boundaries, the general area of concern where quality improvement should begin, and why work on the improvement is a priority.

**Process**
A series of actions (or activities) that transform inputs (or resources) into a desired product, service, or outcome.

**Process definition chart**
A tool that assists in identifying the key components of a process.

**Qualitative methods**
Ways of collecting information on the knowledge, attitudes, beliefs, and behaviors of the target population. In general, information gathered using qualitative methods is not given a numerical value.

**Quality**
Quality in a person, object, or process refers to a distinguishing characteristic that enhances a subject's distinctiveness, or may denote some degree of achievement or excellence. Quality in management often refers to the "reduction of variability" or "compliance with specifications". Measurement of what we do, how well we do it and using that information to improve.

**Quality assessment**
Determination of how processes and services correspond to current standards.

**Quality improvement**
An approach to the study and improvement of the processes that provide services to meet needs of customers. A quality improvement program is a group of activities undertaken to identify op-

portunities for improvement and to take action to improve the quality of the services and their outcomes.

### Quality indicator
An agreed-upon process or outcome measure that is used to determine the level of quality achieved. A measurable variable (or characteristic) that can be used to determine the degree of adherence to a standard or achievement of quality goals.

### Range
The difference between the maximum and minimum values of data in a sample.

### Rate
A special form of proportion that includes specification of time. For example, the case-fatality rate of cerebral malaria is the number of cases of cerebral malaria where the individuals died over a period of time divided by the total number of cases of cerebral malaria in the same time period.

### Ratio
The relationship between two numbers. For example, the ratio of males to females (known as the sex ratio) in a country is the number of males divided by the number of females. Any fraction, quotient, proportion, or percentage is a ratio.

### Reliability
The extent to which the same result is achieved when a measure is repeatedly applied to the same group.

### Root cause
The underlying reason for the occurrence of a problem.

### Run chart
A visual display of data that enables monitoring of a process to determine whether there is a systematic change in that process over time.

### Sample
A subset of the population. To the extent possible, a sample should possess all salient characteristics of the population from which it is drawn so that it is representative of the whole.

**Sampling**
A procedure by which to infer the characteristics of a large body of people (a population) by surveying only a few (the sample).

**Sampling frame**
Complete list of all people in the target population.

**Sampling, Haphazard or convenience**
A type of nonprobability sample in which the sample is chosen based on convenience such as choosing your friends to make up a sample of a specific age group. Another convenience sampling technique is volunteer sampling, where people in the sample volunteer their services for the study.

**Sampling, Judgment**
A type of non-probability sampling in which you make use of special expertise to select units for the study. This can be used to obtain a balance of viewpoints or to select knowledgeable respondents.

**Sampling, Non-probability**
A sample in which the probability of a population unit being chosen is unknown. The selection of population units is based in part on the judgment of the researcher or field interviewer. There are five basic kinds: haphazard or convenience, judgment, quota, snowball, and stratified.

**Sampling, Probability**
A method for drawing a sample from a population where each member of the population has a known probability of being selected in the sample. The chance of a unit being included in a sample can be calculated. Also called random sampling. Probability samples are more costly to obtain, but are more accurate.

**Sampling, Quota**
A sample similar to stratified sampling in which you first divide the population into classes (such as males and females) and then obtain a haphazard sample within each class or sample to adhere to certain proportions within each class.

**Sampling, Snowball**
A type of non-probability sample where you start by sampling one person, then ask that person for the names of other people you might interview, then interview them and obtain referrals from them, and so on.

**Sampling, Stratified**
A sampling method in which the population is divided according to a common characteristic or attribute or subpopulations (strata) and a probability sampling is then conducted within each group.

**Scatter diagram**
A graphic display of data plotted along two dimensions. Scatter diagrams are used to rapidly screen for a relationship between two variables.

**Specification**
A description of the expectations to which a product or service must conform.

**Stakeholders**
People, groups, or organizations with a significant interest in how well a program performs or with an interest in the results of the assessment and what will be done with results. Stakeholders may be staff members, supervisors, administrators, sponsors, funders, personnel who do parallel functions in the company, or the users or customers of the service. They may be internal or external to the organization and may not actually use the service being evaluated.

**Standard**
Something that can be used as a model or example to be followed, such as a practice or a product, and that is widely recognized, employed, or established by authority or by custom, especially because of its excellence; an acknowledged measure of comparison for quantitative or qualitative value; a criterion.

**Standard deviation**
Calculated boundaries that describe how data are dispersed around their mean.

**Steering committee**
While a team is a group of interacting individuals sharing a common goal and the responsibility for achieving it, a steering committee is a special type of team that is usually interdisciplinary and includes stakeholders from different levels. It takes a broader view of the project and helps guide its development and implementation. Some members might be advisory, and some might be part of a working group.

**Strategic planning**
A practical, action-oriented planning process with set goals and resource allocation plans that will affect strategic issues of vital

importance to the organization that have been identified by the study of internal and external factors.

**Stratify**
To break down a whole into its component parts.

**Survey**
Information collected directly from people in a systematic, standardized way at one point in time. Surveys use questionnaires that ask the same question in the same way to all respondents with the same set of possible responses. Surveys may be conducted by interview (in person or by telephone) or by questionnaire.

**SWOT analysis**
An abbreviation used for the analysis of an organization's strengths, weaknesses, opportunities, and threats. The SWOT analysis is part of the internal/external assessment to analyze and evaluate internal conditions (strengths and weaknesses) and external factors (opportunities and threats) that affect the organization; also known as an environmental scan.

**System**
The arrangement of organizations, people, materials, and procedures associated with a particular function or outcome. A system is usually made of inputs, processes, and outcomes.

**Target**
A numeric representation of the required performance level of a process.

**Total quality management (TQM)**
A management strategy aimed at embedding awareness of quality in all organizational processes. It is a systemic approach to continuous improvement of the quality of all products and services using qualitative and quantitative methods and involving all stakeholders with a special emphasis on the customer.

**Trend**
A general direction (rising or falling) demonstrated through observation of data and/or indicators over time, including long term; a pattern that is evident from past events.

**Validity**
The degree to which an indicator accurately measures what it is intended to measure.

**Value**

The importance or preciousness of something, the perception of actual or potential benefit.

**Variance**

Any nonconformance to specifications.

**Variation**

Differences in the output of a process resulting from the influences of people, equipment, materials, and/or methods.

# BIBLIOGRAPHY FOR GLOSSARY

Biblarz, D., S. Bosch, and C. Sugnet. *Guide to Library User Needs Assessment for Integrated Information Resource Management and Collection Development*. Lanham, MD: Scarecrow Press, 2001.

CHLA/ABSC Task Force on Standards for Library & Information Services in Canadian Healthcare Facilities. CHLA/ABSC Task Force on Hospital Library Standards. *Standards for Library & Information Services in Canadian Healthcare Facilities*. 2nd ed. Toronto, Canadian Health Libraries Association/Association des bibliothèques de la santé du Canada, 1995.

Glossary Index. Audience Dialogue, Adelaide, South Australia. Last Updated: June 26, 2006; Accessed: 8 August 2006. www.audiencedialogue.org/gloss.html

Glossary of Terms Commonly Used in Health Care. AcademyHealth. Last Updated: 2004; Accessed: August 8, 2006. www.academyhealth.org/publications/glossary.htm.

Glossary: Program Evaluation for Comprehensive Tobacco Control Programs. Introduction to Program Evaluation for Comprehensive Tobacco Control Programs. Last Updated: February 7, 2005; Accessed: August 8, 2006. www.cdc.gov/tobacco/evaluation_manual/glossary.html

Gluck J. C., et al. "Standards for Hospital Libraries." *Journal of the Medical Library Association*, 90, no. 4 (2002): 465–472.

Indiana University Purdue University Indianapolis, Institute for Museum and Library Services, and E. Kryder-Reid. "Shaping Outcomes: Glossary." Last Updated: 2006; Accessed: January 4, 2007. www.shapingoutcomes.org/course/glossary/index.htm.

Quality Assurance Project, Bureau for Global Health, U.S. Agency for International Development's (USAID). "A Glossary of Useful Terms." Last Updated: n.a.; Accessed: September 22, 2006. www.qaproject.org/methods/resglossary.html.

Rossi, P. H., M. W. Lipsey, and H. E. Freeman. *Evaluation: A Systematic Approach*. 7th ed. Thousand Oaks, CA: Sage, 2004.

# INDEX

(Page numbers for boxes are followed by b, and figures by f.
Locators for CD-ROM content are in boldface, e.g., CDch2.)

# ABOUT THE AUTHOR

Rosalind Farnam Dudden is the Health Sciences Librarian and Library Sciences Director at the National Jewish Medical and Research Center in Denver, Colorado. She has worked in a hospital library setting since 1971. A member of the Medical Library Association (MLA) and the Colorado Council of Medical Librarians (CCML) since 1971, Dudden has been a leader in many of the technology and evaluation efforts of both groups. She has served on more than 60 elected or appointed committees at the national, chapter, and section and local levels. She is a Distinguished Member of the Academy of Health Information Professionals, a Fellow of the Medical Library Association and a former member of the MLA board. She served as president of the MLA Hospital Libraries Section and the CCML.

Committed to sharing the knowledge that she has gained throughout her career, Dudden has taught more than 15 courses and presented many papers and posters. Some of her accomplishments over the years include work in standards, surveys, and technology. She was instrumental in the development of the 1984 edition of the MLA's *Hospital Library Standards* during her tenure as chair of the Hospital Library Standards and Practices Committee. The committee also wrote a paper on the Joint Commission on Accreditation of Healthcare Organizations (JCAHO) standards, which received the MLA Ida and George Eliot Prize in 1981.

Dudden worked on the successful MLA Benchmarking Network Task Force and project since 1999, helping with the analysis of the 2002 and 2004 surveys. The benchmarking efforts have given the MLA and its members an opportunity to learn more about benchmarking, compare data, establish best practices, and identify and work with a benchmarking partner. For her invaluable role in supporting the vision, development, and implementation on the Benchmarking Network, she received the MLA President's Award in 2003. With colleagues, she recently published two articles in the April 2006 issue of *Journal of the Medical Library Association* chronicling the MLA Benchmarking Network and proposing uses for the results.

With CCML members, Dudden has worked on surveys of interlibrary loan activity since 1977, a series of surveys designed to analyze usage patterns and promote balanced resource sharing. She and the survey committee members wrote a research article about the 1997 survey. For her work with these and other CCML efforts, she received the CCML Marla Graber Award for Excellence and Achievement in Health Sciences Librarianship in 2005. With a career-long interest in technology and being a promoter of its use in libraries, Dudden worked on projects locally that promoted the use of e-mail for interlibrary loan in as early as 1980 and was instrumental in expanding the shared integrated library system with a National Library of Medicine (NLM) grant in 1991. For many years, she chaired the committee that produced the CCML *Journal Locator* as a computerized union list of serials starting in 1977, which is now online. In the early 1980s she promoted MEDLINE searching and taught several courses that allowed CCML members to get access. For her work in collaborative technology projects through the years, she received the ISI/Frank Bradway Rogers Information Advancement Award from the MLA in 1995.

Dudden created Denver's first hospital Web site in 1995, writing or loading more than 300 pages, and was hospital Webmaster until 2000. She also served as Webmaster of both the MLA's Hospital Libraries Section and the Consumer and Patient Health Information Section (CAPHIS). Her work contributed to the *CAPHIS Top 100 List: Web Sites You Can Trust* for consumers. During her career Dudden also received two awards from the Midcontinental Chapter of the Medical Library Association: the Barbara McDowell Award for Hospital Librarianship in 1988 and the Outstanding Achievement Award in 1995. The faculty at National Jewish awarded her the first Friend of the Faculty Award in 2002, and she was commended for dragging them kicking and screaming into the Internet age. In October 2004 she was awarded an NLM publications grant for two years to research and write this book. Dudden's resume and CV can be found on the Web at http://roz.dudden.com/.